Technology-Driven Evolution of the Corporate Social Responsibility Ecosystem

Kuldeep Singh
School of Management, Gati Shakti Vishwavidyalaya, Vadodara, Gujarat, India

Jitendra Yadav
Indian Institute of Management, Bodh Gaya, India

Rebecca Abraham
Nova Southeastern University, USA

IGI Global
PUBLISHER of TIMELY KNOWLEDGE

Published in the United States of America by
IGI Global
Business Science Reference (an imprint of IGI Global)
701 E. Chocolate Avenue
Hershey PA, USA 17033
Tel: 717-533-8845
Fax: 717-533-8661
E-mail: cust@igi-global.com
Web site: http://www.igi-global.com

Library of Congress Cataloging-in-Publication Data

CIP DATA PROCESSING

2024 Business Science Reference

ISBN(hc): 9798369332382
ISBN(sc): 9798369348031
eISBN: 9798369332399

British Cataloguing in Publication Data
A Cataloguing in Publication record for this book is available from the British Library.

Advances in Human Resources Management and Organizational Development (AHRMOD) Book Series

Patricia Ordóñez de Pablos
Universidad de Oviedo, Spain

ISSN:2327-3372
EISSN:2327-3380

MISSION

A solid foundation is essential to the development and success of any organization and can be accomplished through the effective and careful management of an organization's human capital. Research in human resources management and organizational development is necessary in providing business leaders with the tools and methodologies which will assist in the development and maintenance of their organizational structure.

The **Advances in Human Resources Management and Organizational Development (AHRMOD) Book Series** aims to publish the latest research on all aspects of human resources as well as the latest methodologies, tools, and theories regarding organizational development and sustainability. The **AHRMOD Book Series** intends to provide business professionals, managers, researchers, and students with the necessary resources to effectively develop and implement organizational strategies.

Coverage

- Human Resources Development
- Employee Relations
- Succession Planning
- Worker Behavior and Engagement
- Recruitment Process
- Upward Feedback
- Coaching and Mentoring
- Work-Life Balance
- Human Relations Movement
- Organizational Development

IGI Global is currently accepting manuscripts for publication within this series. To submit a proposal for a volume in this series, please contact our Acquisition Editors at Acquisitions@igi-global.com or visit: http://www.igi-global.com/publish/.

The (ISSN) is published by IGI Global, 701 E. Chocolate Avenue, Hershey, PA 17033-1240, USA, www.igi-global.com. This series is composed of titles available for purchase individually; each title is edited to be contextually exclusive from any other title within the series. For pricing and ordering information please visit http://www.igi-global.com/book-series/advances-human-resources-management-organizational/73670. Postmaster: Send all address changes to above address.

Titles in this Series

For a list of additional titles in this series, please visit: http://www.igi-global.com/book-series/advances-human-resources-management-organizational/73670

Cognitive Behavioral Neuroscience in Organizational Settings
K. Jayasankara Reddy (Christ University, India) and Thaddeus Alfonso (Christ University, India)
Business Science Reference • copyright 2024 • 331pp • H/C (ISBN: 9798369318584) • US $345.00 (our price)

ESG and Total Quality Management in Human Resources
Christos Papademetriou (Neapolis University, Pafos, Cyprus) Sofia Anastasiadou (University of Western Macedonia, Greece) Konstantina Ragazou (University of Western Macedonia, Greece) Alexandros Garefalakis (Hellenic Mediterranean University, Greece) and Stylianos Papalexandris (University of Western Macedonia, Greece)
Business Science Reference • copyright 2024 • 305pp • H/C (ISBN: 9798369329917) • US $215.00 (our price)

Enhancing Employee Motivation Through Training and Development
Tricia Mazurowski (Adler University, USA)
Business Science Reference • copyright 2024 • 309pp • H/C (ISBN: 9798369316740) • US $205.00 (our price)

Global Practices on Effective Talent Acquisition and Retention
Bryan Christiansen (Southern New Hampshire University, USA) Muhammad Abdul Aziz (University of Greenwich, UK) and Elle Lily O'Keeffe (Rasmussen University, USA)
Business Science Reference • copyright 2024 • 531pp • H/C (ISBN: 9798369319383) • US $295.00 (our price)

IGI Global
PUBLISHER of TIMELY KNOWLEDGE

701 East Chocolate Avenue, Hershey, PA 17033, USA
Tel: 717-533-8845 x100 • Fax: 717-533-8661
E-Mail: cust@igi-global.com • www.igi-global.com

To Late Fauji Ravinder Singh, father of Dr. Kuldeep Singh, who served with honor in the Indian Army. His dedication and guidance have always inspired us to strive for societal betterment.

Table of Contents

Detailed Table of Contents

This chapter provides a critical look at the definition of CSR based on the subject matter literature available. Because CSR is an emerging term in both definition and reality, this study aims to illustrate CSR in relation to the different stakeholders and entities termed as CSR ecosystem in this study. Furthermore, this study also offers an outline of factors, interactions, and contexts under review, such as CSR, Section 135 of the Indian Companies Act 2013, the effect of the Act on corporate bodies' CSR operations, the impact of CSR on societal and environmental concerns, contrasting CSR schools of thinking, and gaps in the views of management, government, shareholders, and stakeholders.

This study explores how technology influences corporate social responsibility (CSR) practices in management studies. This study examines the growing interest in CSR and sustainability management among academics and practitioners in recent years. With the help of this technology, companies can better understand and address social and environmental issues. Technology provides advanced tools for data analysis, stakeholder engagement, and innovative solutions. However, there are concerns about the ethical use of technology and digital divide in communities. Companies must be mindful of these potential risks and ensure that their use of technology aligns with development goals. The integration of technology into CSR practices creates both opportunities and challenges for businesses. As technology continues to shape CSR, it is crucial for companies to prioritize data privacy, the ethical use of technology, and equitable access to digital resources.

The present study is an attempt to understand the historical development of corporate social responsibility in India. The present study classified the development of corporate social responsibility in five different phases as phase of individual philanthropy, phase of social movement philanthropy, phase of state philanthropy, phase of corporate philanthropy, and finally CSR Law in India. The present study has also highlighted corporate social responsibility violations and penalties associated with. The study analyzed the major challenges in corporate social responsibility implementations in India. The study adopted doctrinal and archival research methodology. The findings indicate that there has been an increase in CSR activities because it has been made compulsory by the law. However, the challenges are still there such as local communities disapproving of firms supporting CSR initiatives due to lack of knowledge and public awareness, businesses being dissatisfied with local agencies' transparency, and lack of funding, etc.

The chapter delves into smart cities, exploring their pivotal role in eco-friendly urban development. Utilizing information and communication technology (ICT), smart cities address urban challenges, enhance quality of life, and champion sustainability. The integration of IoT technology and green practices facilitates real-time data collection, green innovation, and eco-friendly urban development. Technological advancements, spanning renewable energy integration to circular economy solutions, propel environmental sustainability. Sustainable mobility solutions, energy management, and effective environmental monitoring contribute to smart and sustainable urban environments. Citizen engagement, crucial for success, requires inclusive planning and careful technology platform consideration. Challenges in implementing smart city technologies encompass ICT infrastructure, regulations, community participation, costs, and data privacy.

Mr. Prabhu Savant, CEO of Savant Electronics, has to convince the management that sustainability is different from CSR. Savant has to develop a plan to address the local communities ?(tm) CSR (corporate social responsibility) issues he would be facing while setting up the new plant. The case discusses achieving sustainability while deploying CSR as a strategy. The case looks at the Greenfield sustainable manufacturing plant project (electrical and electronics devices) in Madhya Pradesh, India, by Savant Electronics. According to the case study, this would describe the project ?(tm)s provenance, the various stakeholders who participated and what they thought of the project, Savant Electronics ?(tm) involvement, and what they did to achieve a long-term sustainable economic and social assessment of the local community members as well as other beneficiaries who were included in the CSR initiative and became responsible ?ocorporate citizens. ?? The case illustrated Savant Electronics ?(tm) perspective on the social, environmental, and economic sustainability challenges related to this specific project. The case investigated the repercussions of establishing manufacturing units, particularly in developing nations, and critically analyzed corporate-society interaction. The case also evaluates the trade-off between promoting sustainability efforts and the impact of such mega-infrastructure projects on society and the environment. The case also prepares the students to analyze whether sustainability promotion causes more risk than benefits and how managers should mitigate the risks to maximize the benefits.

Foreword

In today's rapidly evolving business environment, corporate social responsibility (CSR) has transcended its traditional role as a mere regulatory compliance requirement to become a cornerstone of strategic corporate management. The intersection of technology and CSR represents a transformative frontier, redefining how businesses engage with their stakeholders, address social and environmental challenges, and contribute to sustainable development. It is within this dynamic context that the book *Technology-Driven Evolution of the Corporate Social Responsibility Ecosystem* emerges as a seminal contribution, offering an in-depth exploration of the ways in which technological advancements are reshaping the CSR landscape.

This comprehensive volume stands out not only for its rigorous analysis and insightful perspectives but also for its practical relevance to a wide range of stakeholders, including business leaders, policymakers, academics, and practitioners. The editors and contributing authors have meticulously compiled a collection of studies and reflections that together provide a nuanced understanding of the multifaceted relationship between technology and CSR. Their collective expertise offers readers a rich tapestry of theoretical insights, empirical evidence, and practical applications, making this book a valuable resource for anyone interested in the future of sustainable business practices.

One of the key strengths of this book lies in its ability to bridge the gap between theory and practice. The chapters provide a thorough examination of how technological innovations such as big data analytics, blockchain, artificial intelligence, and the Internet of Things are being harnessed to enhance CSR initiatives. These technologies enable companies to monitor and report their social and environmental impacts more accurately, enhance transparency, and foster greater accountability. By showcasing real-world examples and case studies, the authors illustrate how these technological tools can be effectively integrated into corporate strategies to drive meaningful and measurable social and environmental outcomes.

Furthermore, the book's focus on the Indian and Global context provides a unique and valuable perspective on CSR. India, with its diverse socio-economic landscape and rapidly growing economy, presents both significant challenges and opportunities for CSR. The book's detailed examination of the CSR ecosystem in India highlights the critical role of regulatory frameworks, stakeholder expectations, and corporate governance in shaping CSR practices. This context-specific analysis offers valuable lessons that can be applied to other emerging markets, making the book relevant not only to Indian readers but also to a global audience.

The chapter on "A Study on CSR Eco-System in India" sets the stage by providing a comprehensive overview of the regulatory environment and the various factors influencing CSR practices in India. This foundational understanding is crucial for appreciating the subsequent discussions on the role of technology in enhancing CSR. The authors adeptly highlight how India's unique socio-economic challenges necessitate innovative and contextually relevant CSR strategies. By doing so, they underscore the importance of adapting global best practices to local contexts, a theme that resonates throughout the book.

In exploring "The Evolution of Corporate Social Responsibility: A Technology Driven Approach in the Management Studies Institution," the book delves into the critical role of education in shaping future business leaders who are well-versed in leveraging technology for CSR. The integration of CSR principles into management education is essential for fostering a new generation of leaders who can navigate the complexities of sustainable business practices. This chapter provides valuable insights into how academic institutions can incorporate technological tools into their curricula, thereby preparing students to address the social and environmental challenges of the future.

The practical implications of technology-driven CSR are further elaborated in chapters such as "Challenges and Opportunities within the Evolving CSR Landscape in India" and "Organizational Technological Innovation and Environmental Sustainability Regulations." These chapters offer a nuanced understanding of how businesses can navigate the dynamic CSR landscape by leveraging technology to overcome challenges and seize opportunities. The discussions on regulatory compliance, stakeholder engagement, and resource allocation provide practical strategies for companies looking to align their CSR efforts with their broader business objectives. By emphasizing the role of innovation and continuous improvement, these chapters highlight the importance of a proactive approach to CSR.

The book also addresses sector-specific challenges and opportunities, as illustrated in the chapter on "Corporate Environmental Responsibilities of Auto Manufacturers in the Chennai Auto Industry." This detailed case study provides a deep dive into the unique environmental challenges faced by the automotive industry in Chennai and showcases how companies are leveraging technology to address these issues. By highlighting best practices and innovative solutions, the authors offer valuable insights for other industries seeking to enhance their environmental responsibility and achieve greater sustainability.

A particularly forward-looking aspect of the book is its exploration of the evolution of digital technologies and their impact on CSR disclosure, as discussed in the chapter "The Development of Web 1.0 to Web 2.0 CSR Disclosure of Data." The transition from static websites to interactive platforms has transformed the way companies communicate their CSR initiatives, enabling greater transparency and stakeholder engagement. This chapter provides a thorough analysis of the benefits and challenges associated with digital CSR disclosure, offering practical recommendations for companies looking to enhance their online communication strategies.

The relevance of technology in addressing urban sustainability is another critical theme explored in the book. The chapter on "Technology's Role in Sustainable Urban Development in Smart Cities" highlights how smart city initiatives are leveraging technology to address urban challenges such as congestion, pollution, and resource management. By examining the role of public-private partnerships, community engagement, and innovative technologies, the authors illustrate the potential of technology to create more livable, resilient, and sustainable urban environments. This discussion is particularly timely as cities around the world grapple with the complexities of urbanization and seek sustainable solutions.

Moreover, the book does not shy away from examining the ethical dimensions of CSR, as evidenced in the chapter "Dynamics of Sustainable and Ethically Responsible Business Practices in Corporate Social Responsibility." This chapter underscores the importance of integrating ethical considerations into CSR strategies and highlights the role of technology in facilitating transparent and accountable business practices. By providing a comprehensive overview of sustainable and ethical business practices, the authors offer a roadmap for companies looking to enhance their CSR initiatives and achieve lasting positive impact.

The book also addresses the critical role of consumer rights and protection in the context of CSR. The chapter "Empowering Consumer Rights: Unveiling the Impact of Big Data Analytics in Upholding Consumer Protection" explores how big data analytics can be leveraged to protect consumer rights, enhance transparency, and promote ethical business practices. This discussion is particularly relevant in today's digital age, where consumers are increasingly demanding greater accountability and transparency from businesses. By highlighting the potential of big data to drive more informed decision-making and empower consumers, the authors underscore the importance of integrating consumer protection into CSR strategies.

In conclusion, *Technology-Driven Evolution of the Corporate Social Responsibility Ecosystem* is a timely and essential contribution to the field of CSR. The book's comprehensive examination of the intersection of technology and CSR offers valuable insights for a wide range of stakeholders, including business leaders, policymakers, academics, and practitioners. By bridging the gap between theory and practice, the authors provide a nuanced understanding of how technological advancements are reshaping the CSR landscape. The book's focus on the Indian context, combined with its global relevance, makes it a valuable resource for readers around the world.

As a leading expert in the field, I highly recommend this book to anyone interested in understanding the future of CSR and the critical role of technology in driving sustainable and ethically responsible business practices. The insights and recommendations provided in this book will undoubtedly help businesses, policymakers, and other stakeholders navigate the complexities of the modern CSR landscape and leverage technology to achieve greater social and environmental impact. I congratulate the editors and contributing authors for their outstanding work and for providing a valuable resource that will undoubtedly shape the future of CSR.

Prasanna Kolar
JAIN University, Bangalore, India

Preface

The realm of corporate social responsibility (CSR) has undergone significant transformation over the past few decades, driven primarily by advancements in technology. This edited volume, titled *Technology-Driven Evolution of the Corporate Social Responsibility Ecosystem*, seeks to explore the multifaceted impact of technological innovation on CSR practices globally. As corporations navigate the complexities of the modern world, the integration of technology into CSR strategies has become not only advantageous but imperative.

Corporate Social Responsibility encompasses the practices and policies undertaken by businesses to manage their impact on society, the environment, and the economy. Traditionally, CSR activities have included philanthropy, ethical labor practices, and environmentally sustainable operations. However, the digital revolution has helped in a new era of CSR, where technology plays a crucial role in enhancing transparency, efficiency, and accountability. This book delves into how emerging technologies are reshaping the CSR landscape.

In today's interconnected and rapidly evolving world, the role of corporations extends beyond profit maximization. Stakeholders, including consumers, employees, investors, and regulators, demand greater accountability and responsible conduct from businesses. Technology has become a pivotal enabler in meeting these demands. From improving environmental sustainability through smart technologies to enhancing transparency with new technologies, the integration of technology into CSR strategies is a critical development. This book examines these trends within the global context, with a particular focus on the unique challenges and opportunities faced by businesses.

This book is designed for a diverse audience, including academics, researchers, and students in the fields of business management, corporate governance, and environmental studies. Additionally, it is a valuable resource for corporate executives, CSR professionals, policymakers, and technology innovators who are involved in or interested in the intersection of technology and corporate social responsibility. By providing a comprehensive analysis of the evolving CSR ecosystem, this book aims to inform and inspire stakeholders across various sectors to adopt and advocate for more responsible and sustainable business practices.

The chapters provide a foundational understanding of the current state of CSR

A Study on CSR Ecosystem in India: This chapter provides a foundational understanding of the current state of CSR in India. It explores the regulatory framework, key players, and major CSR initiatives in the country, setting the stage for subsequent discussions on technological integration.

The Evolution of Corporate Social Responsibility: A Technology-Driven Approach in the Management Studies Institution: This chapter examines how management institutions are incorporating technology into their CSR curriculum. It highlights the importance of educating future business leaders on the role of technology in driving responsible business practices.

Challenges and Opportunities within the Evolving CSR Landscape in India: This chapter addresses the specific challenges faced by Indian companies in implementing technology-driven CSR initiatives. It also identifies opportunities for innovation and growth within this evolving landscape.

Organizational Technological Innovation and Environmental Sustainability Regulations: This chapter explores how technological innovations can help organizations comply with environmental sustainability regulations. It discusses various technological tools and approaches that can enhance regulatory compliance and promote sustainable practices.

Dynamics of Sustainable and Ethically Responsible Business Practices in Corporate Social Responsibility: This chapter delves into the dynamics of integrating sustainability and ethical considerations into business practices. It examines case studies of companies that have successfully implemented such practices through technological advancements.

Corporate Environmental Responsibilities of Auto Manufacturers in the Chennai Auto Industry: Focusing on the auto industry in Chennai, this chapter analyzes the environmental responsibilities of auto manufacturers. It highlights the role of technology in reducing the environmental footprint of automotive operations and promoting sustainability.

The Development of Web 1.0 to Web 2.0 CSR Disclosure of Data: This chapter traces the evolution of web technologies and their impact on CSR data disclosure. It discusses how the transition from Web 1.0 to Web 2.0 has enhanced transparency and stakeholder engagement in CSR reporting.

Technology's Role in Sustainable Urban Development in Smart Cities: This chapter explores the intersection of technology and urban development, focusing on smart cities. It examines how technological innovations are contributing to sustainable urban development and improving the quality of life for urban residents.

Savant Electronics Sustainability or Corporate Social Responsibility: This chapter provides a case study of Savant Electronics, analyzing its sustainability and CSR initiatives. It highlights the company's use of technology to drive its CSR agenda and achieve its sustainability goals.

Empowering Consumer Rights: Unveiling the Impact of Big Data Analytics in Upholding Consumer Protection: This chapter discusses the role of big data analytics in protecting consumer rights. It examines how businesses can leverage big data to enhance consumer protection and build trust with their stakeholders.

The integration of technology into the CSR ecosystem is not just a trend but a necessary evolution in the face of global challenges such as climate change, social inequality, and economic instability. This book contributes to the field by providing a comprehensive analysis of how technology is reshaping CSR practices across various industries and regions. By highlighting case studies, regulatory insights, and innovative practices, it offers valuable knowledge and practical guidance for stakeholders aiming to create a more responsible and sustainable future. The insights presented in this volume underscore the critical role of technology in driving positive social, environmental, and economic outcomes through enhanced corporate responsibility.

Kuldeep Singh
Gati Shakti Vishwavidyalaya, India

Jitendra Yadav
Indian Institute of Management, Bodh Gaya, India

Rebecca Abraham
Nova Southeastern University, USA

Acknowledgment

The successful completion of this book, "Technology-Driven Evolution of the Corporate Social Responsibility Ecosystem," would not have been possible without the invaluable contributions and support of several individuals and institutions.

First and foremost, we would like to express our deepest gratitude to Prof. Madhvendra Misra, currently serving as Professor at the Indian Institute of Information Technology Allahabad, India. Prof. Misra's expertise in Corporate Social Responsibility and his extensive body of work published in recognized journals have been a constant source of inspiration. His insightful guidance, constructive feedback, and unwavering support have significantly enriched the quality and depth of this book. We are profoundly grateful for his mentorship and for sharing his profound knowledge and experience with us.

We would also like to extend our heartfelt thanks to the Indian Institute of Information Technology Allahabad, India, for providing the essential research support that enabled the completion of this book. The resources and facilities made available by the Institute were instrumental in facilitating our research and writing process. Their commitment to academic excellence and support for scholarly endeavors have been truly commendable.

Additionally, we would like to acknowledge the support of Gati Shakti Vishwavidyalaya, a Central University under the Ministry of Railways, Government of India. The research environment provided by the University was conducive to the development of this book. The University's dedication to fostering an atmosphere of intellectual curiosity and academic rigor was crucial in bringing this work to fruition.

We are also grateful to our authors team, colleagues, peers, and the editorial team at IGI Global for their encouragement, assistance, and professional support throughout the writing and publication process. Their expertise and dedication have been invaluable in ensuring the high standards of this publication.

Lastly, we would like to thank our families and friends for their constant encouragement and understanding. Their support and patience have been a source of strength and motivation throughout this journey.

This book is a testament to the collaborative efforts of many individuals and institutions, and we are deeply appreciative of the support and contributions that have made it possible.

Thank you all for your invaluable support.

Prof. Kuldeep Singh

Prof. Jitendra Yadav

Prof. Rebecca Abraham

Introduction

Kuldeep Singh
Gati Shakti Vishwavidyalaya, India

Jitendra Yadav
Indian Institute of Management, Bodh Gaya, India

Rebecca Abraham
Nova Southeastern University, USA

Corporate social responsibility (CSR) is a broad concept that encompasses a company's efforts to operate in an ethical and sustainable manner while contributing to the well-being of society and the environment. It involves integrating social and environmental concerns into business operations and interactions with stakeholders on a voluntary basis. At its core, CSR is rooted in the recognition that businesses do not exist in a vacuum but are part of a larger ecosystem that includes communities, employees, customers, suppliers, and the natural environment. By embracing CSR principles, companies acknowledge their responsibility to create value not only for shareholders but also for these broader stakeholder groups.

CSR initiatives can take many forms, including environmental sustainability programs, ethical labor practices, community development initiatives, philanthropic endeavors, and responsible governance structures. Companies may undertake these efforts to address specific social or environmental issues, enhance their reputation and brand image, attract and retain top talent, or simply because they believe it is the right thing to do. However, CSR is not merely a matter of charitable giving or occasional community outreach efforts. Rather, it involves embedding social and environmental considerations into the core business strategy and decision-making processes. This requires a long-term commitment, effective stakeholder engagement, transparent reporting, and a willingness to hold the company accountable for its impact on society and the planet.

CSR is about striking a balance between economic growth, social progress, and environmental protection – the three pillars of sustainable development. By adopting a CSR mindset, companies can contribute to the creation of a more equitable, inclusive, and sustainable future while also enhancing their competitiveness and long-term viability.

On the other hand, technology is the application of scientific knowledge and techniques to solve practical problems, create products, or optimize processes. In the context of the CSR ecosystem, technology plays a crucial role in enabling companies to enhance their social and environmental initiatives and drive positive change more effectively. From big data analytics and artificial intelligence to blockchain and the Internet of Things (IoT), emerging technologies are offering new tools and capabilities for companies to gain insights, streamline operations, and raise transparency and accountability in their CSR efforts. For instance, big data analytics can help companies analyze vast amounts of data from various sources, such as supply chain operations, customer feedback, and social media interactions, to identify patterns, trends, and areas of concern related to their social and environmental impact. This information can then inform targeted strategies and data-driven decision-making to address these issues more effectively. Similarly, artificial intelligence (AI) and machine learning algorithms can be leveraged to optimize resource allocation, predict potential risks or opportunities, and automate certain processes related to CSR initiatives, such as monitoring labor practices or tracking carbon emissions. Blockchain technology, with its decentralized and immutable ledger system, offers a powerful solution for enhancing supply chain transparency and traceability. By recording transactions and tracking the movement of goods and materials across the supply chain, blockchain can help companies ensure responsible sourcing practices and reduce the risk of contributing to environmental degradation or human rights exploitations. Furthermore, the Internet of Things (IoT), which enables the interconnectivity of physical devices and sensors, can play a vital role in monitoring and optimizing resource consumption, reducing waste, and improving operational efficiency – all of which contribute to a company's environmental sustainability efforts. However, the integration of technology into the CSR ecosystem is not without its challenges. Issues such as data privacy, algorithmic bias, and the digital divide must be addressed to ensure that these technologies are deployed in an ethical and inclusive manner, upholding the principles of responsible business practices.

Nonetheless, the potential for technology to drive positive social and environmental change is immense. By leveraging these cutting-edge tools and solutions, companies can gain deeper insights, enhance transparency, streamline processes, and ultimately amplify the impact of their CSR initiatives, contributing to a more sustainable and equitable future.

Stakeholder engagement is a critical component of effective CSR strategies. It involves actively involving and collaborating with various groups and individuals who have a stake or interest in a company's operations and impacts, such as employees, customers, suppliers, local communities, non-governmental organizations (NGOs), and regulatory bodies. Effective stakeholder engagement is essential for several reasons. Firstly, it enables companies to gain a deeper understanding of the concerns, expectations, and perspectives of their stakeholders, which can inform and shape their CSR initiatives to better address the most pressing social and environmental issues. Secondly, it nurtures transparency and accountability, as companies are required to disclose and communicate their CSR efforts and performance to stakeholders, building trust and credibility. Thirdly, it facilitates collaboration and collective action, enabling companies to leverage the expertise, resources, and networks of stakeholders to drive more impactful and sustainable change.

Stakeholder engagement can take various forms, such as stakeholder consultations, focus group discussions, community forums, online platforms for feedback and dialogue, and regular reporting and disclosure mechanisms. The specific approach and methods should be tailored to the unique needs and contexts of the stakeholder groups involved. However, meaningful stakeholder engagement goes beyond merely informing or consulting stakeholders; it involves actively involving them in decision-making processes and co-creating solutions. This requires a genuine commitment to listening, understanding, and incorporating diverse perspectives, as well as a willingness to adapt and adjust strategies based on stakeholder feedback. Technology has played a pivotal role in enhancing stakeholder engagement in the CSR ecosystem. Social media platforms, online forums, and interactive dashboards have opened new channels for companies to communicate their CSR initiatives, solicit feedback, and foster meaningful dialogues with stakeholders. Additionally, advanced data analytics and visualization tools can help companies better understand and analyze stakeholder sentiments, concerns, and priorities, enabling more targeted and responsive engagement strategies. Effective stakeholder engagement not only contributes to the development of more impactful and sustainable CSR initiatives but also helps companies build trust, credibility, and social license to operate. By actively involving and collaborating with stakeholders, companies can ensure that their CSR efforts are aligned with the needs and expectations of the communities and environments in which they operate, ultimately creating shared value for all.

The concept of CSR has undergone a profound transformation in recent years, driven by the rapid advancements in technology and the increasing pressure from stakeholders for companies to adopt sustainable and ethical practices. This book delves into the involved interplay between technology and CSR, exploring how emerging technologies are reshaping the way businesses approach and implement their social and environmental initiatives. In the digital age, technology has become an crucial tool for companies to enhance their CSR efforts, enabling them to gather and analyze data, streamline processes, and engage with stakeholders more effectively. From leveraging big data analytics and artificial intelligence to monitor supply chain sustainability to harnessing blockchain technology for transparent and secure tracking of responsible sourcing practices, the potential applications of technology in the CSR realm are vast and ever-evolving. However, the integration of technology into CSR practices is not without its challenges. Issues such as data privacy, algorithmic bias, and the digital divide raise important ethical considerations that companies must navigate. This book examines these challenges and provides insightful perspectives on how to strike a balance between technological innovation and ethical responsibility. Moreover, the book explores the role of technology in fostering stakeholder engagement and transparency, two critical pillars of effective CSR strategies. Social media platforms, online reporting tools, and interactive dashboards have revolutionized the way companies communicate their CSR initiatives, enabling them to build trust and credibility with their stakeholders. Through a comprehensive analysis of case studies, industry best practices, and cutting-edge research, this book offers a holistic understanding of the technology-driven evolution of the CSR ecosystem. It serves as a valuable resource for business leaders, CSR professionals, policymakers, and academic researchers seeking to navigate the complex intersection of technology and corporate social responsibility in the 21st century.

In the contemporary landscape of corporate governance and social consciousness, the evolution of CSR stands as a testament to the dynamic interplay between societal expectations, technological advancements, and organizational strategies. This book delves into the multifaceted dimensions of CSR, guided by a central theme: the transformative influence of technology on the CSR ecosystem. Across its chapters, this book embarks on a journey through the annals of CSR evolution, from its nascent stages rooted in individual philanthropy to its current manifestation as a strategic imperative shaped by digitalization, data analytics, and emerging technologies. At its core, the exploration seeks to unravel the involved relationship between technology and CSR, elucidating how innovations in the digital sphere have redefined corporate responsibilities, stakeholder engagement, and sustainability practices. Each chapter in this book offers a unique lens through which to examine the convergence of technology and CSR. Whether scrutinizing the impact of digital platforms on stakeholder collaboration, dissecting the ethical implications of AI-driven decision-making, or exploring the role of blockchain in enhancing supply chain transparency, the chapters collectively paint a rich tapestry of insights and perspectives. Furthermore, the thematic unity of the book extends beyond mere technological discourse. It delves into the ethical dilemmas, regulatory challenges, and strategic imperatives that accompany the integration of technology into CSR practices. Through a synthesis of theoretical frameworks, empirical research, and case studies, the book endeavors to provide a holistic understanding of the opportunities and constraints inherent in this evolving landscape. Finally, this book serves as a beacon for scholars, practitioners, and policymakers navigating the complex terrain of CSR in the digital age. By elucidating the synergies between technology, corporate behavior, and societal impact, it aims to inspire a new wave of innovation, collaboration, and responsible leadership in the pursuit of sustainable development and social progress. Through collective introspection and concerted action, it is our collective endeavor to forge a future where technology serves as a force for good, enriching lives, empowering communities, and preserving the planet for generations to come.

However, the technology-driven evolution of the CSR ecosystem is not without its challenges. As companies increasingly rely on algorithms and automated decision-making systems, concerns surrounding algorithmic bias and privacy have come to the forefront. Ensuring that these technologies are designed and implemented with ethical considerations in mind is paramount to maintaining public trust and upholding the principles of responsible business practices. Furthermore, the digital divide poses a significant obstacle, as access to technology and digital literacy remains uneven across different socioeconomic groups and geographic regions. Companies must be mindful of this gap and strive to ensure that their technology-driven CSR initiatives are inclusive and accessible to all stakeholders, regardless of their technological proficiency or access to resources. Despite these challenges, the potential for technology to drive positive social and environmental change is undeniable. Innovative solutions such as renewable energy technologies, sustainable manufacturing processes, and smart city initiatives are reshaping the way companies operate, reducing their environmental footprint and contributing to the development of more sustainable communities. As we move further into the digital age, the convergence of technology and corporate social responsibility will continue to evolve, presenting both opportunities and challenges for businesses. It is imperative that companies remain agile, adaptable, and committed to ethical practices, leveraging the power of technology as a tool to create lasting positive impact while upholding the highest standards of responsibility and accountability.

Technology-Driven Evolution of the Corporate Social Responsibility Ecosystem, this book can be helpful for different stakeholders, specifically businesses and society, and how it can serve as a link between the two:

For Businesses:

The book provide businesses with insights into how leveraging technology can enhance their CSR efforts, leading to improved brand reputation, customer loyalty, and stakeholder trust. This can ultimately translate into a competitive advantage in the market.

By presenting case studies, best practices, and cutting-edge research, the book offer strategic guidance to businesses on how to effectively integrate technology into their CSR initiatives, enabling them to optimize resource allocation, streamline processes, and maximize impact.

The book provides valuable insights into leveraging technology for effective stakeholder engagement, enabling businesses to foster transparency, build trust, and collaborate with stakeholders to co-create sustainable solutions.

For Society:

The book raise awareness about the role of technology in driving positive social and environmental change, empowering individuals, communities, and organizations to advocate for responsible business practices and hold companies accountable.

By addressing the digital divide and emphasizing the importance of inclusive and accessible technology solutions, the book contributes to ensuring that the benefits of technology-driven CSR initiatives are equitably distributed across society.

Through its exploration of technologies such as renewable energy, sustainable manufacturing, the book inspires and inform society about sustainable practices and solutions that can be adopted at individual, community, and governmental levels.

The book serve as a valuable resource for educational institutions, civil society organizations, and policymakers, providing insights and knowledge to build capacity and develop effective strategies for leveraging technology in addressing social and environmental challenges.

Linking Business and Society:

The book establishes a common language and framework for understanding the intersection of technology, corporate social responsibility, and sustainable development. This shared understanding can facilitate more effective dialogue and collaboration between businesses and societal stakeholders.

By highlighting the potential for technology-driven CSR initiatives to create shared value for both businesses and society, the book encourages a mindset of mutual benefit and collaboration, rather than viewing them as separate or conflicting interests.

The book explore how technology can enable collaborative platforms and ecosystems where businesses, civil society organizations, governments, and communities can come together to co-create and implement innovative solutions to complex social and environmental challenges.

1. By addressing ethical considerations and providing guidance on responsible and inclusive technology practices, the book serve as a bridge, aligning the interests and values of businesses and society, ensuring that technological advancements contribute to the greater good.

Below are the all 10 chapters' insights:

1. A study on CSR eco-system in India

This chapter delves into the intricate landscape of CSR in India, exploring the various stakeholders, regulatory frameworks, and cultural nuances that shape the CSR ecosystem within the country. It provides a comprehensive analysis of the evolution of CSR practices in India, tracing its roots from the traditional concept of philanthropic giving to the modern, strategic approach that aligns social and environmental initiatives with business objectives.

The chapter examines the critical role played by the Indian government in promoting and regulating CSR through legislation such as the Companies Act of 2013, which mandates that companies above a certain size and profitability allocate a portion of their profits towards CSR activities. It also highlights the unique challenges faced by Indian companies in implementing effective CSR programs, including issues related to poverty, inequality, and infrastructure gaps.

Furthermore, the chapter explores the influence of cultural and societal factors on CSR practices in India. It delves into the traditional Indian values of philanthropy, social responsibility, and environmental stewardship, and how these values have shaped the CSR landscape. The chapter also examines the role of non-governmental organizations (NGOs), civil society groups, and local communities in collaborating with businesses to address social and environmental challenges.

The chapter provides insights into the best practices and innovative approaches adopted by leading Indian companies in various sectors, such as healthcare, education, environmental conservation, and rural development. It also highlights the challenges faced by smaller companies and those operating in resource-constrained environments in implementing CSR initiatives.

This chapter serves as a comprehensive resource for understanding the unique dynamics of the CSR ecosystem in India, offering valuable insights for businesses, policymakers, and researchers seeking to navigate and contribute to the sustainable development of the country.

2. The Evolution of Corporate Social Responsibility: A Technology Driven Approach in the management studies institution

This chapter explores the intersection of CSR and technology within the context of management education institutions. It examines how these institutions, which play a crucial role in shaping future business leaders and decision-makers, are embracing technology to enhance their CSR initiatives and foster a culture of responsible and sustainable business practices.

The chapter begins by tracing the evolution of CSR in management education, from its traditional focus on philanthropy and community outreach to its current emphasis on integrating social and environmental considerations into the core curriculum and institutional operations. It highlights the growing recognition among management institutions of the need to equip students with the knowledge, skills, and mindset required to navigate the complex challenges of sustainable development and stakeholder engagement.

Furthermore, the chapter delves into the various ways in which technology is being leveraged by management institutions to drive their CSR efforts. This includes the use of online platforms and digital tools for student engagement, virtual case studies and simulations to foster critical thinking and problem-solving skills, and data analytics to measure and report on the institution's social and environmental impact.

This chapter serves as a valuable resource for management educators, students, and institutional leaders seeking to understand and leverage the power of technology to embed CSR principles into the fabric of management education, ultimately shaping a generation of responsible and sustainable business leaders.

3. Challenges and opportunities within the evolving CSR landscape in India

This chapter delves into the dynamic and rapidly evolving landscape of CSR in India, exploring the key challenges and opportunities that businesses and stakeholders face in this rapidly changing environment. It provides a comprehensive analysis of the various factors driving the transformation of CSR practices in the country, including regulatory changes, shifting societal expectations, and the growing awareness of environmental and social issues.

The chapter examines how businesses are adapting their strategies to address these complexities and ensure their efforts are relevant, inclusive, and impactful. Furthermore, the chapter highlights the opportunities presented by the growing emphasis on transparency, accountability, and stakeholder engagement within the CSR realm. It explores how companies are leveraging technology, such as digital platforms and advanced data analytics, to enhance their reporting and disclosure practices, fostering greater trust and credibility with stakeholders.

The chapter also delves into the emerging trends and innovative approaches shaping the future of CSR in India, such as the integration of the United Nations Sustainable Development Goals (SDGs) into corporate strategies, the rise of impact investing, and the increasing focus on employee engagement and volunteerism.

4. Organizational technological innovation and environmental sustainability regulations

This chapter explores the relationship between organizational technological innovation and environmental sustainability regulations, examining how companies are leveraging technological advancements to comply with and even exceed regulatory requirements while driving sustainable business practices.

The chapter begins by providing an overview of the global regulatory landscape related to environmental sustainability, highlighting key international agreements, such as the Paris Agreement and the United Nations Sustainable Development Goals (SDGs), as well as regional and national laws and policies. It examines the role of these regulations in setting standards, establishing benchmarks, and incentivizing businesses to reduce their environmental footprint and adopt sustainable practices.

Furthermore, the chapter delves into the various technological innovations that organizations are embracing to meet and surpass these regulatory requirements. This chapter provides a comprehensive understanding of the interplay between organizational technological innovation and environmental sustainability regulations, serving as a valuable resource for businesses, policymakers, and researchers seeking to navigate the complexities of sustainable development and drive positive change through the responsible integration of technology.

5. Dynamics of Sustainable and Ethically Responsible Business Practices in Corporate Social Responsibility

This chapter delves into the multifaceted dynamics of sustainable and ethically responsible business practices within the realm of corporate social responsibility (CSR). It examines the intricate interplay between economic, environmental, and social considerations, and how companies are adopting holistic approaches to integrate sustainability and ethical principles into their core business strategies and operations.

The chapter begins by exploring the evolution of the sustainability paradigm, tracing its roots from the early environmental movements to the present-day emphasis on the triple bottom line of economic, social, and environmental performance. It highlights the growing recognition among businesses that sustainability is not just a moral imperative but also a strategic necessity for long-term competitiveness and value creation.

Furthermore, the chapter delves into the ethical foundations of responsible business practices, examining the various philosophical and moral frameworks that guide corporate decision-making and stakeholder engagement. It explores concepts such as stakeholder theory, utilitarianism, and virtue ethics, and how these principles shape the development and implementation of CSR initiatives.

6. Corporate Environmental Responsibilities of Auto Manufacturers in the Chennai Auto Industry

In Chapter 6, the focus is on the corporate environmental responsibilities of auto manufacturers within the Chennai auto industry. This sector, being a significant contributor to both economic growth and environmental degradation, faces increasing scrutiny regarding its environmental impact. The chapter delves into the strategies and initiatives undertaken by auto manufacturers in Chennai to mitigate their environmental footprint. It explores various aspects such as adoption of eco-friendly technologies, waste management practices, and compliance with environmental regulations. By examining the challenges faced and the solutions implemented, the chapter offers insights into how the auto industry in Chennai is striving to balance economic growth with environmental sustainability.

7. The Development of Web 1.0 to Web 2.0 CSR Disclosure of Data

Chapter 7 traces the evolution of Corporate Social Responsibility (CSR) disclosure from the static Web 1.0 era to the interactive Web 2.0 landscape. It explores how the advent of Web 2.0 technologies has transformed the way companies communicate their CSR activities and engage with stakeholders. The chapter discusses the shift from traditional CSR reporting methods to more dynamic and interactive platforms, such as social media and corporate websites. It also examines the benefits and challenges associated with this transition, including increased transparency, stakeholder engagement, and the potential for greenwashing. By analyzing the development of CSR disclosure in the digital age, the chapter provides valuable insights into the changing dynamics of corporate sustainability reporting.

8. Technology's Role in Sustainable Urban Development in Smart Cities

Chapter 8 investigates the role of technology in promoting sustainable urban development within the context of smart cities. It examines how advancements in technology are being leveraged to address key challenges faced by modern urban centers. The chapter explores various initiatives and innovations aimed at improving resource efficiency, enhancing mobility, and reducing environmental impact in smart cities. It also discusses the potential benefits of smart city technologies, including increased energy efficiency, improved public services, and enhanced quality of life for residents. By highlighting the intersection of technology and urban sustainability, the chapter offers valuable insights into the future of smart city development.

9. Savant Electronics Sustainability or Corporate Social Responsibility

In Chapter 9, the focus is on Savant Electronics and its approach to sustainability and corporate social responsibility (CSR). The chapter examines the various initiatives and practices adopted by Savant Electronics to integrate sustainability into its business operations. It explores the company's efforts to minimize environmental impact, promote ethical labor practices, and engage with local communities. The chapter also discusses the challenges faced by Savant Electronics in implementing sustainability initiatives and the strategies employed to overcome them. By analyzing Savant Electronics' sustainability journey, the chapter provides valuable lessons for other organizations seeking to enhance their CSR performance and contribute to positive social and environmental outcomes.

10. Empowering Consumer Rights: Unveiling the Impact of Big Data Analytics in Upholding Consumer Protection

Chapter 10 explores the impact of big data analytics on consumer protection and empowerment. It examines how companies are utilizing big data technologies to gain insights into consumer behavior, preferences, and needs. The chapter discusses the potential benefits of big data analytics in improving consumer rights protection, such as detecting fraudulent activities, personalizing consumer experiences, and enhancing product safety and quality. It also addresses the ethical and privacy concerns associated with the use of big data in consumer protection efforts. By shedding light on the opportunities and challenges of big data analytics in upholding consumer rights, the chapter contributes to the ongoing discourse on responsible data usage and consumer empowerment in the digital age.

Chapter 1
A Study on CSR Eco-System in India

Kuldeep Singh
https://orcid.org/0000-0002-8180-4646
School of Management, Gati Shakti Vishwavidyalaya, India

Madhvendra Misra
Indian Institute of Information Technology, Allahabad, India

G. Vinodini Devi
https://orcid.org/0009-0006-4061-3604
Koneru lakshmaiah Education Foundation, India

ABSTRACT

This chapter provides a critical look at the definition of CSR based on the subject matter literature available. Because CSR is an emerging term in both definition and reality, this study aims to illustrate CSR in relation to the different stakeholders and entities termed as CSR ecosystem in this study. Furthermore, this study also offers an outline of factors, interactions, and contexts under review, such as CSR, Section 135 of the Indian Companies Act 2013, the effect of the Act on corporate bodies' CSR operations, the impact of CSR on societal and environmental concerns, contrasting CSR schools of thinking, and gaps in the views of management, government, shareholders, and stakeholders.

DOI: 10.4018/979-8-3693-3238-2.ch001

INTRODUCTION

The study gives an overview of variables, associations, and contexts under study, such as CSR, Section 135 of Indian Companies Act 2013, the impact of the Act on CSR activities of corporate bodies, the effect of CSR on societal and environmental issues, conflicting schools of thought in relation to CSR, and difference in perceptions of managers, government, shareholders, and stakeholders towards CSR activities. This study seeks to examine the effect that the enforcement of Section 135 of Indian Companies Act 2013 has had on CSR spending of firms and firm performance. Thus, this study gives an overview of CSR spending of firms before and after the enforcement of Section 135, and its effect on firm performance.

CSR is a complex subject, especially when the various complications related to CSR definition, scope and performance are taken into consideration. For example, the stakeholder perspective of CSR advocates that multiple stakeholders must be served, but the question then arises, the interests of how many stakeholders may be served by a firm, and to what extent? This would lead to some areas receiving more attention and others, less so. This in turn would lead to a gap in the expected or intended service and actual service rendered. The present study seeks to examine this gap along with issues mentioned in preceding sentences, and this study gives brief descriptions of the same.

In the aspect of business organizations, James Moore's use of the term "ecosystem" that included buyers, intermediaries (marketing channels, agents, and those producing similar goods and services), suppliers, and industry itself. In the context of this study, the effect and association of CSR on and with multiple elements such as environment, society, shareholders, stakeholders, and the firm itself are examined, and these elements form a larger part of the CSR ecosystem. Thus, this study is a comprehensive study of the CSR ecosystem in India in light of the enforcement of Section 135 of Companies Act 2013.

In the following section, the objectives of the study are listed. Next, the study establishes the context of the study which broadly revolves around Section 135 of Companies Act 2013. The section begins by establishing that formal focus on CSR at the policy level concluded with the enactment of Section 135 of the Companies Act 2013 (MCA, 2013), which made CSR spending and disclosure mandatory for firms falling in certain categories. The section goes on to specify conflicts and opinions that arose due to the enforcement of Section 135 and attempts to objectively evaluate these opinions and schools of thought. The debate whether CSR is voluntary or mandatory, especially after nations such as Indonesia, Denmark, France, Philippines, Spain, Argentina, Brazil, India, Norway, and European Union enforced laws related to CSR, has been highlighted. Elements affecting participation of firms in CSR activities, such as firm size and motivation are discussed. The need, significance and interpretation of CSR and its role in relation and conjunction with government responsibility and duty are examined in the section and later in the study. The section also discusses how the absence of a clear definition of CSR may lead to undesirable outcomes and practices. The difference in the nature of CSR in developed and developing countries and its effect on CSR activities actually being carried out in the two different contexts are considered. It is these issues that lead to gaps in intended and actual services rendered under CSR. As mentioned earlier, firm size and motivation play important roles in how and to what extent firms are engaged in CSR. Voluntary and mandatory CSR and their outcomes and implications are discussed in the section. The section specifically explains and discusses performance driven and stakeholder-oriented approaches of CSR. Financial performance would certainly be a very important consideration for all firms, and the relation between CSR and financial performance is one of significant interest. The section discusses the association through findings of studies on the topic. The section also attempts to highlight the nature and extent of CSR activities and spending of firms before and after Section 135. The point of view that mandating CSR is indeed an implicit tax has been considered.

The following sections provide definitions of CSR, an overview of CSR in India and explanation of the CSR ecosystem. The study further identifies research gap and establishes the need for the study. Study-wise organization of the present study is provided before conclusion.

Objectives of the Study

The objectives of the present study are as follows:

- To evaluate the impact of the enforcement of Section 135 of Indian Companies Act 2013 on CSR spending and organizational performance.
- To assess the impact of firms' CSR practices on social inclusion (Positive societal change).
- To analyze the gap between CSR practices adopted by companies and societal/environmental issues.
- To identify processes that companies follow to perform CSR.
- To assess managerial perceptions towards CSR.
- To assess the perceptions of beneficiaries towards CSR as practiced by companies.

Context

After the global financial crisis that took place in the 2000s, mandatory CSR reporting gained prominence as an issue (KPMG-UNEP, 2010). CSR governance became stricter to make corporations disclose how they acted towards the welfare and benefit of stakeholders and community at large. The formal focus on CSR at the policy level started in the year 2009 by issuance of CSR voluntary guidelines by Ministry of Corporate Affairs (MCA, 2009) that become the base of the legitimate Corporate Social Responsibility resulted in the enactment of Section 135 of the Indian Companies Act, 2013, making 2% of average profit of past three years for specific types of business organizations (MCA, 2013). Regulation of CSR is a fairly controversial topic. Majority of existing definitions emphasize that CSR is voluntary in nature (Dahlsrud, 2008) and associate CSR with acts not legally prescribed (e.g., "CSR is beyond that which is required by law," McWilliams & Siegel, 2001, p. x), a few occurrences related to mandatory CSR have brought the voluntary nature of the notion under scrutiny (Waagstein, 2011). The debate whether CSR is voluntary, or mandatory has intensified (Waagstein, 2011) especially after nations such as Indonesia, Denmark, France, Philippines, Spain, Argentina, Brazil, India, Norway and European Union enforced laws related to CSR.

In India, Section 135 of Companies Act 2013 gave birth to conflicting opinions. According to some, mandatory CSR is an opportunity for corporate bodies to work with government and civil society towards national growth and sustainable development; others view it as a middle path that balances regulatory and liberal aspects of the state to achieve growth and social stability. Yet others opine that mandatory CSR actually is an initiative of the government to make the private sector pay for the government's own failures. This argument may however be countered by the view that CSR, especially in context of developing nations, supplements government resources and assists in filling up gaps in governance, particularly where central and state governments 'reachability is minimum, dishonest, and under-resourced, and other institutions are also fragile (Matten and Moon, 2008; Blowfeld and Fyrnas, 2005; Visser, 2008). Another argument made is that while CSR has been made mandatory, in the absence of a clear definition of the same, corporate bodies would find ways to circumvent the law and feign activities to fulfil legal requirements. The essential question in this context would then be the actual fulfilment of the welfare gap in India.

An important aspect to be borne in mind is that the nature of CSR and associated issues differ in developed and developing nations. Developing nations face more problems related to society, environment and sustainability; these are further affected by global challenges, financial crisis, economic growth, investment, savings and developing economic movements (Visser, 2007). Accordingly, CSR in low-income nations focuses on alleviation of poverty, healthcare, education and development of infrastructure (Amaeshi et al. 2006). Contrarily, developed nations are confronted by concerns related to society, green marketing, fair trade, environment and climate change and ethical responsible investments. In the Indian context, CSR is oriented towards socio- economic activities aimed at development of the nation, though not necessarily at the expense of the economic objectives of corporate bodies. However, given the number, diversity and intensity of environmental, societal and economic issues facing India, it would not be reasonable to expect CSR activities, whether voluntary or mandatory, to resolve all problems immediately.

Besides regulation, the motivation behind firms' performance of CSR is also of great significance; it determines how firms view CSR and associated activities. This is clear by the fact that companies in India voluntarily engaged in CSR activities even before CSR was made mandatory. Such firms truly wish to work towards the welfare of the people and the environment and give back to the society in which they operate. Studies identify two motivations for firms engaging in CSR - 'performance driven' and 'focus on stakeholders' (Basu and Palazzo, 2008; van der Wees, 2009). Firms engaging in performance driven CSR are motivated by the notion that CSR would, in the long run, translate into corporate financial performance. Here, expenses on CSR are in line with the objective of maximization of shareholders' wealth with no compromise between shareholder interests and business social responsibility. Stakeholder-oriented CSR, on the other hand, is motivated by the firm's desire to serve all stakeholders' interests. This approach reconciles the social and economic objectives of a firm motivated by serving the society's interests (van der Wees, 2009). Again, the stakeholder perspective has been criticized through the argument that maximization of stakeholder value does not align with operational efficiency of the firm. Further, due to the presence of multiple objectives and stakeholders, it becomes unclear what the manager must seek to maximize. Also, without a clear rationale to perform CSR, the exercise may be used for personal gain, dishonest practices, and irresponsible managerial behavior. Firm size is another factor that decides a firm's participation in CSR activities. Before the enforcement of Section 135, majority of medium-sized Indian firms were not involved in CSR activities. However, for medium sized Indian firms, private returns from CSR activities are smaller. Thus, it can clearly be seen why relatively smaller firms would be hesitant to engage in CSR activities.

Again, it is noteworthy that from the perspective of public policy, mandatory reporting becomes necessary when firms see CSR as non-paying and not converting into financial performance (all the more so in the short run), but CSR remains valuable to society. Further, mandatory reporting may evoke positive CSR response in greater likelihood as opposed to voluntary reporting (where it could hypothetically be zero). Mandatory reporting could help decrease irregularities in information which is vital to stakeholder engagement and establishing corporate accountability (Hung et al., 2013).

Amidst all this debate, a question that arises is that while CSR does benefit society, does it really benefit the firm clearly, if not in measurable terms? Studies show that CSR improves corporate governance, transparency, and accountability to stakeholders, and assists in nation building (Shetty, V. S, 2014). Reported benefits from contribution to CSR include enhanced financial performance, decreased operating cost, better brand image and reputation, increased sales and customer loyalty, product safety, material recyclability and greater utilization of renewable resources (Gautam, A.S, 2010). Disclosure of CSR activities also yields similar benefits (Gautam, A.S, 2010). Thus, communication of CSR activities by a firm could lead to better social responsiveness. Enhanced CSR performance has also been shown to lead to better access to finance and help decrease capital constraints and improve stakeholder engagement (Cheng et al., 2013). Studies further show that CSR reduces the need to advertise as CSR activities act as a very good substitute to advertising. Ferrell, Liang and Renneboog (2016) found better governance to be associated with greater CSR expenditures, indicating that CSR may be attributed to efforts to enhance firm value. Whether CSR affects firm performance is a question that concerns many. Significant research has been conducted on CSR and its effect on the financial performance of the firm, and studies have yielded mixed results. It has been reported that CSSR positively affects net profits but shows no effect on EPS and ROA. Further, CSR showed greater impact on profits if the firm spent more on CSR; this also led to sustainable development of the firm and society (Bafna, A, 2017). (Singh and Misra, 2021) stated that CSR positively impacted organizational performance of Multinational companies in India; organizational performance adopted by the study included managerial perceptions. The study by Abu Bakar & Ameer, 2011; Orlitzky, Schmidt, & Rynes, 2003; Van Beurden & Gössling, 2008 gave similar results. In addition to the positive link between CSR and financial performance (ROC, ROE, ROA, net profit etc.), studies show a positive relation between CSR and non-financial parameters like job satisfaction, employee commitment and internal reputation (Truptha, S.2016). Studies show that after the implementation of Section 135 of Companies Act, 2013, firms, on average spend 2% towards CSR, and that CSR positively and significantly impacts a firm's overall financial performance (PBT, ROC, ROE, and ROA). While it has been reported that overall, firms have increased their CSR spending after Section 135, an interesting outcome of Section 135 has been that large firms that spent less than 2% before the law came into force enhanced their CSR activities thereafter, while firms spending more than 2% before the law took effect reduced their CSR expenditure. Studies assert that increased contribution to CSR enhances a firm's financial performance, and vice versa. In light of the above, it may be said that CSR does have a reasonably clear effect on overall firm performance, though it might not significantly impact individual indicators of firm performance. Here, it may be argued that whether motivated by strategic concerns or the desire to serve all stakeholders, a firm would benefit from voluntarily disclosing the CSR activities in which it is engaged.

With respect to Section 135, arguments are made that imposing the Section is actually the imposition of an implicit tax on firms. While many would view this as such, an important distinguishing factor here is that existing CSR provisions serve as a centralized tax for decentralized use by private parties mainly for project execution. This perceived indirect tax indeed gives firms control over how to disburse their funds and resources; firms can choose projects that align with their operations. The money and resources accumulated by the government would be used for CSR and other purposes cannot be guaranteed under explicit taxation.

It may be concluded that while amendments in the Companies Act seek a balance between firm and shareholder interests and welfare of society and stakeholders, continuous research would be needed to determine the degree to which the objectives were achieved and the actual gap between the two. Of course, the level of achievement and width of gap may increase, decrease or fluctuate with time. This only underscores the need for constant research and monitoring of the phenomenon.

BACKGROUND

Economic expansion and population growth have exerted significant pressure on already depleting natural resources and contributed to environmental degradation. In light of these issues, business organizations have been forced to manage and use their resources more efficiently and responsibly. Business has been widely accepted as a unit of society, and the responsibility thereof towards society almost universally acknowledged. It is argued that a business is responsible towards society because first, business operations impact society and environment, and second, the business becomes a very part of that society in which it operates. Therefore, considering raising concerns about the environment worldwide and the impact of business operations thereupon, there is a clear need to change conventional ways of doing business. A business organization is an organ of society, and the impact of business operations on not just shareholders, but also the environment and members of the community must be considered by management. This is the principle on which CSR (corporate social responsibility) is based. While most organizations have been engaged in acts of social responsibility of some kind, the pressure to establish CSR as a business discipline and achieve positive outcomes relevant to business (as a result of CSR initiatives) has increased lately. This view emphasizes that the value of a firm is entirely based on the firm's capability to create wealth for its shareholders, and that any social or environmental initiative not making profits for the firm is a waste of corporate resources. While this line of thought may be questioned, one reason for such an opinion could be that manager's worry that emphasis on CSR would translate into more duty and think that CSR must be carried out by the government. Another reason is that mangers opine that carrying out CSR initiatives would increase operating costs (cost of improving working conditions of staff, increasing employee benefits, and cost of environmental protection equipment) which would in turn reduce profit margins. One more reason is that some managers view CSR as charity, and strongly believe that firms are not for charity originations and under no obligation to solve social problems; thus, CSR is an unwanted burden on firms.

However, the profit only perspective has received significant criticism. People are increasingly of the view that firms should not conduct business only for selfish reasons; business organizations should conduct operations without harming public interest and the environment. Businesses must manufacture quality products that don't harm the environment and adopt processes that keep the environment clean by minimizing effluent release and waste generation, and recycling waste. Further, businesses must take care of the welfare and security of employees. Firms must inform all stakeholders about steps taken towards the betterment and welfare of the environment and society. Corporations today are legally bound to carry out CSR activities. Firms also experience tremendous pressure due to public opinion and campaigns led by non-government organizations. In 2013, the Indian government mandated that the latest provision in Companies Act 2013 (Shedule VII, section-135) be applied for financial year 2013-2014 according to which, every business firm with net worth of Rs. 500 crore or more, or turnover of Rs. 1000 crore or more, or net profit of Rs. 5 crores or more, had to expend at least 2% of average net profits during the last three financial years on CSR activities. According to law, CSR activities are set to have a positive impact on society as a whole.

After CSR being made compulsory by law, many companies have been involved in development of infrastructure, production of food grains, advancements in science and technology, and imparting education. However, several pressing problems, especially in the Indian context, remain, such as those related to sustainable development, climate change, environmental protection, pollution, etc. Clearly, CSR should focus on inclusive growth and betterment of society, environment, and all stakeholders.

The present study analyzes the current CSR ecosystem in the Indian context and examines the effect of mandating CSR reporting with characteristic features and operative issues of CSR. **Corporate Social responsibility (CSR) Defined**

Corporate Social responsibility (CSR) is a key concept in organization-society association. CSR, stakeholder management and business ethics have received much research and corporate attention over the last century. The notion that businesses have a responsibility beyond just generating wealth for themselves has been emphasized for a long time. It was, however, in the 1950s and 1960s that the significance, influence and study of CSR grew (Carroll and Shabana, 2010). Sir Howard Bowen's text in his book "Social Responsibilities of the Businessman" (1953) is

regarded by many researchers and academicians as a noteworthy starting point to the discussions and arguments that have taken place in literature. Howard Bowen argued that large corporations actually and significantly impacted citizens' lives (Carroll, 1999), and emphasized their responsibility. With time, the notion of CSR underwent modification and transformation into different other concepts such as positive societal change, business ethics theory, stakeholder theory, corporate governance, corporate citizenship, triple bottom line (TBL) social reporting, and more recently, CSR 2:0 (Donaldson and Pretson, 1995; Carroll, 1999, Visser, 2008).

Michael Hopkins (2003) defined CSR in terms of treating a firm's stakeholders responsibly and ethically. While the words 'ethically' and 'responsibly' imply treating shareholders such that is acceptable in civilized societies, the term CSR entails economic responsibility also. Stakeholders may be internal to a firm or external. Indeed, the natural environment is also a stakeholder. The broader objective of corporate social responsibility is to fashion higher standards of living (for people within the firm and without) while conserving firm profitability.

Kotler and lee (2005) explained CSR in terms of dedication towards improving the well-being of the community through appropriate business practices and assistance in the form of business resources.

The World Business Council for Sustainable Development (WBCSD) defines CSR as "the commitment of business to contribute to sustainable economic development, working with employees, their families and the local communities" (WBCSD, 2001). It may thus be concluded that primarily, the notion of CSR entails business corporations' obligation to work towards fulfilling a broad set of stakeholder needs (Clarkson, 1995; Waddock et al., 2002). In general terms, CSR may be seen as a group of management practices seeking to ensure maximum positive effects of a firm's operations on society. Thus, CSR implies that a business should seek to function in a manner that fulfills and goes beyond the legal, ethical, commercial, and public expectations that members of society have of the business (BSR, 2001). It is also noteworthy that while governments have been conventionally responsible for improving the living conditions of their populations, needs have often exceeded governments' abilities. This has led to the debate on responsibilities of businesses towards society and environment. Business firms themselves have assumed responsibility and engaged in CSR activities which has in turn helped firms to differentiate themselves from competitors in the eyes of stakeholders.

Furthermore, the expectations of local community members and the society in which a business organization exist, are continuously changing, mostly determined by the economic and social theories, different political and cultural events, socio-economic behavior, environment, and transformation in the knowledge of society that really puts a burden on the domestic as well as multinational business organizations. Social progress and success of business are interrelated. As social progress depends on the success of businesses in that society, businesses too depend on the stability of society to thrive. Thus, corporate bodies should reconsider and restructure their roles considering the interdependence of business and society and engage in CSR activities accordingly.

Dahlsrud (2008) identified key themes considered by several definitions that were used by CSR researchers to forward a synthesis of the position of CSR definitions by way of content analysis of present definitions. The first theme is based on the relationship between business and society (such as CSR can "contribute to positive societal change", "community welfare", and "social inclusion"). The second theme related to environmental concerns such as "carbon footprint", "ecological balance", and "climate change" (Van Marrewijk, 2003). The third theme comprised financial and economic aspects related to firm's responsibilities such as "contribution toward economic development", "sustainable development", and "organizational performance" (World Business Council for Sustainable Development, 2000). Another important theme is based on organizational links with stakeholder groups such as "how business firms interact with their suppliers, customers, employees and community members" (Lea, 2002). Out of all these themes the final common portion is the voluntary nature of Corporate Social Responsibility such as "CSR could be beyond the legitimate requirement", "voluntary support to the local community needs", and "voluntary support to the natural environment" (McWilliams & Siegel, 2001). In a study, made by Dahlsrud's (2008) emphasized the importance of voluntary aspects of corporate social responsibility. In his study Dahlsrud's (2008) found that 21 out of thirty-seven CSR definitions were based on the voluntary dimension, and no single definition considered any mandate characteristics.

While the above argument may be made to emphasize the voluntary nature of CSR, the voluntary perspective may be criticized on the basis that it promotes irresponsible behavior and fails to establish accountability. On the other hand, mandatory aspects of CSR could help in creating awareness and may priorities CSR as an appropriate policy intervention (Cominetti & Seele, 2016). Horrigan (2007) stated that mandatory provision may enable the regulatory environment for assessable socially responsible indicators that might be valuable not only for one state but the whole nation.

CSR in India

Being the country known by its largest democracy, also the second most populous nation (around 1.2 billion) reported by (CIA, 2012) and has been achieved the significant economic growth in terms of global comparison, the role of businesses in India must be examined not only with respect to economic growth, but also social welfare, especially considering the country's diverse social, cultural and economic background. After 1991, India's economy gained momentum, especially when the GoI dismantled the Licence Raj. It also has been predicted that by 2035, the country would be the third largest economy in the global world after US and China (Wilson and Purushothaman, 2006; Kaplinsky and Messner, 2008). In spite of bright expectations and predictions, India is heavily over-populated, home to nearly 33 percent of the world's chronically malnourished, and faces serious issues such as widespread poverty, corruption, and environmental degradation (CIA, 2012). In light of the above, CSR assumes greater importance in the Indian context and warrants greater research attention and examination. Practices, barriers, drivers and responsibilities associated with CSR in India must be studied so that CSR may offer more value to the nation not only in terms of economic growth, but also societal and environmental well-being and preservation.

CSR's history in India can be traced back to the days of the Kings. According to Arthashasthra by Kautilya, "the welfare of the king lies in the welfare of the people and his happiness in their happiness" (cited in Jose et al., 2003). The nineteenth century saw attempts for mutual wellbeing by traders and religious/ethnic groups; certain advantages even flowed beyond the community (Jose et al., 2003). Charity and faith have been closely connected in India; people in India are normally raised with the belief that giving is pleasant (Jose et al., 2003). Businesses made valuable contributions to schools, hospitals, and rural development projects long before India's independence in 1947, even big corporations especially public sector companies carried out state- sponsored CSR operations since independence (Mohan, 2001). CSR in India could be seen as an integral part of long-term market growth initiatives over the last couple of years (Balasubramanian et al., 2005).

Awareness about CSR among stakeholders and activities associated therewith by business firms have been growing; this may be seen as a result of government regulations, expectations of the public (Mohan, 2001) and also corporate will, nevertheless, CSR is still evolving. Regulators and the government have also shown interest in CSR institutionalization in recent years. In 2009 and 2011, voluntary guidelines on CSR were introduced by the Government of India. In 2011, in accordance with the voluntary guidelines on CSR set out in the same year, SEBI directed the top 100 listed companies to submit details of their CSR activities in a Business Responsibility Report accompanying the annual report. And then, the Government of India made mandatory provisions for CSR spending, reporting, policy and governance under the Companies Act, 2013. According to Section 135 of Companies Act, 2013 every company with any of the three - 1) net worth of Rs. 5000 million or more; 2) turnover of Rs. 10000 million or more; or 3) net profit of Rs. 50 million or more –

Figure 1. CSR spending criteria for Indian companies

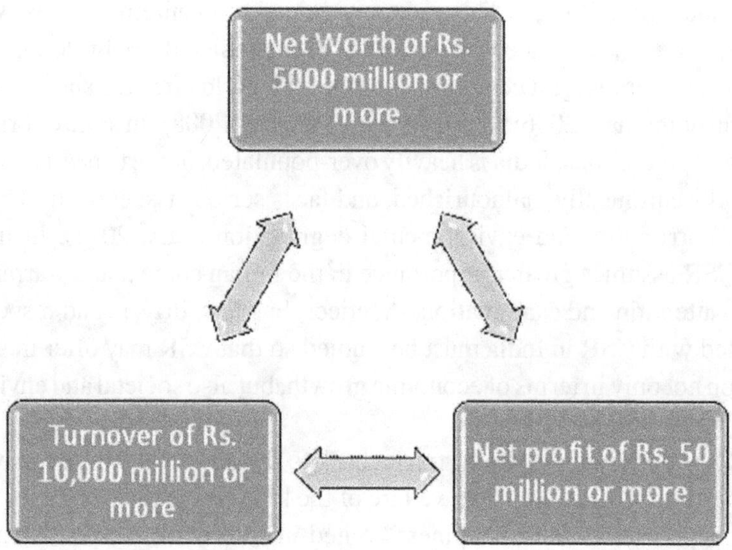

A governing CSR committee of at least three senior board members must be established by all businesses falling within the scope of this law, where one would be an independent director from outside the company. CSR procedures, architecture and activities will be controlled by this board. This task should specifically include the broad goals of the CSR, implementation processes for developing relationships with other organizations, as well as audit and monitoring duties. The activities expressly included in this Act to be eligible for CSR Spending include (As on 31st Jan 2021):

- *(i) "Eradicating hunger, poverty and malnutrition, promoting health care including preventive health care and sanitation including contribution to the Swatch Bharat Kosh set-up by the Central Government for the promotion of sanitation and making available safe drinking water".*
- *(ii) "Promoting education, including special education and employment enhancing vocation skills especially among children, women, elderly and the differently abled and livelihood enhancement projects".*

- *(iii) "Promoting gender equality, empowering women, setting up homes and hostels for women and orphans; setting up old age homes, day care centers and such other facilities for senior citizens and measures for reducing inequalities faced by socially and economically backward groups".*
- *(iv) "Ensuring environmental sustainability, ecological balance, protection of flora and fauna, animal welfare, agroforestry, conservation of natural resources and maintaining quality of soil, air and water including contribution to the Clean Ganga Fund set-up by the Central Government for rejuvenation of river Ganga".*
- *(v) "Protection of national heritage, art and culture including restoration of buildings and sites of historical importance and works of art; setting up public libraries; promotion and development of traditional art and handicrafts".*
- *(vi) "Measures for the benefit of armed forces veterans, war widows and their dependents".*
- *(vii) "Training to promote rural sports, nationally recognized sports, Paralympic sports and Olympic sports".*
- *(viii) "Contribution to the prime minister's national relief fund or any other fund set up by the central govt. for socio economic development and relief and welfare of the schedule caste, tribes, other backward classes, minorities and women".*
- *(ix) "Contribution to incubators funded by Central Government or State Government or any agency or Public Sector Undertaking of Central Government or State Government, and contributions to public funded Universities, Indian Institute of Technology (IITs), National Laboratories and Autonomous Bodies (established under the auspices of Indian Council of Agricultural Research (ICAR), Indian Council of Medical Research (ICMR), Council of Scientific and Industrial Research (CSIR), Department of Atomic Energy (DAE), Defense Research and Development Organization (DRDO), Department of Biotechnology (DBT), Department of Science and Technology (DST), Ministry of Electronics and Information Technology) engaged in conducting research in science, technology, engineering and medicine aimed at promoting Sustainable Development Goals (SDGs)".*
- *(x) "Rural development projects".*
- *(xi) "Slum area development. Explanation.- For the purposes of this item, the term `slum area' shall mean any area declared as such by the Central Government or any State Government or any other competent authority under any law for the time being in force".*
- *(xii) "Disaster management, including relief, rehabilitation and reconstruction activities".*

The Act further describes "fraud" with the creation of a separate entity to investigate where appropriate, the law seeks to plug loopholes in the system to create "a better business environment". The amended company law reinforces balance of power in the governance system of companies, enables greater transparency to decisions of the board, and enhances responsibility of firms' directors and auditors. The legislation requires firms to rotate auditors and clarify the supervision of firms accepting public fund deposits and intra-company loans.

In the Indian sense, empirical literature on the existence of corporate-initiated CSR is minimal. There exist a few case studies that focus on best practices. Most of these case studies emphasize that structural and strategic association between the industry and financial and non-financial stakeholders is key to successful outcomes of stakeholder engagement. Some literature mentions elements that possibly explain enhancement in performance, like greater number of activities and expending 2% of firm's net profit. Others suggest a lack of analytical data on the effects of CSR in India on the types of interventions that include expanding business performance simultaneously or shifting their CSR routes to paths of community growth. In the Indian background, however, there is a notable lack of detailed studies on the relationship between CSR (strategy and scope) and corporate success and sustainability. There is a clear need for a study on CSR ecosystem which may contribute to finding CSR as a link between business and society.

CSR Ecosystem Defined

"In the context of business firms, James Moore introduced the term "ecosystem" and defined it as comprising "customers, market intermediaries (including agents and networks, and those selling complementary goods and services), suppliers, and, of course, the organization itself. Moore's concept of business ecosystem considered the firm linked to its larger environment and emphasized the role of individual firms and the collective health of the system in which the firm existed (Moore, 2006).

We refine and extend Moore's original concept to highlight the necessity of generating value for society through CSR. With respect to CSR in India, three drivers are key – coordination bodies (government and infrastructure provider/funders), beneficiaries (local communities) and awareness creators (annual reports, news, and media). These three drivers have an impact on multiple stakeholders in business and society and combine with them to create CSR ecosystem. In terms of interconnectedness of stakeholders, CSR may be defined as follows:

"A CSR ecosystem is a mutually dependent system interconnected by various ecosystem members, including industry, government, society, and awareness creators".

Business firms' impact and act as enablers in CSR ecosystem. However, the interrelatedness between stakeholders forms the core of the CSR ecosystem. In future, this CSR ecosystem could extend to participation in or leveraging broader social activities. Society would determine the context at the macro-level within which CSR policies would be established and developed at the micro level.

Drivers of the CSR ecosystem

Figure 2. CSR ecosystem reference for critical parts of an eco-system has been taken from Indian philanthropy report, 2014, by Bain & Co.

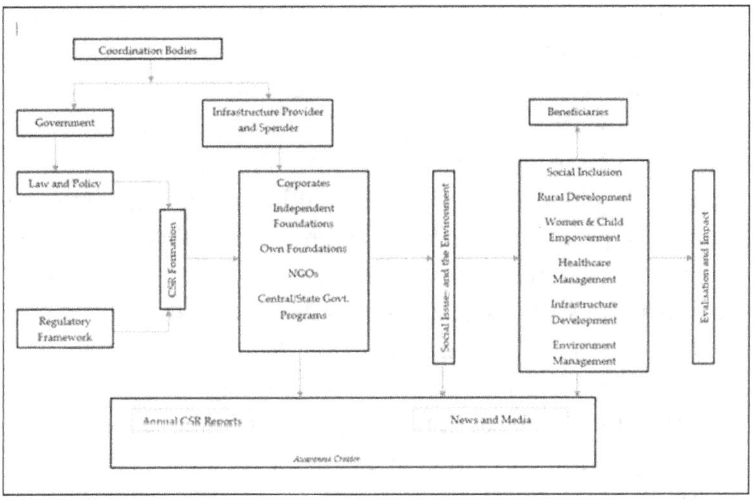

(Sheth & Singhal, 2014)

Coordination Bodies: Coordination bodies make sure that CSR is practiced as laid down by law and doesn't clash with accepted cultural norms. These bodies assist in communication on legal procedures and follow CSR activities to enforce social justice and protect the environment. The main coordination bodies in CSR ecosystem are as follows:

Governments: Governments ensure that firms act as per law and established CSR norms (Neha, 2014). Government action is vital to creating an environment that reduces risk, cost and barriers to operations, and rewards and offers competitive and responsible organizations opportunities to grow. Hence, the role of governments in CSR initiatives by firms is significant. Government bodies, when promoting a CSR agenda, face problems associated with identifying priorities, creating awareness, offering incentives and support, and mobilizing resources through cross- sectoral cooperation (Neha, 2014). Key roles of governments when supporting CSR include (but are not limited to) the following:

i. ***Regulation*** – This applies to the rules and penalty provisions therein and other mechanisms for regulating the practices and operations of business. Governments regulate firm behavior and practice by establishing minimum standards for business performance, appointing enforcers and inspectorates to oversee business conduct, establishing codes or laws to restrict undesirable business conduct, granting licenses to operate and mandating environmentally friendly industrial systems.

ii. ***Facilitating*** – Governments facilitate firms' engagement in CSR activities to promote social and environmental well-being. Governments may also provide tax incentives and impose penalties to promote responsible business practices. Other measures for facilitation may include steps to ensure that firms may access required information; dissemination of information about minimum legal requirements for carrying out responsible business practices; formulate policies for CSR activities to be carried out by firms; Providing, where appropriate such as capacity development, business consulting services and industry technical assistance; or, promoting supply chain programs and voluntary certification,

iii. **Brokering** - Government may act as a broker between partnering public sector bodies, businesses, civil society organizations and other stakeholder groups to address complex social and environmental challenges. Government may initiate dialogue in multi- stakeholder processes and engage in government-industry collaboration towards capacity building and developing sectoral CSR guidelines. The role of government can expand to engaging stakeholders in the setting of standards, fostering public-private community development collaborations, and mobilizing capital.

In this position as broker, government may also facilitate the involvement of key players in a CSR agenda by, for example, providing research funding or leading initiatives, collaborating, and disseminating information, teaching, or raising awareness.

iv. **Instigating** - It can take various kinds, including dedication to the application of international principles; education or awareness-raising programs; official policy documents; publicity of good CSR activities carried out by other leading companies; unique award schemes related to CSR (such as the National Green Business Award); or support of specific metrics, rules, frameworks, and criteria for pro-CSR.

Infrastructure Providers/Funders

Companies seek to fill some gaps through reinforcing social infrastructure - a part of the infrastructure sector – and developing social services like schools, universities, hospitals, prisons and community housing. Several providers and stakeholders confirm their active role in such CSR activities; this role goes beyond the conventional role of being a mere funds provider.

A few modes of being a provider are given below:

In-house Implementation: A firm sets up an internal department to work directly with communities towards designing and implementing projects.

Formation of Own Foundations: Several large stipulated corporations spend through their own foundations which become a repository for the firm's CSR fund. In recent years, this practice has gained prominence and become more compliant to the requirements of the statute.

Third Party Implementation: A firm may choose to involve a local or an international NGO as third party to work with local communities on CSR projects; this may include supporting or assisting in an existing initiative being carried out by others.

Multi-stakeholder Partnership: A firm may set up or join a voluntary or collaborative alliance, network, or partnership to share risk, responsibilities, resources, and competencies; such an alliance shares a common cause and commitment thereto.

Hybrid:*A firm employs a combination of two or more implementation models to deliver the various components of its CSR* program.

Clearly, there are several ways in which a firm may choose to discharge its duties related to CSR, but an increasingly large number of companies today prefer to establish their own foundations to carry out CSR.

In India, the law allows firms to engage in CSR through a registered trust or society which has at least three years of experience in a given area, a foundation (Section 25 Company) set up by the

firm or a subsidiary/associate company. Most large companies such as Tata Motors Ltd and Marico Ltd adopt a mixed model of CSR; they carry out projects themselves as well as establish foundations and work through non-profit organizations. Organizations such as State Bank of India (SBI) and Reliance Industries Ltd prefer the foundation route.

A company must follow a through and stringent selection process to ensure that that the organizational business responsibility goals are being achieved in the most transparent, effective and efficient manner.

Maximum transparency should be ensured during the selection process. A Company before appointing an organization should check background of organization to ensure that it is able to implement its" Corporate Social Responsibility" programs.

Beneficiaries

According to literature, CSR beneficiaries act as important sources of information and offer managers key insights into firm behavior and attitude towards CSR practices. In India, several firms engage with local communities near their area of operations; these communities become the beneficiaries of CSR activities.

Husted and Allen (2006) asserted that the key difference between global and local CSR was the community demanding it. Local CSR focuses on a firm's obligations towards the standards of the local community, while global CSR concerns itself with a firm's obligations that relate to hyper norms or universal standards to which all societies can be held (Husted and Allen, 2006).

CSR is not limited to philanthropy, abiding by international codes of conduct, or disseminating them across supply chains; CSR, in essence, seeks to bring about a visible difference in lives and livelihoods of people, develop local capability and fulfil needs and aspirations of locals (World Business Council for Sustainable Development, 2001).

Studies have shown that before CSR legitimation in India, local communities believed that while firms contributed towards societal development through social infrastructure investments, the impact of such efforts remained marginal in terms of capacity building or decreasing inequality

among communities. However, after the enforcement of the new Companies Act, contribution of businesses towards socio-economic and environmental initiatives has increased. Education, healthcare, livelihood, and skill development have been the recipients of the majority of CSR funds.

Awareness Creator

A valid argument is that if a firm displays strong commitment towards CSR, but that commitment is not acknowledged or recognized, then does engagement in CSR activities yield any benefit to the firm? Stakeholder perception of a firm's CSR activities is vital as such perception leads to customer loyalty and firm reputation. Over the years, CSR awareness has increased in developing Asian nations (Levine, 2008). There also has been increased acknowledgement among Indian firms of the importance of CSR in the resolution of societal and environmental issues and the benefits CSR offers in terms of value creation, effective management of the triple bottom line and employee engagement. Benefits such as positive brand image and reputation bestowed by CSR could act as a competitive advantage in the marketplace (Gupta, 2002). However, these rewards may be secured only when stakeholders know of the firm's CSR endeavors (McWilliams and Siegel, 2001). Multinational firms are increasingly adopting the practice of not only carrying out CSR activities, but also reporting them on company websites and annual reports (Holcomb, Upchurch, and Okumus 2007). Media has an important role to play in the dissemination of information related to CSR. Dissemination of information may inspire others to either engage or increase engagement in social causes; it is also necessary to highlight initiatives that are inspired as such.

Companies like ITC and Vedanta have conducted impressive advertising campaigns to highlight their values and communicate their CSR initiatives. Organizations such as Shell have devised innovative methods to make people aware of their CSR initiatives. The belief that CSR offers a competitive edge in the highly competitive marketplace is becoming increasingly prevalent among firms. Firms must consider communicating with as many stakeholders as possible, including constituent bodies, public and private enterprises, academic institutions, media, government support organizations and individuals to strengthen the CSR ecosystem and devise initiatives that offer maximum value to stakeholders while aligning with firm objectives.

CONCLUSION

The Corporate Social Responsibility (CSR) ecosystem in India is a complex and evolving landscape that plays a crucial role in addressing the country's multifaceted social, economic, and environmental challenges. Given India's status as the world's largest democracy and the second most populous nation, CSR initiatives hold significant potential to drive positive change and contribute to sustainable development. The country's journey towards economic growth, particularly post-1991 following the dismantling of the Licence Raj, has highlighted the need for businesses to not only focus on economic advancement but also on social welfare and environmental sustainability.

The historical roots of CSR in India are deeply embedded in the cultural and philanthropic traditions of the country. From the days of the kings, as noted in Kautilya's Arthashastra, to the 19th century when traders and religious groups undertook mutual well-being initiatives, the ethos of giving and community support has been integral to Indian society. This tradition continued through India's independence and into the modern era, with businesses contributing to various social causes such as education, healthcare, and rural development. The post-independence period saw public sector companies leading state-sponsored CSR operations, which have since been complemented by private sector initiatives.

In recent years, the Indian government has taken significant steps to institutionalize CSR through regulations and guidelines. The introduction of voluntary guidelines in 2009 and 2011, followed by the mandatory CSR provisions under the Companies Act, 2013, marked a pivotal shift in the CSR landscape. These regulations mandate that companies meeting specific financial criteria allocate a portion of their profits to CSR activities, thereby ensuring that businesses contribute to social and environmental causes. The Companies Act outlines various activities eligible for CSR spending, ranging from eradicating hunger and promoting education to ensuring environmental sustainability and protecting national heritage.

The CSR ecosystem in India is driven by multiple stakeholders, including coordination bodies, beneficiaries, and awareness creators. Coordination bodies, such as the government and infrastructure providers, play a vital role in ensuring that CSR activities are conducted in compliance with legal requirements and societal norms. They facilitate and broker partnerships, provide necessary incentives, and create an enabling environment for CSR initiatives. The government's role in regulating, facilitating, brokering, and instigating CSR activities is crucial in promoting responsible business practices and fostering cross-sectoral collaboration.

Beneficiaries, particularly local communities, are central to the CSR ecosystem. Businesses often engage with communities near their areas of operation, addressing their needs and aspirations through various social initiatives. The focus on local CSR, as opposed to global CSR, underscores the importance of addressing community-specific issues and fostering sustainable development at the grassroots level. The impact of CSR on local communities has been significant, particularly in areas such as education, healthcare, and livelihood enhancement.

Awareness creation is another critical aspect of the CSR ecosystem. Effective communication of CSR initiatives helps build a positive brand image, enhance reputation, and secure stakeholder loyalty. The increasing recognition of CSR's importance in resolving societal and environmental issues has led to greater transparency and reporting of CSR activities by businesses. Media plays a key role in disseminating information about CSR initiatives, inspiring other firms to engage in similar activities and raising public awareness about the benefits of CSR.

REFERENCES

Abu Bakar, A. S., & Ameer, R. (2011). Readability of corporate social responsibility communication in Malaysia. *Corporate Social Responsibility and Environmental Management*, 18(1), 50–60. 10.1002/csr.240

Amaeshi, K., Adi, A. B. C., Ogbechie, C., & Amao, O. O. (2006). Corporate social responsibility in Nigeria: Western mimicry or indigenous influences? *Available atSSRN* 896500. 10.2139/ssrn.896500

Bafna, A. (2017). A Study on the Impact of CSR on Financial Performance of Companies in India. *International Journal of Engineering Technology. Science and Research*, 4(12), 325–331.

Balasubramanian, N. K., Kimber, D., & Siemensma, F. (2005). Emerging opportunities or traditions reinforced? An analysis of the attitudes towards CSR, and trends of thinking about CSR, in India. *Journal of Corporate Citizenship*, 2005(17), 79–92. 10.9774/GLEAF.4700.2005.sp.00010

Basu, K., & Palazzo, G. (2008). Corporate social responsibility: A process model of sensemaking. *Academy of Management Review*, 33(1), 122–136. 10.5465/amr.2008.27745504

Blowfield, M., & Frynas, J. G. (2005). 'Editorial: Setting New Agendas - Critical Perspectives on Corporate Social Responsibility in the Developing World. *International Affairs*, 81(3), 499–513. 10.1111/j.1468-2346.2005.00465.x

Bowen, H. (1953). *Social responsibilities of the businessman*. Harper.

BSR. (2001). *Business for Social Responsibility, Introduction to Corporate Social Responsibility*. BSR. https://www.bsr.org/bsrresources/WhitePapers_IssueArea.cfm

Carroll, A. B. (1999). Corporate social responsibility: Evolution of a definitional construct. *Business & Society*, 38(3), 268–295. 10.1177/000765039903800303

Carroll, A. B., & Shabana, K. M. (2010). The business case for corporate social responsibility: A review of concepts, research and practice. *International Journal of Management Reviews*, 12(1), 85–105. 10.1111/j.1468-2370.2009.00275.x

Cheng, B., Ioannou, I., & Serafeim, G. (2014). Corporate social responsibility and access to finance. *Strategic Management Journal*, 35(1), 1–23. 10.1002/smj.2131

CIA. (2012). *The World Fact Book: India*. CIA. www.cia.gov/library/publications/the- worldfactbook/geos/in.html

Clarkson, M. E. (1995). A stakeholder framework for analyzing and evaluating corporate social performance. *Academy of Management Review*, 20(1), 92–117. 10.2307/258888

Cominetti, M., & Seele, P. (2016). Hard soft law or soft hard law? A content analysis of CSR guidelines typologized along hybrid legal status. *uwf UmweltWirtschafts-Forum, 24*(2), 127- 140.

Dahlsrud, A. (2008). How corporate social responsibility is defined: An analysis of 37 definitions. *Corporate Social Responsibility and Environmental Management*, 15(1), 1–13. 10.1002/csr.132

Donaldson, T., & Preston, L. E. (1995). The stakeholder theory of the corporation: Concepts, evidence, and implications. *Academy of Management Review*, 20(1), 65–91. 10.2307/258887

Ferrell, A., Liang, H., & Renneboog, L. (2016). Socially responsible firms. *Journal of Financial Economics*, 122(3), 585–606. 10.1016/j.jfineco.2015.12.003

Gautam, R., & Singh, A. (2010). Corporate social responsibility practices in India: A study of top 500 companies. *Global Business and Management Research*, 2(1), 41–56.

Gupta, S. (2002). Strategic dimensions of corporate image: corporate ability and corporate social responsibility as sources of competitive advantage via differentiation. [Doctoral dissertation, Temple University]. http://proquest.umi.com/ pqdweb?-did1/4727401921&Fmt1/47&clientId1/469955&RQT1/4309&VName1/4PQD,

Holcomb, J. L., Upchurch, R. S., & Okumus, F. (2007). Corporate social responsibility: What are top hotel companies reporting? *International Journal of Contemporary Hospitality Management*, 19(6), 461–475. 10.1108/09596110710775129

Hopkins, M. (2003). The business case for CSR: Where are we? *International Journal of Business Performance Management*, 5(2-3), 125–140. 10.1504/IJB-PM.2003.003261

Hung, M., Shi, J., & Wang, Y. (2013, September). The effect of mandatory CSR disclosure on information asymmetry: Evidence from a quasi-natural experiment in China. In *Asian finance association (AsFA) 2013 conference.*

Husted, B. W., & Allen, D. B. (2006). Corporate social responsibility in the multinational enterprise: Strategic and institutional approaches. *Journal of International Business Studies*, 37(6), 838–849. 10.1057/palgrave.jibs.8400227

Jose, P. D., Bandi, R., & Mehra, M. (2003). Corporate social responsibility in the information and communication technologies sector: Discussion. *IIMB Management Review*, 15(4), 61–75.

Kaplinsky, R., & Messner, D. (2008). Introduction: The impact of Asian drivers on the developing world. *World Development*, 36(2), 197–209. 10.1016/j.worlddev.2007.06.006

Kotler, P., & Lee, N. (2005). Best of breed: When it comes to gaining a market edge while supporting a social cause,"corporate social marketing" leads the pack. *Social Marketing Quarterly*, 11(3-4), 91–103. 10.1080/15245000500414480

KPMG. U. (2010). Carrots and Sticks–Promoting Transparency and Sustainability. *An update on trends in Voluntary and Mandatory Approaches to Sustainability Reporting*.

Lea, R. (2002). *Corporate Social Responsibility, Institute of Directors (IoD) member opinion survey*. IoD: London. http://www. epolitix.com/data/companies/images/Companies/Institute-of- Directors/CSR_Report.pdf [23 June 2003].

Levine, M. A. (2008). China's CSR expectations mature. *The China Business Review*, 35(6), 50–53.

Matten, D., & Moon, J. (2008). "Implicit" and "explicit" CSR: A conceptual framework for a comparative understanding of corporate social responsibility. *Academy of Management Review*, 33(2), 404–424. 10.5465/amr.2008.31193458

MCA. (2009). *Corporate Social Responsibility Voluntary Guidelines in 2009 by the Ministry of Corporate Affairs*. Government of India.

MCA. (2013). *Companies Act, 2013, Ministry of Corporate Affairs, Government of India, New Delhi*. MCA. http://www.mca.gov.in/Ministry/pdf/CompaniesAct2013.pdf

McWilliams, A., & Siegel, D. (2001). Profit maximizing corporate social responsibility. *Academy of Management Review*, 26(4), 504–505.

Mohan, A. (2001). *'Corporate Citizenship: Perspectives from India', Journal of Corporate Citizenship*. Greenleaf Publishing. 10.9774/GLEAF.4700.2001.su.00012

Moore, J. F. (2006). Business ecosystems and the view from the firm. *Antitrust Bulletin*, 51(1), 31–75. 10.1177/0003603X0605100103

Orlitzky, M., Schmidt, F. L., & Rynes, S. L. (2003). Corporate social and financial performance: A meta-analysis. *Organization Studies*, 24(3), 403–441. 10.1177/0170840603024003910

Sheth, A., & Singhal, M. (2014). *India Philanthropy Report 2014*. Bain, Incorporated.

Shetty, V. S. (2014). Corporate Social Responsibility: An Analysis and Implications under Companies Act 2013. *Asian Journal of Humanities and Social Studies, 2*(5).

Singhal, N. (2014). Corporate social responsibility-Role of government. *International Journal of Computing and Corporate Research*, 4(1), 16–21.

Van Beurden, P., & Gössling, T. (2008). The worth of values–a literature review on the relation between corporate social and financial performance. *Journal of Business Ethics*, 82(2), 407–424. 10.1007/s10551-008-9894-x

van der Wees, M. (2009) *Why firms invest in Corporate Social Responsibility: A study in the Dutch bank and insurance industry,* [Master Thesis, University of Matricht].

Van Marrewijk, M. (2003). Concepts and definitions of CSR and corporate sustainability: Between agency and communion. *Journal of Business Ethics*, 44(2), 95–105. 10.1023/A:1023331212247

Visser, W. (2007). Corporate social responsibility in developing countries. In Crane, A., Mcwilliams, A., Matten, D., Moon, J., & Siegel, D. (Eds.), *The Oxford handbook of corporate social responsibility* (pp. 473–499). Oxford University Press.

Visser, W. (2008). Corporate social responsibility in developing countries. In *The Oxford handbook of corporate social responsibility*. Oxford Press. 10.1093/oxfordhb/9780199211593.003.0021

Waagstein, P. R. (2011). The mandatory corporate social responsibility in Indonesia: Problems and implications. *Journal of Business Ethics*, 98(3), 455–466. 10.1007/s10551-010-0587-x

Waddock, S. A., Bodwell, C., & Graves, S. B. (2002). Responsibility: The new business imperative. *The Academy of Management Perspectives*, 16(2), 132–148. 10.5465/ame.2002.7173581

WBCSD. (2001). *Measuring Eco-efficiency—A Guide to Reporting Company Performance*. WBCSD.

Wilson, D., & Purushothaman, R. (2006). 1. Dreaming with BRICs: the path to 2050. *Emerging economies and the transformation of international business: Brazil, Russia, India and China (BRICs), 1*.

World Business Council for Sustainable Development WBCSD. (2000). *Corporate Social Responsibility: Making Good Business Sense*. WBCSD.

KEY TERMS AND DEFINITIONS

Corporate Social Responsibility (CSR): Corporate Social Responsibility (CSR) is a self-regulatory business model that enables companies to be socially accountable to themselves, their stakeholders, and the public. By practicing CSR, companies can be conscious of the impact they have on all aspects of society, including economic, social, and environmental factors. CSR goes beyond compliance with regulatory requirements and involves voluntarily adopting policies and practices that contribute to societal goals, particularly those that are ethical and sustainable. The concept of CSR can be traced back to the early 20th century, but it gained significant traction in the 1950s and 1960s with the rise of environmental awareness and social movements. Howard Bowen, often referred to as the "father of CSR," laid the groundwork with his seminal work "Social Responsibilities of the Businessman" in 1953. He argued that large corporations had significant power and influence, and thus, a responsibility to use that influence to benefit society. There are various frameworks and theories associated with CSR, including the Triple Bottom Line (TBL) and Stakeholder Theory. The Triple Bottom Line, popularized by John Elkington, posits that companies should commit to focusing on social and environmental concerns just as they do on profits. Hence, the three pillars of TBL are "People, Planet, and Profit." Stakeholder Theory, introduced by R. Edward Freeman, expands the focus from shareholders to include all parties affected by corporate activities, such as employees, customers, suppliers, and the broader community. Implementing CSR involves a range of activities. These can include environmental efforts such as reducing carbon footprints, waste management, and sustainable resource use; philanthropic initiatives like donating to charities and community projects; ethical labor practices including fair wages, safe working conditions, and child labor policies; and volunteerism where companies encourage their employees to volunteer for causes. The benefits of CSR extend beyond mere compliance and risk management. Companies that effectively implement CSR can experience enhanced brand reputation, customer loyalty, and employee satisfaction. A robust CSR strategy can also result in operational cost savings through eco-efficiency measures, improved investor relations, and access to new markets. Moreover, CSR can drive innovation as companies seek out new, sustainable business practices and products. Despite its benefits, CSR is not without challenges. One of the primary issues is the perception of CSR as a form of window-dressing or greenwashing, where companies superficially engage in CSR activities to improve their image rather than make substantive changes. Additionally, integrating CSR into the core business strategy requires significant commitment and can pose challenges in aligning with short-term financial goals.

CSR Ecosystem: The CSR ecosystem refers to the network of interconnected stakeholders and entities involved in the realm of Corporate Social Responsibility (CSR). This ecosystem includes businesses, government bodies, non-governmental organizations (NGOs), communities, consumers, employees, and the environment. Understanding the CSR ecosystem is crucial because it highlights the interdependencies and relationships that influence how CSR is implemented, managed, and perceived. At the center of the CSR ecosystem are businesses, which are the primary drivers of CSR activities. Companies engage in CSR to achieve various objectives, such as improving brand reputation, gaining customer loyalty, enhancing employee engagement, and contributing to societal well-being. Within the company, various departments, including HR, marketing, and sustainability teams, play roles in designing and implementing CSR strategies. Governments are key stakeholders in the CSR ecosystem. They establish the regulatory framework within which businesses operate. For instance, in India, the enforcement of Section 135 of the Indian Companies Act, 2013, mandates that certain companies spend a portion of their profits on CSR activities. Governments can also provide incentives, guidelines, and support for CSR initiatives, thereby influencing corporate behavior towards more sustainable and socially responsible practices. Non-Governmental Organizations (NGOs) and civil society organizations are crucial in the CSR ecosystem. They often act as watchdogs, ensuring that companies adhere to their CSR commitments and do not engage in practices such as greenwashing. NGOs can collaborate with businesses on various projects, bringing in expertise, grassroots connections, and credibility. These collaborations can enhance the impact and reach of CSR initiatives. Communities and consumers are direct beneficiaries of CSR activities. Companies engage with local communities through various initiatives such as education programs, healthcare services, and infrastructure development. Consumers, increasingly aware of social and environmental issues, can drive CSR by choosing to support companies with strong CSR commitments. This consumer behavior creates a market incentive for businesses to engage in CSR. Employees are also significant stakeholders in the CSR ecosystem. Companies that prioritize CSR often see higher levels of employee satisfaction and engagement. Employees take pride in working for socially responsible companies, and CSR initiatives can enhance recruitment and retention. Moreover, involving employees in CSR activities, such as volunteer programs, can foster a sense of purpose and community within the organization. The environment is an integral part of the CSR ecosystem. Environmental sustainability is a major focus of CSR, with companies adopting practices to reduce their carbon footprint, manage waste, and use resources efficiently. Environmental NGOs and regulatory bodies work to ensure that businesses comply with environmental standards and contribute positively to environmental conservation efforts. The CSR ecosystem is dynamic and complex, with various stakeholders influencing and being influenced by corporate actions. Effective CSR requires businesses to navigate this ecosystem thoughtfully, balancing the needs and expectations of different stakeholders. This involves transparent communication, genuine engagement, and a commitment to continuous improvement.

Performance-Driven CSR: Performance-driven Corporate Social Responsibility (CSR) is a strategic approach where companies engage in CSR activities with the expectation that these efforts will ultimately enhance their financial performance. This perspective aligns CSR with business objectives such as profit maximization and shareholder value enhancement, viewing social and environmental initiatives as investments that can yield measurable returns. The premise of performance-driven CSR is that socially responsible behavior can lead to tangible business benefits. These benefits can include improved brand reputation, increased customer loyalty, enhanced employee engagement, cost savings through operational efficiencies, and better risk management. By strategically integrating CSR into their core business operations, companies can create value not only for society but also for themselves. One of the primary drivers of performance-driven CSR is the growing consumer preference for socially responsible companies. Consumers today are more informed and concerned about the social and environmental impacts of their purchases. They tend to support brands that demonstrate a commitment to ethical practices, sustainability, and community engagement. This shift in consumer behavior creates a competitive advantage for companies that prioritize CSR, leading to increased sales and market share. Employee engagement is another critical aspect of performance-driven CSR. Companies that are perceived as socially responsible often enjoy higher levels of employee satisfaction and retention. Employees take pride in working for organizations that align with their values and contribute positively to society. CSR initiatives, such as volunteer programs and sustainable business practices, can foster a sense of purpose and community among employees, enhancing their motivation and productivity. Operational efficiency is a significant benefit of performance-driven CSR. Companies that adopt sustainable practices, such as reducing energy consumption, minimizing waste, and optimizing resource use, can achieve substantial cost savings. For instance, implementing energy-efficient technologies or recycling programs can lower operational costs and improve profitability. Additionally, sustainable practices can mitigate risks associated with environmental regulations and potential liabilities. Risk management is another crucial element of performance-driven CSR. By proactively addressing social and environmental issues, companies can reduce the risk of negative publicity, legal disputes, and regulatory penalties. Effective CSR strategies can enhance a company's reputation and build trust with stakeholders, making it more resilient in the face of crises and challenges. To implement performance-driven CSR effectively, companies need to adopt a strategic and systematic approach. This involves setting clear goals and metrics, integrating CSR into the company's business model, and continuously monitoring and reporting on progress. Companies often use frameworks such as the Global Reporting Initiative (GRI) or the United Nations Sustainable Development Goals (SDGs) to guide their CSR activities and measure their impact. However, performance-driven CSR is not without its challenges. One of the main criticisms is the potential for companies to prioritize profit over genuine social impact. This can lead to superficial or insincere CSR efforts, commonly known as greenwashing, where companies engage in CSR activities primarily for positive publicity rather than meaningful change. To avoid this, companies must ensure that their CSR initiatives are authentic, transparent, and aligned with their core values.

Section 135 of the Indian Companies Act, 2013: Section 135 of the Indian Companies Act, 2013, marks a significant milestone in the legal framework governing Corporate Social Responsibility (CSR) in India. It mandates that certain categories of companies spend a minimum percentage of their profits on CSR activities. This legislation represents a shift from voluntary to mandatory CSR, aiming to ensure that businesses actively contribute to social and environmental welfare. The introduction of Section 135 was driven by the need to formalize CSR activities and ensure that companies are accountable for their social and environmental impacts. According to this section, any company with a net worth of INR 500 crore or more, a turnover of INR 1000 crore or more, or a net profit of INR 5 crore or more during any financial year must constitute a CSR Committee. This committee is responsible for formulating and recommending CSR policies, deciding on the CSR activities to be undertaken, and monitoring the implementation of these activities. The law requires eligible companies to spend at least 2% of their average net profits of the preceding three years on CSR activities. If a company fails to spend this amount, it must specify the reasons for not doing so in its annual report. This provision ensures transparency and accountability, compelling companies to justify their CSR expenditure or lack thereof. Section 135 outlines specific areas where CSR funds can be allocated. These include activities related to eradicating hunger and poverty, promoting education, enhancing vocational skills, ensuring environmental sustainability, and contributing to the national heritage. The act encourages companies to focus on local areas where they operate, thereby addressing community-specific needs and fostering local development. The impact of Section 135 has been significant. It has institutionalized CSR in India, making it a strategic priority for businesses. Many companies have established dedicated CSR departments and appointed CSR professionals to ensure compliance with the law. The mandatory nature of the law has led to increased CSR spending and more structured and impactful CSR initiatives. However, the legislation has also sparked debates and challenges. Critics argue that mandatory CSR can be seen as an implicit tax on businesses, potentially diverting resources from core business activities. Some businesses may engage in CSR merely to comply with the law, without genuine commitment to social responsibility. Additionally, the lack of a clear and comprehensive definition of what constitutes CSR can lead to varied interpretations and implementations. Despite these challenges, Section 135 has been a catalyst for positive change. It has brought CSR to the forefront of corporate strategy and governance, encouraging companies to integrate social and environmental considerations into their business models. The law has also promoted greater collaboration between companies, NGOs, and government bodies, leading to more effective and impactful CSR projects.

Stakeholder-Oriented CSR: Stakeholder-oriented Corporate Social Responsibility (CSR) focuses on the company's responsibility to serve the interests of all its stakeholders, not just its shareholders. This approach emphasizes ethical business practices, social equity, and environmental sustainability, aiming for a balance between economic goals and societal welfare. Stakeholder-oriented CSR is rooted in the belief that businesses have a duty to consider the impacts of their actions on all parties involved or affected by their operations. The foundation of stakeholder-oriented CSR lies in Stakeholder Theory, which was developed by R. Edward Freeman in the 1980s. Freeman argued that businesses should create value for all stakeholders, including employees, customers, suppliers, communities, and the environment, rather than focusing solely on maximizing shareholder returns. This theory challenges the traditional view of shareholder primacy and promotes a more inclusive and ethical approach to business management. Employees are a key focus of stakeholder-oriented CSR. Companies that prioritize the well-being of their employees tend to offer fair wages, safe working conditions, opportunities for professional growth, and inclusive workplaces. Engaging employees in CSR activities, such as community service projects or sustainability initiatives, can enhance their sense of purpose and loyalty to the organization. A satisfied and motivated workforce is more productive and contributes positively to the company's overall performance. Customers are another critical stakeholder group. Stakeholder-oriented CSR involves ensuring product safety, quality, and ethical marketing practices. Companies that demonstrate a commitment to social and environmental responsibility often enjoy greater customer loyalty and trust. In today's market, consumers increasingly prefer to support brands that align with their values and contribute positively to society. This preference drives companies to adopt responsible practices, such as using sustainable materials, reducing environmental impact, and supporting social causes. Suppliers and business partners are also essential stakeholders. Ethical supply chain management is a crucial aspect of stakeholder-oriented CSR. Companies must ensure that their suppliers adhere to fair labor practices, environmental standards, and ethical sourcing guidelines. Building strong, transparent, and mutually beneficial relationships with suppliers can lead to improved product quality, reduced risks, and enhanced corporate reputation. Communities where companies operate are significantly impacted by corporate activities. Stakeholder-oriented CSR emphasizes giving back to these communities through initiatives such as education programs, healthcare services, infrastructure development, and environmental conservation. Engaging with local communities and addressing their needs can enhance the company's social license to operate, fostering goodwill and long-term sustainability. The environment is a non-human stakeholder that plays a central role in stakeholder-oriented CSR. Companies are increasingly recognizing the importance of sustainable practices to mitigate their environmental impact. This includes reducing greenhouse gas emissions, minimizing waste, conserving natural resources, and promoting biodiversity. Environmental sustainability not only benefits the planet but also reduces operational costs and regulatory risks for businesses. Implementing stakeholder-oriented CSR requires a holistic approach that integrates ethical considerations into all aspects of the business. Companies must engage in regular dialogue with stakeholders to understand their needs and expectations, set clear CSR goals, and measure and report on their progress transparently. Tools such as stakeholder mapping, materiality assessments, and sustainability reporting frameworks can aid in this process. While stakeholder-oriented CSR offers numerous benefits, it also presents challenges. Balancing the diverse and sometimes conflicting interests of various stakeholders can be complex. Companies must navigate these complexities thoughtfully, ensuring that their CSR efforts are genuine and aligned with their core values. Additionally, there is a risk of superficial or symbolic actions, known as "CSR-washing," which can undermine stakeholder trust and corporate credibility.

Stakeholders: Stakeholders are individuals, groups, or organizations that have an interest in or are affected by a company's operations, decisions, and activities. The concept of stakeholders is central to Corporate Social Responsibility (CSR) and business ethics, emphasizing the importance of addressing the needs and expectations of various parties involved with or impacted by a business. The term "stakeholder" was popularized by R. Edward Freeman in his 1984 book "Strategic Management: A Stakeholder Approach." Freeman's Stakeholder Theory argues that businesses should create value for all stakeholders, not just shareholders. This approach challenges the traditional shareholder-centric view, which prioritizes maximizing shareholder returns, by advocating for a more inclusive perspective that considers the interests of all parties affected by business activities. Stakeholders can be broadly categorized into two groups: internal and external stakeholders. Internal stakeholders include individuals and groups within the organization, such as employees, managers, and shareholders. Employees are crucial stakeholders as they are directly involved in the company's operations and can influence its success. Ensuring fair wages, safe working conditions, and opportunities for professional development are essential aspects of CSR related to employees. Managers are responsible for decision-making and strategic planning, and their actions significantly impact the company's direction and performance. Shareholders, or owners, invest in the company and expect returns on their investments, making their interests aligned with the company's financial success. External stakeholders encompass entities outside the organization that are affected by its activities. These include customers, suppliers, communities, government bodies, and the environment. Customers are vital stakeholders whose satisfaction and loyalty are critical to the company's success. CSR initiatives aimed at ensuring product safety, quality, and ethical marketing practices are essential for maintaining customer trust and loyalty. Suppliers provide the necessary goods and services for the company's operations, and fostering ethical and sustainable supply chain practices is crucial for maintaining positive relationships and ensuring long-term sustainability. Communities are significantly impacted by corporate activities, especially in areas where companies have a physical presence. CSR initiatives that support local education, healthcare, infrastructure, and environmental conservation can enhance community well-being and strengthen the company's social license to operate. Government bodies regulate business activities and ensure compliance with laws and regulations. Engaging with government stakeholders and adhering to regulatory requirements is essential for maintaining operational legitimacy and avoiding legal issues. The environment is a non-human stakeholder that is increasingly recognized in CSR and sustainability discourse. Companies impact the environment through resource extraction, emissions, waste generation, and land use. Sustainable business practices that minimize environmental harm and promote conservation are critical components of CSR. These practices include reducing carbon footprints, managing waste effectively, and utilizing renewable resources. Effective stakeholder management involves identifying key stakeholders, understanding their interests and concerns, and engaging with them through transparent communication and collaboration. Companies use various tools and frameworks to manage stakeholder relationships, such as stakeholder mapping, which helps identify and prioritize stakeholders based on their influence and interest.

Chapter 2
The Evolution of Corporate Social Responsibility:
A Technology-Driven Approach in the Management Studies Institution

Shri V. Niranchana
https://orcid.org/0000-0003-3342-3352
REVA University, India

ABSTRACT

This study explores how technology influences corporate social responsibility (CSR) practices in management studies. This study examines the growing interest in CSR and sustainability management among academics and practitioners in recent years. With the help of this technology, companies can better understand and address social and environmental issues. Technology provides advanced tools for data analysis, stakeholder engagement, and innovative solutions. However, there are concerns about the ethical use of technology and digital divide in communities. Companies must be mindful of these potential risks and ensure that their use of technology aligns with development goals. The integration of technology into CSR practices creates both opportunities and challenges for businesses. As technology continues to shape CSR, it is crucial for companies to prioritize data privacy, the ethical use of technology, and equitable access to digital resources.

DOI: 10.4018/979-8-3693-3238-2.ch002

INTRODUCTION

The essay "The Evolution of Corporate Social Responsibility: A Technology-Driven Approach in the Management Studies Institution" (Taneja et al., 2011) examines how technology influences students' beliefs about innovation and creativity in the context of corporate social responsibility. This study investigates the impact of developing technologies on students' perspectives and comprehension of corporate social responsibility (CSR) and sustainability, as well as the consequences for education. (Kouatli, 2019) The kids ought to enhance their skills. As technology becomes more integrated into many areas of business and society, it is crucial to comprehend how it affects the way corporate strategies are perceived and put into action (Jali et al., 2017). The concept of accountability is discussed by Brennan & Johnson in 2004. This essay explores how technology-driven techniques are changing the teaching landscape in management institutes. In addition, we examine the changing significance of students' ingenuity and originality within the framework of corporate social responsibility (CSR), as well as the impact of technical progress on their perception of sustainability. The reference is Schulz et al., 2018. The citation "Ismail et al., 2013" refers to a study conducted by Ismail and colleagues in 2013.

We examine case studies and instances where technologies have impacted students' viewpoints on corporate social responsibility (CSR), and we explore how these observations might be used in educational environments. (Moratis et al., 2006) In addition, we analyze the difficulties and possibilities that arise from the combination of technology and corporate social responsibility (CSR) at management studies institutions.

This analysis provides valuable information for educators and administrators as they navigate through this fast-evolving environment. (Filho et al., 2008) By understanding the influence of emerging technologies on students' perspectives and comprehension of corporate social responsibility, educators and administrators can modify their curriculum and instructional approaches to better equip students for the future of business and ensure that they can address the ethical and social dilemmas of a technology-driven society. The reference "González-Zamar et al., 2020" is provided. The reference is Sobczak et al., 2006. Moreover, the dependence on technology can potentially lead to a transition towards more environmentally friendly and ethically responsible economic strategies (Duho et al., 2019). Management study institutions can empower students to discover new solutions for environmental and social concerns by integrating technology into their curriculum. This method not only equips students for the future job market but also fosters a sense of accountability towards society and the environment. The reference is from Sobczak et al. (2006).

Overall, the incorporation of new and developing technology into educational institutions specializing in management studies significantly influences how students perceive and comprehend the concept of corporate social responsibility (Duho et al., 2019). It is important for educators and administrators to acknowledge and utilize the power of technology in influencing students' understanding, abilities, and attitudes towards corporate social responsibility (CSR) and sustainability (Karabasevic et al., 2016). This will ultimately facilitate the growth of a future cohort of business executives who possess the necessary skills to effectively navigate the intricate obstacles and possibilities presented by a swiftly changing technological environment. Moreover, these leaders will be dedicated to promoting beneficial social and environmental transformations (Duho et al., 2019).

LITERATURE REVIEW

The concept of corporate social responsibility has undergone substantial transformation in recent years, primarily due to the progress made in technology. The reference is from Taneja et al., 2011. The reference "Figueiró & Raufflet, 2015" is provided. Multiple studies have emphasized the significant influence of technology on how corporate social responsibility (CSR) is seen and practiced in management studies schools. The citation (McWilliams et al., 2006) An examination of current research indicates that developing technologies have not only impacted students' comprehension of sustainability and corporate social responsibility (CSR) but have also completely transformed the methods by which these topics are incorporated into the curriculum and educational process. (Moratis et al., 2006) The increasing incorporation of technology has resulted in a change in students' thinking, prompting them to think creatively and imaginatively about how organizations might function in a socially responsible and sustainable way. The citation (McWilliams et al., 2006)

The literature emphasizes the importance of equipping students with the necessary technological skills and knowledge to competently tackle CSR concerns in their future professions. (Rodríguez-Gómez et al., 2020). In light of the increasing importance of technology in company operations, it is crucial for management study institutes to provide their students with the necessary skills and knowledge to effectively utilize technology for ethical and sustainable business practices. The citation for the source is "Reavis & Tucci, 2020." Moreover, the literature emphasizes the importance of educators and administrators keeping up to date with technological innovations and understanding their consequences for corporate social responsibility (CSR). This requires an adaptable and proactive approach to designing the curriculum, guaranteeing that students are introduced to the most recent technical advancements and their possible uses in the field of corporate social responsibility. The reference is from the study conducted by González-Zamar et al. in 2020. Carrión-Martínez et al., 2020 are the references cited. By integrating case studies and tangible instances of technology-driven corporate social responsibility (CSR) activities, instructors can stimulate and encourage students to delve into the convergence of technology and its effects on society. Overall, the research has shown the significance of comprehending students' perceptions of developing technology in the context of corporate social responsibility (CSR) and sustainability. (Duho et al., 2019) The literature study emphasizes the crucial role of technology in influencing the comprehension and application of corporate social responsibility within academic institutions specializing in management studies. (Tuuli and colleagues, 2023) Given the ongoing impact of technological progress on the business world, it is critical for educators and administrators to adopt a technology-focused strategy that enables students to develop into ethical and socially conscious leaders in a constantly changing global market. The reference is from the study conducted by Rodríguez-Gómez and colleagues in 2020. In the current technological era, it is evident that incorporating technology into management studies institutions is not only advantageous, but also necessary for equipping students to tackle the challenges of corporate social responsibility and sustainability in the business world (Schulz et al., 2018). The citation is from Tickell et al. (2017).

Furthermore, educators and administrators must prioritize the cultivation of an environment that promotes innovation and creativity among students, while also recognizing the influence of developing technology on their perspectives and comprehension of corporate social responsibility (CSR).

(Source: Fleacă, 2017) (Erskine & Johnson, 2012) By promoting innovative thinking and encouraging students to investigate technical solutions for corporate social responsibility (CSR) concerns, educational institutions can have a significant impact on building a future generation of business executives who are dedicated to creating beneficial social and environmental transformations (Wieland & Fitzgibbons, 2013). Overall, the research emphasizes the significance of incorporating ethics, corporate social responsibility, and sustainability into management education in order to tackle the intricate difficulties that society confronts (Goby & Nickerson, 2011). Furthermore, the literature emphasizes the importance of equipping students with the necessary technology skills and knowledge to competently tackle CSR concerns in their future professions. (Rodríguez-Gómez et al., 2020) In light of technology's increasing significance in business operations, it is imperative for management study institutes to provide their students with the necessary tools and skills to effectively utilize technology for ethical and sustainable business practices. The reference is from Christensen et al. (2007).

To progress, management studies institutes must adopt a proactive and innovative approach to curriculum development. The reference "Rodríguez-Gómez et al., 2020" is cited. This entails integrating case studies and real-life illustrations of technology-driven corporate social responsibility (CSR) projects, which aim to inspire and encourage students to delve into the convergence of technology and social change. The reference "Rodríguez-Gómez et al., 2020" is provided. The reference is Schulz et al., 2018. By providing management education, students can be equipped to effectively utilize emerging technology to bring about positive social, environmental, and economic results for both enterprises and society.

This education empowers students to become catalysts for change. The citation "González-Zamar et al., 2020" refers to a publication by González-Zamar and colleagues in the year 2020. Further research is required to gain a deeper understanding of the effects of using technology in management education and its influence on students' ideas and attitudes towards CSR. (Rodríguez-Gómez et al., 2020) Saxena and Mishra (2017) are the references. By integrating ethics, sustainability, and technology into management education, we may cultivate a new cohort of socially conscious leaders who possess the skills to effectively address the intricate challenges of a swiftly evolving world. These leaders will possess the requisite skills and expertise to effectively tackle urgent social and environmental concerns while also demonstrating a profound comprehension of ethical principles (Rodríguez-Gómez et al., 2020).

(Córdoba & Campbell, 2008) To summarize, the literature emphasizes the crucial role of technology in influencing the comprehension and application of corporate social responsibility in management studies institutions. Given the ongoing impact of technological breakthroughs on the business world, it is critical for educators and administrators to adopt a technology-focused strategy that enables students to develop into ethical and socially conscious leaders in a constantly changing global marketplace. The citation "Rodríguez-Gómez et al., 2020" refers to a publication by Rodríguez-Gómez and colleagues in the year 2020.

Basu and Palazzo's CSR sense-making framework and stakeholder theory provide the theoretical groundwork for this investigation. Theoretically, these frameworks shed light on how various parties involved in the development of new technologies comprehend and interpret CSR. This qualitative study sought to gather empirical data by conducting in-person and over-the-phone interviews with relevant parties.

To fully understand how new technology impacts CSR and sustainability views, it is necessary to delve into the viewpoints and experiences of stakeholders. This method can help achieve this goal. To evaluate and interpret the empirical data obtained from the qualitative interviews, the study approach incorporates a theoretical perspective derived from stakeholder theory and a CSR sense-making framework created by Basu and Palazzo. The purpose of this qualitative study is to investigate the intricate dynamics between stakeholders and new technology, drawing on stakeholder theory and a CSR sense-making framework.

THEORY

This study adheres to the tenets of Basu and Palazzo's CSR sense-making framework and stakeholder theory. Within the framework of corporate social responsibility (CSR), these theories help us make sense of the complicated web of relationships between social, economic, and environmental challenges.

Educators, students, and the community at large are all considered stakeholders according to stakeholder theory, which means that management schools must take their interests into account when making decisions.

This study's theoretical foundation is strengthened by the CSR sense-making framework, which allows us to see how students' grasp and application of CSR concepts are impacted by new technology. This model considers educational practices and technological developments as two of the numerous factors that could influence individuals' interpretation of CSR in their daily lives. In 2008, Córdoba and Campbell This study intends to examine how technology influences management students' views and attitudes towards corporate social responsibility (CSR) and sustainability, based on these theoretical frameworks (Saxena & Mishra, 2017). This study adds to the expanding amount of literature on the topic of technology and corporate social responsibility (CSR) in management education by providing theoretical grounds for comprehending the intricacies of how incorporating technology into the classroom can influence students' views and sentiments towards CSR (Rodríguez-Gómez et al., 2020). Sustainability frameworks, theories, and corporate social responsibility (CSR) classes can influence students' worldviews and make them more cognizant of environmental and societal problems. In 2020, Rodríguez-Gómez and colleagues Rodriguez-Gómez et al. (2020) Additionally, this study seeks to fill a need in the literature by investigating the ways in which students' views of CSR and sustainability are influenced by developing technologies within the framework of their educational experiences. This study enhances our understanding of students' perceptions and attitudes towards CSR and sustainability by incorporating a 10-Likert scale, which introduces variability (Duho et al., 2019). In conclusion, the purpose of this research is to find out how students' views on sustainability and corporate social responsibility change when new technology becomes a part of their management education.

QUESTION FOR RESEARCH

The literature study shed light on how students' exposure to and use of technology in management education programs affect their CSR awareness and practice. "How does the integration of technology influence students' beliefs and attitudes towards corporate social responsibility in management education?" is the research topic that builds on this foundation.

Examining how students' views of CSR and sustainability change as a result of technological advancements, and how this in turn influences their strategy for tackling social and ethical issues in their future corporate endeavours is the primary goal of this research.

The study also aims to determine whether and to what extent students' perceptions of the interrelatedness and complexity of social, economic, and environmental issues are impacted by new technology (Duho et al. 2019).

The study topic is addressed by collecting and analysing data using a rigorous methodology. The focus is on how technology in management education affects students' views and attitudes towards corporate social responsibility. To do this, a mixed-methods strategy is employed, which merges quantitative and qualitative techniques to offer a thorough grasp of the subject. To get quantitative data, a sample of management students were asked to fill out surveys or questionnaires. In contrast, interviews or focus groups will be convened with teachers and students to collect qualitative data, which will provide a more nuanced picture of their perspectives and experiences. The quantitative data was analysed using statistical techniques, while the qualitative data was analysed using thematic analysis. The results of this methodology will reveal how students' knowledge and attitudes towards corporate social responsibility (CSR) in management education are influenced by technology. It will also reveal how students' comprehension and application of CSR principles in their future business practices could be affected by emerging technologies.

The purpose of this research is to examine how management studies programs use technology to teach their students about and model CSR practices. To establish a theoretical perspective, the research methodology began with a thorough literature analysis that cantered on stakeholder theory and Basu and Palazzo's CSR sense-making framework. Qualitative methods, including in-person and over-the-phone interviews with relevant parties, were used to gather empirical data (Baker, 2012).

DESIGN OF RESEARCH

The researchers in this study used a mixed-methods strategy, which means they used both quantitative and qualitative techniques. This method will provide a more complete picture of the topic by including not just students' views and attitudes, but also any changes in behavior that may occur because of using technology in CSR education.

INFORMATION GAIN

1. Polls: Students enrolled in management education programmes will fill out a standardised questionnaire that asks about their thoughts on corporate social responsibility (CSR) and how they feel technology has influenced their views on the topic.

Part 2: Interviews To better understand the complexities of students' involvement with technology-driven CSR education, we will do in-depth interviews with chosen teachers and students.

Analysing Data

To find out how students feel about CSR and how technology is influencing their views, we will use statistical tools to examine the quantitative data collected from the questionnaires. Thematic analysis will be used to unearth rich contextual insights into how technology influences students' ideas and perceptions based on the qualitative data collected from the interviews.

CONSIDERATIONS OF ETHICS

To guarantee the preservation of participants' rights and privacy, ethical clearance was sought before data was collected. All participants will be kept anonymous during the reporting and distribution of the findings, and their informed consent will be obtained.

Research Question

R1: What does this study mean?

The purpose of this research is to add to what is already a substantial amount of literature on the topic of how management programs incorporate CSR and technology. Curriculum development and pedagogical techniques can be informed by this study, which seeks to enable students to become proactive and socially responsible participants in the business landscape by shining light on the impact of technology on students' views and attitudes regarding CSR. In addition, this study's results can help teachers, school leaders, and lawmakers better understand how to incorporate CSR and sustainable business practices into management education using technology. By delving into the research question, we can gain a better understanding of how CSR education is changing considering technological developments.

This study's methodology provides a strong and thorough approach to understanding how technology affects students' beliefs and attitudes towards corporate social responsibility (Duho et al., 2019). It includes surveys, interviews, data analysis using statistical methods, theme analysis, and more. Another way to make sure that data is consistent and comparable between researchers is to modify current questionnaires and Likert scales to evaluate CSR and sustainability. Moreover, by combining text mining with statistical methods, educational datasets can be analysed to gain a better grasp of how teaching and learning models are structured and how they affect students' perceptions and viewpoints (Okoye et al., 2023).

In sum, this research fills a major need in the existing literature by investigating how new technology influences students' views and opinions on corporate social responsibility and sustainability.

Research Design

This study lays a solid theoretical and conceptual groundwork for future research on the complex interplay of stakeholders, new technology, and corporate social responsibility (CSR) in management education. Flaăcă (2017) says that this study will look into the complicated ways that technology affects how community members, teachers, and students feel and think about corporate social responsibility (CSR). It will do this by combining stakeholder theory with the CSR sense-making framework that Basu and Palazzo made (Rodríguez-Gómez et al., 2020). As per the findings of Schulz et al. (2018),

Interviews with important stakeholders, both in-person and over the phone, provide a wealth of information about their viewpoints and experiences and are a crucial component of the qualitative methodology used in this study. This method not only allows for the collection of many perspectives and experiences, but it also enriches our knowledge of how new technology influences stakeholders' views of CSR and sustainability. Rodriguez-Gómez et al. (2020)

Furthermore, the research methodology can be improved by incorporating stakeholder theory and the CSR sense-making framework. This will lead to a more thorough and rigorous analysis and interpretation of the empirical data obtained from qualitative interviews (Carrión-Martínez et al., 2020). As a result, the ramifications for pedagogical methods, curriculum creation, and the larger CSR landscape of management education can be better understood, as can the intricate relationship between stakeholders and new technology.

This study adds to the existing literature on the topic of how technology affects stakeholders' views of corporate social responsibility and sustainability. Its theoretical and conceptual framework, in conjunction with its qualitative approach, positions it to make a substantial contribution to our understanding of this topic. By investigating students' views on new technology considering corporate social responsibility and environmental protection, this research hopes to close a knowledge gap in the current literature.

Research Methodology

Using a quantitative methodology, future studies could expand on this one by investigating how students feel about the effects of new technology on corporate social responsibility and environmental sustainability. Considering the rapid development of new technology, it would be instructive to study how various educational strategies can influence students' attitudes and actions towards corporate social responsibility (CSR) and sustainability. To achieve this, it may be necessary to perform experiments or surveys with a larger sample size to collect quantitative data that can be statistically analysed and applied to a broader context. In addition, studies in the future could investigate how various forms of new technology, including blockchain and artificial intelligence, influence stakeholders' views on CSR and sustainability.

CONCLUSION

In conclusion, when designing curricula and training the next generation of managers to adapt to a dynamic corporate environment, it is critical to have a firm grasp of students' perspectives on new technology and its effects on corporate social responsibility and sustainability. López-Pérez et al. (2017) state that institutions can better prepare students to promote sustainable business practices by incorporating sustainability frameworks and theories into management curricula, teaching about corporate social responsibility, and investigating the impact of new technology. Both students and enterprises will gain from this; the former will be better equipped to meet society's expectations, while the latter will be able to contribute to sustainable growth.

REFERENCES

Bihari, A., & Shajahan, P. (2023). Changing CSR practices of corporates – a study of institutionalization of mandated corporate social responsibility in India. *International Journal of Law and Management*. .10.1108/IJLMA-09-2022-0198

Brennan, L., & Victoria, E. J. (2004, January). Technology Management for Corporate Social Responsibility. *IEEE Technology and Society Magazine*, 23(1), 40–48. 10.1109/MTAS.2004.1273471

Carrión-Martínez, J. J., Luque de la Rosa, A., Fernández-Cerero, J., & Rueda, M. M. (2020, April). Information and Communications Technologies (ICTs) in Education for Sustainable Development: A Bibliographic Review. *Sustainability (Basel)*, 12(8), 3288–3288. 10.3390/su12083288

Christensen, L. J., Peirce, E. R., Hartman, L. P., Hoffman, W. M., & Carrier, J. Ethics, CSR, and Sustainability Education in the Financial Times Top 50 Global Business Schools: Baseline Data and Future Research Directions. *Journal of Business Ethics*, *73*(4). 10.1007/s10551-006-9211-5

Córdoba, J.-R., & Campbell, T. (2008, May). Learning to Deal with CSR Issues in the Classroom. *Systems Research and Behavioral Science*, 25(3), 427–437. 10.1002/sres.898

Cuervo-Carabel, T., & Repiso, R. (2023). Presence and Impact of the Articles on Corporate Social Responsibility in the Different Research Areas. *SAGE Open*, 13(1). 10.1177/21582440231158262

Duho, K. C. T., Onumah, J. M., Samuel, N. Y. S., & Onumah, R. M. "Emerging Technologies, Corporate Social Responsibility and Sustainability: The Perception of Business Students in Ghana," August 2019. https://scite.ai/reports/10.31219/osf.io/pg94b10.31219/osf.io/pg94b

Elembilassery, V. (2023). *Evolutionary influences on corporate social responsibility literature: a review and prognosis*. Society and Business Review. 10.1108/SBR-05-2022-0136

Erskine, L., & Johnson, S. D. (2012, January). Effective Learning Approaches for Sustainability: A Student Perspective. *Journal of Education for Business*, 87(4), 198–205. 10.1080/08832323.2011.590162

Figueiró, P. S., & Raufflet, E. (2015, November). Sustainability in Higher Education: A Systematic Review with Focus on Management Education. *Journal of Cleaner Production*, 106, 22–33. 10.1016/j.jclepro.2015.04.118

Filho, W. L., Manolas, E., & Pace, P. (2008, November). Education for Sustainable Development: Current Discourses and Practices and Their Relevance to Technology Education. *International Journal of Technology and Design Education*, 19(2), 149–165. 10.1007/s10798-008-9079-z

Fleacă, E. (2017). Study on Social Responsibility Learning Needs to Capacitate the Responsible Education in Business Engineering. *Balkan Region Conference on Engineering and Business Education*. IEEE. 10.1515/cplbu-2017-0053

Goby, V. P., & Nickerson, C. (2011). Introducing Ethics and Corporate Social Responsibility at Undergraduate Level in the United Arab Emirates: An Experiential Exercise on Website Communication. Scite Press. https://scite.ai/reports/10.1007/s10551-011-1025-4

González-Zamar, M.-D., Abad-Segura, E., López-Meneses, E., & Galán, J. G. (2020, October). Managing ICT for Sustainable Education: Research Analysis in the Context of Higher Education. *Sustainability (Basel)*, 12(19), 8254–8254. 10.3390/su12198254

Ismail, M., Ratna, F. A. J., Rasdi, R. M., & Alias, S. N. (2013, July). School as Stakeholder of Corporate Social Responsibility Program: Teacher's Perspective on Outcome in School Development. *The Asia-Pacific Education Researcher*, 23(2), 321–331. 10.1007/s40299-013-0107-8

Jali, M. N., Abas, Z., & Ariffin, A. S. (2017). Corporate Social Responsibility and Corporate Social Innovation: A Conceptual Understanding. *SHS Web of Conferences*. IEEE. 10.1051/shsconf/20173401001

Karabasevic, D., Petrović, G., & Maksimovic, M. (2016). *The Impact of the Levels of Education on the Perception of Corporate Social Responsibility*. Scite. https://scite.ai/reports/10.5937/poseko10-12322

Karagiannopoulou, S., Sariannidis, N., Ragazou, K., Passas, I., & Garefalakis, A. (2023). Corporate Social Responsibility: A Business Strategy That Promotes Energy Environmental Transition and Combats Volatility in the Post-Pandemic World. *Energies*, 16(3), 1102. 10.3390/en16031102

Koi-Akrofi, J. (2023). *CSR Paradigms, Consumer Behaviour, and Business Performance: A Literature-Based Analysis*. TEXILA INTERNATIONAL JOURNAL OF MANAGEMENT. 10.21522/TIJMG.2015.09.01.Art003

Kouatli, I. (2019, October). The Contemporary Definition of University Social Responsibility with Quantifiable Sustainability. *Social Responsibility Journal*, 15(7), 888–909. 10.1108/SRJ-10-2017-0210

López-Pérez, M. E., Melero, I., & Javier Sesé, F. (2017). *Does Specific CSR Training for Managers Impact Shareholder Value? Implications for Education in Sustainable Development*. Scite Press. https://scite.ai/reports/10.1002/csr.1418

Mazur, B., Walczyna, A., & Cichorzewska, M. (2023). The Place of the Natural Environment in Activities for Social Responsibility in the Opinion of Students of Electrical Engineering. *Sustainability (Basel)*, 15(2), 1306. 10.3390/su15021306

McWilliams, A., Siegel, D. S., & Wright, P. M. (2006, January). Corporate Social Responsibility: Strategic Implications*. *Journal of Management Studies*, 43(1), 1–18. 10.1111/j.1467-6486.2006.00580.x

Mohammadi, E., Vagnani, G., & Maleki, H. (2023). *Corporate social responsibility and satisfaction in service industries: a systematic review and integrative framework*. Society and Business Review., 10.1108/SBR-05-2022-0133

Moratis, L., von den Hoff, J., & Reul, B. (2006, March). A Dual Challenge Facing Management Education. *Journal of Management Development*, 25(3), 213–231. 10.1108/02621710610648150

Reavis, M., & Tucci, J. E. (2020, November). Sustainability Effort Acceleration as Measured by Increased Propensity of Corporate Social Responsibility. *Journal of Management and Sustainability*, 10(2), 121–121. 10.5539/jms.v10n2p121

Rodríguez-Gómez, S., Sánchez, R. G., Arco-Castro, M. L., & María, V. L. P. (2020, December). Does the Use of Social Media Tools in Classrooms Increase Student Commitment to Corporate Social Responsibility? *Frontiers in Psychology*, 11, 589250. 10.3389/fpsyg.2020.58925033424704

Saxena, M., & Mishra, D. K. (2017, June). CSR Perception: A Global Opportunity in Management Education. *Industrial and Commercial Training*, 49(5), 231–244. 10.1108/ICT-12-2016-0085

Schulz, K.-P., Finstad-Milion, K., & Janczak, S. (2018, October). Educating Corporate Sustainability – A Multidisciplinary and Practice-Based Approach to Facilitate Students' Learning. *Journal of Cleaner Production*, 198, 996–1006. 10.1016/j.jclepro.2018.06.104

Sobczak, A., Debucquet, G., & Havard, C. (2006, August). The Impact of Higher Education on Students' and Young Managers' Perception of Companies and CSR: An Exploratory Analysis. *Corporate Governance (Bradford)*, 6(4), 463–474. 10.1108/14720700610689577

Sun, R. (2023). Corporate social responsibility and green innovation: Based on the perspective of corporate strategic management. *International Journal of Multidisciplinary Research and Growth Evaluation*. .10.54660/.IJMRGE.2023.4.2.46-49

Taneja, S., Taneja, P., & Gupta, R. K. (2011, January). Researches in Corporate Social Responsibility: A Review of Shifting Focus, Paradigms, and Methodologies. *Journal of Business Ethics*, 101(3), 343–364. 10.1007/s10551-010-0732-6

Tickell, G., Paz, V., & Rahman, M. (2017, December). Teaching Corporate Social Responsibility In An MBA Program. *Journal of Sustainability Management*, 5(1), 1–10. 10.19030/jsm.v5i1.10153

Tuuli, M. M., Fusheini, K., & Salia, H. (2023, June). Corporate Social Responsibility (CSR) Effect on Teaching and Learning: Evidence from an Emerging Economy. *International Journal of Innovation in Teaching and Learning*, 9(1), 1–19. 10.35993/ijitl.v9i1.2570

Wieland, J. R., & Fitzgibbons, D. E. (2013, December). Integrating Corporate Sustainability and Organizational Strategy Within the Undergraduate Business Curriculum. *Organizational Management Journal*, 10(4), 255–266. 10.1080/15416518.2013.859059

Chapter 3
Challenges and Opportunities Within the Evolving CSR Landscape in India

Md Safiullah
Chanakya National Law University, Patna, India

Anchal
Chanakya National Law University, Patna, India

Md Ismail Iqbal
University of Technology and Applied Science, Nizwa, Oman

Neha Parveen
Indian Institute of Technology, Dhanbad, India

ABSTRACT

The present study is an attempt to understand the historical development of corporate social responsibility in India. The present study classified the development of corporate social responsibility in five different phases as phase of individual philanthropy, phase of social movement philanthropy, phase of state philanthropy, phase of corporate philanthropy, and finally CSR Law in India. The present study has also highlighted corporate social responsibility violations and penalties associated with. The study analyzed the major challenges in corporate social responsibility implementations in India. The study adopted doctrinal and archival research methodology. The findings indicate that there has been an increase in CSR activities because it has been made compulsory by the law. However, the challenges are still

DOI: 10.4018/979-8-3693-3238-2.ch003

there such as local communities disapproving of firms supporting CSR initiatives due to lack of knowledge and public awareness, businesses being dissatisfied with local agencies' transparency, and lack of funding, etc.

INTRODUCTION

The idea of "Corporate Social Responsibility" (CSR) is an important part of business thought and practice worldwide. Indian businesses have included CSR for quite some time. Both the public and private sectors have made long-term and short-term efforts to inculcate a culture of ethics in our company culture. (Briefin, 2022)

But these efforts haven't been planned well, they've targeted just one entity, and they might not even know what they're trying to do. Recently, there have been indications that things are starting to change. Concern and commitment to the idea of "corporate social responsibility" have grown for a number of reasons, such as the proliferation of worldwide business operations, the importance of climate change initiatives, the adoption of the "Millennium Development Goals", and others. The government's aims are reflected in the new enterprises Act, which went into effect in 2013 and mandates CSR spending for a particular group of corporate enterprises. (Acharya, 2023)

This has significantly boosted corporate CSR programs, many of which have gone above and beyond the letter of the law. In keeping with natural happening, there have also been efforts to incorporate CSR into business strategy with the goal of obtaining and retaining a competitive advantage. In the present study, we'll look at how CSR has evolved in India. Government initiatives to incorporate CSR into company operations and the difficulties of CSR in India will also be covered in the study.

BACKGROUND

Development of CSR in India

"Corporate Social Responsibility" originates from the boundary between the realm of knowledge and the realm of uncertainty. Kotchen and Moon (2007)

The development is divided into five phases. Each of phases has contributed to the development of numerous CSR concepts that align with the nation's historical context. Nevertheless, there are variations between the stages, and characteristics from one phase to another.

The First Phase (Individual Philanthropy)

Initially, philanthropy and altruism were the primary motivations behind CSR. Corporate social responsibility has been influenced by factors such as industrialization, family values, religion, society, and tradition. Wealthy individuals during the pre-industrial era (1800-1855) constructed temples for religious purposes and allocated a portion of their wealth for the benefit of the public. During the time, social and economic factors exerted significant influence on industrial dynasties like as the Birla, Singhania, Modi, Bajaj, Tata, and Godrej families. (Tilt, 2009)

The Second Phase (Societal Movement Philanthropy)

The struggle for independence, Indian manufacturers faced increasing demands to demonstrate their commitment to societal improvement. "Mahatma Gandhi" (Indian independence activist and leader) propagated the concept of "trusteeship," advocating that business magnates should utilize their influence to improve the world. (Khanna and Palepu, 2005)

Due to his influence, businesses facilitated the establishment of training and study facilities, as well as endowments for schools and colleges. The trusts primarily operated their enterprises in accordance with Gandhi's measures that aimed to advance rural development, empower women, and end untouchability.

The Third Phase 1948 – 1990 (State Philanthropy)

The government established Public Sector Undertakings (PSUs) with the aim of ensuring equitable distribution of resources, such as food, financial assistance, and other commodities, to the underprivileged population. However, the public sector was not able to fully maximize its potential. Given the shift in public expectations, it became imperative for the private sector to assume a more prominent role in the nation's social and economic advancement. In 1965, Indian intellectuals, politicians, and entrepreneurs organized a national CSR conference to foster peace. The significance of being socially responsible, maintaining openness, and engaging in regular dialogues with stakeholders was emphasized. Regardless of the efforts made, the CSR was unable to acquire momentum.

The Fourth Phase-1991 - 2013 (Corporate Philanthropy)

The expansion of the economy of India commenced in the 1991. Globalization has led to India becoming as a significant hub for transnational corporations (*TNCs, i.e a company operating in more than one country*) to conduct business and manufacturing operations. Indian companies engaged in manufacturing and exporting goods to developed nations. Concerns over the working conditions and environmental standards in emerging nations are growing in the Western markets. (Agarwal, 2011)

After the economic liberalization MNCs and Indian corporations shifted their approach to CSR by incorporating it into their strategies for operating a sustainable business.

The Fifth Phase 2013 Until Present (Law Enforced CSR)

The Companies Act 2013 is an Act of the Parliament of India which forms the primary source of Indian company law. It received presidential assent on 29 August 2013, and largely superseded the Companies Act 1956. "Under Section 135 of the Indian companies act 2013", companies must set up a CSR group, give a certain amount to charity, and work to solve problems like poverty, poor health, and environmental damage in order to be eligible. There are further developments & amendments bring in later year as depicted in the flowchart as following.

ANALYSIS

Figure 1. Metamorphosis of "Companies Act 2013"

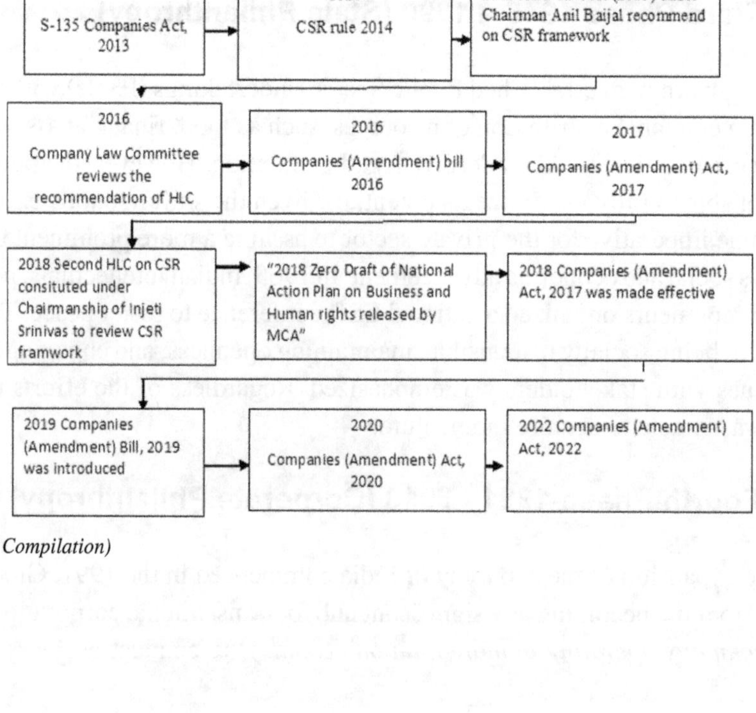

(Author Compilation)

Table 1. Amendments and developments in Indian "companies act 2013"

Sec-135 of Companies Act, 2013	In 2013 Companies Amendment Act was brought which came into force in 2014. Section 135 states that companies having a net worth of 500cr or more net worth, profit or turnover will have to establish a CSR committee. (Ramesh, 2021)
CSR RULE FRAMED IN 2014.	
Rule (3)	1) All firms that meet subsection (1) of section 135 and have branch offices or project offices in India, including their "holding or subsidiary companies" and foreign corporations described under section (42) of section 2 of the Act, are required to abide by section 135 and the following guidelines: Under clause (a) of sub-section (1) of sections 381 and 198, a foreign firm's net worth, turnover, and net profit will be disclosed on the balance sheet and profit and loss account. 2) A firm that is not covered by "subsection (1) of section 135 of the Act for three consecutive financial years is not required to create a CSR Committee or follow sub-sections (2) to (5)" until it meets subsection (1).
Rule (4)	(1) Except for ordinary business operations, the company shall conduct CSR projects, programs, or activities (new or existing) according to its CSR Policy. (2) "The business's Board may choose to carry out its CSR activities, which the CSR Committee has authorized, through a registered trust, society, or company established by the company, its holding company, subsidiary, or associate company under section 8 of the Act, or by other means. (Ramesh, 2021) A trust, society, or firm that is not created by the corporation or its holding, subsidiary, or associate company must have three years of experience with such programs or projects". (3) To enable their CSR Committees to provide independent reports by these guidelines, a company may collaborate with other businesses to complete projects or engage in CSR activities. (4) Under paragraph (5) of section 135 of the Act, only Indian CSR projects, programs, or activities comprise CSR spending. (Indulia, 2021) (5) CSR projects, programs, and activities that benefit only firm employees and their families are exempt from Section 135 of the Act. Institutions with at least three financial years of experience can help companies strengthen their personnel and implement agencies' CSR. (6) "The Companies (Corporate Social Responsibility Policy) Amendment Rules, 2014", effective 12-9-2014, restrict such charges, including administrative overheads 5% of annual corporate CSR spending. (7) Section 182 political party donations are not CSR activities 129. (Indulia, 2021)
Rule (5)	(1) Rule 3 companies will form the CSR Committee: "A foreign company covered by these rules must have at least two CSR Committee members, while a public company that is not listed or a private company covered by section 135(1) of the Act that is not required to appoint an independent director (*non-executive director of a company who helps the company in improving corporate credibility and governance standards)* under section 149(4) must have its CSR Committee without such director." (2) "The CSR Committee shall provide a clear monitoring structure for firm CSR projects, programs, and activities."

continued on following page

Table 1. Continued

Sec-135 of Companies Act, 2013	In 2013 Companies Amendment Act was brought which came into force in 2014. Section 135 states that companies having a net worth of 500cr or more net worth, profit or turnover will have to establish a CSR committee. (Ramesh, 2021)
Rule (6)	(1) The company's CSR Policy will specify Schedule VII-covered CSR initiatives or programs, their implementation timeframes, and a monitoring methodology. The Board of Directors must ensure that the Corporate Social Responsibility Policy's actions comply with Schedule VII of the Act for non-routine CSR activities. (2) Business revenues will not include extra income from CSR projects, programs, and activities.
Rule (7)	CSR expenditures cannot contain items that do not comply with Schedule VII of the Act. CSR expenditures include corpus donations for Board-approved CSR projects or programs recommended by the CSR Committee.
Rule (8)	(1) CSR reports will be in Annexure for fiscal years beginning after April 1, 2014. (2) A foreign corporation's financial sheet under paragraph (b) of sub-section (1) of section 381 should include and CSR report
Rule (9)	The Board of Directors will approve CSR Policy proposals from the CSR Committee. The company's website will post the policy if relevant, as per Annexure 145. CSR policy Corporate Social Responsibility disclosures shall follow the Companies (Corporate Social Responsibility Policy) Rules, 2014 annexure, under Rule 9 of the Companies (Accounts) Rules, 2014.
2015 HLC(High level committee) on CSR (2015) under Chairman Anil Baijal:	He recommend on the CSR framework Be expanded to include Limited Liability Partnerships (LLPs), which fall under the MCA's jurisdiction, in the scope of CSR applicability
Companies Amendment Act 2016:	It amends to add the clauses related to CSR and giving the greater clarity in the role and responsibilities of directors and its committees.
Companies Amendment Act 2017:	It added the eligibility criteria for the purpose constituting the CSR committees and its applicability in CSR expenditure. (*Lxmikumaran and Sridharaan Attorneys*, 2017)
HLC on CSR (2018):	Aimed at reviewing the CSR framework and offering suggestions for creating a more solid and cohesive CSR regulatory and legislative framework, as well as an underlying ecosystem(MCA, 2018).
Companies Amendment Act 2019: continued on following page	Major modifications to Section 135 of the Companies Act were made in 2019 by the Companies (Amendment) Act in an effort to improve corporate accountability and guarantee the efficient use of monies allotted for CSR initiatives. The change permits businesses to compute their CSR expenditure commitments by taking into account the time that they haven't completed three fiscal years since their establishment. Additionally, it requires businesses to transfer any unused funds to one of the funds listed in Schedule VII within six months of the end of the fiscal year, unless they are part of an ongoing project. After the fiscal year ends, the corporation must transfer any unused funds from an ongoing initiative to a unique account known as the "Unspent CSR Amount" and use the funds in accordance with CSR policy within three fiscal years following the date of transfer.

Table 1. Continued

Sec-135 of Companies Act, 2013	In 2013 Companies Amendment Act was brought which came into force in 2014. Section 135 states that companies having a net worth of 500cr or more net worth, profit or turnover will have to establish a CSR committee. (Ramesh, 2021)
Companies Amendment Act 2022	In response to the 2014 rule that funds had to go to CSR projects, many ideas were put forward. The Companies (CSR policy) amendment Rules, 2022 ("Amendment rules") are one set of changes that were made public on September 20, 2022, by the Ministry of Corporation Affairs. Because of the Amendment Rules, the following changes have been made: There should be a corporate social responsibility committee in every company to make sure that their CSR tasks are carried out and that any money in their "unspent corporate social responsibility account" is used properly. (Radhakrishnan, 2022) As long as the money is used within three fiscal years, companies can keep any funds in this account that aren't used for corporate social responsibility. The CSR group is in charge of how it is used. Additionally, the new laws have taken away the exception that let businesses skip setting up a CSR Committee if they stopped following the rules. (Taxmann, 2022) Before the CSR Regulations, up to 5% of all CSR costs or 50 lakh rupees, whichever was less, could have been used to pay for impact studies. According to the new rules, the most that can be spent on social impact assessments (SIAs) in a fiscal year is 2% of the total amount of money that was made, or 50 lakh rupees, whichever is greater .

Table 2. Development phases of CSR

Development phases of CSR					
	Please I	**Please II**	**Please III**	**Please IV**	**Please V**
Individual Philanthropy					
Social Movement Philanthropy					
State Philanthropy					
Corporate Philanthropy					
CSR Law					

Source: Author Compilations

CSR Violations

In Companies Act, 2013; Implementing rules serve as the foundation for violations of CSR. These consist of quantitative non-compliance with obligatory CSR spending standards, improper funding distribution, non-formation of CSR committees, and insufficient and non-disclosing reporting. The most obvious criterion is quantitative non-compliance, where businesses don't spend the minimal amount of 2% of their average net income for the three years prior to the current year. A more complex criterion is misallocation of funds, since businesses must coordinate their

CSR initiatives with the industries specified in Schedule VII of the Companies Act 2013(Indian act). ***(Rose 2020, Radhakrishnan, 2020)***

It is improper to form or give sufficient authority to CSR committees; this is a procedural infraction that suggests there are insufficient internal oversight systems. Inadequate reporting or the non-disclosure of CSR operations is illegal, and businesses are required to release thorough CSR reports so that interested parties can obtain complete data.

Penalties

Penalties for failing to transfer unspent CSR monies are outlined in the corporations Act and include fines for both corporations and officers in default. Even if unused money are subsequently moved to Schedule VII funds or Unspent CSR Accounts, post-transfer penalties still apply. The only provision that addresses penalties for failing to transfer unspent CSR funds is Section 135(7). Non-adherence to additional clauses, including Sections 134(8), 450, and 454(8), pertains to violations of the Companies Act/Rules or terms and limits that do not carry particular penalties. If adjudicating officers or regional directors fail to pay fines within ninety days, there may be jail time, corporate fines, fines ranging from INR 25,000 to INR 1 lakh, or both.

Roles and Liabilities of Directors (Oversees the Management of the CSR Activities)

An organization's CSR policy (turnover as specified in the companies act 2013), which is authorised by the business and has to be compliant with regulatory requirements and company values, is heavily influenced by the Board. Directors are required to make the policy available to stakeholders and declare it in the business report. To ensure that at least 2% of average net earnings over the previous three years is allocated to CSR, the Board supervises the implementation of CSR activities. Penalties may result from deficiencies, which must be explained in the annual report. The Board, in particular the directors, is responsible for overseeing CSR money and assessing the results of programmes. In order to ensure openness for stakeholders, the Board shall include an explanation in the annual report if the company is unable to meet the standards for CSR spending. (Majithiya, 2021)

FINDINGS AND DISCUSSIONS

CSR Implementation

One of the most important components of a business's attempts to improve society is its commitment to corporate social responsibility, or CSR. Corporate social responsibility (CSR) is a crucial approach for businesses to create a strong reputation, attract media attention, build a strong brand, and compete in the market. It involves not only distributing charity and funds but also well-planned, socially-driven projects. CSR is essential for a company's reputation, media coverage, brand value, market differentiation, and competitiveness.

In India, laws have been enacted to regulate CSR, including the formation of a CSR committee, policy development, implementation oversight, linking social-economic issues, and self-reporting and auditing. The Ministry of Corporate Affairs (MCA) is the national standard-setting body in India, which issues the industry-specific CSR compliance guidelines. Ministry of Corporate Affairs publishes guidelines and interpretation directions to help businesses follow the principle of uniformity in the interpretation and application of directives. By focusing on CSR, businesses can achieve a prominent position and maintain a strong reputation in the competitive market.

One of the reasons behind this is the fact that the MCAs have reviewed their CSR system, which led to the inclusion of CSR standards in the Off-Shore Legislation system. Thus, the modifications took place through notification 2021 containing CSR guidelines and rule relaxation which allowed carry forward of not-utilized CSR fund in some conditions. Along with the legal text document, there is a set of standards that city business has to follow; just like the National standards for Environmental and Social Responsibility of corporate.

Such as the MCA, compliance is shown with the recent amendment of the Companies Act in 2019 which let it being possible to conduct CSR offenses investigation. On the other hand, we must not disregard the efficiency of the policy and see to it this is studied more profoundly. However, the implementation of the regulations guarantees that the decision makers are not biased at local level which creates a foundation of uniformity and transparency regardless of place and local issues

The Companies Act of 2013 and the Companies rule 2014 regulate CSR expenditures. The calculation of average net profit for CSR purposes is outlined in Section 198, and administrative overheads are permitted up to 5% of the total amount spent on CSR. Costs associated with capital asset transfers are allowable CSR expenses. Subject to Rule 7(3), excess CSR expenditures may be deducted from the required 2% expenditure over the next three years.

According to the Indian Income Tax Act of 1961, CSR expenditures are not tax deductable business expenses, and in-kind CSR contributions are not monetizable. The use of funds is limited to Schedule VII activities, and while employee participation in CSR is encouraged, it is not monetizable.

Major Challenges

Local communities disapprove of firms participating in or supporting CSR initiatives. The primary factor is the lack of knowledge and understanding of CSR among the local population. The primary cause of this issue is the lack of engaging initiatives aimed at increasing public awareness of corporate social responsibility. Businesses are dissatisfied with the local operating agencies' lack of transparency on their programs, audit subjects, impact evaluations, and fund utilization. It is challenging to locate Non-Governmental Organizations (NGOs) that can accurately determine the community's requirements and collaborate effectively with businesses to ensure the success of their CSR projects. India's substantial and concentrated population makes it a preferred destination for many firms to concentrate their CSR initiatives. Research indicates that community members are unwilling to endorse or participate in the local corporate social responsibility initiatives of firms. Several non-governmental organizations perform commendable jobs. Research indicates that India faces a unique challenge due to the difficulty in locating these groups in remote and rural areas. These groups can use their expertise to identify the genuine needs of communities and collaborate with businesses to implement CSR projects. (Shyam and Rosencranz, 2002)

- Companies continue to see CSR in a limited way. They do not consider CSR comprehensively, which acknowledges its impact on stakeholders, society, and the global community. Businesses must be informed about new opportunities and seize them to address societal issues. They should strive to create shared value by aligning their corporate objectives with initiatives that benefit both society and the environment. India is rife with instances of green washing.
- The CSR project inadequately addresses inequality and lacks a robust mechanism for ensuring compliance. CSR might inadvertently promote greenwashing at a national level by lacking clarity and creating the illusion of progress. This is a primary obstacle that hinders the effectiveness and legality of CSR.
- Other challenges lie around effectively communicating knowledge and demonstrating the link between the objective and the overall achievement of a diverse company.

- Inefficient utilization of resources such as human, financial, and technical capital. Individuals in this industry must possess a diverse skill set due to the relatively recent integration of CSR practices in the maritime sector.
- Implementing CSR in the maritime sector is challenging due to a lack of skilled individuals with the necessary education and experience. While not all of CSR's objectives have been achieved, its effectiveness has been demonstrated. One of the primary issues is the ineffective implementation of these policies. It is not logical to adhere rigidly to them. Identifying dependable projects that these firms can finance while fulfilling their CSR obligations is somewhat challenging. (Barnett et.al, 2007)
- The effectiveness of CSR is bias rooted in geographical location. Most firms have a fundamental propensity that explains this discrepancy. The company funded projects in close proximity to its headquarters. Ultimately, this leads to increased industrialization in both industrialized and developing regions. The government intervened with 284 companies and sent 5832 letters to corporations that failed to comply with the mandatory CSR payments, as reported by The Economic Times (*an Indian newspaper*). Indian companies attempt to evade payment for CSR initiatives by disclosing minimal information regarding their financial contributions.
- Individuals are utilizing CSR funds for personal development rather than achieving societal objectives. Businesses utilize philanthropic contributions to cover their corporate social responsibility expenses.
- Many corporations are exempt from adhering to CSR regulations as they contribute their funds to major initiatives initiated or supported by the ruling political party *(the government regulating the country*). It is feasible to get these monies to assist the government in covering its increased expenses. The primary objective is to ensure that the government shields these corporations from legal action for violating CSR regulations. The Finance Act of 2014 reduces tax incentives for expenses related to CSR, which may discourage corporations from fulfilling CSR obligations mandated by law. Most firms are not fond of the impact that CSR regulations have on them. They disagree with its rules. This section critically examines part 135 of the 2013 Companies Act. These proposals aim to enhance the existing service by addressing any deficiencies or improving its quality. Lacking sufficient criminal statutes or the authority to implement them: If you avoid making mistakes, no negative consequences will occur. (Zakaria, M., Hassan, T., Sherief, L., & Erhabor, O. (2023, November 22).
- # ## Corporate social responsibility may be compromised if firms discover methods to evade the financial obligations associated with it. Clarify Businesses are required to adhere to regulations and allocate funds towards corporate social

responsibility. If they are unable to do so, they must justify their inability. The current matter involves determining the responsible party for providing justifications for non-compliance 9not functioning) with regulations and the adequacy of those justifications. What factors are considered when making this decision? Can the corporation seek a third appeal if it's dissatisfied with the second one Requires attention. There is no guidance on what constitutes a valid or lawful justification for not using the funds. Tilt, C. A. (2009). Consequently, the board report lacks any guidelines for a legitimate justification for the unspent funds. Both the corporation and its board of directors bear responsibility even if they opt not to discuss well-completed CSR efforts. Schedule VII of the Companies Act contains a somewhat restricted list as follows: Several activities listed in Schedule VII of the Act are classified as CSR projects. (Bhat et.al, 2010)

- Some projects focus on curing diseases, establishing social enterprises, eradicating poverty and hunger, and improving educational institutions. This list does not include funding for non-governmental organizations (NGOs), human rights advocacy, and other charitable causes. The scope of actions covered under Schedule VII is ambiguous as the list appears to be exhaustive rather than illustrative. The two exemptions in Section 135 are especially concerning. Priorities the business's location. This method may only allocate resources to certain local communities, neglecting other regions that are still in the process of development and lack corporate presence. Most firms and their production facilities are located in states that are still in the process of development.

CONCLUSION

Companies are increasingly compelled to engage in CSR to support communities, the environment, and ethical standards. Today, brand names rely on factors beyond quality, price, and distinctiveness. Their dependence also relies on their interactions with the community, employees, and the organization as a whole. CSR is a practice that firms can engage in to contribute to their long-term growth. Historically, there was a belief that industrialization was indicative of a country's development and wealth. Nevertheless, it has also led to numerous issues in society. CSR in India, including what it means to be a nation like India, how it relates to sustainability in India, and how it has developed throughout the years in Indiana thorough overview of Indian legislation pertaining to corporate social responsibility had been difficult to achieve. Therefore, different phases are highlighted, showing the gradual development in India. Laws need to continuously adjust to the swiftly evolving social landscape. CSR in India has progressed through many stages and is currently in its early stages. Progress has begun, and increasing pressure from informed stakeholders will ensure that the concept spreads rapidly and extensively throughout all companies. Moreover, the regulations are evolving rapidly, especially concerning disclosures to the public. Many innovative corporations that acknowledge their societal responsibilities have initiated significant corporate social responsibility projects. The companies have demonstrated their patriotism to other nations and have willingly taken on the significant responsibility of creating a beneficial impact on societal progress. Corporate social responsibility has changed over time in terms of its extent and nature.

REFERENCES

Acharya, M. (2023, September 22). *Corporate Social Responsibility Under Section 135 of Companies Act 2013*. Cleartax. https://cleartax.in/s/corporate-social-responsibility

Agarwal Sanjay, K. (2011). Corporate Social Responsibility in India. *Response Business Books*. SAGE. www.sustainability.com

Briefing, I. (2022, October 10). *Corporate Social Responsibility in India*. India Briefing News. https://www.india-briefing.com/news/corporate-social-responsibility-india-5511.html/

Companies (Amendment) Act. 2017 – An analysis. (n.d.). *Lxmikumaran and Sridharaan Attorneys*, https://www.lakshmisri.com/insights/articles/companies-amendment-act-2017-an-analysis/#, Divan, S., Divan, S. A. S., & Rosencranz, F. D. J. S. O. E. A. S. A. (2022, October 22). *Environmental Law and Policy in India*. Oxford University Press. http://books.google.ie/books?id=uKBEAAAQBAJ&printsec=frontcover&dq=Diwan+Shyam+and+Armin+Rosencranz,+(2002)+Environmental+Law+and+Policy+in+India,+2nd+ed,+New+Delhi:+Oxford+University+Press&hl=&cd=1&source=gbs_api

Dr Bhat, K. N. (2010). *Prof. Misra Suresh and Chadha Sapna*. Consumer, Consumerism, and Consumer Protection- Indian Context, Indian Institute of Public Administration in Collaboration with Abhijit Publications.

Indulia, B. (2021, July 30). Companies (Corporate Social Responsibility Policy) Amendment Rules, 2021. *SCC Times*. https://www.scconline.com/blog/post/2021/02/06/companies-corporate-social-responsibility-policy-amendment-rules-2021/

Khanna, T. (2005) *The Evolution of Concentrated Ownership in India*. Nber.org. https://www.nber.org/system/files/chapters/c10272/c10272.pdf

Mc Barnett, D., Voiculescu, A., & Campbell, T. (2007). *The New Corporate Accountability: Corporate Social Responsibility-The Law*. Cambridge University Press.

MCA. (2018). Report of the high level committee on corporate social responsibility. *Government of india ministry of corporate affairs august,* MCA. https://www.mca.gov.in/ministry/pdf/csrhlc_13092019.pdf

Ramesh, S. (2021, September 30). A Comparative Analysis of Companies Act, 1956 and Companies Act, 2013 in India. (pp. 25–31). *Journal of Legal Subjects*, .10.55529/jls.11.25.31

Taxmann (2022, June 7). *Key Highlights of the Company Law Committee Report (2022) | CLC-2022*. Taxmann Blog. https://www.taxmann.com/post/blog/key-highlights-of-the-company-law-committee-report-2022-clc-2022

Tilt, C. A. (2009). *Corporate Responsibility, Accounting and Accountants*. Springer Berlin Heidelberg. 10.1007/978-3-642-02630-0_2

Zakaria, M., Hassan, T., Sherief, L., & Erhabor, O. (2023, November 22). *Thalassemia Syndromes - New Insights and Transfusion Modalities*. BoD – Books on Demand. http://books.google.ie/books?id=PL7mEAAAQBAJ&pg=PA200&dq=https://www.ncbi.nlm.nih.gov/books/NBK2682/&hl=&cd=1&source=gbs_api

KEY TERMS AND DEFINITIONS

"Trusteeship": an idea that people should be satisfied with what the god has given to them: ensuring equal distribution of wealth in the society

Altruism: moral obligation to serve others

Board of Directors: a collective body of independent.non-independent and other directors of the company)

Companies act 2013: The Act consolidates and amends the law relating to companies

CSR Committee: A committee involved in allocation of funds for CSR activities

CSR: Corporate social responsibility is a business model that helps a company be socially accountable to itself, its stakeholders, and the public.

Directors: Oversees the management of the CSR activities)

Ethical standard: The principles that promote trust, good behavior, fairness and governing the conduct of a person

Globalisation: An interdependence of the world' economics, culture etc.

Philanthropy: Charitable help in return of consideration

Public Sector Undertakings: (PSUs i.e. brought in 1956 to develop infrastructure and economy in India

Transnational corporations: TNCs, i.e a company operating in more than one country

Chapter 4
Organizational Technological Innovation and Environmental Sustainability Regulations

José G. Vargas-Hernandez
Tecnológico Nacional de México, ITSF, Mexico

Janet M. Barrientos-Lujàn
Tecnològico Nacional de Mèxico, ITSF, Mexico

Francisco J. González-Àvila
Tecnològico Nacional de Mèxico, ITSF, Mexico

Omar C. Vargas-González
http://orcid.org/0000-0002-6089-956X
Tecnológico Nacional de Mexico, Ciudad Guzmán, Mexico

ABSTRACT

This study tends to analyze the technological innovation infrastructure system supported by the environmental sustainability regulations. It is assumed that the technological innovation infrastructure in organizations has a positive relationship with environmentally sustainable regulations to improve the contribution of companies with an impact on the efficiency of green sustainable development. The method employed is the analytic-reflective based on a conceptual, theoretical, and empirical literature review. It is concluded that the technological innovation infrastructure system improves the efficiency of innovation supported by environmental sustainability regulations such as by protecting property rights.

DOI: 10.4018/979-8-3693-3238-2.ch004

INTRODUCTION

The rapid global diffusion of innovative technologies has modernized the various economic sectors (primary, secondary, and tertiary) that contribute to environmental pollution and other health risks, which in turn limits the development of green solutions. For Amburgey & Rao (1996), the advances in organizational sociology represent a key element to understand the relational nature of aspects such as culture and organizational change, two fundamental aspects to understand the interdependence established between the organization and society.

In the words of Salimath & Jones (2011), the solution aims to study the relationship between sustainability and the socio-ecology of the population. In other words, the theoretical proposal is built on the theories of organizational choice, the theory of resource dependence (Pfeffer & Salancik, 1978) until reaching the ecological theory of organizations focusing on the specificities of the sector as exercise of choices.

The Evolutionary Theory of Being Human examined from the paradigm of subsistence, development, and preservation, are the notions of sustainability established in its own origins. Humanity's progress is limited to the conservation of its ecosystem given that planetary resources are finite. Hence, the expression "sustainability" can be defined as the socio-ecological relationship that seeks the conservation and stability of an environment to maintain an ideal state oriented to future scenarios based on a balance. This is why natural and social systems present constant changes associated with evolutionary dynamics, for this reason it is necessary to balance and regulate different human actions so that future generations can enjoy the same or better benefits and resources than nature. today offers. (Quiroz, J.2023).

Thus, from the theoretical framework of organizational socio-ecology and sociological theory, ecological principles are applied to organizational study. Starting from the notion that both organizational sociology and socioecological theory serve as tools to formulate and implement socioecological principles through organizational strategies with the objective of strengthening those organizations that present low performance, resulting in new economic and social environments. characterized by non-linear development.

Socio-ecology theory assumes that there is a convergence between the organizational socio-ecology paradigm and the sociological perspectives that drive organizational research. Because the foundation of socio-ecology rests on the differentiation of organizational populations. At the same time, it addresses contemporary issues such as climate change, environmental responsibility, planetary balance, etc., and links them with other disciplines of organizational thinking. The link in question arises from the incorporation of methodological innovations such as strategic simulation models.

And although the study of socio-ecology has been widely accepted in recent decades, it has been heavily criticized because it assumes that organizational destiny is a controllable variable. However, from practice it has been shown that organizational socio-ecology is dynamic and is based on the methodology of the analysis of temporal events, which helps to extract and interpret representative situations of the underlying relationships between the data and allows to different extents with different confidence. The data is extrapolated or interpolated, and thus scenarios are predicted.

It should be noted that the so-called green revolution not only failed to provide food for the world's population but was created under invalid premises: abundant and cheap water and energy, and a non-changing climate. In some cereal regions, the rate of yield increase is declining despite increased use of agrochemicals, as crops reach the point of declining yields. Given the absence of ecological regulation mechanisms, monocultures that cover 80% of the world's arable land are highly dependent on pesticides and fertilizers and, given their genetic homogeneity, are very vulnerable to pests and climate change. Today there are more than one billion hungry people in the world, but hunger is due to poverty and inequality and not to scarcity or lack of production. The world already produces enough food to feed an expected 9 billion people by 2050.

There is no doubt that humanity needs a new paradigm of agricultural development, one that promotes more biodiverse, resilient, and socially just forms of agriculture. The basis of these new agrarian systems are the indigenous-peasant agricultural styles developed by the majority of the 1.5 billion small farmers who manage some 350 million small farms and who produce on 30% of the arable land, no less than 50%. of food for domestic consumption in the world. As an applied science, agroecology uses ecological principles to optimize farming systems and to develop new sustainable agro-ecosystems, where external inputs are replaced by natural processes such as soil fertility and biological control. The global south has the potential to produce enough food per capita to sustain the current population and potentially a larger population, but on the same arable land base, with less oil and amid a changing climate (Altieri & Nicholls, 2012).

On the other hand, the theory of population socio-ecology is considered as the instrument for the theoretical and empirical analysis of organizational phenomena, constituting a perspective of convergent intersection with sustainability that integrates dimensions, levels, and analysis of results. (Birnholtz & Hoch, 2007) define the socio-ecology of routines as the ability to regenerate a socio-ecology of action patterns.

Research in socio-ecology is relevant for its contribution to the analysis of the interactions of organizational populations and for its contribution to sustainable development. This contribution arises from the application of principles and assumptions of socio-ecology to the study of the sustainability of organizations. (Dimaggio & Powell, 1983) describe the theory of organizational socio-ecology as an analysis of the alterations, difficulties, and restrictions of organizational populations in the conditions of application based on social Darwinism, that is, based on competition between individuals. Specifically, the fight for survival.

Regarding research in ecological theory of the population, this is consolidated in the theory of socio-ecology of the population in coordination and convergence with organizational sustainability, considering that there are several areas conducted with the sustainability of populations that potentially contribute to its sustainability (Salimath & Jones, 2011). Variables such as controlling greenhouse gas emissions, reducing energy consumption, green technology innovation, institutional quality, economic growth, and the benefits of urbanization are all considered interdependent and co-integrated. That is, they are considered part of the process by which society can meet its needs and improve its quality of life without endangering the ability of future generations to meet their own needs.

This demonstrates the close relationship that exists between environmental regulation and green innovation. Which makes it necessary to assign values to environmental regulations since these lead to the performance of green innovation. An archetype contrary to what is indicated here occurs when the environmental regulation system is weak, with a tendency to maximize company profits. Where, as compensation, governments apply environmental taxes to try to balance the cost of lack of regulation.

Furthermore, it is necessary to point out that the world's environment has changed and unknown phenomena, never seen before, are becoming widespread, even in rich countries, and not only the poor ones, receive the greatest volume of natural attacks, floods that affect agriculture and the working class., poisoning of the soil that makes the land unproductive. Pollution of rivers, lakes and seas, chemical waste from industries, agriculture, and cities, increase in the disappearance of species in the process of extinction, erosion of productive areas produced by winds and waters, increasingly polluting activities (Hermosillo, 2023).

In fact, delving into the environment requires knowledge of other sciences, which makes it a very specialized and highly technical discipline, due to its transversality for its normative, systematic, and conceptual study.

The effects and consequences of COVID-19 are, until today, indeterminable regardless of the economy and human health. For this research, the protection of forests, lands and waters is of interest, due to their natural wealth for the environment and its biodiversity. Toxic waste and dangerous waste, produced by laboratories, hospitals, treatment plants for this material, funeral homes, crematoriums and pantheons, some open-air activities in clandestine places or wastewater discharges without any sanitary control or legal permits for proper operation, with competent professional supervision of how these establishments operate, which are a new threat to ecosystems and environmental pollution, a product of the global health catastrophe (Hermosillo, 2023).

This is why it is important to have indicators that allow us to measure the impact of the pandemic that occurred in past years, with the intention of proposing strategies that allow us to propose environmental regulations appropriate to the current situation.

Regarding research on green innovation, it focuses on the creation and commercialization of environmentally improved technologies, as well as the dissemination and adoption of these technologies. At the same time, it addresses learning about environmental management systems, the development of technological systems adopted by organizations and the adoption of innovative technologies related to the integration of environmentally friendly practices. It should be noted that green innovation is supported by normative and regulatory institutions, science, and technological development.

Green growth consists of creating new sources of growth through innovations and new markets, based on innovative financial and business models that succeed with or without financial support.

The use of eco-innovations is decisive for promoting this growth since these include both economic and environmental as well as social and technological aspects that contemplate the care of the environment through less harmful technologies. For this to happen, it is necessary to create synergies between those involved, to take advantage of the technological potential. A contextual analysis is required to identify the origin of the problems and guide changes towards sustainability in a coordinated manner (Velazquez & Castro, 2023)

It is necessary to know the specific characteristics and needs of each economic sector to project and improve the benefits of each of those involved, instead of focusing on individual privileges. Eco innovation will provide the bases to reorganize the way in which functions or services are conducted to achieve more competitive functions. Other fundamental aspects are 1) exploration of the impact of environmental regulation, as it is an environmental policy instrument that aims to prevent, mitigate, and restore damage to the environment, as well as regulate activities to mitigate negative effects on the environment. and human health, 2) incentives in socio-ecological and green technological innovation, conditioning or inducing behaviors towards organizational, technological, and productive innovation activities.

Next, some implications of organizational socio-ecology will be addressed with the aim of developing a framework to understand the relational nature of aspects such as leadership, culture and organizational change and the interdependence established between the organization and society. Organizational green technological innovation will also be analyzed to determine the impact of environmental regulation policies and incentives.

ORGANIZATIONAL SOCIO-ECOLOGY

Socio-ecology proposes the study of the behavior of individuals in interaction with their environmental systems. Hence its implications for organizational theories. Promotes the emergence of models that value resources and external influences. Authors such as Hu et al. (2020) and Chen et al. (2021) state that organizations are restricted by internal factors, such as capital, investment in R&D, and inclusion factors such as interest groups and bureaucratic advances in environmental regulation policies. However, the above situation is not the case for SMEs, since in most cases strict environmental policies incline them to invest in improving pollution control instead of betting on the development of green technologies, since the latter imply greater investments.

Regarding population ecology, most organizational theories propose that companies tend as much as possible to differentiate themselves from their competitors to achieve better access to system resources. However, the theory of population ecology maintains that companies directed by the forces of market selection tend in the long term to homogenize, so that a single business style remains, in each sector or population of organization: the more appropriate to the situation and the demands of the environment at that time. His work aims to describe in broad strokes the possible strategies to be adopted by organizations in different environmental situations (homogeneous, multiple, and variable), always considering the business vision and the consequences that derive from ecological theory.

Finally, the theory of population ecology explains the existence of diverse types of organizations; Environmentalists fixed their response on the rates of creation and death of organizations (Guerrero, 2024).

That is, the end or survival does not result from its capacity to change, but from the capacity of the environment to select and retain certain organizations and discard others. From the socioecological organizational theory, organizational size is studied, arguing that SMEs are immersed in a greater number of problems to obtain investments or credits and thus capitalize, which is why they are more likely to dissolve.

It is through organizational socio-ecology that the organization-environment assumption is broken since the analysis focuses on aggregate propositions at the population level and not on the individual organization. As in socio-ecology theory, the classical approach to environment and contingency theory seeks to evaluate existing scenarios through objective data and thus create plans to adapt to the needs of the organization. Thus, contingency theory states that there is no single way to solve problems, but rather that organizational change must be based on the capacity for adaptability and aligned adjustment between the organization and the internal and external environment of the organization.

Socio-ecology suggests that organizations tend to compete for resources and positioning against their competitors. The previous situation is explained from the theory of niche width, understood as a category of general theory, that is, of organizational socio-ecology. As for the theory of niche breadth, it is based on the survival possibilities of organizations in the face of environmental changes (Hannan & Freeman, 1977). Thus, from organizational socio-ecology, plans arising from the ecological contingencies imposed by the demands of the environment are necessary.

Aldrich & Auster (1986) state that organizational socio-ecology examines the characteristics of the vital manifestations of organizational populations, such as disappearance, considering individual situations such as their size and age, two elements associated with survival. Thus, the socio-ecology of the population reflects the changes that populations undergo over time. As a social demand, organizational socio-ecology exceeds internal limits and affects the influence on human beings and the natural environment. Consequently, corporate social responsibility is integrated into the fields of organizational socio-ecology, along with the establishment of socioecological and environmental measures (Oller, 2021).

In relation to the construction of an organizational socio-ecology to learn the management model of professional development, the latter should be based on guidance and not on control as is thought (Le Boterf, 1999). Furthermore, the organizational socioecological framework uses its knowledge to formulate and implement organizational strategies for change, which requires consensus for the cumulative generation of knowledge.

Regarding routines at the company level, as well as the notion of organizational character from organizational socio-ecology, these configure the capabilities of the participants to regenerate a coherent socio-ecology of action patterns (Birnholtz, Cohen & Hoch, 2007). For Pentland (2004) organizational routines are synonymous with ecologies. Since organizational routines are characterized by being organizational habits that arise from past experiences of the organization itself and make up the so-called organizational memory, thus conditioning future actions. Meanwhile, ecologies make up the relationships of living beings among themselves with the environment in which they live, from which they constantly learn.

The interdependence between routines challenges scholars to find the interactions in a socio-ecology between routines considering that routines never operate in a vacuum (Howard- Grenville et al. 2016) but are ubiquitous in organizations (Becker, 2008), configured in interdependently as a network. (Feldman et al., 2016; Pentland, 2011; Sele & Gran, 2016; Spee, Jarzabkowski & Smets, 2016). According to Howard- Grenville et al. (2016) routines are intertwined by actions, artifacts and people linked to other routines. And they are located at a particular level of macro and micro analysis of actors and activities.

Considering the above, authors such as Dietz et al. (2003), Eckerberg and Joas (2004), Folke et al. (2005) and Ostrom (2005) state that adaptive governance of ecosystems and socioecological systems serves as a gear in the search for changes in the stability properties of ecological interactions. Where the implications of chaos-induced dispersal in continuous-time models for socio-ecology are important (Sole and Bascompte, 1995).

Regarding sustainability practices, these converge with the socio-ecology of the population, composing a tool for the analysis of macro-organizational phenomena that tracks their use in theoretical and empirical research aimed at studying actions that help reduce the negative impact at a global level. . . that derive from productive practices (Salimath, & Jones, 2011). An archetype of the above is the industrial structure, since it has effects on regional economic growth and ecological well-being (Zhao et al., 2020; Huang et al., 2021) and the technological innovation infrastructure system by improving the innovation efficiency. protecting property rights.

The opposite of sustainability practices could be the culture that most developing countries have around the pursuit of rapid economic growth based on dependence on non-renewable energy consumption, resulting in significant carbon dioxide emissions. carbon. of carbon with adverse effects on the quality of the environment. It is a fact that currently economic growth is promoted through the substantial consumption of fossil fuels with harmful influence on the environment. And that companies seek to increase their production above environmental concerns. For this reason, in recent decades, multiple methods have emerged to evaluate environmental performance (Zhou et al., 2008; Sueyoshi & Goto 2012; Wu et al., 2019).

Environmental performance is characterized by a lack of green development, where polluting emissions are present in most geographic spaces. Currently, the theory of population ecology has relevant recognition since it has theoretical and ontological foundations that are widely accepted by academia and by the science that studies organizations; Its main precursors, Hannan & Freeman, focused their first studies on populations as objects of analysis, then in 1984 their objective was to also study companies, highlighting that the environment is the most determining and influential factor in subsistence or extinction. of companies, postulate the statement that it is the environment or environment that autonomously selects the characteristics of the companies that will be successful and eliminates the weakest ones. In this way, a parallel is made with animal populations, stating that organizations are similar to these populations where the environment is a place where they coexist and fight to survive and where only the strongest and those who manage to adapt to changes in the environment survive, while those that do not become extinct, that is, they disappear, since organizations compete among themselves for resources that, according to this theory, are limited and that organizations must compete for them with their peers.

Annual scientific production on the theory of the ecological of populations and labor inclusion is still low and although it is a topic of utmost importance in today's society, it is observed in the figure that in Latin America in the last two years there was no scientific production in this regard, which denotes a debt of academia and science with this very important topic. (Aguilar 2023)

ORGANIZATIONAL GREEN TECHNOLOGICAL INNOVATION

Green growth consists of creating new sources of growth through innovations and new markets, based on innovative financial and business models that succeed with or without financial support. The use of eco-innovations is decisive for promoting this growth since these include both economic and environmental as well as social and technological aspects that contemplate caring for the environment through less harmful technologies. For this to happen, it is necessary to create synergies between those involved, to take advantage of the technological potential. (Velasquez 2023)

It is necessary to conduct a contextual analysis that allows identifying the origin of the problems and guiding changes towards sustainability in a coordinated manner. It is necessary to know the specific characteristics and needs of each economic sector to project and improve the benefits of each of those involved, instead of focusing on individual privileges.

Over the past three decades, the concept of green ergonomics has gained relevance in the context of green technological innovation, including the development of products and services aimed at achieving ecological benefits and reducing organizational environmental impacts (Bernroider, 2002; Damanpour, 1992). This ergonomics focuses on the study of environmental factors, which constitute the environment of the system formed by the connection between humans and nature, taking and reducing the environmental impact, linking the design of innovative products and services aimed at reducing emissions. and contamination with other pro-nature benefits (Mandavilli, Rys & Russell, 2008; Sanquist, 2008; Hilliard & Jamieson, 2008).

The specialized literature has long presented a consensus on the relevance of the generation of innovation processes to achieve economic growth and development, and on the importance of public intervention to promote technological change and innovation. But the need to offer a conceptual framework that allows including in the analysis the effects and possible environmental mitigations that technological change can promote has more recently induced novel studies and conceptualizations (Zheng & Cai, 2022, among others).

It should be noted that currents of thought often differ regarding how innovation processes are conceived and, consequently, regarding the foundations and purpose of innovation policy. As well as with respect to the forms of intervention, which is what is most relevant for this work. In the following sections we will then dedicate ourselves to presenting this theoretical debate, considering these points of comparison and the incorporation of the green agenda in the approaches.

In the opinion of Sneideriene & Rugine (2019), Kousar et al. (2017), Weng & Lin (2011) and Lin & Ho (2011) organizations seek to create and commercialize better technologies from an environmental point of view, since the use of technological innovations can affect the diffusion and adoption of these technologies. Likewise, the government encourages organizations to adopt and develop green technological technology, and contributes to this objective through technical assistance services, financing, or training for its adoption.

However, efforts by the government and organizations are not always necessary, since in most cases organizations tend to adopt technological innovation with elevated levels of environmental uncertainty, since they do not always develop by taking technological innovation. as a banner. green (Zilani, Iranmanesh, Nikbin and Jumadi, 2014). Even when the adoption of said innovation reduces the negative organizational impacts of the processing of technological systems and internal administrative processing. In some cases, attempts to adopt this type of innovation are repeated, even before their final adoption, which means that they are costly and unattractive for organizations (Baines, Brown, Benedettini & Ball, 2012).

Furthermore, green innovation of organizations is related to life cycles by constituting a set of technology-related practices that focus on sustainability. Well, it leads to offering ecological, dependable, environmentally friendly products and services at competitive prices and delivered on time (Thatte, 2007). Elements such as company ownership structure, life cycle, size, etc., affect environmental regulations which in turn affect green innovation. And these, having a direct positive relationship with green technological innovation, can hinder or prolong the pollutant reduction or patenting processes (Amore & Bennedsen, 2016; Fujii & Managi 2016). As Rogers (2003) states, organizational innovation is characterized by traceability, which forms a stage of creativity based on information collected, and a series of tests before the use and implementation of the innovation in question due to the degree of uncertainty.

The theoretical development of green organizations is framed in the study of sustainable businesses, based on Acquier 's postulates. et al., (2019) research has focused on topics ranging from the description of dimensions, characteristics, and specific typologies of business models, through theoretical perspectives on this area of research, to the design and organizational capabilities required to the development of sustainable business models. In this sense, it is worth highlighting that in the category of description, characteristics and typologies of sustainable business models, a set of studies dedicated to aspects of sustainable business models that focused on the evolution of the elements of the concept were identified.

A second study topic analyzes scalability based on the drivers and barriers in adoption, and the third category focuses on how value creation and the value proposition occur in sustainable business models (Acquier et al., 2019, p. The implementation, incorporation or exploitation of an innovative product, production process, service or management or marketing approach for the organization, whether by developing or adopting it, that leads to a decrease in the environmental impact, pollution, and other negative effects of consumption of resources throughout their life cycle. Then it can be stated that environmental innovation is an element of value relationship that must be incorporated into the development of green businesses, as an element that generates competitive advantages in the current context that seeks business solutions to global environmental problems. (Quiroz 2024)

It is for this reason that interest arises in the study of eco-innovation and its impact on business and sustainability. Fernando et al., (2018) state that "green growth cannot be achieved without promoting green innovation."" This means that knowledge enables the design of new green products and services that can meet a company's objectives of generating wealth and satisfy the requirements of environmentally and ethically conscious customers. Likewise, it can be said that green growth implies prosperity focused on quality, reduced carbon footprint, lower energy consumption and energy efficiency, with a business approach aimed at creating value using clean technologies. (Quiroz 2024)

The research finds that relative advantage is related to the adoption of green innovation. Relative advantage is the perception of the characteristics of organizational technological innovation in terms of price, quality, satisfaction, use and useful life over its costs. Authors such as Lin & Ho (2011), Rogers (2003), Kousar et al. (2017) and Grandon & Pearson (2004) agree that if the organizational perception of the relative advantage of the innovation is greater than the cost and better than the current technology, the organization can adopt the innovation.

On the other hand, innovation management is related to internal and external practices. Regarding the externalities of innovation, Bi et al. (2006), Li et al. (2018) and Liu et al. (2020), state that these are addressed through government subsidies for research and development. R&D, as well as human capital and gross domestic product per capita, have effects on the development of green innovation, which in turn influences human capital and gross domestic product and the development of green innovation. The previous situation shows the latent need for high investments in R&D, human capital, and gross domestic product by organizations to consolidate better performance in green innovation.

Investments in R&D are essential to improve the organization's technological innovation capabilities. However, for these to go hand in hand with sustainable development, they must be allocated to initiatives that prioritize energy conservation and environmental protection. The latter is the responsibility of governments (Li et al., 2015; Jiang et al., 2020; Wang & Jiang, 2021). Well, it is the governments that oversee deploying policies focused on the development of a more sustainable economy.

Grossman and Krueger (1995) maintain that regional economic development is an operation related to the level of investment in innovation. Well, it is understood as the process of socioeconomic and environmental change whose central objective is to improve the well-being of the population of the territory where it is limited. That is, local governments are responsible for investing in organizations with the objective of promoting the development of innovative activities through the technological benefits of foreign investment and incentives for competition.

Regarding the complexity of the innovation, it depends on the degree of organizational perception of the technological innovation in terms of use. In other words, if the complexity of the innovation increases due to difficulties in innovation diffusion and knowledge sharing, adoption decreases.

Thus, the perception of organizational complexity is negatively related to green innovation. Otherwise, when innovation spreads and knowledge is shared, where the organization tends to adopt technological innovation. It should be noted that Kousar et al (2017), Etzion (2007), Rogers (2003), Tornatzky & Klein (1982), Deng & Ji (2015) and Bradford & Florin (2003) state that innovation requires skills and efforts that increase complexity while the level of adoption decreases. Furthermore, Li, Pan, Kim, Linn, and Chiang (2015) clarify that there is a lack of green technological innovations in developing countries compared to developed nations.

Technological innovation is adopted after observing the impacts (Shahrul & Normah, 2015; Tan & Eze, 2008). Therefore, it is considered visible for adoption, reflecting the expected observation outcome or perceived observability (Rogers, 2003). Thus, the perception of observability is positively related to green innovation, as stated by Hatimtai & Hassan (2018) and Rogers (2003), considering it a significant characteristic of green innovation because it allows organizations to identify the benefits of innovation. green. innovation. innovation with high possibilities of being adopted by organizations.

Chen, Shih, Shyur, and Wu (2012) and Chen and Hsu (2009) classify green innovation into green management, green process, and green product. Enterprises are promoting green technology innovation capabilities, green product innovation capabilities, followed by green process innovation capabilities and governance technology capabilities of enterprises. Wang et al. (2019) argue that green innovation capabilities, green product innovation, green process innovation, and governance technological capabilities should be implemented based on enterprises' green technology innovation capabilities. Thus, organizational innovations compatible with the organization's capabilities have positive effects on the environment (Etzion, 2007). Thus, the perception of organizational compatibility is positively related to green technological innovation.

Antonioli, Mancinelli and Mazzanti (2013) state that green process innovation is related to updates in systems, methods and processes, and process innovation aims to produce green goods and services to satisfy ecological concerns and environmental objectives. Regarding the innovation capabilities of a green process, these are measured through indicators such as strengthening transformation processes and improving protection design processes, eliminating pollution, and reviewing the green process. Meanwhile, government environmental regulatory actions have effects on investments in pollution elimination.

Companies' green technology innovation capabilities are related to the elements of green product innovation, process innovation, and technological governance. Accordingly, Li (2019), Wang et al. (2018) and Saud et al. (2019) state that organizations should intensify green technology innovation to meet technical specifications and green emissions standards set by governments, improve technology governance capabilities through waste and product innovation capabilities. and green processes and develop innovation in green technology.

Organizational learning represents an alternative capable of transforming information into knowledge, but, like innovation, it thrives in informal environments (Gunderson, 1999). Likewise, Teece (2016) maintains that the internal fit of a learning organization has a positive relationship with organizational innovation, and this with organizational performance. Therefore, organizational learning intention has effects on innovation capacity and this on organizational performance.

Therefore, organizational learning guides organizational innovation in knowledge-intensive organizations. For Rahim, Eldwiah & Rahman (2013), the knowledge-based view expands the resource-based view and is being used in various studies on stakeholder theory, open innovation, microdata, outsourcing and offshoring (Hoskisson, Gambeta, Green, & Li, 2018; Santoro, Vrontis, Thrassou & Dezi, 2018; Specifically, individual and organizational learning leads to innovation that improves organizational performance. Organizational learning guides organizational innovation (Visser & Togt, 2016).

Authors such as Toffler (1970) and Mintzberg (1979) propose the adhocratic organizational structure to promote creativity and innovation. Since the adhocracy model is flexible, organic, innovative, and collaborative. Additionally, you can merge different disciplines into a project team while avoiding the dangers of bureaucratic structures such as division of labor and coordination because of interactions.

From the perspective of motivation, green innovation must be worked in a disjointed manner with technological innovation. Well, it is considered that organizational behaviors are classified according to their motivations into symbolic strategic environmental actions of cooperation and substantive environmental actions, or substantive and cooperative strategies (Delmas & Montes Sancho, 2010; Neumann, 2021; Truong et al., 2021).

ENVIRONMENTAL REGULATION POLICIES AND INCENTIVES

The mechanism of environmental regulation policy influences the motivation of green innovation enterprises to differentiate between green innovation behaviors in regulation and the regulated objects of the government enterprise. In other words, government environmental support increases the adoption of green innovation through the implementation of environmental production methods (Lin & Ho, 2010; Gadenne, Kennedy & McKeiver, 2009). Government environmental support shapes systems that take the form of environmental regulations, policies, standards, and interventions that tend to reduce environmental impact and encourage companies to engage in environmental technological innovation (Eidat, Kelly, Roche & Eyadat, 2008).

The mechanisms of environmental regulation policies affect organizational green innovation in different green innovation behaviors. Promoting the conservation and rational use of goods and services that reduce the environmental impact in the world. Zhou et al. (2017) and Bai et al (2019), in a study on state ownership and business innovation in China, found that state-owned enterprises assume responsibilities that non-state-owned enterprises do not assume in the implementation of green innovation development under the limitations of the environmental regulations. Consequently, state-owned enterprises do better after the implementation of environmental regulations since, due to the policy of restricted environmental regulations,

For small businesses, regulatory policies mean improved pollution control, while for growing businesses, they mean access to abundant funds for R&D investments in green innovation to improve environmentally friendly production. environment. the environment and green technology (Cao & Cao, 2019). For this reason, environmental policy formulation must consider specific measures for the pollution control capabilities of companies according to their ownership structure, size, life cycle, etc.

The policy on environmental regulations is of immense importance, considering the commercial value of carbon, since it has a strong incentive effect to improve the green innovation of organizations. However, openness does not have a significant impact on green innovation because the effect is indirect. Dauda et al. (2021) and Ko et al. (2021) value technological innovation in organizations as a process capable of reducing carbon emissions and improving environmental quality. Since in practice it has been shown that green innovation significantly reduces energy consumption and, consequently, the emission of CO2 gas.

The carbon emissions trading market should be liberalized by placing organizations' emissions into pricing mechanisms to stimulate green technological innovation activities. In other words, a higher level of CO2 emissions and environmental pollution as causal links requires the establishment of effective institutional quality for green innovation. That is, the causal link between energy consumption and institutional quality is established. Thus, there is a relationship between green innovation and institutional quality.

Research has found causal relationships between variables ranging from CO2 emissions to economic growth, CO2 emissions to green innovation and institutional quality, urbanization and energy consumption to economic growth and institutional quality. In turn, the research points to the existence of a bidirectional link between economic growth and gas emissions. Therefore, institutional quality and urbanization in developing countries can increase CO2 emissions.

The influence of environmental regulations on green technology innovation by mature and growing companies achieves the greatest impact, while green technology innovation by emerging companies has severe financial constraints, struggles to meet capital needs, and faces an elevated level of risk taking that leads to lower ones. impact (Shahzad et al., 2019). The mechanism between good capital allocation, green development and technological innovation leads to a more efficient socio-ecological environment. Incorporating capital allocation in technological innovation into an analytical framework promotes the efficiency of regional green development. Regarding heterogeneity, the effect of capital allocation is significant (Schmidt et al., 2020; Gao et al., 2019). Since, capital allocation has a positive relationship with technological innovation that improves the contribution of companies with an impact on the efficiency of green development.

Government intervention on misallocated capital can lead to environmental degradation. In the words of Zhang & Lu (2017), if there is price distortion in the market, capital allocation cannot be optimized. Enterprises find it difficult to obtain the capital needed for technological innovation, which weakens the motivation to conduct research and development (Gao et al., 2019). If the price of capital is controlled by the government, firms tend to seek rents for low-cost factors that attract funds for research and development and reduce the efficiency of innovation (Murphy et al., 1993). The intervention of external factors can destroy the capital price mechanism, reducing the costs of production factors for polluting industries. Technological innovation has a mediating role with capital allocation in the efficiency of green development.

Technological innovation increases the use of clean processes by reducing environmental pollution (Hua et al. 2018). At the same time, it stimulates enterprises to use efficient resources, adopt equipment, and promote the improvement of industries (Sun et al. 2020b). And it tends to facilitate the development of green economy and has a mediating role in capital allocation for green economic efficiency, while capital allocation improves the efficiency of green development. For these reasons, technological innovation plays a mediating rôle with capital allocation and improves the efficiency of green development.

Another element that contributes to the development of green innovation in organizations is green finance (Luo et al., 2021). They motivate organizations to invest in green technological innovation and are the driving force for the green transformation of polluted companies through participation in green innovation activities. Whereas environmental regulation enhances the effects of green finance on green innovation.

It is thought that companies tend to adopt conservative strategies to invest in green technological projects with intense environmental regulations and minimal risk. This is where green finance and environmental regulations have positive effects on green innovation. The moderating effects of environmental regulation promote the effects of green finance on this type of innovation, as low levels of environmental regulations lead to higher innovation performance as green finance performance increases. (Chávez, et al. 2024)

It is about being responsible for social issues within the organization, while business criteria aim to collect and measure environmental, social and governance data that is relevant to the business objectives of each company. They are important for organizations that prioritize sustainability and for investors who want their resources to be allocated to organizations that are responsible towards society. To achieve sustainable status, companies must design and implement a program, create adequate visibility through program participation, and achieve metrics that matter to investors making decisions based on long-term profit. In short, the objective is to establish the duty of business due diligence for the integration of Sustainability criteria. With this adoption, companies will be obliged to identify, prevent, mitigate, or even put an end to actions that negatively affect human rights or the environment. (Chávez, et al 2024)

The emphasis on green innovation outcomes by companies requires more efficient green financing to produce green innovation. And the results of this innovation can be achieved by encouraging organizations to use green finance and investments and avoiding time-consuming projects. This type of financing is subject to the implementation of environmental regulations, as they enhance the effects of green finance on green innovation.

Large companies have more resources and tend to improve the quality of green technological innovation. At the same time, they have a more mature development of organizational systems, achieving high innovation management (Yu et al., 2022b). Well, they have access to abundant innovation resources such as capital, R&D, patents, and technological talents (Gupeng & Xiangdong, 2012; Hu et al., 2017). Of the above-mentioned resources, green patent application is a measure that has green finance effects to boost green technological innovation. And the use of these patents to measure innovative behavior is not exhaustive for the different motivations in green innovation options.

Both large companies and small companies limit themselves to promoting green technological innovation. Large companies face complex scenarios because of environmental regulations, while small companies, being more restricted by capital, technology, talent, etc., have more difficulties in promoting green innovation. And although the behavior of companies must be limited by environmental regulations to develop green technological innovation. The implementation of intense environmental regulations improves green innovation considering that the limitations of companies may not lead to the transformation of technologically innovative production.

Green innovation as a dependent variable can be measured by the number of patent applications associated with energy intensity (Wurlod & Noailly, 2018). Green patent applications indicate the advancement of green innovation (Tolliver et al. 2021) and are giving rise to innovation activities without institutional preferences or time lags, which are used as indicators to evaluate green innovation (Fujii & Managi 2016; Cho & Sohn, 2018; Fuji 2016). Environmental regulation has a positive impact on green innovation patents and green utility model patents, although from an influence perspective, the impact of environmental regulation on green innovation may decrease if companies have not phased out the green innovation strategy. For Westwood & Low (2003) innovation strategies in green technologies must be formulated and implemented with sensitivity considering the cultural differences that have an impact on innovation processes.

Environmental regulations influence government subsidies to eliminate compliance costs by enhancing green innovation with minimal impact on green innovation behaviors. And the latter must be classified into diverse types to determine the effect on choices of innovative behaviors with different motivations. That is why government innovation subsidy policies should be more specific and flexible according to the qualifications of the companies that need them and the suitability of the subsidies, coinciding with the development stage in the life cycle to improve core competitiveness. and achieve positive effects on the environment. technological innovation.

Regulatory capture and government subsidies are moderating variables. Grants enable organizations to conduct green innovation aligned with the government's technological innovation goals (Boeing, 2016; Bai et al., 2019). Although they promote green innovation; Regulatory capture has a negative role in the regulatory process of environmental regulation that promotes green innovation by companies. Even so, the increase in green subsidies leads to companies having more resources and funds to invest in the development of green technologies, improving technological governance, process innovation and green product capabilities (Saud et al., 2019; Lin et al., 2020). Consequently, regulatory capture behavior requires more precise indicators to verify the results on the impact of green innovation effects.

And while regulatory capture leads to different green innovation behaviors, it has a distorting effect on substantial high-quality incentives that lead to economic consequences of environmental regulations. That is, it has a negative effect on environmental regulation in the promotion of companies as an explanation of the different behaviors of green innovation. Since, they can expire due to regulatory rigor as the main cause of environmental accidents that intentionally balance profits (Graham et al., 2011; Steinzor, 2012). Therefore, firms that adopt a profit maximization orientation may have more potential benefits from regulatory capture behavior than those that have strong motivational behavior for regulatory capture (Li et al., 2021; Zhang et al., 2021).).

When talking about policy evaluation, specifically in environmental matters, and when environmental policy is studied, most of the attention is focused on the performance of public officials, since they appear as the source of that policy. However, it is necessary to keep in mind that it is private parties, companies, and consumers, who with their decisions determine the scope and extent of environmental impacts and that the incentives faced by these private parties specify how and where these impacts will be reduced. Consequently, an extremely important criterion that must be used to evaluate any environmental policy is whether that policy provides a strong incentive for individuals and groups to find new and innovative ways to reduce their impacts on the natural environment (Cossío 2023).

Therefore, it can be said that it is possible for the existence of policies that have been developed in accordance with what is established in the constitution and the laws or that have even been implemented under rigorous management control systems and, however, have not achieved all the objectives. objectives for which they were implemented or that the substantial number of undesirable effects overshadows the fulfillment of their objectives. Environmental regulations tend to influence green innovation of mature and growing companies at the highest level, while the startup stage has the lowest impact due to available resources in capital, technology, and talent.

CONCLUSIONS

In general terms, this analysis concludes that there is a direct relationship between the incentives of environmental regulation and socio-ecological and green technological innovation in organizations. And that the socio-ecology of the organizational population has implications for sustainability. Besides that, institutional reforms are essential to reduce green emissions and achieve climate change targets.

It was also found that enterprises perform high-quality green innovation behaviors to promote green technology and gain competitive advantage. And that green innovation companies reach their highest level during periods of growth and maturity, when they improve green technological innovation and develop a keen sense of social responsibility for more active innovation activities.

Regarding environmental regulation, it affects the company's green innovation through innovation compensation mechanisms and compliance costs. That is why companies that bear excessive environmental costs should lean towards regulatory capture instead of enhancing environmental protection with green technology, which can destroy the incentive mechanism with long time and higher costs. Furthermore, the institutional environment is relevant in the allocation of environmental factors and performance.

As for business differences in ownership, life cycle, size, etc., they have a significant impact on the incentives for green innovation of environmental regulation. Both environmental regulations and green finance have effects on green technological innovation.

On the other hand, green financing levels of green innovation have heterogeneous impacts with a moderating effect on environmental regulations. On the other hand, environmental regulation is a moderator that is used to examine the effects of green innovation, through the level of contribution of green finance and the application of green patents.

In summary, green finance, green innovation, and environmental regulations tend to be stable with fixed effects.

Finally, the research results suggest that subsidies do not explain the gap between green technology innovation behaviors.

RECOMMENDATIONS

The role of technological innovation should be strengthened to improve the efficiency of green development. That is, the organization must implement and review the implementation of green product innovation capabilities, green process innovation capabilities, and technology governance capabilities.

Regarding environmental regulation, the scientific design of environmental regulation policy tools must be strengthened to monitor emissions reductions and conduct green innovation. The intensity of environmental regulation should be increased according to the specific situations of companies.

Governments in policy making and stakeholders should facilitate green organizational strategies to invest in technological innovation projects aimed at reducing environmental pollution. Policymaking must strengthen institutional quality and enact more effective policies to address environmental challenges. The different impacts of institutional settings must be assumed by the research model.

Finally, regarding green financing, governments must support the development of innovative companies with tax incentives and financial subsidies that encourage more capital flows towards green technological innovations and clean processes.

SCOPE OF FUTURE WORK

The critical exercise conducted here leads to considering the role of the principles and assumptions of population socio-ecology in examining organizational sustainability in organizations. As well as the evaluation of the individual effects of government subsidy and regulatory capture mechanisms on the behavior of green innovation with different motivations.

REFERENCES

Aguilar-Hernández, P. A., Acosta-Tzin, J. V., Andino-González, P., Raudales-García, E. V., & Sarmiento-Matute, R. E. (2023). Aprendizaje organizacional orientado a la diversidad laboral desde una perspectiva de la teoría de la ecología de las poblaciones. *UMH - Sapientiae, 4*(1), 25–45. 10.5377/umhs.v4i1.17205

Aldrich, H., & Auster, E. R. (1986). Even dwarfs started small: Liabilities of age and size and their strategic implications. In Staw, B. M., & Cummings, L. L. (Eds.), *Research in Organizational Behavior* (Vol. 8, pp. 165–198). JAI Press.

Altieri, M. Ángel, & Nicholls, C. I. (2012). Agroecología: Única esperanza para la soberanía alimentaria y la resiliencia socioecológica. *Agroecología, 7*(2), 65–83. https://revistas.um.es/agroecologia/article/view/182861

Amburgey, T., & Rao, H. (1996). Organizational ecology: Past, present, and future directions. *Academy of Management Journal*, 39(5), 1265–1286. 10.2307/256999

Amore, M. D., & Bennedsen, M. (2016). Corporate governance and green innovation. *Journal of Environmental Economics and Management*, 75, 54–72. 10.1016/j.jeem.2015.11.003

Antonioli, D., Mancinelli, S., & Mazzanti, M. (2013). Is environmental innovation embedded within high- performance organizational changes? The role of human resource management and complementarity in green business strategies. *Research Policy*, 42(4), 975–988. 10.1016/j.respol.2012.12.005

Bai, Y., Song, S., Jiao, J., & Yang, R. (2019). The impacts of government R&D subsidies on green innovation: Evidence from Chinese energy-intensive firms. *Journal of Cleaner Production*, 233(9), 819–829. 10.1016/j.jclepro.2019.06.107

Baines, T., Brown, S., Benedettini, O., & Ball, P. (2012). Examining green production and its role within the competitive strategy of manufacturers. *Journal of Industrial Engineering and Management*, 5(1), 53–87. 10.3926/jiem.405

Becker, M. C. (Ed.). (2008). *Handbook of organizational routines*. Cheltenham, UK: Edward Elgar Publishing Becker, M. C. (Ed.). (2008). *Handbook of organizational routines*. Cheltenham, UK: Edward Elgar Publishing. 10.4337/9781848442702

Bernroider, E. (2002). Factors in SWOT analysis applied to micro, small-to-medium, and large software enterprises: An Austrian study. *European Management Journal*, 20(5), 562–573. 10.1016/S0263-2373(02)00095-6

Bi, K., Huang, P., & Wang, X. (2016). Innovation performance and influencing factors of low-carbon technological innovation under the global value chain: A case of Chinese manufacturing industry. *Technological Forecasting and Social Change*, 111, 275–284. 10.1016/j.techfore.2016.07.024

Birnholtz, J. P., Cohen, M. D., & Hoch, S. V. (2007). Organizational character: On the regeneration of Camp Poplar Grove. *Organization Science*, 18(2), 315–332. 10.1287/orsc.1070.0248

Boeing, P. (2016). The allocation and effectiveness of China's R&D subsidies—Evidence from listed firms. *Research Policy*, 45(9), 1774–1789. 10.1016/j.respol.2016.05.007

Boubakri, N., Cosset, J. C., & Saffar, W. (2013). The role of state and foreign owners in corporate risk-taking: Evidence from privatization. *Journal of Financial Economics*, 108(3), 641–658. 10.1016/j.jfineco.2012.12.007

Bradford, M., & Florin, J. (2003). Examining the role of innovation diffusion factors on the implementation success of enterprise resource planning systems. *International Journal of Accounting Information Systems*, 4(3), 205–225. 10.1016/S1467-0895(03)00026-5

Cao, X., Deng, M., Song, F., Zhong, S., & Zhu, J. (2019). Direct and moderating effects of environmental regulation intensity on enterprise technological innovation: The case of China. *PLoS One*, 14(10), e0223175. 10.1371/journal.pone.022317531589643

Chen, C. C., Shih, H. S., Shyur, H. J., & Wu, K. S. (2012). A business strategy selection of green supply chain management via an analytic network process. *Computers & Mathematics with Applications (Oxford, England)*, 64(8), 2544–2557. 10.1016/j.camwa.2012.06.013

Chen, H. L., & Hsu, W. T. (2009). Family ownership, board independence, and R&D investment. *Family Business Review*, 22(4), 347–362. 10.1177/0894486509341062

Chen, Z., Zhang, X., & Chen, F. (2021). Do carbon emission trading schemes stimulate green innovation in enterprises? Evidence from China. *Technological Forecasting and Social Change*, 168, 120744. 10.1016/j.techfore.2021.120744

Chiu, Y. B., & Lee, C. C. (2020). Effects of financial development on energy consumption: The role of country risks. *Energy Economics*, 90, 104833. 10.1016/j.eneco.2020.104833

Cho, J. H., & Sohn, S. Y. (2018). A novel decomposition analysis of green patent applications for the evaluation of R&D efforts to reduce CO2 emissions from fossil fuel energy consumption. *Journal of Cleaner Production*, 193, 290–299. 10.1016/j.jclepro.2018.05.060

Cossío Blandón, F. C., & Hinestroza Cuesta, L. (2023). La evaluación y seguimiento de las políticas ambientales: Una etapa en el olvido. *Advocatus*, 2(29), 87–104. 10.18041/0124-0102/advocatus.29.1671

Damanpour, F. (1992). Organizational size and innovation. *Organization Studies*, 13(3), 375–402. 10.1177/017084069201300304

Dauda, L., Long, X., Mensah, C. N., Salman, M., Boamah, K. B., Ampon-Wireko, S., & Dogbe, C. S. K. (2021). Innovation, trade openness and CO2 emissions in selected countries in Africa. *Journal of Cleaner Production*, 281, 125143. 10.1016/j.jclepro.2020.125143

Delmas, M. A., & Montes-Sancho, M. J. (2010). Voluntary agreements to improve environmental quality: Symbolic and substantive cooperation. *Strategic Management Journal*, 31(6), 575–601. 10.1002/smj.826

Deng, Q., & Ji, S. (2015). Organizational green IT adoption: *Concept and evidence. Sustainability (Basel)*, 7(12), 16737–16755. 10.3390/su71215843

Dietz, T., Ostrom, E., & Stern, P. L. (2003). The Struggle to Govern the Commons. *Science*, 302(5652), 1907–1912. 10.1126/science.109101514671286

DiMaggio, P., & Powell, W. W. (1983). The iron cage revisited: Collective rationality and institutional isomorphism in organizational fields. *American Sociological Review*, 48(2), 147–160. 10.2307/2095101

Eckerberg, K., & Joas, M. (2004). Multi-level Environmental Governance: A Concept under Stress? *Local Environment*, 9(5), 405–412. 10.1080/1354983042000255315

Eiadat, Y., Kelly, A., Roche, F., & Eyadat, H. (2008). Green and competitive? An empirical test of the mediating role of environmental innovation strategy. *Journal of World Business*, *43*(2), 131–145. doi:. jwb.2007.11.01210.1016/j

Etzion, D. (2007). Research on organizations and the natural environment, 1992-present: A review. *Journal of Management*, 33(4), 637–664. 10.1177/0149206307302553

Feldman, M. S. (2016). Past, Present, and future. In J. Howard-Grenville, C., Rerup, A., Langley, & H., Tsoukas (Eds.). *Organizational Routines: How They are Created, Maintained, and Changed* (pp. 23-46) Oxford: Oxford University Press

Folke, C., Hahn, T., Olsson, P., and Norberg, J. (2005). Adaptive Governance of Social–ecological Systems. *Annual Review of Environment and Resources.*

Fujii, H. (2016). Decomposition analysis of green chemical technology inventions from 1971 to 2010 in Japan. *Journal of Cleaner Production*, 112, 4835–4843. 10.1016/j.jclepro.2015.07.123

Fujii, H., & Managi, S. (2016). Research and development strategy for environmental technology in Japan: A comparative study of the private and public sectors. *Technological Forecasting and Social Change*, 112, 293–302. 10.1016/j.techfore.2016.02.012

Gadenne, D. L., Kennedy, J., & McKeiver, C. (2009). An empirical study of environmental awareness and practices in SMEs. *Journal of Business Ethics*, 84(1), 45–63. 10.1007/s10551-008-9672-9

Gao, X., Lyu, Y., Shi, F., Zeng, J., & Liu, C. (2019). The impact of financial fac-tor market distortion on green innovation efficiency of high-tech industry. *Ekoloji*, 28(107), 3449–3461.

Graham, B., Reilly, W., Beinecke, F., Boesch, D., Garcia, T., Murray, C., & Ulmer, F. (2011). *Deep water: The Gulf oil disaster and the future of offshore drilling. Report to the President*. National Commission on the BP Deepwater Horizon Oil Spill and Offshore Drilling.

Grossman, G. M., & Krueger, A. B. (1995). Economic growth and the environment. *The Quarterly Journal of Economics*, 110(2), 353–377. 10.2307/2118443

Guerrero Sánchez, P., Hernández Jaimes, B. G.., Bonilla Sánchez, F. de J.., Sánchez Guevara, I.., & Guerrero Grajeda, J. (2024). Las estrategias de sobrevivencia de las microempresas en México durante la pandemia. *Revista Universidad Y Empresa, 26*(46), 1–30. https://doi.org/10.12804/revistas.urosario.edu.co/empresa/a.13581

Gunderson, L. (1999). Resilience, Flexibility and Adaptive Management: Antidotes for Spurious Certitude? *Conservation Ecology*, 3(1), 7. http://www.consecol.org/vol3/iss1/art7. 10.5751/ES-00089-030107

Gupeng, Z., & Xiangdong, C. (2012). The value of invention patents in China: Country origin and technology field differences. *China Economic Review*, 23(2), 357–370. 10.1016/j.chieco.2012.02.002

Hannan, M. (2005). Ecologies of Organizations: Diversity and Identity. *The Journal of Economic Perspectives*, 19(1), 51–70. 10.1257/0895330053147985

Hannan, M. T., & Freeman, J. (1989). *Organizational Ecology*. Harvard University Press. 10.4159/9780674038288

Hannan, M. T., & Freeman, J. H. (1977). The Population Ecology of Organizations. *American Journal of Sociology*, 82(5), 929–963. 10.1086/226424

Hatimtai, M. H., & Hassan, H. (2018). The relationship between the characteristics of innovation towards the effectiveness of ICT in Malaysia productivity corporation. *Malaysian Journal of Communication*, 34(1), 253–269. 10.17576/JKMJC-2018-3401-15

Hermosillo Hernández, Luis. (2023). Necesidad de replantear la jurisdicción ambiental en México. *Derecho global. Estudios sobre derecho y justicia, 8*(24), 15-45. 10.32870/dgedj.v8i24.395

Hilliard, A., & Jamieson, G. A. (2008). Winning solar races with interface design. *Ergonomics in Design*, 16(2), 6–11. 10.1518/106480407X312374

Hoskisson, R. E., Gambeta, E., Green, C. D., & Li, T. X. (2018). Is my firm-specific investment protected? Overcoming the stakeholder investment dilemma in the resource-based view. *Academy of Management Review*, 43(2), 284–306. 10.5465/amr.2015.0411

Howard-Grenville, J., Rerup, C., Langley, A., & Tsoukas, H. (2016). Introduction: Advancing a process perspective on routines by zooming out and zooming in. In J. Howard-Grenville, C., Rerup, A., Langley, & H., Tsoukas (Eds.). *Organizational routines: how they are created, maintained, and changed* (pp.1-22.) Oxford: Oxford University Press.

Hu, A. G. Z., Zhang, P., & Zhao, L. (2017). China as number one? Evidence from China's most recent patenting surge. *Journal of Development Economics*, 124, 107–119. 10.1016/j.jdeveco.2016.09.004

Hua, Y., Xie, R., & Su, Y. (2018). Fiscal spending and air pollution in Chinese cities: Identifying composition and technique effects. *China Economic Review*, 47, 156–169. 10.1016/j.chieco.2017.09.007

Huang, M., Ding, R., & Xin, C. (2021). Impact of technological innovation and industrial-structure upgrades on ecological efficiency in China in terms of spatial spillover and the threshold effect. *Integrated Environmental Assessment and Management*, 17(4), 852–865. 10.1002/ieam.438133325155

Jiang, Z., Wang, Z., and Lan, X. (2021). How Environmental Regulations Affect Corporate Innovation? Coupling Mechanism of Mandatory Rules and Voluntary Management. *Technol. Soc.,65*, 101575. doi:. 2021.10157510.1016/j.techsoc

Ko, Y.-C., Zigan, K., & Liu, Y.-L. (2021). Carbon capture and storage in South Africa: A technological innovation system with a political economy focus. *Technological Forecasting and Social Change*, *166*, 120633. . techfore. 2021. 12063310. 1016/j

Kousar, S., Sabri, P. S. U., Zafar, M., & Akhtar, A. (2017). Technological factors and adoption of green innovation- moderating role of government intervention: A case of SMEs in Pakistan. *Pakistan Journal of Commerce and Social Sciences*, 11(3), 833–861.

Le Boterf, G. (1999). *L'ingénierie des compétences*. Éditions d'Organisation.

Li, J., Pan, S. Y., Kim, H., Linn, J. H., & Chiang, P. C. (2015). Building green supply chains in eco-industrial parks towards a green economy: Barriers and strategies. *Journal of Environmental Management*, 162, 158–170. 10.1016/j.jenvman.2015.07.03026241931

Li, N. B. (2019). Environmental Regulation and Corporate Green Technology Innovation - a Conditional Process Analysis. *Inn. Mong. Soc. Sci. Chin. Ed*, 40(6), 109–115. 10.14137/j.cnki.issn1003-5281.2019.06.016

Li, S., Song, X., & Wu, H. (2015). Political connection, ownership structure, and corporate philanthropy in China: A strategic-political perspective. *Journal of Business Ethics*, 129(2), 399–411. 10.1007/s10551-014-2167-y

Li, Z., Liao, G., Wang, Z., & Huang, Z. (2018). Green loan and subsidy for promoting clean production innovation. *Journal of Cleaner Production*, 187, 421–431. 10.1016/j.jclepro.2018.03.066

Lin, C. Y., & Ho, Y. H. (2010). The influences of environmental uncertainty on corporate green behavior: An empirical study with small and medium-size enterprises. *Social Behavior and Personality*, 38(5), 691–696. 10.2224/sbp.2010.38.5.691

Lin, Y. X., Sha, K. C., & Wang, J. (2020). Practical Experience and Inspiration of Foreign Emission Permit System. Environ. Impact. *Assess, 42*(1), 14–16. CNKI: SUN:SXHS.0.2020-01-004.

Liu, J., Zhao, M., & Wang, Y. (2020). Impacts of government subsidies and environmental regulations on green process innovation: A nonlinear approach. *Technology in Society*, 63, 101417. 10.1016/j.techsoc.2020.101417

Liu, Y., Wang, A., & Wu, Y. (2021). Environmental regulation and green innovation: Evi-dence from China's new environmental protection law. *Journal of Cleaner Production*, 297, 126698. 10.1016/j.jclepro.2021.126698

Luo, Y., Salman, M., & Lu, Z. (2021). Heterogeneous impacts of environmental regulations and foreign direct investment on green innovation across different regions in China. *The Science of the Total Environment*, 759, 143744. 10.1016/j.scitotenv.2020.14374433341514

Mandavilli, S., Rys, M. J., & Russell, E. R. (2008). Environmental impact of modern roundabouts. *International Journal of Industrial Ergonomics*, 38(2), 135–142. 10.1016/j.ergon.2006.11.003

Mintzberg, H. (1979). *The structuring of organizations: A synthesis of the research.* Prentice Hall.

Murphy, K. M., Shleifer, A., & Vishny, R. W. (1993). Why is rent-seeking so costly to growth? *The American Economic Review*, 83(2), 409–414. https://www.jstor.org/stable/2117699

Neumann, T. (2021). Does it pay for new firms to be green? An empirical analysis of when and how different greening strategies affect the performance of new firms. *Journal of Cleaner Production*, 317, 128403. 10.1016/j.jclepro.2021.128403

Oller Alonso, M. (2021). *La Responsabilidad Social Corporativa de las empresas del mármol en la comarca del Almanzora, Almería (2019-2021): análisis de sus estrategias de comunicación integral.* [Doctorado en Gestión de la Información y de la Comunicación en las Organizaciones Universidad de Murcia Escuela Internacional de Doctorado].

Ostrom, E. (2005). Understanding Institutional Diversity. *Princeton University Press*. Princeton New Jersey, USA.

Pentland, A. (2004, October). *Social Dynamics: Signals and Behavior. International Conference on Developmental Learning*, Salk Institute, San Diego, CA

Pentland, B. T., Hærem, T., & Hillison, D. (2011). The (N)Ever-Changing World: Stability and Change in Organizational Routines. *Organization Science*, 22(6), 1369–1383. 10.1287/orsc.1110.0624

Pereira, V., Munjal, S., & Ishizaka, A. (2019, October). Outsourcing and offshoring decision making and its implications for businesses- A synthesis of research pursuing five pertinent questions. *Journal of Business Research*, 103, 348–355. 10.1016/j.jbusres.2019.07.009

Pfeffer, J., & Salancik, G. (1978). *The External Control of Organizations: A Resource Dependence Perspective*. Harper & Row.

Quiroz Carvajal, J. (2023). *Análisis de la relación de la ética ambiental corporativa y la innovación verde sobre el desempeño organizacional y ambiental*. Universidad Nacional de Colombia.

Rahim, A., Eladwiah, R., & Abdul Rahman, A. (2013). Resource-based framework of green IT capability toward firms 'competitive advantage. *Resource (Saint Joseph, Mich.)*, 6, 18–2013.

Rogers, E. M. (2003). Elements of diffusion. *Diffusion of Innovations*, 5, 1–38.

Salimath, M., & Jones, R.III. (2011). Population ecology theory: Implications for sustainability. *Management Decision*, 49(6), 874–910. 10.1108/00251741111143595

Sanquist, T. F. (2008). Human factors and energy use. *HFES Bulletin*, 51(11), 1–3.

Santoro, G., Vrontis, D., Thrassou, A., & Dezi, L. (2018). The Internet of Things: Building a knowledge management system for open innovation and knowledge management capacity. *Technological Forecasting and Social Change*, 136, 347–354. 10.1016/j.techfore.2017.02.034

Saud, S., Chen, S., Haseeb, A., Khan, K., & Imran, M. (2019). The Nexus between Financial Development, Income Level, and Environment in Central and Eastern European Countries: A Perspective on Belt and Road Initiative. *Environmental Science and Pollution Research International*, 26(16), 16053–16075. 10.1007/s11356-019-05004-530968296

Schmidt, C., Schneider, Y., Steffen, S., & Streitz, D. (2020). Capital misal-location and innovation. *Available atSSRN* 3489801. 10.2139/ssrn.3489801

Sele, K., & Grand, S. (2016). Unpacking the dynamics of ecologies of routines: Mediators and their generative effects in routine interactions. *Organization Science*, 27(3), 722–738. 10.1287/orsc.2015.1031

Shahrul, N. S., & Normah, M. (2015). Digital version newspaper: Implication towards printed newspaper circulation in Malaysia. *Malaysian Journal of Communication*, 31(2), 687–701.

Shahzad, F., Lu, J., & Fareed, Z. (2019). Does firm life cycle impact corporate risk taking and performance? *Journal of Multinational Financial Management*, 51, 23–44. 10.1016/j.mulfin.2019.05.001

Sneideriene, A., & Rugine, H. (2019). Theoretical approach on the green technologies development. *Regional Formation and Development Studies*, 2(28), 124–134.

Sole, R. V., & Bascompte, J. (1995). *Spatial Self Organization Self-Organization incomplex Ecosystems* Princeton University Press.

Spee, P., Jarzabkowski, P., & Smets, M. (2016). The influence of routine interdependence and skillful accomplishment on the coordination of standardizing and customizing. *Organization Science*, 27(3), 759–781. 10.1287/orsc.2016.1050

Steinzor, R. (2012). The case for abolishing centralized white house regulatory review. *Michigan Journal of Environmental & Administrative Law*, 1(1.1), 209. 10.36640/mjeal.1.1.case

Sueyoshi, T., & Goto, M. (2012). Efficiency-based rank assessment for electric power industry: A combined use of data envelopment analysis (DEA) and DEA-discriminant analysis (DA). *Energy Economics*, 34(3), 634–644. 10.1016/j.eneco.2011.04.001

Sun, X., Zhou, X., Chen, Z., & Yang, Y. (2020b). Environmental efficiency of electric power industry, market segmentation and technologi-cal innovation: Empirical evidence from China. *The Science of the Total Environment*, 706, 135749. 10.1016/j.scitotenv.2019.13574931940733

Tan, K. S., & Eze, U. C. (2008). An empirical study of internet-based ICT adoption among Malaysian SMEs. *Communications of the IBIMA*, 1, 1–12.

Teece, D. J. (2016). Dynamic capabilities and entrepreneurial management in large organizations: Toward a theory of the (entrepreneurial) firm. *European Economic Review*, 86, 202–216. 10.1016/j.euroecorev.2015.11.006

Thatte, A. A. (2007). *Competitive advantage of a firm through supply chain responsiveness and SCM practices* [Doctoral dissertation, The University of Toledo].

Toffler, A. (1970). *Future shock*. Random House.

Tolliver, C., Fujii, H., Keeley, A. R., & Managi, S. (2021). Green innovation and finance in Asia. *Asian Economic Policy Review*, 16(1), 67–87. 10.1111/aepr.12320

Tornatzky, L. G., & Klein, K. J. (1982). Innovation characteristics and innovation adoption-implementation: A meta-analysis of findings. *IEEE Transactions on Engineering Management*, 29(1), 28–45. 10.1109/TEM.1982.6447463

Truong, Y., Mazloomi, H., & Berrone, P. (2021). Understanding the impact of symbolic and substantive environmental actions on organizational reputation. *Industrial Marketing Management*, 92, 307–320. 10.1016/j.indmarman.2020.05.006

VELÁZQUEZ CASTRO. (2023). *JUDITH ALEJANDRA; CRUZ CORIA, ERIKA; BRIONES JUÁREZ, ABRAHAM INNOVACIÓN Y CRECIMIENTO VERDE, UNA REVISIÓN DESDE LA PERSPECTIVA TURÍSTICA Turismo y Sociedad* (Vol. 33). Universidad Externado de Colombia., 10.18601/01207555.n33.09

Visser, M., & Togt, K. (2016). Learning in Public Sector Organizations: A Theory of Action, Approach. *Public Organization Review*, 16(2), 235–249. 10.1007/s11115-015-0303-5

Wang, F. Z., Jiang, T., & Guo, X. C. (2018). Government Quality, Environmental Regulation and Corporate Green Technology Innovation. *Sci. Res. Manage.39*(1), 26–33. CNKI:SUN:KYGL.0.2018-01-004.

Wang, K., & Jiang, W. (2021). State ownership and green innovation in China: The con-tingent roles of environmental and organizational factors. *Journal of Cleaner Production*, 314, 128029. 10.1016/j.jclepro.2021.128029

Wang, Y., Sun, X., & Guo, X. (2019). Environmental regulation and green productivity growth: Empirical evidence on the Porter Hypothesis from OECD industrial sectors. *Energy Policy*, 132, 611–619. 10.1016/j.enpol.2019.06.016

Weng, M. H., & Lin, C. Y. (2011). Determinants of green innovation adoption for small and medium-size enterprises (SMES). *African Journal of Business Management*, 5(22), 9154–9163.

Westwood, R., & Low, D. R. (2003). The multicultural muse: Culture, creativity, and innovation. *International Journal of Cross Cultural Management*, 3(2), 235–259. 10.1177/14705958030032006

Wu, H. Y., Tsai, A., & Wu, H. S. (2019). A HYBRID MULTI-CRITERIA DECISION ANALYSIS APPROACH FOR ENVIRONMENTAL PERFORMANCE EVALUATION: AN EXAMPLE OF THE TFT-LCD MANUFACTURERS IN TAIWAN. [EEMJ]. *Environmental Engineering and Management Journal*, 18(3), 597–616. 10.30638/eemj.2019.056

Wurlod, J. D., & Noailly, J. (2018). The impact of green innovation on energy intensity: An empirical analysis for 14 industrial sectors in OECD countries. *Energy Economics*, 71, 47–61. 10.1016/j.eneco.2017.12.012

Xu, Z., Frankwick, G. L., & Ramirez, E. (2016). Effects of big data analytics and traditional marketing analytics on new product success: A knowledge fusion perspective. *Journal of Business Research*, 69(5), 1562–1566. 10.1016/j.jbusres.2015.10.017

Yu, Z., Khan, S. A. R., Ponce, P., & Jabbour, A. B. L. (2022). Factors affecting carbon emissions in emerging economies in the context of a green recovery: Implications for sustainable development goals. *Technological Forecasting and Social Change*, 176, 121417. 10.1016/j.techfore.2021.121417

Zailani, S., Iranmanesh, M., Nikbin, D., & Jumadi, H. B. (2014). Determinants and environmental outcome of green technology innovation adoption in the transportation industry in Malaysia. *Asian Journal of Technology Innovation*, 22(2), 286–301. 10.1080/19761597.2014.973167

Zhang, D. G., & Lu, Y. Q. (2017). Impact of market segmentation on energy efficiency. *China Popul Resour Environ*, 27(1), 65–72.

Zhang, W., He, L., & Yuan, H. (2021). Enterprises' decisions on adopting low-carbon technology by considering consumer perception disparity. *Technovation*, 102238. Advance online publication. 10.1016/j.technovation.2021.102238

Zhao, X., Shang, Y., & Song, M. (2020). Industrial structure distortion and urban ecological efficiency from the perspective of green entre-preneurial ecosystems. *Socio-Economic Planning Sciences*, 72, 100757. 10.1016/j.seps.2019.100757

Zheng, X., & Cai, Y. (2022). Transforming Innovation Systems into Innovation Ecosystems: The Role of Public Policy. *Sustainability (Basel)*, 14(12), 7520. 10.3390/su14127520

Zhou, K. Z., Gao, G. Y., & Zhao, H. (2017). State Ownership and firm innovation in China: An integrated view of institutional and efficiency logics. *Administrative Science Quarterly*, 62(2), 375–404. 10.1177/0001839216674457

Zhou, P., Ang, B. W., & Poh, K. L. (2008). Measuring environmental performance under different environmental DEA technologies. *Energy Economics*, 30(1), 1–14. 10.1016/j.eneco.2006.05.001

Chapter 5
Dynamics of Sustainable and Ethically Responsible Business Practices in Corporate Social Responsibility

Harshi Garg
https://orcid.org/0009-0005-2790-5111
IIMT University, India

George Nwokike Ike
Girne American University, Cyprus

Mohammad Kashif
https://orcid.org/0000-0002-4940-8264
Graphic Era University (Deemed), Dehradun, India

Md Sikandar Azam
https://orcid.org/0000-0001-8630-8425
ICFAI Business School (IBS), Hyderabad, India

ABSTRACT

This book chapter constitutes a securing examination of the subject of corporate social responsibility (CSR), getting into the complicated circumstances surrounding company conduct. It carefully evaluates CSR's converting route, establishing its historical foundations and establishing available changes. All living things on the earth are directly or indirectly bound to the community, and the single most essential

DOI: 10.4018/979-8-3693-3238-2.ch005

thing is the human being, who bears the greatest duty to the community to which the individual is a citizen. The objective of the study is to explain in thoroughly the growth of CSR in India, and to evaluate the changing shift of CSR, which will offer information into how businesses have evolved their tactics and targets. The chapter offers to serve as an informative manual, creating an extremely prepared road for users who seek to recognize and effectively operate in the rapidly evolving field of sustainability.

INTRODUCTION

Corporate social obligation (CSR) or social business engagement remains an example regarding self- regulations for international companies that seeks to add to communal causes of a philanthropic, or charitable nature through involvement with, or advancing expert service helping others within free of charge applications, developing communities, conducting economic funding to charities groups during the societal advantage, or carrying out responsibly focused investment and business. Although it was originally once probable to define CSR as a policy within an organization or a business morals tactics equivalent to what is currently referred to as a social and governance responsibility, ESG, that era has arrived because different enterprises have made commitments to do beyond what is required and beyond what is expected or have been imposed or motivated by authorities to make a beneficial effect on the communities they serve (Brammer et al., 2012; Wang et al., 2016). Likewise, National and international guidelines, laws, and financial structures have been developed to encourage and foster this event. Multiple groups have taken advantage of their power to broaden it transcend particular or nationwide (Elkington, 1997). Conversely, it was initially viewed simply an instance of business autonomy; nevertheless, in the past few years, or so, it has changed drastically from independent choices at the scale of individual corporations to requisite applications at the national and globally sectors. Further, educators and businessmen are using the phrase "developing common value" a variant of social responsibility, to refer to approaches for running commerce in an ethical way whilst continuing a profit (Kashif, et al., 2017).

At the level of the company, CSR is often seen as an important initiative which enhances the image of a company. To be successful, initiatives related to social responsibility have to be rationally linked and seamlessly and integrated with a company's approach. In accordance to specific theories, an organization's execution of CSR extends beyond complying with regulations and participates on " deeds that seem to promote to a social cause, despite the aims of the company as well as that is imposed under law. Additionally, companies could participate in CSR for economic or moral reasons. According to a business viewpoint, CSR may increase company earnings, particularly when firms proactively report data both the beneficial and adverse effect of their actions (Fu & Deshpande, 2014; Grindrod, 2016). Those advantages are originated in predominantly from establishing suitable public image and maintaining high standards of ethics with the goal to minimize corporate and legal hazards by embracing the liability of company behaviors (Asante Antwi, 2020; Sagar, 2023).

CSR campaigns encourage businesses to make a positive effect on the natural world and the people they serve, such as staff, investors, neighbourhoods, and more. Certain companies will develop CSR procedures and standards according to their upper management 's moral principles; for instances, the top executive is a violation of ethics (Martha, et al., 2024). analysts state that embracing a CSR perspective improves future- earnings, while opponents believe that it redirects concentration toward a business financial accountability (De Olde & Valentinov, 2019). A study conducted in 2000 equated present economic research on the connection among the social and financial success, completing that the divergent findings of prior research expressing benefits, disadvantages, and favorable monetary consequences were caused by incomplete empirical evaluations & maintained when the study is effectively specified, CSR provides an insignificant impact upon economic results. Analysts have pointed out such lofty and at times unreal goals of CSR, arguing that it is a combination of facade- building or a scheme to foresee politicians' duty as monitors over global companies (Banerjee and Dean, 2008; Brejnholt, 2022). In agreement with this essential viewpoint, economic and social institutions have an interest in CSR in the backdrop of internationalization, and the final stage of capitalism.

Background of the Study

Sustainability has increased its relevance in the modern corporate environment as society grows increasingly worried concerning issues like global warming, disparities in society, and responsible business procedures. The beginnings of CSR may be linked towards the bringing of the 20th century, when companies started participating in philanthropy and fundraising. Nevertheless, it was not till the 1950s and 1960s that the idea of social obligation started to take shape, alongside environmental and social initiatives (Loorbach and Wijsman, 2013; Nidumolu et al., 2009). Throughout the year 1970 to 1980s, the concept of corporate citizenship started to acquire significance, stressing the civic and moral responsibilities of companies. Through the 1990s and 2000s, there has been an upward movement regarding an increased focus on durability and offering common advantage for every stakeholder.

Presently, CSR is an essential component for businesses of every kind, with businesses seeking for better connections with staff, workers, and other stakeholders by resolving their issues while simultaneously assisting both community as well as natural world (Metcalf & Benn, 2013). Early variations of CSR focused primarily with philanthropy and charities. In the starting of 20th century, prosperous executives employed their wealth to contribute a range of non-profit organizations, particularly medical care, and health (Baker-Shelley et al., 2017). One of the greatest cases of beginning philanthropy was the establishment of libraries, which were funded by Andrew Carnegie and enabled the everyone with unlimited availability of books and other source for learning (Iatridis et al., 2022).

Corporate Social Responsibility in Indian Context

Upon their founding, business enterprises have begun assisting the others via philanthropy and charity activities through their organizations. The provision of section 135 of CSR rules indicates that all business in the country with a total asset of 500 crore, or a company with a turnover 1k crore, followed by net profit 5 crore, must commit at least a maximum of 2% of its average net revenue over the previous 3 serving years to charitable giving. Indian overall sustainability reporting reached by 27% in 2015, providing it the highest growth among 44 nations related to the act. Many Indians firms have begun to realize the importance of executing CSR initiatives.

Figure 1. Estimated CSR by Indian companies in the year 2021-22

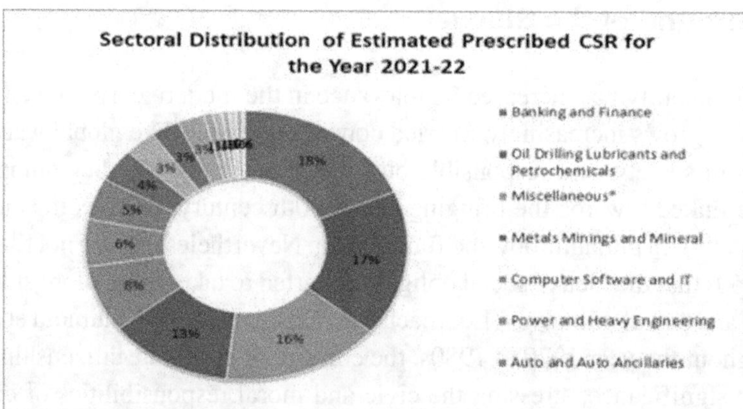

(Atchuta Sai Gowtham, 2023)

The main purpose of CSR is to maximize the businesses entirely effect on consumers. Business is growing increasingly aware about their ethical responsibilities. This is due to a rising realization these individuals, as an essential part of the community may assist to its improvement and development. As a consequence, companies have established separate groups that create tactics, norms, and goals for their CSR tasks.

Figure 2. Component of CSR

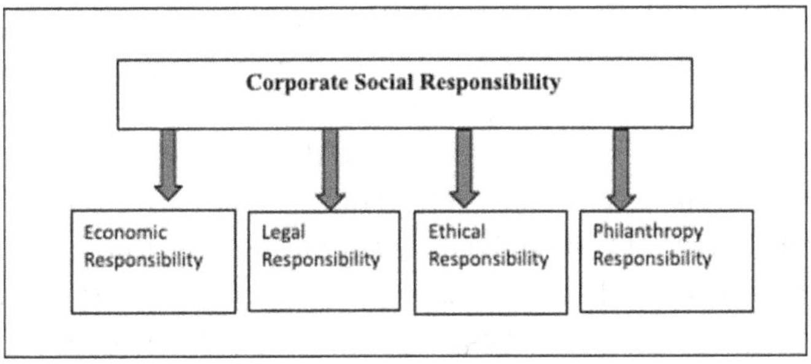

(Authors)

LITERATURE REVIEW

This section has been divided into following two sections:

Theoretical Concepts

The basic concepts that motivate the integration of creativity and environmental practices in the commercial sphere indicate an ongoing relationship that extends over typical profit- driven systems. The theoretical roots of ethical innovation illustrate the numerous relationships between business in an expanded biosphere.

Triple Bottom Line (TBL) framework, introduced by Elkington in 1997 (Elkington, 1997). In the earlier times, organizations just concerned about their economic financial bottom line. TBL was initially suggested in 1994 by novelist and entrepreneur John Elkington in a move to transform a monetary based company structure toward an integrated one that evaluates performance and consequences. TBL or its execution contributed to an awareness within specific csompanies of the link between a company's profitability, adaptability, and overall social or the condition of the environment. Corporations are required to altogether reconcile for every expense associated with operating their company so as to acquire an accurate assessment of their operations, above whatever is shown in their financial and accounts figures. TBL expands the application of standard business- related metrics by including the company's achievements to global welfare, social wellness, and economy. TBL consists of three distinct domains, but it's important to bear in forefront that they are not separate from each other. Under the point of view of the theory of systems, every single one of the 'p' are linked. Considering the concept of systems is the foundation of long- term viability, any endeavor that relates to humanity, atmosphere or finance will additionally have a footprint on the remaining.

Corporate Social Responsibility (CSR) plays as a significant conventional guide for firms as they negotiate their societal Jobs. The conceptual framework is Carroll's pyramid, (Carroll, 1991). The original publication of the presenting four- part outline of CSR dates back to 1979. Carroll adopted the four- part model and constructed them into a CSR Triangle. The structure of the pyramid was created to emphasize the fundamental element of CSR and to demonstrate how the four foundation elements are depend upon each other. The shape of the pyramid was selected as a form of geometry since it is intuitive to comprehend, excellent, and persistent. As a consequence, because fiscal accountability is an essential requirement in business, it was placed at the bottom of the triangle. Sustaining prosperity is required to satisfy the community's other standards of firms, exactly as a building's foundations must be present to sustain its whole construct. The most significant aspect to keep in mind is the fact that economically solid and resilient business acts as a basis for the CSR network. At the same time, community conveys with companies that it is required to adhere to the rules comply by laws, as these reflect community's establishment of the basic rules that dictate how business is expected to operate in a democracy. Whenever involves CSR in emerging markets, for example, the existence or lack of a regulatory and legal structure has a major effect on whether or not large companies invest there or not.

The Global Reporting Initiative (GRI) it serves around the world, self- sufficient, charitable group that offers a widely recognized system for reporting on sustainability. Its objective is to ethically transform the mankind through enabling companies to comprehend and convey the effects of their operations on individuals and the natural world. The GRI was established in 1997 via an arrangement among the UNEP and the alliance for ecologically sustainable business (Halkos and Nomikos, 2021). The GRI contains numerous significant parts. Initially, the GRI is carried out via multi stakeholder ownership. The guidelines established by GRI are produced within an approach which includes contribution from an extensive array of entities, notably firms, grassroots organizations, unions, and educational institutions. GRI reporting is particularly deep. The GRI Guidelines, particularly covers an extensive number of ecological, fiscal, and cultural issues, offer a comprehensive basis for reporting on sustainability.

Research data strongly supports underlying theories, highlighting the advantages of linking invention with ecology for business success. (Porter and Linde, 1995) revealed a significant connection among sustainable conscious actions, savings in the economy and boosting edge over rivals. This indicates how sustainability may encourage productivity and creativity without inflicting unfounded financial costs. Besides validating this view, the research examined the link amongst green innovations and business results, indicating that corporations that embrace green procedures not only showcase a stronger reaction to natural issues, but also achieve a higher financial stream (Schaltegger and Wagner, 2006).

CSR acts as a basis for realizing every aspect of ecological innovation. Empirical Study, as evidenced by the publications of (Porter and Linde,1995; Schaltegger and Wagner, 2006; Macarthur and Heading, 2019), and initiatives as GRI, presents compelling proof of the beneficial implications.

Historical Roots of CSR

The involvement of society throughout company conduct can be established through to antique Roman regulations and is prevalent organization that include shelters, residences, for the homeless and elderly people medical facilities, and charities (Jerab & Mabrouk, 2023). Throughout the medieval era, educational, public, and faith- based organization maintained to see firms as charitable organization under the laws of England. Subsequently, it developed in the 16th and 17th centuries through the guidance of the English crown, which considered firms as an instrument for improving society (Lescrauwaet et al., 2022). In the centuries that followed, as the British Empire extended and captured new regions, the king of England established business law to its American subjects, wherein business organizations maintained the community to certain extant. Throughout the 18th and 19th centuries, spirituality theology as well as reactions to the enduring social setting were seen as an answer to humanity's ethical losing, which was resulted in misery between all people in the realm of England and certain regions of France. This biblical standpoint led the foundation for social changes and Victorian charity, which witnessed a variety of social problems such as revolved around lack of education, ignorance, and child labor (Carroll 2008). The spiritual origins of the Victorian era provided British benefactors an elevated sense of optimism and humanity, as well as the end of the 1800s, the charitable contributions were shifting to the workers and the establishment of welfare programs, with instances observed in action both in Europe and in the USA (Kotler and Lee, 2008; Sagar, 2023).

Method of Research

This research is being conducted exploratory in Nature. This meant acquiring secondary data source from many sources accessible through on the web, mostly Shodhganga, ResearchGate, Academia etc. and many other web pages, in addition to employing content analysis to evaluate the CSR policies.

Emerging Trends in Corporate Social Responsibility

Increasing transparency, expenditure on environmentally friendly innovations, local neighbourhood involvement, and initiatives to promote inclusion and diversity initiatives constitute some of the most significant CSR themes.

Increased transparency has been partly due because of increasing administration leadership, such as GDPR. It additionally occurs because of the ever- increasing, almost immediate access to earlier unobtainable knowledge. Corporations are offering additional details regarding their social, governance, activities as a component of an economic method that promotes ethical behavior. Buyers are becoming less delighted with fraudulent company procedure and secret motives, and they are asking for more detail concerning formerly confidential subjects.

The environment remains to be an explosive subject in the world of business, and numerous sustainability trends communicate within it. The available resources become increasingly scarce and the world addresses the threshold of a 2- level increase in the mean temperature, ethical companies, are making investment in environmentally friendly innovations, decreasing their dependence on resources that are not renewable, and looking for more alternatives the components to do companies (Kashif et al., 2023a). Regardless of whether the rule is clothing manufacturing investigating different materials such as the species or reused water glasses, creating neat gases via stricter equipment testing for emissions, or just getting licensing like LEED for their structures, environmentally friendly is certain to become an increasing concern trend for companies seeming to boost their responsibility to the community.

Manufacturers working on an international level recognize the worth of regional markets and supply networks. This goal is not merely to reduce emission of carbon related to shipping or procurement costs but also to gain insight into regional expertise & alternatives. Many businesses with kindness select associations who work alongside with local politicians and experience versus shipment in cookie- cutter solution. Moreover, CSR initiatives are constantly looking to take part in endeavors that both assist the communities they serve and produce money for the company. Contributing in neighbourhood groups can boost worker satisfaction whereas simultaneously offering advertising gains. CSR initiatives, including specifically employing individuals with from challenging financial or academic backgrounds, eventually empower the local workforce, provide various viewpoint, surface constitute a movement that will persist. Consideration of disparities in wages and the financial restrictions that workers face a rising CSR trend. Compensation equality for female and male, assessment the earning gap among the highest- paid and lowest- paid personal at an organization.

Identifying Obstacles and Opportunities in CSR Implementation

The integration of creativity and environmental responsibility within companies provides an environment full of both challenges & opportunities.

Opportunities

i. **Employee Engagement:** Studies indicates that CSR and an overwhelming feeling of workplace mission contribute to boost worker engagement (Chandani, et al., 2016; Saks and Gruman, 2014; Kular, et al., 2008). This can be essential since when workers get involved, an organization's output increase by 17%, revenues improve by 21%, and truancy decreases by 41%. An interested environment promotes creativity. In economic phase, disinterested staff members lose companies around $450 billion per year.

ii. **Increased Revenue:** Whenever it involves obtaining approval from management for a CSR scheme, accounting records are tended to be the deciding elements. Investors need to understand if this endeavor will bring about an advantageous return on investment (ROI)

iii. **CSR supports global communities:** Notwithstanding the wonderful advantages that your business gets through advertising its CSR efforts, it is difficult to give up focus on reasons why it was established in the primary place. CSR equips people with the required power and opportunity for making an impact in the communities they live and work in. Firms tend to be made from compatible, skilled people, who collaborate to accomplish a bigger objective. If you may create an environmental sustainability initiative that matches with your business's opinions, you will be given the chance to exercise an enormously advantageous impact.

iv. **Increased Investment Opportunities:** Presently, worldwide environmentally friendly investment surpasses $30 trillion, boosting 68% from 2014. Chairman of Blackrock, recited this in an email addressing to CEO, asserting that global warming has grown into an essential component in companies long future prospects.

v. **CSR present press opportunity:** Successful CSR may garner your excellent press focus. Having an environment that earns you recognized could boost your brand recognition overall online customer loyalty. CSR doesn't seem is regarded as environmental marketing if your project seems to far removed from your goals and principles, consumers might wonder about the reason, regardless of whether it's thoughtful.

Obstacles

i. **Defining the scope of CSR:** The majority of the initial obstacles when developing an approach to CSR is figuring out what it includes for the persons company or sector. CSR may include an extensive variety of issues, encompassing rights for human, labor laws, protection of the environment, inclusive and diverse, charity work, and ethical purchasing. Nevertheless, not certain challenges are equally important or crucial to each company. As a consequence, companies have to determine their primary participants, analyze the real impacts, and establish their CSR targets in relation to their goal.
ii. **Measuring CSR Performance:** A further Obstacle when developing a CSR strategy is the reporting and measurement and tracking and providing the information on the outcomes and effects of CSR efforts. Organizations have to establish precise and pertinent metrics, gather accurate and uniform data, and convey their growth and accomplishments to consumers. Nevertheless, assessing and giving feedback on the achievements of CSR can prove challenging and costly, especially for medium sized enterprise. Who lack the required funds and understanding. Additionally, there is no worldwide or controlled organization for reports on CSR, leaving it harder to measure and assess performance in CSR.
iii. **Engaging with Stakeholders:** Another difficulty in implementing a CSR approach is interacting and connecting amongst the all of the parties that are affected by concerned with the firm's performance in CSR. visitors, vendors, staff, charities, media outlets, and neighbourhoods were a variety of users. Firms have to comprehend customer needs and requirements involve stakeholders in the CSR selection and execution procedure, and address any possible disputes or compromises. Yet, integrating and harmonizing with various groups can prove laborious and challenging.
iv. **Integrating CSR into the business approaches:** The fourth Obstacle when creating a CSR plan is how to integrate it into the company's overall approach and activities. CSR shouldn't be considered as a separate or different operation, but rather as a deliberate & integrated part of the organisation's propositions, lifestyle, and edge over competitors. Companies have to align their CSR goals with their company's general targets, consist of CSR values and approaches into

their procedures and guidelines, and foster an environment friendly amongst their top managers. Yet, implementing CSR into basic company goals can be difficult and annoying, particularly if it requires substantial modifications to the company's operating management or corporate architecture.

v. **Adapting to CSR Landscape:** The problem with developing an approach to CSR plan involves adapting to the changing CSR environment. CSR definitely not a stable or established notion, rather a concept that develops accordance with shifting community & market demands and desires. Companies have to track and anticipate future developments and issues that will affect their CSR effectiveness, as global warming, digitization, equality for all, and consumer action. In addition, companies have to be flexible and creative in the CSR procedure, and have the ability to modify and enhance their CSR approach and procedures as required.

vi. **Balancing the Cost and Benefit of CSR:** A sixth Obstacle in implementing a CSR plan involves reconciling the costs with the benefits of CSR. It may bring many advantages to a company, like enhanced image, client devotion, staff participation, mitigation of risk, creativity, and prosperity. Yet, CSR may come at an expensive price, involving higher expenditures, cost of operation, legal requirements, so firms must check and analyze the monetary return of CSR activities.

Real World Case Studies

The case studies that follow a number of sectors and methods, giving an in depth understanding of the wide variety of possibilities available in the area of imaginative preservation.

PwC: PricewaterhouseCoopers International Limited

A leading company worldwide through advisory services that include the auditing process, assessments, and guidance, has frequently shown adaptability in its social responsibility tasks. By changing applications, PwC emphasized gadgets participation, centered upon promoting digital competence for communities that are underrepresented via connections to institutions. Following the covid- 19 pandemic, the business instantly modified its CSR commitment to emphasize worker happiness, creating work schedules wellness, and funding regional medical programs. Pwc has additionally incorporates sustainable development within its CSR efforts, increasing energy utilization and reducing its environmental impact. This adaptability places Pwc as an innovator in ethical company behavior. Furthermore, acknowledging the importance of learning, Pwc proposed the learning development risk, offering aid, facilities, and grants for low- income kids in collaboration that concerning Schools, showing its devotion to modifying learning and community. (Carlsson and Åkerstöm, 2008).

Tesla: Revolutionizing Mobility Through Sustainable Transportation

Driven by entrepreneur Elon Musk, Tesla is changing the automobile industry through its dedication to environmentally development. Developing electric automobiles, Tesla confronts the ecological issues associated with conventional engineered combustion. Tesla dedication to environment goes outside the Evs itself; its gigantic facilities employ clean energy resources, and the network of supercharger network provides distant EV mobility (Maraveas, et al., 2022). The company's results prove that sustainable development not solely fixes ecological problems yet additionally presents its business as a leader in the established business sector. (Sperling, 2018).

Walmart: Cooperative Sustainability Programs Within the Supply Chain

Walmart, an acknowledged worldwide retailing powerhouse, recently begun initiatives to promote sustainability that stretch beyond its own walls, engaging vendors through its complicated chain of custody. Walmart has established ambitious targets for its vendor partners to enhance energy consumption, minimize waste, and encourage environmentally friendly operations via joint efforts. Walmart showcases how beneficial unions could lead to major modifications during a single sector by combining its substantial power and vast volume. The firm's dedication towards ecology not simply matches the demands of consumer, but it additionally contributes in reduced expenses and permanent commerce stability. (Jacob, 2024).

These real- life instances demonstrate that innovative sustainability along with CSR is not restricted to a particular area or business style.

Socially Responsible Business Strategies

Efficient models for CSR consist of socioeconomic and ecological variables within a ln organization's opinion and activities, that relate to its purpose. These examples may function as guidance for businesses wanting to carry out environmentally friendly efforts.

i. **Global Reporting Initiative:** This is a worldwide, autonomous guidelines initiative that promotes enterprises, authorities, and other groups in grasping and conveying the effects they have on matters such as mankind, environmental issues. GRI is a national charitable group with an interconnected organization.

GRI develops permitted reporting specifications in order to assist all companies and agencies reports on their commercial, social.

ii. **AA1000:** It is the governor approach employed by professionals in sustainability for environmentally related certification assignments, evaluating a company's compliance to the responsibility standards. This is a globally developed, principles - based paradigm that assists firms identify, rank highest and reply to issues concern with a goal to boost their long- term viability. Accountability is dedicated to improving worldwide availability and the application of the responsibility rules, and a result has worked together with corresponded groups in the ESG ecosystems, such as earth academy.

iii. **Social Accountability 8000 (SA8000):** It is a transparent accreditation criterion which motivates companies to develop, repair, and carry out environmentally Friendly methods of operation. It was originated in 1997 by social responsibility initiative, members of labor, nonprofit organizations, groups representing civil society and corporations. It evaluates companies' achievements in 8 primary areas of professional moral responsibilities: kid labor, exploitation of labor, security and health, liberty, and labor negotiation, prejudice, regulatory, hours of operations, and compensation. Sustainable corporate in America involves with an enterprise's foundation of values and an ethical approach to managing enterprise. This requires operating with methods this, at the least, satisfy primary duties in the subjects of equality in workforce, atmosphere.

iv. **United Nations Global Compact:** This is the globe's biggest company sustainability and accountability scheme, with more than twenty thousand operations stakeholders and participants from 167 different nations. The group is composed of a globally organizations and regional networks or entities in every nation that participates.

v. **Caux Round Table (CRT):** The rules are founded upon three ethical pillars for accountable company behavior and an equitable and efficient culture as a whole: ethical leadership, working and living for the common good, and valuing and safeguarding and upholding and preserving. (Bardas, et al., 2013).

RECOMMENDATIONS/ SUGGESTIONS AND CONCLUSION

Increasing the general understanding of social responsibility initiatives is essential to boosting their success. Other stakeholders, including the press, could employ this technique to bring attention to the beneficial task that businesses carry out. This endeavor, via novel approaches, could motivate other companies to get into the organizations and perform crucial parts in addressing difficulties like medical care, schooling, Job, among an enormous percentage of Indians. Only major and small businesses engage in social responsibility initiatives in some areas. This matter requires the commitment of larger corporations in initiatives related to CSR. In order to tackle the problem of accessing a border demographic, the contribution of small and medium sized companies in the CSR industry is vital. It is suggested that a marketing initiative be started to increase expansive understanding of CSR as well as to urge SMEs to take part more involved in CSR efforts.

Organizations are employing different strategies to fight the difficulties arise. Employers and non- profit- organizations, on the opposite hand, ought to strive more to combine their assets and establish alliances so as to implement CSR standards while creating novel approaches which assist a bigger number of individuals, this will improve the detrimental effect of their actions on the lives of ordinary humans. Numerous CSR programs and initiatives are carried out primarily in cities. Precisely, these schemes have little effect on those who are impoverished or excluded in the countryside. Despite emphasizing on cities, business must take into account agricultural health, and labor- intensive, which directly benefit humanity's poorest residents. It is recommended that CSR be established as an integral order or subject in company universities and schools so as to educate pupils regarding both social and development difficulties, alongside how to utilize of CSR in helping businesses in affecting a suitable equilibrium within their respective positions & societal duties. Having an agenda should encourage young individuals to become ready for future growth shortcomings and in search for innovative responses to the problems of poor. The premise of CSR is currently deeply rooted in the worldwide business discourse. Getting from concept to simulate necessitates tackling several challenges. Among the greatest worries affecting organizations includes the demand for president measurement of CSR execution, along with the growth of CSR tactics. Openness, discussions, and sincerity will render an organization seem more reliable whilst growing as well the standard for rival businesses.

The CSR accountability represents definitely an important development when it comes to making sure that the advantages obtained by firms in the nation at large are properly passed into to humanity. The attempt by the government to maintain the sorts of conduct allowed within these conditions as wide as possible are noteworthy. In addition, clearly and informally connecting CSR efforts to the SDG goals guarantees that CSR investment coincides with, and enhances federal goals. But, notable shortcomings in the CSR enforcement have been detected, which must be promptly solved soon in order to have most beneficial effect on communities near you. First, business organization ought to change the emphasis from satisfying their statutory duty to proactively identifying and creating sustainable consequences endeavors that represent their beliefs.

Furthermore, there needs to be swift explanations and simpler details regarding the conduct allowed by the regulations. Across the globe, project recognition methods have to be established. It will help the allocation of CSR funds to regions getting the greatest benefit. The exchange board of India's request for creating a sustainable exchange represents an excellent move. this system will make it possible for more improved CSR finance installation, program effect confirmation, and a transfer of excess, contributions to CSR through firms. In the end, there is a critical requirement to make certain that CSR donations achieve an indirect impact on neighbourhoods in relation to financial, economic, and benefits for the environment. This will implies simultaneously evaluating the long- lasting impacts of CSR spendings and actually engaged. Supporting research and technological development centers offers an extensive list of possible implications. Firms, both big and small, based in India or exterior, are starting to add to the efforts of the government by copying their CSR efforts. It is anticipated that the identical passion and operational tactical emphasize will continue following the epidemic has passed. Eligible categories and the authorities ought to collaborate jointly to encourage companies pursuing significant CSR Possibilities as a component strategy.

REFERENCES

Asante Antwi, H. (2020). Beyond COVID-19 Pandemic: A Systematic Review of the Role of Global Health *in the Evolution and Practice of Corporate Social Responsibility*. 10.21203/rs.3.rs-40212/v1

Baker-Shelley, A., van Zeijl-Rozema, A., & Martens, P. (2017). A conceptual synthesis of organisational transformation: How to diagnose, and navigate, pathways for sustainability at universities? In *Journal of Cleaner Production* (Vol. 145, pp. 262–276). Elsevier Ltd., 10.1016/j.jclepro.2017.01.026

Banerjee, S. B., & Dean, A. (2008). Corporate Social Responsibility: The Good, The Bad and The Ugly. *Critical Sociology*, 34(1), 51–79. 10.1177/0896920507084623

Bardas, P., & Rotaru, S., Ghiţă, M., & Cocosila, M. (2013). The Caux Round Table Principles: A Solution For The International Economic And Social Crisis? *Review of General Management*, 17(1).

Brammer, S., Jackson, G., & Matten, D. (2012). Corporate social responsibility and institutional theory: New perspectives on private governance. *Socio-economic Review*, 10(1), 3–28. 10.1093/ser/mwr030

Brejnholt, A. (2022). Institute for International Management Navigating Plurality, *in The State and Corporate Social Responsibilities: A collection of research papers.*

Carlsson, J., & Åkerstöm, R. (2008). Corporate Social Responsibility: a case study of Öhrlings PricewaterhouseCoopers.

Carroll, A. B. (1991). The pyramid of corporate social responsibility: Toward the moral management of organizational stakeholders. *Business Horizons*, 34(4), 39–48. 10.1016/0007-6813(91)90005-G

Chandani, A., Mehta, M., Mall, A., & Khokhar, V. (2016). Employee engagement: A review paper on factors affecting employee engagement. *Indian Journal of Science and Technology*, 21(4), 256–272. 10.17485/ijst/2016/v9i15/92145

De Olde, E. M., & Valentinov, V. (2019). The Moral Complexity of Agriculture: A Challenge for Corporate Social Responsibility. *Journal of Agricultural & Environmental Ethics*, 32(3), 413–430. 10.1007/s10806-019-09782-3

Elkington, J. (1997). The triple bottom line. *Environmental management: Readings and cases, 2*, 49-66.

Fu, W., & Deshpande, S. P. (2014). The Impact of Caring Climate, Job Satisfaction, and Organizational Commitment on Job Performance of Employees in a China's Insurance Company. *Journal of Business Ethics*, 124(2), 339–349. 10.1007/s10551-013-1876-y

Gowtham, A. S. (2023). The changing landscape of Corporate Social Responsibility in India Pre & Post Covid-19. *International Journal for Multidisciplinary Research*, 5(6), 113–127.

Grindrod, P. (2016). Beyond privacy and exposure: Ethical issues within citizen-facing analytics. *Philosophical Transactions. Series A, Mathematical, Physical, and Engineering Sciences*, 374(2083), 20160132. Advance online publication. 10.1098/rsta.2016.013228336804

Hair Jr, J. F., Wolfinbarger Celsi Arthu, M., & Page, M. J. (n.d.). *ESSENTIALS OF Business Research Methods SECOND EDITION*.

Halkos, G., & Nomikos, S. (2021). Corporate social responsibility: Trends in global reporting initiative standards. *Economic Analysis and Policy*, 69, 106–117. 10.1016/j.eap.2020.11.008

Iatridis, K., Gond, J. P., & Kesidou, E. (2022). How Meaningfulness and Professional Identity Interact in Emerging Professions: The Case of Corporate Social Responsibility Consultants. *Organization Studies*, 43(9), 1401–1423. 10.1177/01708406211035506

Jacob, A. T. (2024). *Assessing the effectiveness of Green Supply Chain Management in Enhancing Sustainability in the UK retail industry: A focused study on Walmart Inc* (Doctoral dissertation, Dublin Business School).

Jerab, D. A., & Mabrouk, T. (2023). The Role of Leadership in Changing Organizational Culture. SSRN *Electronic Journal*. 10.2139/ssrn.4574324

Kashif, M., Kumar, P., Ghai, S., & Kumar, S. (2023b). Disruptive Technologies in Computational Finance. In *Algorithmic Approaches to Financial Technology: Forecasting, Trading, and Optimization* (pp. 46-60). IGI Global.

Kashif, M., Shajar, S. N., Singhal, N., & Kumar, P. (2023a). Achieving sustainable investment practices through green finance: Challenges and opportunities. In *Sustainable Investments in Green Finance*. 10.4018/979-8-3693-1388-6.ch016

Kashif, M., Sridharan, P., & Thiyagarajan, S. (2017). Impact of economic growth on international reserve holdings in Brazil. *Revista de Economia Política*, 37(3), 605–614. 10.1590/0101-31572017v37n03a08

Kotler, P., & Lee, N. (2008). *Corporate social responsibility: Doing the most good for your company and your cause*. John Wiley & Sons.

Kular, S., Gatenby, M., Rees, C., Soane, E., & Truss, K. (2008). *Employee engagement: A literature review*.

Lescrauwaet, L., Wagner, H., Yoon, C., & Shukla, S. (2022). *Adaptive Legal Frameworks and Economic Dynamics in Emerging Technol-ogies: Navigating the Intersection for Responsible Innovation. 16*(3), 202–220. https://journals.ristek.or .id/index.php/LE/index

Loorbach, D., & Wijsman, K. (2013). Business transition management: Exploring a new role for business in sustainability transitions. *Journal of Cleaner Production*, 45, 20–28. 10.1016/j.jclepro.2012.11.002

Macarthur, E., & Heading, H. (2019). How the circular economy tackles climate change. *Ellen MacArthur Found*, 1, 1–71.

Maraveas, C., Piromalis, D., Arvanitis, K. G., Bartzanas, T., & Loukatos, D. (2022). Applications of IoT for optimized greenhouse environment and resources management. *Computers and Electronics in Agriculture*, 198, 106993. 10.1016/j.compag.2022.106993

Martha Adaga, E., Efe Egieya, Z., Kuzankah Ewuga, S., Abiola Abdul, A., Oluwaseun Abrahams, T., & Author, C.Ejuma Martha AdagaZainab Efe EgieyaSarah Kuzankah EwugaAdekunle Abiola AbdulTemitayo Oluwaseun Abrahams. (2024). Philosophy In Business Analytics: A Review Of Sustainable And Ethical Approaches. *International Journal of Management & Entrepreneurship Research*, 6(1), 69–86. 10.51594/ijmer.v6i1.710

Metcalf, L., & Benn, S. (2013). Leadership for Sustainability: An Evolution of Leadership Ability. *Journal of Business Ethics*, 112(3), 369–384. 10.1007/s10551-012-1278-6

Nidumolu, R., Prahalad, C. K., & Rangaswami, M. R. (2009). Why sustainability is now the key driver of innovation. *Harvard Business Review*, 87(9), 56–64.

Porter, M., & Van der Linde, C. (1995). Green and competitive: ending the stalemate. *The Dynamics of the eco-efficient economy: environmental regulation and competitive advantage, 33*, 120-134.

Sagar, S. (2023). Innovation and Sustainability in Business: Navigating the Future Landscape, *12(25)*, 51–60. https://doi.org/10.9790/487X-2512055160

Saks, A. M., & Gruman, J. A. (2014). What do we really know about employee engagement? *Human Resource Development Quarterly*, 25(2), 155–182. 10.1002/hrdq.21187

Schaltegger, S., & Wagner, M. (2006). Integrative management of sustainability performance, measurement and reporting. *International Journal of Accounting. Auditing and Performance Evaluation*, 3(1), 1–19. 10.1504/IJAAPE.2006.010098

Sperling, D. (2018). *Three revolutions: Steering automated, shared, and electric vehicles to a better future*. Island Press. 10.5822/978-1-61091-906-7

Wang, H., Tong, L., Takeuchi, R., & George, G. (2016). Corporate social responsibility: An overview and new research directions. In *Academy of Management Journal, 59*(2). Academy of Management. 10.5465/amj.2016.5001

ADDITIONAL READING

Baxi, C. V., & Prasad, A. (Eds.). (2005). *Corporate social responsibility: Concepts and cases: The Indian experience*. Excel Books India.

Brennan, D. (2011). *Corporate social responsibility: The corporate governance of the 21st century*. Kluwer Law International BV.

Chandler, D. (2020). *Sustainable value creation*. Routledge. 10.4324/9781003016199

Chandler, D. (2022). *Strategic corporate social responsibility: Sustainable value creation*. Sage publications.

Crane, A., Matten, D., Glozer, S., & Spence, L. J. (2019). Business Ethics: Managing Corporate Citizenship and Sustainability in the Age of Globalization. (5th ed.). Oxford University Press. Andriof, J., Waddock, S., Husted, B., & Rahman, S. S. (2017). Unfolding stakeholder thinking: Theory, responsibility, and engagement. Routledge. 10.1093/hebz/9780198810070.001.0001

Crane, A., McWilliams, A., Matten, D., Moon, J., & Siegel, D. S. (Eds.). (2008). *The Oxford handbook of corporate social responsibility*. OUP Oxford. 10.1093/oxfordhb/9780199211593.001.0001

Harrigan, B. (2010). *Corporate social responsibility in the 21st century: Debates, models, and practices across government, law, and business*. Edward Elgar Publishing. 10.4337/9781849805278

Kotler, P., & Lee, N. (2008). *Corporate social responsibility: Doing the best for your company and your cause*. John Wiley & Sons.

Moon, J. (2014). *Corporate social responsibility: A very short introduction* (Vol. 414). Oxford University Press. 10.1093/actrade/9780199671816.001.0001

KEY TERMS AND DEFINITIONS

Sustainability: This deals with the way current activities shape upcoming possibilities. If materials are utilized at the moment, they are no longer obtainable for utilization in the future, and that's particularly relevant while the assets are finite. Hence, extract resources, including steel, and copper, are scarce in quantity and cannot be regenerated. Therefore, options for the contemporary capabilities available through such assets will be needed in the years to come. This could happen in the distant future, but the more significant is the reality that once assets are drained, the expense of securing the ones that remain increases to rise, because of the operational expenses of the firm.

Accountability: This revolves around a group comprehending that its decisions influence the outside world and consequently assuming accountability for the effects of those behaviors. The concept indicates an analysis of the effects of decisions within the organization. Further, the idea demands conveying certain metrics to all entities concerned by the behavior.

Transparency: This indicates that the outside effect of the company's conduct can be ascertained from its disclosure, and the appropriate details are not concealed throughout it. This means that all of the implications of the organization's deed, such as outside effects, must become obvious to every individual by using the data given by the company's monitoring techniques. Visibility is particularly vital for other consumers of this type of substance, who have the contextual information and comprehension that internal consumers have. Accessibility is thus recognizable as proceeding from the other two values and similarly as an element of the method of acknowledging on the part of the company the external effects of its activities.

Distributable sustainability: We deliberately apply the expression accessible sustainability to emphasize a single of the primary points of this case. This implies that authentic environmental sustainability is defined not only through how tasks affect subsequent choices but also through the way the outcomes of those- behaviors - both constructive and negative- are separated among the parties involved. A significant component of our framework is the belief that for business operations to be viable, it needs to not only responsibly funds to help proprietors, but additionally, take into account the effects on every stakeholder and redistribute these in a manner that is agreeable to them, both currently and in the future. This is an innovative transformation of commercial operations.

CSR: This can be referred to as the connection between international companies, and personal citizens. Essentially, the phrase addresses the partnership between a company and the community wherever it belongs or functions.

Ethics: This explains the way an entity ought to run its whole company and tasks. Concerns of passion, remain fundamental to corporate ethics. Organizations seek to achieve maximum earnings while addressing concerns of accountability and human duty. Morality is a set of regulations that decide what is beneficial or detrimental, acceptable or unacceptable for individuals. In simple terms, morality pertains to the rules which act as a basis for interpersonal interactions, in addition to the essence and product of being socially upright or vile, the company Ethics include decency, admiration, reverence, and equal behavior throughout every situation. Nevertheless, principles such as courtesy, regard, and assurance are fairly broad concepts with no obvious limits.

Utilitarianism: This relies on the concept that the consequences are the only thing that exists in expressing the concept of benefit, arguing that a community attains its greatest good by every person following his or her own best interests. According to the theory, the combined effect of each of these motives will ultimately end in the greatest benefit for the community as a whole. Some rationalists have changed the idea to claim that the authorities must have a part in balancing such distinct events in an attempt to be responsible for the reality that certain needs are most effectively met together.

Corporate Behaviour: Corporate behavior is essential for the financial performance of a business along with its connection between corporation and business goals, defining corporate conduct with no roots in ethics and sustainability, governing by regulations, moral codes, and social duty, revolving on all of these elements, which involve regulations, morality.

Corporate Reputation: This represents a novel Obstacle for companies: maximizing the unlimited possibilities of their company. In modern markets, companies depend on intangible characteristics for survival and promote what they offer in a marketplace defined by sudden shifts. The image of a company is often the most critical factor for developing an advantage over competitors along with creating commercial and cultural success.

Market Integration: Foreign standards and rules seek to liberalize all of these marketplaces. The markets demand banking systems that are capable of handling the greater risk that exists. The stock market has to be deep, and fluid, only the nation's economic systems are sufficiently large to provide this structure of finance in the worldwide market, involving both international and financial sector expansions. Several instances of market consolidation are the consequence of growing economic rivalry. The integration events occur frequently in firm combination deals.

Moral Risk: this happens when it is challenging or expansive for owners to observe or estimate the level of energy put ahead by leaders. Directors feel obligated to refrain from working under the confines of the mutually agreed-up labor agreement as individuals have no way to examine the real picture. Executives might also have the motivation and capacity to hide the 'absolute view' by distorting the real outcomes provided to the investors.

Chapter 6
Corporate Environmental Responsibilities of Auto Manufacturers in the Chennai Auto Industry

Arokiaraj David
https://orcid.org/0000-0002-9591-2410
ATMS, Swiss Business School, UAE

Md Sikandar Azam
https://orcid.org/0000-0001-8630-8425
ICFAI Business School (IBS), Hyderabad, India

M. Banumathi
Pondicherry Central University, India

ABSTRACT

This study addresses the escalating global concern regarding environmental deterioration caused by automobile emissions, which requires investigation practice of corporate environmental responsibilities (CER) of auto manufacturers. Chennai auto-industry major contributor to India's auto production, the research comprehensively examines the environmental impact of the entire automobile lifecycle, underscoring emissions like CO, CO2, NOx, SOx, HC, PM, Pb, and VOCs and its effects on human health and environment. Data analysis reveals notable CER practices, emphasizing cost-cutting, waste management, vehicle life extension, and adherence to emission control standards. The study evaluates the implementation of environmental management systems, green procurement, and manufacturing efficiency. The findings indicate a substantial level of CER among surveyed auto

DOI: 10.4018/979-8-3693-3238-2.ch006

assemblers, driven by governmental regulations and market competition. It is concluded that establishing dedicated environmental departments, eco-awareness campaigns, and organized dismantling units.

INTRODUCTION

Unfortunately, recent years have witnessed a rapid surge in worldwide industrialization, accompanied by a consequential deterioration of the environment (Yann Arthus et al., 2009). Industrial effluents have wreaked havoc on our surroundings, leading to severe pollution and ozone depletion, consequently impacting agricultural yields (Nemry et al., 2008). Environmental issues such as greenhouse gas emissions, ozone depletion, and acid rain transcend national boundaries, encompassing air, water, and soil contamination. Contributing factors to this environmental crisis include population explosion, unplanned urbanization, rapid industrialization, scientific and technological advancements, and deforestation (Archana & Neeru, 2006).

The impact of environmental issues is not just limited to the environment but also has a profound human cost. Environmental causes contribute to an estimated 13 million deaths annually, with one-third occurring in developing countries alone (World Health Organization, WHO). The severity of this issue is starkly illustrated by the fact that major Southeast Asian cities are grappling with severe air pollution that claims approximately 7 million lives annually out of a total of 9 million in 2024. The situation is particularly dire in developing countries, where approximately 900 million people will be exposed to unhealthy levels of pollutants due to motor vehicle emissions (Faiz, 1993). A study by the World Resources Institute (WRI) reveals that 12% (Parul & Popli, 2010) of artificial Greenhouse Gas emissions (2.5 million metric tons) stem directly from vehicle usage on roads as per the 2024 record.

While vehicles emit relatively small quantities of Hydrocarbons (HCs) and Volatile Organic Compounds (VOCs) during operation, significant emissions occur during the manufacturing process, particularly during painting (Santos et al., 2010; Alvarez et al., 2008). Groundwater pollution around auto components and assembling units compounds environmental concerns (R.N. Wahal, 2006). The Environmental Outlook Baseline (OECD) projects millions of premature deaths by 2050 due to particulate matter and indoor air pollution, with groundwater pollution posing comparatively lesser risks to human health. Motor vehicles have emerged as key contributors to the world's most pressing environmental issues (Sagar, 1995). Vehicle pollution escalates rapidly due to both the emissions per vehicle and the increasing number of cars per mile.

Auto Industry and Environmental Responsibility

The automotive industry is poised to increase emissions substantially, which are projected to rise by 40% by 2030 (Beltramello, 2012), primarily due to the proliferation of vehicles (Sagar, 1995). Throughout the lifecycle of automobiles, from production to disposal (known as Cradle-to-Grave), various pollutants are emitted, including VOCs, Particulate Matter (PM), Lead (P_b), Carbon Monoxide (CO), HC, Carbon Dioxide (CO_2), Sulphur Oxides (SO_x), Nitrogen Oxides (NO_x), and at varying levels (Banumathi & Arokiaraj, 2011). During the user stage, vehicles significantly impact the environment, contributing to ozone layer depletion, greenhouse gas emissions, climate change, and other atmospheric concerns (Stephan, 2011). The auto industry is considered one of the primary reasons for air pollution, with each liter of petroleum/diesel combusted releasing approximately 2,640 grams (or 2.64 kilograms) of CO_2 into the atmosphere (UNEP, 2011; Popli & Gupta, 2010).

Numerous studies have delved into the social responsibility practices of large corporations, revealing a strong sense of responsibility embedded within their operations and reflected in their strategies, marketing plans, and core values (Kärnä et al., 2003). Corporate Environmental Responsibility (CER) goes beyond mere compliance with legal requirements; it entails voluntary engagement in environmentally friendly practices, going the extra mile to protect and preserve the environment (Lyon & Maxwell, 2007). It encompasses the three R's: Reduce, Recycle, and Reuse, aimed at fostering a sustainable environment. Milton Friedman famously asserted that "the basic mission of any business is thus to produce goods and services at a profit, and in doing this, business is making its maximum contribution to society and being socially responsible" (Friedman et al., 2008). In contemporary times, company managers are not only tasked with objectives such as reducing lead times, enhancing quality, and lowering costs but are also increasingly expected to exhibit environmental responsibility (Irajpour et al., 2012).

This research examines the Corporate Environmental Responsibility (**CER**) practices of leading auto assemblers in the Chennai auto industry. The study will evaluate the environmental impact of the entire automotive lifecycle, focusing on emissions and their societal effects. Additionally, it seeks to benchmark the industry's global environmental standards, propose future emission standards alignment, and identify effective strategies and technologies that auto-assemblers employ for environmental sustainability. By applying a descriptive and qualitative approach, the study will conclude CER levels and provide recommendations to enhance environmental responsibility, including establishing dedicated environmental departments and collaborating with NGOs.

REVIEW OF LITERATURE

Effects on Human and Environment

A diverse array of chemicals is employed throughout the lifecycle of automobiles, from the manufacturing of components to the dismantling of vehicles. These chemicals, both directly and indirectly, pose significant risks to human health. They can cause damage to internal and external organs, leading to various sicknesses (Arokiaraj, 2015). Each chemical component exerts its distinct effects on society, further influencing the quality of air, water, soil, and overall environmental health. Automobile emissions, including those from gasoline combustion, adversely affect crops, livestock, and human health, leading to respiratory problems, lung cancer, chronic asthma, and pulmonary diseases. The potential ecological and human health concerns and their corresponding impacts are delineated in Table 1 (Madaan et al., 2021; Feleen et al., 2021).

Table 1. Effects of the automotive sector on environmental and human well-being

Contents	Effects on Environment	Effects on Human Health
Copper	Air pollution during melting and processing.	Coma, hypertension, sporadic fever.
Mercury	Land pollution due to improper disposal.	Cancer, diarrhea, headache, chest pain.
Chromium	Severe impact on the environment and natural resources, especially water and soil.	Central nervous system disorders, ulcers in gastrointestinal tracts, cancer.
Coal burning and Sulphide ore	Affects air quality.	Gastrointestinal disorders.
Manganese	Contaminates soil and water sources.	Neurological disorders.
Lead	Soil contamination affects plant growth and wildlife habitats.	Dysfunctions in blood circulation, brain damage, learning disabilities, poor mental development, irritability, reduced appetite, damage to central nervous systems, nausea, fatigue, impaired kidneys and reproductive systems, and reduced lung abilities.
Volatile organic compounds (VOCs)	Soil and water pollution contribute to ozone layer depletion and smog formation.	Headaches, throat and nasal irritation, liver damage, kidney malfunction, brain and central nervous system malfunction.

continued on following page

Table 1. Continued

Contents	Effects on Environment	Effects on Human Health
Nitrites	Water pollution, eutrophication, and aquatic ecosystem disruption.	Damage to respiratory and vascular systems, overabundant bacteria, decreased oxygen levels in deep water, and climate change.
Oxide of nitrogen	Contributes to smog formation, acid rain, and nitrogen deposition, affecting ecosystems and water quality.	Respiratory tract irritation, bronchial hyperactivity, impaired lung defenses.
Heating & cooling systems	Increases energy consumption and contributes to the urban heat island effect.	Skin disease, eye problems, and ecosystem impact.
Carbons	Contributes to global warming, climate change, and ocean acidification.	Chest pain, congestion, dizziness, headache, impaired visibility and consciousness, fatigue, permanent cardiovascular damage, heart diseases, and impaired fertility.
Nitrogen oxides (fossil-fuel combustion, highway vehicles, surface coating, organic solvents, solid-waste disposal) / Photochemical oxidant	Contributes to ground-level ozone formation, acid rain, and atmospheric pollution.	Respiratory issues, lung diseases, nasal and eye irritation, blood hemoglobin disintegration.
Sulphur oxides	Contributes to acid rain, smog formation, and respiratory illnesses.	Reduced visibility, runny nose, vomiting, headache, lung disease, respiratory ailments, cardiovascular damage, chronic obstructive pulmonary diseases.
Hydrocarbons	Contributes to ground-level ozone formation, smog, and carcinogenic air pollutants.	Headaches, throat and nasal irritation, liver damage, kidney malfunction, brain and central nervous system malfunction.
Particulate matter	Airborne particles contribute to respiratory diseases, cardiovascular problems, and climate change.	Respiratory issues, skin damage, heart diseases, asthma, reduced visibility, lung malfunctions, premature deaths, bronchial problems, lung cancer, reduced life expectancy
Running engines, Power trains, Cooling and Exhaust systems	Noise pollution disrupts ecosystems and wildlife habitats.	Stress and fatigue.
Electroplating wastes	Soil contamination, water pollution.	Cancer
Waste and engine oils	Contaminates water sources, such as soil, and affects aquatic and terrestrial ecosystems.	Bone degeneration, severe hypertension.

continued on following page

Table 1. Continued

Contents	Effects on Environment	Effects on Human Health
Lead acid battery	Contributes to soil and water pollution and disrupts ecosystems and wildlife habitats.	Skin diseases, loss of aquatic life, forest dieback, reduced lung function, cardiac and respiratory problems, & material degradation.
Ferrous metals (Iron, steel, etc.)	Contributes to land pollution and affects soil and water quality.	Respiratory issues, occupational hazards.
Non-ferrous metals (Aluminum, stainless steel, copper, brass, lead, magnesium, zinc, nickel, etc.)	Land and water pollution, habitat destruction.	Neurological disorders, carcinogenic effects, reproductive issues.
ASR (Plastic, glass, rubber, foam, carpet, textile)	Pollution of soil, water, and air endangers wildlife and marine life.	Respiratory issues, skin irritation, hormonal disruption.

Source: From Dieter Schwela,1996; Arokiaraj, 2015; R.N. Wahal, 2006; David, 2015; Madaan et al., 2021; Feleen et al., 2021.

The global automotive industry, a dynamic landscape dominated by key players such as China, the USA, and Japan, has profound economic implications. India, a significant contender, ranks 4th in automobile production with over 4 million units (OICA, 2024). Approximately 40% of global car production is attributed to Japan, Canada, and the USA (Kumar & Subrahmanya, 2010). While the industry was initially concentrated in the USA and parts of Europe, globalization has blurred trading boundaries, resulting in the proliferation of automobile industries in southeastern regions like China, Japan, and Korea. This expansion has generated approximately 90 million job opportunities worldwide (David, 2018; Kalburgi et al., 2023; Sankar et al., 2024), with associated sectors such as aluminum, textiles, plastics, rubber, glass, iron, and steel, contributing to further employment opportunities globally (Arokiaraj, 2015). In tandem with production growth, passenger car sales (Arokiaraj, 2015) have reached around 75 million vehicles in 2024, with China and the USA emerging as the major markets. India, holding the fourth position in production and 5th in global sales, signifies its growing significance in the automotive arena.

Global Scenario of Auto Industry: (Motorization Rate)

The motorization rate, a key metric reflecting vehicle ownership per capita, showcases Japan and South Korea as the leaders with 1070 vehicles per 1000 people, followed by Australia (869), NAFTA (722), and the European Union (309), among others. In stark contrast, India's motorization rate stands at a mere 33 per 1000, with 17 being the lowest value on the map, significantly below the global average despite ranking as the fourth largest producer worldwide.

Figure 1. Motorisation rate of world, 2024

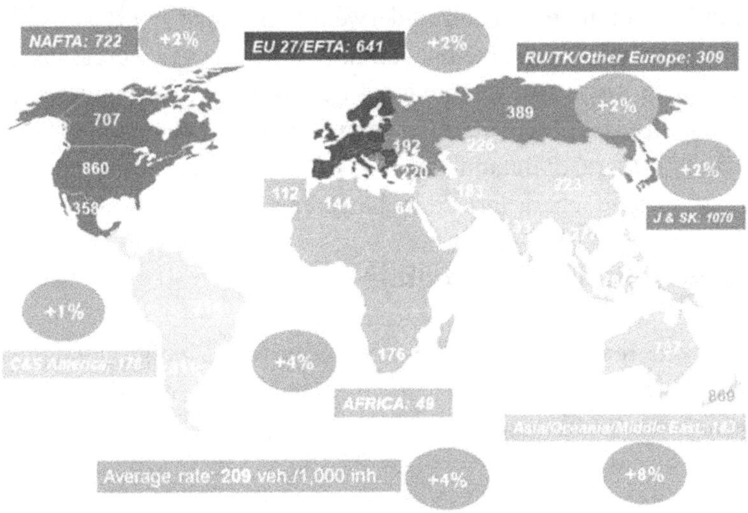

(OICA, 2024)

Analyzing the production trends depicted in Figure 1, sourced from OICA (2020), it becomes evident that passenger car production surpasses other vehicle types and exhibits steady growth. China's ascendancy to the top position occurred post-1990s, surpassing the USA, while Japan, the second largest producer, witnessed a significant increase after the 1980s. India's trajectory, propelled by economic liberalization in the 1990s, saw it rise to the fourth position in global production despite its delayed entry into the market (David, 2020a). Passenger car production outpaces commercial vehicles, further cementing China's dominance in automobile production, trailed by the USA and Japan.

Perspective From the Indian Automobile Sector

Notable milestones and substantial transformations characterize the history of the Indian automotive sector. Initially, in the 1940s, global giants like General Motors and Ford Motors held sway over the Indian automotive landscape. Concurrently, homegrown players such as Hindustan Motors and Premier Motors emerged, drawing upon the expertise inherited from their predecessors. In the 1950s, indigenous manufacturers such as Ashok Leyland, Bajaj, Mahindra, and Mahindra Auto began producing two- and four-wheelers (Arokiaraj, 2015), contributing to the diversification of the market (Pankaj Vashisht, 2008; David, 2020b).

The 1960s saw the inception of native automobile component manufacturing, bolstering the industry's indigenous capabilities. However, it was during the 1990s that the Indian automotive sector underwent a profound transformation following economic liberalization and the dismantling of the license raj regime. This pivotal period heralded a wave of international collaborations and joint ventures as the sector was delicensed, particularly in the passenger car segment, fueling a surge in production (Arokiaraj & Banumathi, 2015). Subsequently, many Indian automobile companies emerged, characterized by heightened competitiveness and innovation.

Evolution of Indian Automobile

These stages represent the dynamic evolution of the Indian automotive industry, outlining its progression from its beginnings to its current position as a significant participant in the global automotive landscape, as depicted in Table 2 below.

Table 2. Timeline of the Indian automobile industry

Year	Timeline	Year	Timeline
1897	The first car owner in India, Mr Foster, acquired a vehicle	1996	Hyundai Motors
1901	Jamshedji Tata became the first Indian to own a car	1997	Establishment of Toyota Kirloskar Motors in India
1905	Mrs. R.D. Tata became the first woman driver in India	1997	Fiat Motors re-entered the Indian market
1905	Fiat Motors entered the Indian market	1998	Introduction of San Motors
1911	The first taxi service was introduced in India	1998	Entry of Mitsubishi Motors into the Indian automotive sector
1924	Traffic police units were established.	2001	Launch of Skoda Auto in India
1928	Chevrolet Motors began operations in India.	2003	Introduction of Chevrolet vehicles in the Indian market
1942	Hindustan Motors	2008	Mahindra unveiled the first electric car, while Honda introduced a hybrid vehicle.
1944	Premier Auto Limited	2009	Tata Nano, the world's cheapest car, was introduced
1945	Tata Motors	2014	Ashok Leyland diversified into passenger car production
1947	Mahindra Motors	2015	Toyota introduced its first fuel-cell vehicle powered by compressed hydrogen gas.
1948	Ashok Motors	2016	Ford launched its first electric SUV
1948	Standard Motors	2017	Nissan introduced its fully autonomous vehicle
1974	Sipani Motors	2018	Volkswagen unveiled its first electric car in the ID series
1981	Maruti Suzuki	2019	BMW launched its first fully electric SUV
1994	Rover Motors	2020	Tesla achieved record sales with its Model 3

continued on following page

Table 2. Continued

Year	Timeline	Year	Timeline
1994	Mercedes Benz, Opel	2021	Hyundai announced plans for mass production of flying cars
			Mercedes-Benz announced plans to expand its electric vehicle lineup with new models.
			Ford revealed its plans to invest heavily in electric and autonomous vehicle technology.
			Toyota introduced its hydrogen-powered truck, the Hino Project Z.
			Honda unveiled its concept for an all-electric crossover vehicle.
1995	Ford Motors Honda SIEL	2022	Renault introduced its first hydrogen-powered commercial vehicle
			Porsche introduced its first all-electric sports car, the Taycan.
			Volvo pledged to transition into a fully electric automobile company by 2030.
		2023	Audi unveiled its concept for a self-driving luxury sedan.
1995	Reva Electric Car Company		General Motors announced its ambitious plan for all-electric future vehicles.
			Jaguar announced its transition to an all-electric brand by 2025.
			BMW unveiled its Vision iNEXT concept, showcasing its vision for the future of electric and autonomous vehicles.
			Audi introduced its electric compact SUV, the Q4 e-tron.
			Ford announced the development of its electric version of the iconic Ford Mustang.
1995	Daewoo Motors	2024	Nissan & Lucid Motors introduced its next-generation electric vehicle platform.
			Chevrolet unveiled its all-electric pickup truck, the Chevrolet Silverado EV.
			Hyundai launched its hydrogen-powered heavy-duty truck, the Hyundai Xcient Fuel Cell.

Source: SIAM – Society of Indian Automobile Manufacturers; ACMA – OICA – International Organization of Motor Vehicle; Automotive Component Manufacturers Association of India; JAMA - Japan Automobile Manufacturers Association, 2024.

The evolution of the Indian automobile industry can be outlined in several distinct phases. Initially, from 1940 to 1950, Phase I marked the emergence of the market, primarily dominated by domestic players. Following this, a regulated market environment characterized Phase II (1960-1970). The subsequent period, Phase III (1970-1980), witnessed a surge of international players entering the Indian market. Phase IV (1990-2000) saw the market maturing as liberalization took hold. Phase V (2001-2008) unfolded with notable shifts when transitioning to a globalized market. Technological advancements and an increasing emphasis on sustainability marked Phase VI (2008-2010). Safety and quality became focal points during Phase VII (2011-2015), whereas Phase VIII (2016-2024) reflects the industry's embrace of digitalization and the burgeoning prominence of electric and mobility services.

India is Asia's fourth largest producer of automobiles and is experiencing rapid growth, trailing closely behind China. However, the industry faces challenges such as inadequate infrastructure, complex tax structures, labor laws, and a need for national policy standardization and harmonization. Indian automotive production is notably concentrated in three primary regions: the South (encompassing Bangalore, Chennai, and Hosur), the North (including Faridabad and Gurgaon), and the West (comprising Pune and Mumbai), (Arokiaraj, 2015) as depicted in Figure 2. Recent policies and tax incentives have also encouraged expansion into other regions of the country (Nihmathullah et al., 2022).

Figure 2. Geographical distribution of automobile manufacturing hubs in India

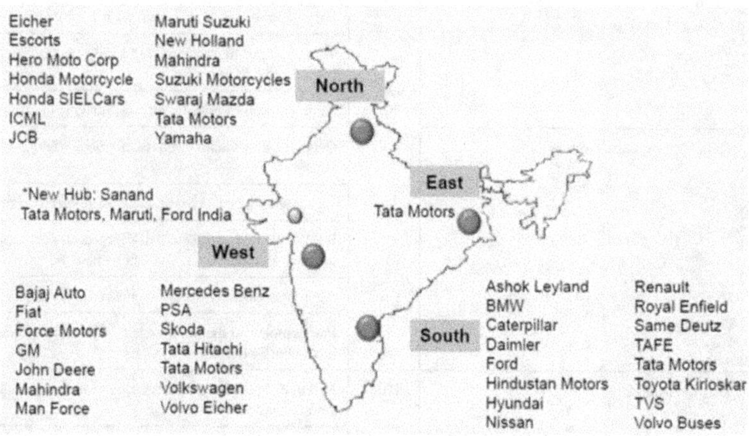

(ACMA, 2024)

The significant automobile players produce a variety of vehicles, which includes Heavy Commercial Vehicles (HCVs), Multi-Utility Vehicles (MUVs), Multi-Purpose Vehicles (MPVs), Medium Commercial Vehicles (MCVs), and Light Commercial Vehicles (LCVs), as mentioned in Table 3. Among the 34 listed companies, approximately 20 are engaged in passenger car production, with only a few manufacturing three-wheelers and buses. Notably, Mahindra and Mahindra stand out as a purely Indian company producing four-, three-, and two-wheeled vehicles (Arokiaraj, 2015).

Table 3. Key players in the Indian automotive industry

Companies	Segments								
	LCV	MCV	HCV	Cars	MUV	MPV	Two	Three	Buses
Ashok Leyland	x	x	x	x					x
Asian Motor Works		x	x						
Bajaj Auto							x	x	

continued on following page

Table 3. Continued

Companies	Segments								
	LCV	MCV	HCV	Cars	MUV	MPV	Two	Three	Buses
BMW India				x	x				
Daimler Chrysler India				x					
Eicher Motors	x	x	x						
Fiat India				x					
Force Motors		x							
Ford India				x	x				
General Motors India				x	x				
Hero Honda Motors							x		
Hindustan Motors	x			x	x				
Honda				x	x		x		
Hyundai Motors				x	x				
Jaguar & Land Rover				x					
Kinetic Motors							x		
Mahindra & Mahindra	x			x	x		x	x	
Maruti Suzuki				x	x	x	x		
Mercedes-Benz India				x					
Mitsubishi				x					
Nissan Motor India				x					
Piaggio	x							x	
Premier Automobiles				x					
Renault India				x					
Royal Enfield Motors							x		
Skoda Auto India				x					
Suzuki Motorcycles							x		
SwarjMazada		x	x		x				x
Tata Motors	x	x	x	x	x				x
Toyota Kirloskar		x		x					
TVS Motor Company							x	x	
Volvo India		x	x						x
Volkswagen India				x					
India Yamaha Motor							x		

Note: LCVs = Light commercial vehicles, MCVs = Medium commercial vehicles, HCVs=Heavy commercial vehicles, MUVs= multi-utility vehicles & MPVs = multi-purpose vehicles.

Source: Maheskumar, 2011.

Automobile Industry in Chennai

Focusing on the automobile industry in Chennai, the city emerges as a pivotal player, contributing around 35% of India's automobile production and 40% of auto components. Forecasts suggest exports are poised to increase by up to 50% by 2024. Chennai is a manufacturing hub for various automobile parts, encompassing brake systems, engine components, castings, forged parts, and electrical components. Notable establishments such as Ashok Leyland in the late 1950s, the TVS group in the 1960s, and organizations engaged in military vehicle production in collaboration with Russia have laid the foundation for Chennai's automotive prowess. Chennai's importance in the industry is underscored by the presence of institutions such as the Vehicle Research and Development Establishment (CVRDE), which is dedicated to engine testing. Labeled the "Detroit of India," Chennai boasts an impressive annual production of three million cars (Arokiaraj, 2015). The emergence of Tamil Nadu as a top manufacturing destination is reinforced by adding new manufacturers such as Hindustan Motors, Hyundai, and Ford (Arokiaraj, 2015; David & Banumathi, 2014_b).

Environmental Standards for the Auto Industry

Various emission standards and corporate environmental responsibility initiatives are crucial in shaping automobile manufacturers' ecological impact and sustainability practices in the global automotive industry. This paper delves into three prominent regulatory frameworks: the EURO standard adopted in Europe, the Corporate Average Fuel Economy (CAFÉ) standard in the United States, and the BHARAT standard implemented in India. Each standard has distinct objectives, methodologies, and implications for reducing carbon emissions and promoting environmentally friendly vehicle technologies.

EURO Standard

Europe has long been at the forefront of regulating vehicle emissions to mitigate environmental pollution. The EURO standard, initiated in 1992 and periodically updated, aims to control emissions of nitrogen oxides (NO_x), non-methane hydrocarbons (NMHC), carbon dioxide (CO_2), and total hydrocarbons (THC) from all types of vehicles except ships and aircraft. Clean vehicles meeting enhanced environmentally friendly vehicle (EEV) criteria are classified under Euro-V and Euro-VI standards. Compliance with EURO standards is mandatory for vehicle manufacturers, and adherence is assessed through engine tests. While the EURO standard does not prescribe specific technologies, meeting predefined emission limits is essential for market access.

CAFÉ Standard

In 1978, the United States implemented the Corporate Average Fuel Economy (CAFÉ) standard, primarily for passenger cars, with subsequent regulations extended to light and heavy-duty vehicles. CAFÉ standards aim to improve fuel efficiency and reduce carbon emissions by setting targets for manufacturers' average fuel economy. The latest iteration, Tier-III, adopted in 2024, aims to reduce carbon emissions further and enhance fuel efficiency. Manufacturers exceeding CAFÉ regulations may earn credits, while non-compliance can lead to penalties. However, the absence of incentives for consumers to prioritize fuel-efficient vehicles poses challenges to widespread adoption.

BHARAT Standard

In India, the auto sector contributes significantly to carbon emissions, prompting the adoption of emission regulations in 1989. In 2003, the National Auto Fuel Policy paved the way for implementing BHARAT emission standards (Arokiaraj, 2015), aligned with EURO norms but tailored to Indian geographic and climatic conditions. The transition from BS-I to BS-VII standards, with BS-VII to be implemented by 2023, signifies India's commitment to reducing vehicular emissions. Despite differences from EURO standards in testing parameters and regulatory approaches, India aims to bridge the gap and achieve parity with European standards by 2025.

* Some cities/regions have more stringent emission standards.

As of January 2013, the following cities have Bharat IV standards: Delhi (NCR), Mumbai, Kolkata, Chennai, Bangalore, Hyderabad, Ahmedabad, Pune, Surat, Kanpur, Agra, Solapur, Lucknow, Ankleshwar, Hisar, Bharatpur, Unnao, Raeareli, Aligarh, Jamnagar, Vapi, Puducherry and Mathura. 50-60 cities implemented Bharat IV standards by 2015.

Figure 3. Light-duty vehicle standard adoption timeline in India and other countries

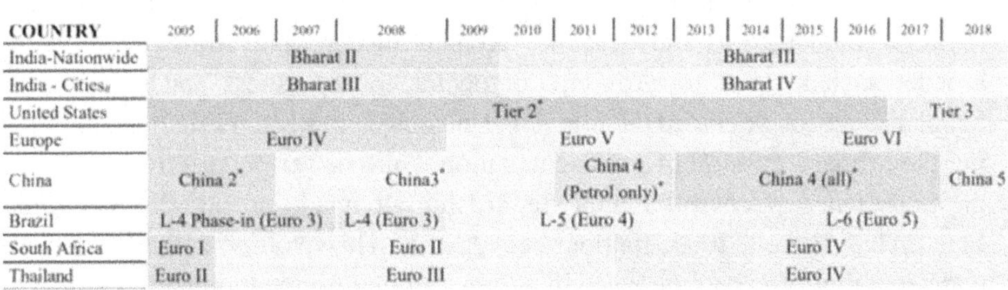

Source: Gaurav Bansal & Anup Bandivadekar, 2013.

Figure 3 illustrates the emission standards adopted by both developed and developing countries. The European Union has implemented the most stringent emission standard, which other countries adhere to under different names (Arokiaraj, 2015). In contrast, India follows two distinct sets of emission standards: one for 17 major cities including Delhi (NCR), Chennai, Kolkata, Mumbai, Bangalore, Pune, Kanpur, Ahmedabad, Hyderabad, Agra, Ankleshwar, Raeareli, Vapi, Surat, Aligarh, Lucknow, Jamnagar, Bharatpur, Unnao, Solapur, Mathura, Hisar, and Puducherry which adhere to advanced emission standards, while the rest of the country follows earlier versions. Therefore, uniformity is needed despite being significantly behind the Euro standards (Arokiaraj, 2015).

All implementation dates are for the beginning of the fiscal year (April 1).

Figure 4. Recommended standards for the future

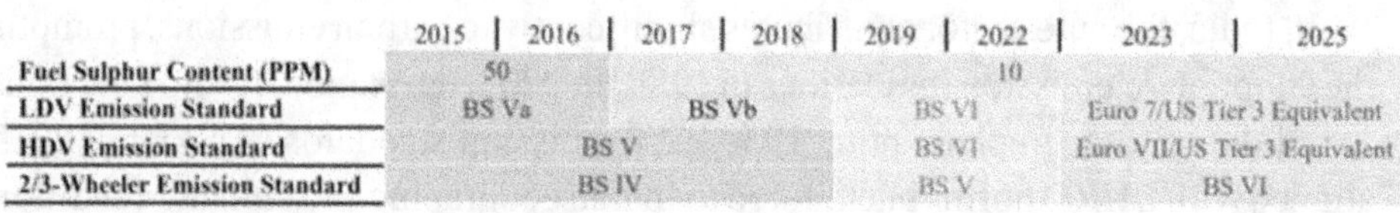

Source: Gaurav Bansa & Anup Bandivadekar, 2013.

As per the International Council on Clean Transportation (ICCT's) Report, Gaurav Bansal, and Anup Bandivadekar (2013) emphasized that future standards would prioritize environmental impact and consider the needs of future generations. These standards apply to all categories of vehicles, including passenger cars, light and heavy-duty vehicles, and two- and three-wheeled vehicles (Arokiaraj, 2011; Sankar & David, 2024). By 2025, India is expected to align its Bharat Stage standards with the European standards of that period, as depicted in Figure 4 above.

Corporate Environmental Responsibility

In contemporary business landscapes, Corporate Environmental Responsibility (CER) has emerged as a critical measurement of corporate strategy, reflecting a broader societal shift towards environmental consciousness and sustainability. Scholars have long debated the role of businesses, with Milton Friedman highlighting the primary mission of profit generation while newer perspectives emphasize the importance of environmental stewardship alongside profitability (Friedman, Fraedrich & Ferrell, 2008; Irajpour et al., 2012). This evolution signifies a deeper understanding of corporate roles in addressing environmental challenges beyond legal obligations. Research indicates (Aragón-Correa & Rubio-Lopez, 2007) that large corporations, especially those in the automotive industry, are increasingly recognizing their environmental impact and taking proactive measures to mitigate it. Studies exploring the social responsibility practices of these corporations reveal a notable emphasis on ecological concerns alongside traditional business objectives (Sudhakar et al., 2017; Karna et al., 2003). This shift in focus underscores a broader trend toward incorporating environmental considerations into corporate decision-making processes. Corporate Environmental Responsibility encompasses a spectrum of initiatives to minimize environmental harm and promote sustainability. Often extending beyond legal requirements, CER initiatives embody voluntary commitments to reduce, recycle, and reuse resources, fostering a more sustainable operational framework (Lyon & Maxwell, 2007). These efforts signify a growing recognition among businesses of their role in safeguarding the environment and contributing to broader sustainability goals.

The study highlights the sector's significant contribution to pollution in the automotive industry context, particularly during the primary production phase. While manufacturers bear a share of this responsibility, end-users also play a crucial role in driving emissions (David et al., 2018; Arokiaraj, 2015). It underscores the importance of comprehensive approaches to environmental responsibility that encompass all stages of the product lifecycle, from production to disposal. Stakeholder pressure, including demands from employees, customers, and regulatory bodies, further incentivizes corporations to prioritize environmental concerns. Companies are increasingly expected to identify and engage with various stakeholders to address environmental challenges effectively (Madsen & Ulhoi, 2001). It underscores the increasing acknowledgement of the interrelation between corporate activities and their broader societal and environmental consequences. Organizations have begun implementing various strategies to proactively enhance environmental performance and engage stakeholders in response to these pressures. It includes conducting orientation programs, training sessions, and green initiative evaluations (Sankar et al., 2023). Such initiatives demonstrate a shift towards more integrated approaches to environmental responsibility, where businesses actively seek to align their operations with sustainability objectives. However, scaling up environmental performance remains challenging for many organizations, particularly Small and Medium Enterprises (SMEs) within the automotive supply chain. Resource constraints and limited capacity hinder SMEs' adoption of sustainable practices (D'Souza et al., 2007; Melnyk et al., 2003), highlighting the need for collaborative efforts and support mechanisms. It underscores the need to foster partnerships and knowledge-sharing initiatives to promote sustainability across the industry. Regulatory advancements and increasing environmental consciousness mark the automotive industry's environmental journey. Government policies and regulations are crucial in incentivizing businesses to adopt environmentally friendly practices (Kel Dummett, 2006; Curkovic & Landeros, 2000). It highlights the interconnected nature of corporate environmental responsibility and regulatory frameworks, underscoring the importance of policy alignment and collaboration between public and private sectors.

The literature on Corporate Environmental Responsibility within the automotive industry reflects a broader societal shift towards sustainability and environmental stewardship. As businesses navigate evolving regulatory landscapes and stakeholder expectations, integrating ecological considerations into corporate strategies becomes imperative for long-term success and societal well-being.

RESEARCH METHODOLOGY

To address the unique characteristics of the Chennai automotive industry, which is characterized by a relatively small population size, a targeted snowball sampling method was chosen for participant selection. The survey enlisted prominent auto assemblers, including Hindustan Motor, Toyota Kirloskar Motor, Ford India, Ashok Leyland, and Renault Nissan Automotive India. The investigation employed direct approaches and mail methods to ensure a comprehensive reach. Survey participants, crucially identified as Environmental or HR Managers, were selected. The study adopted a dual methodology, combining descriptive and qualitative approaches, to intricately explore Corporate Environmental Responsibility (CER) within the Chennai automotive industry. A meticulously designed questionnaire was the primary tool to extract detailed insights into environmental practices (Ganeshkumar et al., 2023). The questionnaire focused on critical areas such as emissions management, waste reduction strategies, vehicle life extension, and compliance with emission control standards.

This approach, integrating both descriptive and qualitative dimensions, facilitated a nuanced exploration of the environmental initiatives undertaken by the surveyed auto-assemblers. Through a focus on qualitative aspects, the research sought to provide a more profound insight into the strategies and practices adopted by these companies (David & Banumathi, 2014_a). Ultimately, this distinctive research methodology sought to offer valuable, original insights into the Corporate Environmental Responsibility landscape of the Chennai automotive sector.

FINDINGS

This section focuses on the key actions and strategies undertaken to address the social imperative of environmental responsibility. The collected data was analyzed and summarized in the subsequent to provide insights into these practices.

Figure 5. Green strategies practiced by auto assemblers

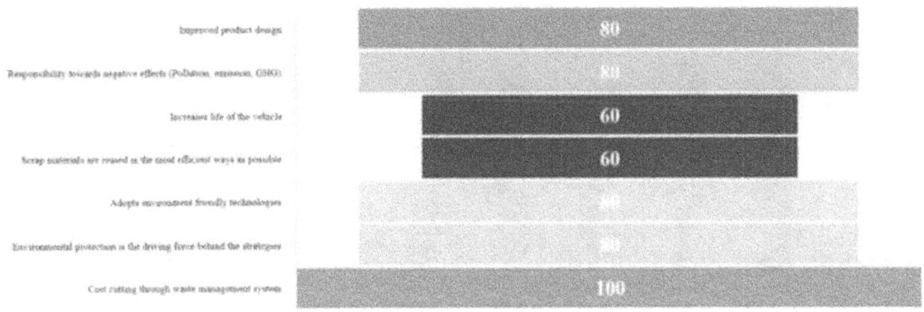

(Author's Original Work)

Figure 6. Corporate governance practiced in auto assembling firms

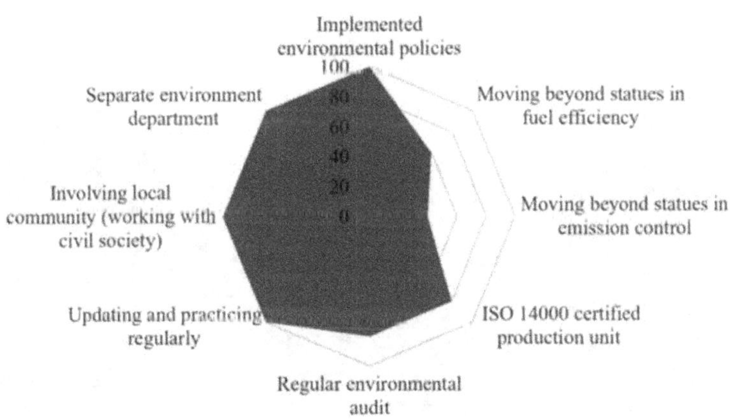

(Author's Original Work)

Figure 7. Auto assemblers environmental management system

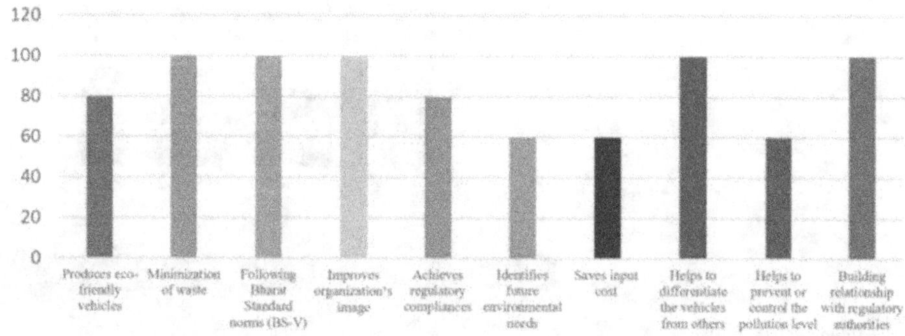

(Author's Original Work)

Figure 8. Green components purchased by auto assemblers

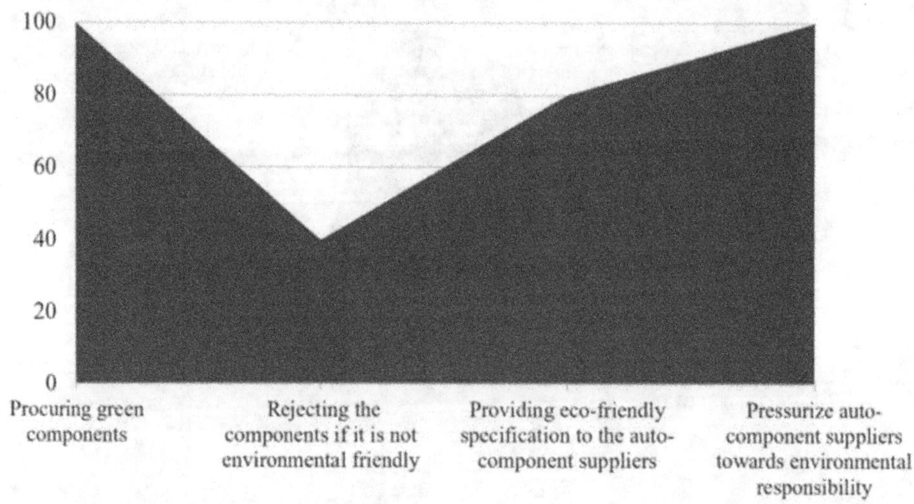

(Author's Original Work)

Figure 9. Auto assemblers environmental friendly manufacturing practices

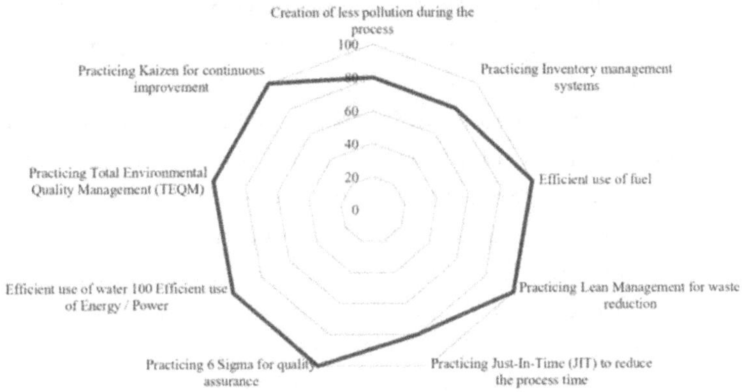

(Author's Original Work)

The surveyed organizations found that 77% have devised green strategies primarily aimed at cost reduction through effective waste management practices. However, a slightly lower percentage, only 60%, have implemented strategies geared towards prolonging vehicle life and repurposing scrap materials. Despite this, most organizations have corporate governance policies addressing environmental management concerns. However, only a minority, approximately 40%, have taken steps beyond legal mandates to control emissions and enhance fuel efficiency. Furthermore, nearly all surveyed organizations have implemented environmental management systems, adhering to BS-V standards and establishing relationships with regulatory bodies to anticipate future requirements. However, the perceived benefits of such systems vary, with only a few organizations reporting cost savings and pollution prevention as tangible outcomes. Regarding procurement practices, most vehicle assemblers prioritize green components and encourage suppliers to provide environmentally friendly parts. However, only 40% of organizations are willing to reject components that do not meet these criteria.

Regarding manufacturing processes, companies are actively working to enhance the utilization of natural resources like energy, fuel, and water. To accomplish this objective, they have adopted advanced technologies such as Just-In-Time (JIT), Lean Management, Six Sigma, Kaizen, Total Quality Environmental Management (TQEM), and Inventory Management Systems (Arokiaraj, 2015). These initiatives demonstrate a commitment to sustainable manufacturing practices and environmental responsibility within the automotive industry.

DISCUSSION

The research indicates significant adherence to key sustainability metrics across various dimensions based on meticulous data analysis and interpretation of the Environmental Practices of Auto Assemblers. Specifically, Green Strategies exhibit a commendable compliance rate of 77.14%, as evidenced in Figure 5. Corporate Governance demonstrates robust performance with an adherence rate of 82.23%, as illustrated in Figure 6. Moreover, Environmental Management Systems (EMS) showcase exemplary compliance at 85.46%, as depicted in Figure 7. Green Components manifest a notable adherence rate of 80%, as shown in Figure 8. Additionally, environmentally friendly manufacturing displays commendable performance, boasting an 83.77% compliance rate, as depicted in Figure 9. These findings underscore the auto assembly industry's proactive commitment to environmental responsibility, providing a clear roadmap for advancing sustainable practices within the sector.

The findings underscore a commendable commitment to Corporate Environmental Responsibility (CER) within the Chennai automotive industry. A substantial majority, approximately 95%, demonstrated a proactive stance by EMS in their operations. Notably, all surveyed auto-assemblers, constituting 100%, implemented Kaizen, TQEM, Six Sigma, and lean management and exhibited efficient resource utilization, including water, energy, and fuel (Arokiaraj, 2015). The unanimous adherence to BS-V norms, regular publication of environmental reports, and fostering relationships with regulatory authorities exemplify a robust commitment to environmental compliance. The auto-assemblers showcased a concerted effort to minimize operational waste. Multinational corporations (MNCs) stood out by implementing corporate governance and influencing their suppliers to adopt environmentally friendly manufacturing practices.

The prevalence of ISO 9001 and ISO 14000 certifications among almost all auto-assemblers signifies a dual commitment to quality management and environmental stewardship. The observed high level of CER is attributed to stringent government regulations and intensified market competition, shaping a landscape where environmental responsibility is not merely a compliance measure but a competitive edge for automotive manufacturers in Chennai. The study's findings reveal a positive shift towards environmental responsibility in Chennai's automotive industry. Critical implications include efficient resource utilization practices like lean management and quality certifications, serving as benchmarks for waste reduction. Collaborating with NGOs for eco-awareness campaigns and establishing specialized environmental departments can integrate sustainability into business strategies. Adherence to stringent regulations and certification standards underscores the competitive advantage of environmental responsibility. Initiatives like structured dismantling units for vehicle disposal align with sustainability goals, promoting a circular economy (Arokiaraj, 2015). Realizing these practical suggestions can drive sustainable practices and ensure long-term viability in the automotive sector.

To strengthen the auto industry's commitment towards environmental responsibility, it is proposed that organizations institute specialized environmental departments alongside existing marketing and human resource structures. As part of Corporate Social Responsibility (CSR), manufacturers should engage with NGOs to orchestrate diverse eco-awareness campaigns, encouraging drivers to embrace environmentally friendly behaviors and drawing inspiration from successful models in developed nations. Furthermore, auto assemblers are encouraged to establish their structured dismantling units, aligning with the contemporary surge in used car sales. This initiative aims to promote sustainable vehicle disposal practices and contribute to the principles of a circular economy.

CONCLUSION

In conclusion, the research reveals a nuanced narrative of environmental responsibility within the Chennai automobile industry. The study navigates through complex terrains, from a microcosmic examination of emissions and industry practices to a macroscopic view of global production dynamics. The challenges faced by the automotive sector, including emissions, waste management, and resource utilization, are acknowledged within the study. However, the research proposes a forward-looking perspective rather than presenting these challenges as insurmountable obstacles. It envisions a future where environmental responsibility transcends mere regulatory compliance to become a fundamental guiding principle shaping the industry's trajectory. It emphasizes integrating environmental considerations into every aspect of industry operations, from production processes to product lifecycle management. Ultimately, the research highlights the potential for the Chennai automobile industry to mitigate its environmental footprint and become a leader in driving sustainable and resilient automobile futures. The sector can pave the way for a greener, more environmentally conscious future where economic prosperity aligns harmoniously with ecological well-being through concerted efforts and collaborative initiatives.

REFERENCES

Alvarez, R., Weilenmann, M., & Favez, P.-Y. (2008). Evidence of increased mass fraction of NO2 within real-world NOx emissions of modern light vehicles — Derived from a reliable online measuring method. *Atmospheric Environment*, 42(19), 4699–4707. 10.1016/j.atmosenv.2008.01.046

Aragón-Correa, J. A., & Rubio-Lopez, E. A. (2007). Proactive corporate environmental strategies: Myths and misunderstandings. *Long Range Planning*, 40(3), 357–381. 10.1016/j.lrp.2007.02.008

Arokiaraj, D. (2011). The green market: The way to save the World. *Business Strategies*, 2(1), 41–44.

Arokiaraj, D., & Banumathi, M. A. (2015). Study on the environmental concern of the passenger car user in Chennai. [IRJBM]. *International Research Journal of Business and Management*, 8(5), 64–70.

Arokiaraj, D., Ganeshkumar, C., & Paul, P. V. (2020). Innovative management system for environmental sustainability practices among Indian auto-component manufacturers. *International Journal of Business Innovation and Research*, 23(2), 168–182. 10.1504/IJBIR.2020.110095

Bansal, G., & Bandivadekar, A. (2013). *Overview of India's vehicle emissions control program*. ICCT.

Banumathi, M., & Arokiaraj, D. (2011). Eco-labeling–The Need for Sustainable Marketing. In *National Conference in the era of Global Recovery-2011 (SGEGR2011* (pp. 511-515). Research Gate.

Beltramello, A. (2012). *Market development for green cars.*

Christmann, P., & Taylor, G. (2001). Globalization and the environment: Determinants of firm self-regulation in China. *Journal of International Business Studies*, 32(3), 439–458. 10.1057/palgrave.jibs.8490976

Criscuolo, C., & Menon, C. (2014). *Environmental policies and risk finance in the green sector: cross-country evidence.*

Curkovic, S., & Landeros, R. (2000). An environmental baldrige? *American Journal of Business*, 15(2), 63–76. 10.1108/19355181200000012

D'Souza, C., Taghian, M., Lamb, P., & Peretiatko, R. (2007). Green decisions: Demographics and consumer understanding of environmental labels. *International Journal of Consumer Studies*, 31(4), 371–376. 10.1111/j.1470-6431.2006.00567.x

David, A. (2018). Towards Mobile Opportunistic in Cloud Computing. *Indian Journal of Scientific Research (IJSR),* 2250-0138.

David, A. (2020$_a$). Air Pollution Control Monitoring & Delivery Rate Escalated by Efficient use of Markov Process in Manet Networks: to Measure Quality of Service Parameters. *Test Engineering & Management.* The Mattingley Publishing Co.

David, A. (2020$_b$). *Corporate and individual environmental responsibility towards automobile*. Book Rivers.

David, A., & Banumathi, M. (2014$_a$). A Study on Eco–Driving Behaviour of Passenger Car Users in Chennai. *TIJ's Research Journal of Social Science & Management (RJSSM), 3*(11).

David, A., & Banumathi, M. (2014$_b$). Factors influencing the purchase decision of passenger cars in Puduchery. *International Journal of Exclusive Management Research (IJEMR),* 2249-2585.

David, A., Muthukumar, A., Ayyappan, D., & Ravi, S. (2020$_a$). Accident Avoidance System by Using Sensors Module. *Test Engineering & Management.* The Mattingley Publishing Co., Inc.

David, A., Nagarjuna, K., Mohammed, M., & Sundar, J. (2020). *Determinant Factors of Environmental Responsibility for the Passenger Car Users. SSRN.*

David, A., Ravi, S., & Reena, R. A. (2018). The Eco-Driving Behaviour: A Strategic Way to Control Tailpipe Emission. *International Journal of Engineering & Technology, 7*(3.3), 21-25.

David, A., Thangavel, Y. D., & Sankriti, R. (2019). *Recover, recycle and reuse: An efficient way to reduce the waste*. Research Gate.

Dummett, K. (2006). Drivers for corporate environmental responsibility (CER). *Environment, Development and Sustainability*, 8(3), 375–389. 10.1007/s10668-005-7900-3

Faiz, A. (1993). Automotive emissions in developing countries – Relative implications for global warming, acidification and urban air quality. *Transportation Research Part A, Policy and Practice*, 27A(3), 167–186. 10.1016/0965-8564(93)90057-R

Feleen, F., David, A., Choudhary, N., & Vivekanand, N. (2021). *Impact of Psychological Capacities on the Work-Life Balance of Entrepreneurs.*

Ferrell, O. C., & Ferrell, L. (2008). A macromarketing ethics framework: Stakeholder orientation and distributive justice. *Journal of Macromarketing*, 28(1), 24–32. 10.1177/0276146707311290

Galitsky, C., & Worrell, E. (2008). *Energy efficiency improvement and cost saving opportunities for the vehicle assembly industry: an energy star guide for energy and plant managers* (No. LBNL-50939-Revision). Lawrence Berkeley National Lab. (LBNL), Berkeley, CA (United States).

Ganeshkumar, C., David, A., & Jebasingh, D. R. (2022). Digital transformation: Artificial intelligence-based product benefits and problems of agritech industry. In *Agri-Food 4.0* (Vol. 27, pp. 141–163). Emerald Publishing Limited. 10.1108/S1877-636120220000027010

Ganeshkumar, C., David, A., Sankar, J. G., & Saginala, M. (2023). Application of Drone Technology in Agriculture: A Predictive Forecasting of Pest and Disease Incidence. In *Applying Drone Technologies and Robotics for Agricultural Sustainability* (pp. 50–81). IGI Global.

Irajpour, A., Golsefid-Alavi, M., Hajimirza, M., & Soleimani-Nezhad, N. (2012). Evaluation of the most effective criteria in green supply chain management in automotive industries using the Fuzzy DEMATEL Method. *Journal of Basic and Applied Scientific Research*, 2(9), 8952–8961.

Kalburgi, N. K., David, A., & Muralidhar, L. B. (2023). Understanding the Perceptions of Students towards YouTube as a Learning Tool-An Empirical Approach. *Central European Management Journal, ISSN*, 2336-2693.

Kärnä, J., Hansen, E., & Juslin, H. (2003). Social responsibility in environmental marketing planning. *European Journal of Marketing*, 37(5/6), 848–871. 10.1108/03090560310465170

Krinke, S. (2011). Implementing life cycle engineering efficiently into automotive industry processes. In *Glocalized Solutions for Sustainability in Manufacturing: Proceedings of the 18th CIRP International Conference on Life Cycle Engineering, Technische Universität Braunschweig,* (pp. 11-16). Springer Berlin Heidelberg.

Kumar, R. S., & Subrahmanya, M. B. (2010). Influence of subcontracting on innovation and economic performance of SMEs in Indian automobile industry. *Technovation*, 30(11-12), 558–569. 10.1016/j.technovation.2010.06.005

Lyon, T. P., & Maxwell, J. W. (2007). Environmental public voluntary programs reconsidered. *Policy Studies Journal: the Journal of the Policy Studies Organization*, 35(4), 723–750. 10.1111/j.1541-0072.2007.00245.x

Madaan, G., Swapna, H. R., Kumar, A., Singh, A., & David, A. (2021). Enactment of sustainable technovations on healthcare sectors. *Asia Pacific Journal of Health Management*, 16(3), 184–192. 10.24083/apjhm.v16i3.989

Madsen, H., & Ulhøi, J. P. (2001). Integrating environmental and stakeholder management. *Business Strategy and the Environment*, 10(2), 77–88. 10.1002/bse.279

Melnyk, S. A., Sroufe, R. P., & Calantone, R. (2003). Assessing the impact of environmental management systems on corporate and environmental performance. *Journal of Operations Management*, 21(3), 329–351. 10.1016/S0272-6963(02)00109-2

Narayanan, G. B., & Vashisht, P. (2008). *Determinants of competitiveness of the Indian auto industry* (No. 201). Working paper.

Nemry, F., Leduc, G., Mongelli, I., & Uihlein, A. (2008). Environmental improvement of passenger cars (IMPRO-car). *Institute for Prospective Technological Studies*, 1(1), 1–216.

Nihmathullah, Z. & Ramasamy, R. (2022). *Event Impact Assessment: A Case of Puducherry*.

Popli, G. S., & Gupta, P. V. (2010). A Study on Cognitive Consistency of Young Passenger Car Consumers Towards Vehicular Pollution by Private Cars: An Empirical Analysis in Indian Context. *Available atSSRN* 1579984. 10.2139/ssrn.1579984

Ravi, S., David, A., & Imaduddin, M. (2018). Controlling & calibrating vehicle-related issues using RFID technology. *International Journal of Mechanical and Production Engineering Research and Development*, 8(2), 1125–1132. 10.24247/ijmperdapr2018130

Sagar, A. D. (1995). Automobiles and global warming: Alternative fuels and other options for carbon dioxide emissions reduction. *Environmental Impact Assessment Review*, 15(3), 241–274. 10.1016/0195-9255(95)91707-F

Sahay, A. (2004). Environmental reporting by Indian corporations. *Corporate Social Responsibility and Environmental Management*, 11(1), 12–22. 10.1002/csr.51

Sankar, J. G., & David, A. (2024). Transforming the Travel Landscape: Smart Contracts in Tourism Management. In *Decentralizing the Online Experience With Web3 Technologies* (pp. 246–266). IGI Global. 10.4018/979-8-3693-1532-3.ch012

Sankar, J. G., David, A., & Shrutimeena, G. (2024). From Hesitation to Integration: Understanding Digital Healthcare Adoption. In *Multi-Sector Analysis of the Digital Healthcare Industry* (pp. 1–32). IGI Global. 10.4018/979-8-3693-0928-5.ch001

Sankar, J. G., David, A., & Valan, P. (2023). Examining User Understanding and Perceptions of E-Commerce Data Privacy, Security, and Protection. In *Confronting Security and Privacy Challenges in Digital Marketing* (pp. 159–185). IGI Global. 10.4018/978-1-6684-8958-1.ch008

Santos, G., Behrendt, H., Maconi, L., Shirvani, L., & Teytelboym, A. (2010). Externalities and economic policies in road transport. *Research in Transportation Economics*, 28(1), 2–45. 10.1016/j.retrec.2009.11.002

Sarkis, J., Zhu, Q., & Lai, K. H. (2011). An organizational theoretic review of green supply chain management literature. *International Journal of Production Economics*, 130(1), 1–15. 10.1016/j.ijpe.2010.11.010

Sudhakar, B. D., Kattepogu, N., & David, A. (2017). Marketing assistance and digital branding-an insight for technology up-gradation for MSME's. *International Journal of Management Studies & Research*, 5(1), 2455–1562.

Sullivan, J. L., Burnham, A., & Wang, M. Q. (2013). Model for the part manufacturing and vehicle assembly component of the vehicle life cycle inventory. *Journal of Industrial Ecology*, 17(1), 143–153. 10.1111/j.1530-9290.2012.00515.x

Thummula, E., Yadav, R. K., & David, A. (2019). A cost-effective technique to avoid communication and computation overhead in vehicle insurance database for online record monitoring. [IJMPERD]. *International Journal of Mechanical and Production Engineering Research and Development*, 9(2), 711–722.

Yann Arthus-Bertrand, (2009, June 5). —*HOME – Documentary film*. Paris: Europa Corp.

Chapter 7 The Development of Web 1.0 to Web 2.0 CSR Disclosure of Data

Sabyasachi Pramanik
https://orcid.org/0000-0002-9431-8751
Haldia Institute of Technology, India

ABSTRACT

The impact of technology developments on corporate social responsibility (CSR) disclosure is examined in this chapter. It looks at how different stakeholders' changing needs for CSR disclosure and the interdependent interactions between them are being shaped by the way new technologies are being used. Understanding the profound effects that technology will have on CSR disclosure as it develops is essential for both companies and society at large. The way businesses engage with stakeholders has been significantly impacted by the development of Internet technology at every step, from the pre-Internet period to Web 2.0. This chapter will critically analyze how technology has transformed CSR disclosure and how stakeholder interaction has been shaped by these technological advancements. Additionally, this chapter offers solutions for related problems in the age of social media.

OVERVIEW

Information technology is dynamic and essential to the growth of economies, industries, and communities. The way companies are conducted has been profoundly impacted by the advent of computers and the growth of networks. Technology has transformed the character of the CSR conversation and expedited and facilitated the CSR debate during the last forty years. When Leung et al. (2013) examine earlier

DOI: 10.4018/979-8-3693-3238-2.ch007

research on media platforms; they find that there aren't many studies that particularly discuss CSR activities on social media. These points to a research hole in the study of how businesses use social media to convey corporate social responsibility. Therefore, it's important to understand how the technology revolution has affected CSR disclosure. The purpose of this chapter is to examine how technology developments affect the channels used for CSR disclosure. It will look at how changing technology and changing stakeholder needs at different phases of technological transformation are intertwined.

Prior to the release of Web 1.0, companies mostly disclosed CSR via annual reports and conventional media (Figure 1). The audience and communication capability are restricted, which limits the distribution of CSR statements. Rather of press releases and marketing, firms officially disclose their CSR information via annual reports, which are auditable. However, depending on how they define their stakeholders, businesses' CSR information and topics differ significantly. For instance, from 1973 to 1974, different FTSE 500 companies provided different CSR information in their annual reports (Abbott & Monsen, 1979). Furthermore, companies are unable to promptly get input and criticism from stakeholders after the disclosure of CSR-related data. As Web 1.0 gained popularity in the 1990s, companies began to include stand-alone reports and online CSR disclosures to their annual reports. The lack of CSR disclosure in traditional annual reports is successfully addressed by these stand-alone reports, which also address the dispersion of CSR data with regard to its breadth and depth. Transparency in CSR information is also increasing because to Web 1.0's introduction of Internet accountability. In addition to increasing public awareness of corporate social responsibility (CSR), the widespread use of Web 1.0 technology has forced businesses to evaluate how accessible CSR content is to a larger range of stakeholders. Web 1.0 represents only the beginning of Internet development; in contrast to the highly dynamic Web 2.0 stage of today, Web 1.0 consisted simply of static web pages devoid of user interaction.

The creation and sharing of knowledge has undergone a major transformation thanks to Web 2.0, a dynamic and interactive online environment (Chen et al., 2011). Business practices have been profoundly impacted by this revolutionary period, particularly with regard to CSR disclosure. Web 2.0 technologies provide two-way communication between people and organizations, hence advancing transparency and authenticity. Businesses' connections with stakeholders have been further impacted by the rise of social networks and the presence of CEOs on these platforms. The transition from Web 1.0 to Web 2.0 represents a change in communication from static, one-way to two-way, real-time, which improves the efficacy and transparency of CSR.

All things considered, CSR disclosure has changed significantly in the fast moving Internet age. Stakeholders, businesses, and legislators must comprehend the profound effects of technology on CSR disclosure. Online social media, or Web 2.0, allows businesses to share information more effectively, but it also presents new and important challenges, like the veracity of CSR information, the practice and disclosure of selective CSR activities, and the divergent preferences in CSR communication channels. This chapter offers related recommendations about these matters as well. The impact of technology changes on CSR disclosure is discussed in detail in the sections that follow.

HISTORY

CSR Conversation and Stroll

Unavoidably, “talk” and “walk” are used to conceptualize CSR, and they are often considered to be the two primary domains of CSR knowledge (Colucci et al., 2020). While CSR walk refers to the particular CSR policies, procedures, and processes that a business adopts, CSR speak refers to the image that a corporation creates of itself via the dissemination of information (Wickert et al., 2016). The academic division of corporate social responsibility (CSR) into talk and walk categories is justified by prior research indicating that companies typically prefer to talk when choosing between the two, and that they are prepared to discuss a significant amount of CSR material in order to achieve their goals (Brunton et al., 2017; Kallio, 2007; Lomborg, 2003).

Over the last 40 years, the use of Internet technology has changed the nature of CSR conversation and expedited and facilitated it. The next segments will examine the development of corporate social responsibility discourse throughout the last four decades, emphasizing the revolutionary influence of Web 1.0 technology before to and subsequent to its launch. The possible effects of this technology on the CSR walk are also covered.

Dawn: Discussion on CSR Prior to the Release of Web 1.0

Prior to the arrival of Web 1.0, the majority of firms' CSR disclosure came via their annual reports and conventional media, such as print ads and press releases (Grey et al., 1995). CSR discourse was only partially disseminated as a consequence of conventional media's and communication channels' constrained dissemination capacities. This implies that there are limits to the amount of CSR information that can be disseminated as well as to the audience that can comprehend and consume it. Within this framework, the primary target audience for CSR disclosure and communication was thought to be a certain demographic, which was thought to have the ability to affect business conduct (Freeman, 1984). "The process of communicating the social and environmental effects of organizations' economic actions to particular interest groups within society and to society at large" (Grey et al., 1988, page 9).

Currently, the majority of CSR discourse consists of disseminating pertinent information via annual reports. For a select few businesses, press releases, print ads, and public lectures and seminars are also used as supplements (Abbott & Monsen, 1979; Grey et al., 1995). Corporate annual reports are considered to be the formal means via which businesses may disclose corporate social responsibility (CSR) information. This is particularly true for listed companies, whose annual reports are subject to examination by the appropriate authorities, namely the stock market (Wilmshurst & Frost, 2000). Furthermore, compared to the supplemental channels previously described, annual reports also subject corporate annual reports to increased regulatory pressure from social responsibility. Corporate annual reports that are not disseminated via other disclosure channels and methodologies have a great degree of credibility because of this accountability pressure (Haniffa & Cooke, 2005; Tilt, 1994).

There is variation in how CSR information is disclosed in yearly reports from firms. As previously stated, the scope of CSR information released by businesses is constrained by the identification of their stakeholders, and the topics and material released by businesses range significantly based on the variations in their stakeholder identification. These themes address a broad variety of subjects, including product quality, community participation, and environmental challenges. Furthermore, at this point, society's perspective of CSR is still developing and changing. Every year, firms' CSR disclosures in their annual reports differed as well. Through a content study, Abbott & Monsen (1979) discovered that during 1973 and 1974, the CSR information that FTSE 500 businesses revealed in their annual reports fluctuated from year to year. Between 1973 and 1974, the sample corporations disclosed 13.4% more environmental information; however, there was only a little increase in disclosure on other areas.

Additionally, businesses employ print ads and press releases to showcase their CSR performance and outcomes (Manheim & Pratt, 1986; Zeghal & Ahmed, 1990) particularly for sectors that are sensitive to the environment, such the energy, extractive, and textile industries. Press releases and commercials, however, are not the main venues for CSR discussion.

CORPORATE RESPONSIBILITY ON THE DIGITAL LANDSCAPE: WEB 1.0

Twilight: Difficulties in Communicating CSR Earlier Than Web 1.0

At the beginning, information was really hard to get by. Annual reports gave stakeholders access to a company's financial and operational information, although they were usually released via public channels with an eye towards certain audiences like analysts and investors. Before Web 1.0 technology, this technique made it difficult for non-specialists to acquire such information. Annual reports were mostly delivered as text documents that had been digitally printed, as Louwers (1996) noted. Due to the related costs, corporations were dissuaded from wider dissemination by this old technique, which sometimes included expensive paper-based reports (Khadaroo, 2005). As such, the restricted accessibility hindered the supervision and participation of wider stakeholder groups in the discussion and application of CSR—also known as CSR "talk" and "walk." This led to a situation where a small number of stakeholders and the firms themselves had the most influence over CSR activity and communication.

Furthermore, CSR information transmission is impeded by company annual report disclosure policies, which may lead to material that is outdated or inconsistent with current corporate business activities (Courtis, 1986). Corporate annual reports have a two-way prohibition on the disclosure of CSR information. Traditional annual report data, as seen by stakeholders, summarizes a company's social and environmental performance across a predetermined time frame, sometimes depriving stakeholders of up-to-date information on the company's most recent performance. On the other hand, after disclosing CSR information, businesses could not quickly seek the opinions and input of stakeholders, which might result in information released in a later time that is inaccurate in addressing stakeholders' concerns. Real-time contact and communication between businesses and stakeholders may not be possible, especially in situations involving unanticipated environmental or societal challenges.

In the past, supplemental channels such as print ads, brochures, and press releases were used to compensate for the delay in distributing corporate social responsibility information via annual reports (Zeghal & Ahmed, 1990). Nevertheless, a company's CSR communication may unintentionally lose its impact due to the oversimplification of messaging in press releases and commercials, which is sometimes required to get the attention of the public. Furthermore, it is unlikely that businesses who disclose data via non-annual reporting channels do so with the intention of promoting societal welfare. A content study of CSR messages that were released in magazine advertising in 1967, 1972, 1975, 1977, and 1984 was done by Lill et al.

(1986). They discovered that rather than focusing more on public services goals, these communications often served commercial purposes.

Beacon: Illuminating Web 1.0 Era CSR Communication

Since the introduction of online 1.0 in the 1990s, corporate CSR discourse has evolved from mostly depending on annual reports to being augmented by stand-alone report releases and online disclosures, with an annual report release serving as the major source of information. Furthermore, the use of Web 1.0 technology has had a significant impact on the promotion and distribution of CSR. The influence of online 1.0 on CSR disclosure will be examined in the next section from the standpoints of online disclosures and standalone CSR reports.

As previously indicated, prior to Web 1.0, businesses could only use yearly reports to share their CSR performance and activities with certain stakeholder groups. However, the widespread use of the Internet has facilitated stakeholder communication (Gowthorpe & Amat, 1999; Thornburg, 1995) and increased public awareness of environmental responsibility and corporate social responsibility (CSR). This has encouraged a wider range of people to participate in CSR talks and walks, including governments, social organizations, and consumers (Esrock & Leichty, 1998).

In addition to raising awareness of corporate social responsibility (CSR), the widespread use of Web 1.0 technology has also compelled businesses to assess how easily accessible CSR information is to a wider range of stakeholder groups. As a result, businesses now understand that the broad range of demands of their audience cannot be satisfied by the conventional disclosures, which are often brief in annual reports. Companies were forced to provide more comprehensive and varied CSR content under Web 1.0 in order to meet the needs of different audiences.

Moreover, the corporation has exclusive control over corporate disclosure in annual reports. According to Parker (1982), the corporate monopoly on CSR information is broken by the development of Internet technology. Through the Internet, stakeholders may get information on the social and environmental performance of suppliers, rivals, partners, and the firms themselves. Bypassing obstacles put up by businesses, this information flow allows stakeholders to confirm the veracity and correctness of the data. Consequently, Web 1.0 technology promotes more openness, which in turn strengthens stakeholder confidence in the data that companies publish on non-annual reporting platforms.

Emergence: Independent CSR Reporting's Ascent

Taking into account the history mentioned above, the first stand-alone report on CSR data was released in 1989 (Kolk, 2004). The "Sustainability Report" was the name given to this. Compared to standard yearly reports, standalone reports provide a more thorough and in-depth presentation of CSR information. A broad variety of themes are covered, including health management, sustainability, local community concerns, air and water pollution, employee involvement, and resource utilization.

Furthermore, with the introduction of Web 1.0 technology, stand-alone reports have not only expanded the amount of information provided but also the number of organizations participating in the disclosure of these issues (KPMG, 1997).The rise of stand-alone reports more than makes up for the disclosure of CSR information that is lacking in conventional annual reports. It also makes up for the amount and depth of CSR information that is dispersed across yearly reports.

Change: New Channels for Online CSR Communication

More significantly, the introduction of Web 1.0 technology has a direct impact on the dissemination of CSR information, in addition to indirectly supporting full disclosure of CSR. The Internet was only a static website at this time, devoid of user interactions, even though Web 1.0 was simply the beginning of Internet growth compared to the highly dynamic Web 2.0 stage today. However, these static webpages gave businesses a new platform to showcase their commercial successes and encouraged them to focus on areas other than profit, such social, environmental, and sustainable development, which was of interest to Internet users.

Businesses may now choose to disclose CSR information on their own websites, moving away from traditional print and distribution routes for CSR reports and towards online disclosure. This significant shift does more than only broadening the audience—which in the conventional reporting format was mostly limited in geography and made up of certain stakeholder groups. It eliminates the geographical and temporal limitations present in the earlier reporting format. Companies may now update and publish their CSR reports from anywhere at any time, making sure that their disclosures in the information age are timely and flexible.

Duality: Web 1.0 CSR Disclosure's Opportunities and Challenges

Increased Openness

One prominent characteristic of the Web 1.0 era is transparency, particularly in CSR disclosure. The complexity and difficulty of accessing information have changed subversively with the emergence of Web 1.0. The flow of CSR information is regulated and managed by businesses and information publishers in the context of CSR disclosure, which is dominated by disclosure via annual reports and conventional media (Parker, 1982). The "information black box" was cracked by the widespread use of Internet technology, and businesses no longer have as much control over the flow of information (Sun & Bhattacherjee, 2014).

The public now has access to social and environmental data, and businesses now pay a hefty price for information blocking and concealment (Gajewski & Li, 2015). According to García-Sánchez and Noguera-Gámez (2017), stakeholders may now actively influence corporate disclosure policy via the use of Internet platforms. If a company claims to have excellent environmental standards, for instance, investors, customers, and supervisors may more readily obtain the related data released by the company in other sources via the Internet and confirm the accuracy of the claim.

Therefore, it is evident that Web 1.0 was essential in improving corporate openness. Businesses must adjust to the growing democratization of information in this era by viewing transparency as a duty as well as a way to deepen relationships with stakeholders. They must also always strive for timeliness, accuracy, and truthfulness when disclosing information.

The Advent of Online Responsibility

Internet users are no longer constrained by time or geography, in contrast to conventional stakeholder groupings that developed with Web 1.0. This group's formation contradicts the initial framework that corporations used to identify stakeholders, which included priorities including urgency, power, and legitimacy (Ryan & Schneider, 2003). This indicates that when disclosing CSR information, businesses must provide a more thorough catering to the demands of non-traditional stakeholder groups (Sriramesh et al., 2013). In the meanwhile, the number of this group has increased geometrically due to the quick adoption of Web 1.0 technology. The views of this group have been amplified and aggregated as a result of the rise in quantity, and this has created an unstoppable force for accountability (Neu et al., 2019). Due to this authority, businesses must not only comply with the group's disclosure requirements when releasing corporate social responsibility (CSR) information, but also recognize and take into account the group's voice.

Developing a Global Corporate Social Responsibility Branding Approach

The Internet age has broken down time and space barriers, as was highlighted many times in the preceding section. This means that the influence of a company's social and environmental performance is no longer restricted to the company's internal and particular stakeholder groups (Palazzo et al., 2020). Businesses may spread these CSR walks over nations and regions via the Internet, developing a global brand impact on social and environmental issues. The CSR brand may expand quickly inside the online user community as a result of the rise in Internet users, surpassing the conventional word-of-mouth effect and resulting in larger image diffusion.

Questions About the Veracity of the Data

However, the Internet also has the intrinsic issue of the validity of information in conventional media (Zhang et al., 2015). The introduction of Web 1.0 technology has realized a communication impact that cannot be accomplished by traditional media. Although Internet technology has made it easier to access and verify information in traditional media, it is still not a foolproof solution to the issue of under- and misreporting of information. Both Internet platforms and users are unable to judge and identify the authenticity of CSR information (Flanagin & Metzger, 2000).

REVOLUTIONISING CSR INFORMATION DISCLOSURE ON WEB 2.0

The Revolution in CSR Social Media

Web 1.0 served mostly as an information repository in the early days of the Internet, offering static web pages with little to no user interaction. During that period, content was published by organizations on the Internet for the purpose of passive consumption, making it more of a one-way street. But when the Web 2.0 era arrived, this environment saw a dramatic change. Thus, the introduction of Web 2.0 represents a significant change in the ways that information is shared, made available, and accessed on the Internet. According to Chen et al. (2011), Web 2.0 represents a dynamic and interactive online ecosystem where users actively participate in generating and sharing content. The Internet's revolutionary phase has had a significant impact on many facets of society, including corporate social responsibility (CSR) disclosure and business practices.

The emergence of the Web 2.0 age, exemplified by social media, has broadened the channels via which businesses may disseminate information on corporate social responsibility. Web 2.0 technologies include a range of interactive tools and platforms, such as blogs, wikis, social media, and websites with user-generated content. Due to the democratization of the internet, people and organizations may now cooperate, exchange information, and communicate in both directions with previously unheard-of ease (Lee et al., 2013). Since 2020, the number of CEOs with social media accounts has significantly increased, and having an online presence is more important than ever. The growing usage of mobile applications during the epidemic has further magnified this tendency. Approximately 70% of Fortune 500 CEOs have accounts on at least one of the main social media networks, such as Facebook, Instagram, Twitter, LinkedIn, or Snapchat, as of August 2022 (Mcivor, 2022).

Consequently, the Web 2.0 era has emerged as a key influence on how businesses interact with their stakeholders, especially when it comes to CSR disclosure (Figure 2). An earlier research (Basil & Erlandson, 2008) shows that business websites are increasingly using CSR. For instance, to encourage consumers to recycle old items in-store and participate in H&M's World Recycle Week sustainability campaign, the fast fashion retailer H&M created an online music video advertisement involving artists (Sutton, 2016). Disney's campaign to encourage its followers to post pictures of them wearing Mickey Mouse ears and pledge to pay $5 to the Make-A-Wish Foundation for each picture is another example (Disney, 2018). Public interest groups like the Red Cross use a variety of platforms, such as websites, blogs, Twitter, and Facebook, in addition to for-profit businesses, to promote connections. According to research by Briones et al. (2011), they place a strong emphasis on volunteer recruitment and retention, provide community updates on disaster planning and response, and interact with the media. These examples highlight social media's impact. Presently, companies mostly use their official social media accounts and the CEOs' personal accounts to disseminate information on corporate social responsibility (CSR) (Zhou et al., 2023). Consequently, the CEO—such as Tim Cook of Apple or Elon Musk of Tesla and SpaceX—or Mark Zuckerberg of Facebook—is sometimes seen as the public face of the company. Mark Zuckerberg, for instance, writes about Facebook's internal and external CSR initiatives on a regular basis. He also shared a post on starting the Chan Zuckerberg Initiative to find treatments for illnesses that affect children. Even if this is an appeal to him personally, it does show Facebook's commitment to corporate social responsibility (Wang & Huang, 2018).

Since social media and CSR development have many interconnected and complimentary links, they should operate in tandem. Businesses may discuss their CSR initiatives more openly and honestly by using social media (Dutot et al.,

2016; Yang et al., 2020). Social media may assist businesses in identifying and addressing CSR-related concerns faster, hence lowering the risk of reputational harm. This increases responsibility by making information about a company's social and environmental commitments more widely accessible, which contributes to the development of trust. Additionally, social media gives stakeholders a platform to provide recommendations, criticism, and opinions, which help businesses, improve their corporate social responsibility (CSR) programs (Briones et al, 2011; Cortado & Chalmeta, 2016; Manetti & Bellucci, 2016; Saxton et al., 2019). Businesses may satisfy social and environmental demands more effectively by optimizing their sustainability plans with the help of these recommendations (Briones et al., 2011). Furthermore, good corporate social responsibility posts on social media may increase brand recognition and cultivate client loyalty (Yan et al., 2010; Kang & Hustvedt, 2014; Jin & Phua, 2014; Dwivedi et al., 2021). Social media platforms enable businesses to communicate with customers more effectively, share CSR success stories, and engage customers in a way that aligns with the brand's essential values (Chu et al., 2020). As a result, improved engagement and deeper connections with a range of stakeholders may result from the combination of social media and corporate social responsibility.

There isn't as much research on social media and CSR disclosure as there is now, and the integrated conversation is still in its early stages. For instance, Briones et al. (2011) provide helpful advice to NGOs on how to strategically utilise social media to develop dialogic connections with stakeholders by adhering to guidelines like offering insightful information, promoting engagement, and keeping an eye on talks. But this is also restricted to nonprofit institutions. This chapter will explore how new technologies have changed stakeholder expectations, changed the dynamics of corporate communication, and modified the tactics used by businesses to convey their commitments to and CSR activities. In order to properly understand how the Web 2.0 age affects CSR disclosure, it is critical to evaluate how online communication has developed, how social media platforms have emerged, and how these factors have influenced corporate responsibility and transparency.

Figure 1. Internet technology's impact on CSR disclosure channels over the years

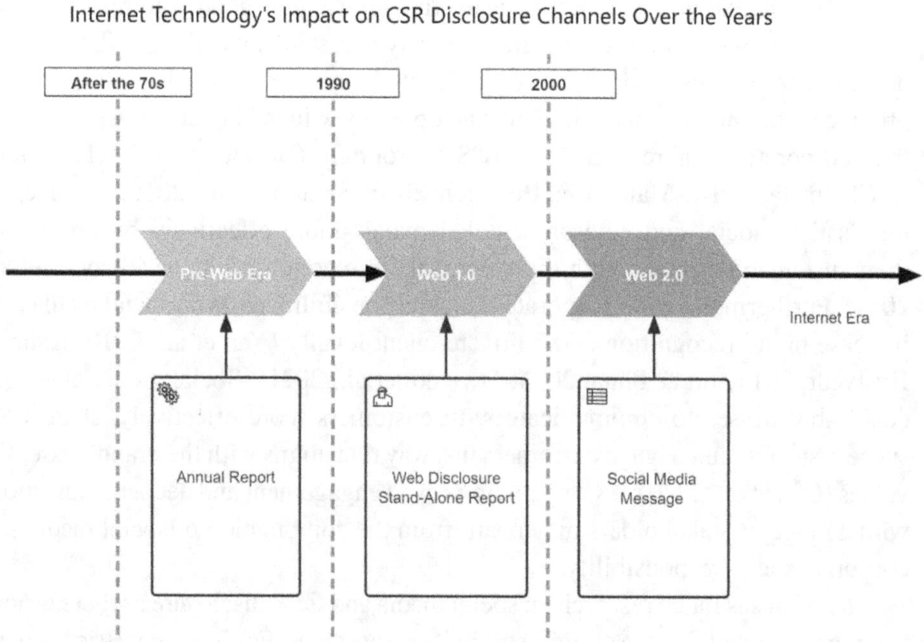

Accepting Web 2.0: Social Media's Benefits for CSR Communication

In the business world, disseminating CSR information via media platforms has been popular lately. The CEO and the company's social media accounts often work together to communicate with the company's stakeholders (Zhou et al., 2023). Social media is a more affordable approach to spread CSR information than conventional CSR reporting techniques (Etter, 2013). It provides for instant changes without the cost of reprinting and does away with the need for expensive print materials. Furthermore, since electronic word-of-mouth is often seen as more reliable than commercial advertising, media platforms are an ideal place for corporate social responsibility (CSR) activities, such as green advertising (Minton et al., 2012) companies are starting to notice this trend for a number of compelling reasons, and it has completely altered the way social media and companies interact.

Redefining Interactive Engagement

One of the most significant changes to the Web between versions 1.0 and 2.0 has been the redefining of interactive involvement. Static websites and one-way communication were the main characteristics of Web 1.0, when businesses published information and CSR reports without engaging in meaningful dialogue with their stakeholders (Brennan & Merkl-Davies, 2018). Businesses and their consumers often experienced a lack of engagement and communication as a consequence of this unidirectional strategy.

Figure 2. Social media disclosure with stakeholder(s)

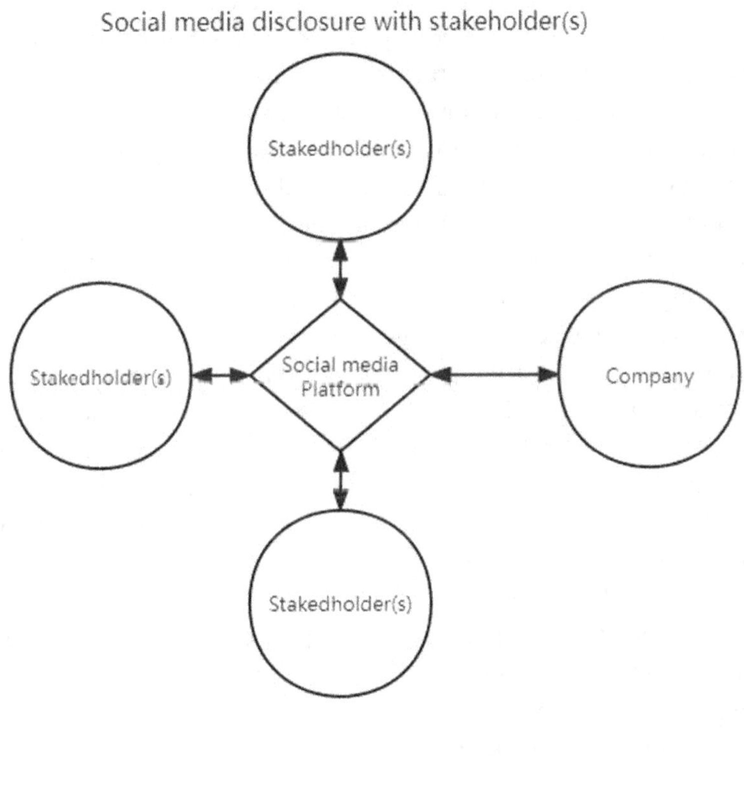

The interactive interaction environment has changed significantly since the release of Web 2.0. Blogs, social media sites, and other Web 2.0 tools have given stakeholders the ability to actively engage in conversations about CSR projects. The bidirectional communication feature of social media may improve the involvement of stakeholders (Du & Vieira, 2012, Lee et al., 2013; Zhang & Lin, 2015; Dutot et al., 2016). Now, users may co-create, share, and even remark on information about the company's CSR initiatives. Real-time dialogues and feedback loops are now possible because to the increased interactivity (Briones et al., 2011; Cortado & Chalmeta, 2016; Manetti & Bellucci, 2016; Saxton et al., 2019). According to Du & Vieira (2012), it is beneficial to use media platforms for CSR communication as they may help reduce public mistrust in CSR. According to this research, social media platforms are helpful for CSR communication because they enable stakeholders to engage in a two-way conversation by providing consumers a say in the companies' CSR initiatives.

Moreover, businesses now understand the importance of this reinterpreted involvement. They have seized the chance to hear the worries and aspirations of their stakeholders in addition to promoting their CSR initiatives. In their 2011 study, Briones et al. investigate how the American Red Cross uses social media to interact and establish relationships with important stakeholders. They discover that social media enables the Red Cross to conduct two-way discussions and exchanges with stakeholders. This promotes interaction, helps the organization obtain input, and raises awareness of its services and objectives. Businesses are now able to more successfully customize their CSR strategies, addressing particular concerns and demonstrating a genuine commitment to social and environmental responsibility thanks to this two-way communication (Chu et al., 2020). According to Men & Tsai (2016), there is a clear correlation between public involvement with the CEO and the quality of public relations reporting. Additionally, Sisson's (2017) research demonstrates that when donors engage with a nonprofit's social media pages; they are more likely to feel that the page is interactive and to contribute social media content to the organization. Zizka(2017), however, finds that social media is mostly used by the hotel sector for one-way CSR communications. This begs the concerns of whether the industry is losing out on the potential advantages of a more participatory and responsive strategy, as well as questioning their commitment to real stakeholder involvement. Therefore, even if the importance of two-way CSR communication is becoming more widely recognized, it is important to carefully evaluate the sincerity, effectiveness, and impact of these programs on resolving social and environmental problems. Businesses should actually commit to ethical practices and being receptive to the concerns of stakeholders, rather than just using this kind of communication as a front.

Instantaneous Understanding for Immediate Effect

Web 1.0's static character was replaced by Web 2.0, which ushered in a new era of real-time participation and information transmission. The transition to real-time updates has strengthened the credibility of disclosures and guaranteed the timeliness and quality of CSR information. This has allowed organizations to engage with their stakeholders more directly and effectively.

Businesses might provide real-time updates on their CSR programs and operations in the Web 2.0 age. Stakeholders are able to remain up to date on the most recent advancements and advances because to this capacity to communicate information as it happens. Real-time updates provide a dynamic and responsive approach to CSR disclosure, whether it's for the purpose of introducing a new sustainability initiative, providing live updates from CSR events, or quickly answering questions from stakeholders. Briones et al. (2011), for instance, discover via interviews that social media public relations techniques are essential and successful. The two most popular social media sites in the USA are Facebook and Twitter, which enable discussion monitoring and real-time involvement. This results in increased media attention, quicker assistance to underserved populations, and feedback to help the organization grow. This new strategy differs from the conventional Web 1.0 strategy, in which data was usually static and only updated in yearly reports.

Annual and standalone CSR reports used to be published once a year on average, which caused a delay in communicating recent accomplishments and actions. Stakeholders were often unaware of the most current CSR initiatives of the companies due to this lag between actions and reporting. Web 2.0 technologies, on the other hand, have closed this gap by enabling businesses to instantly exchange information. Because of this, stakeholders have access to real-time data, which empowers them to hold businesses responsible, make better choices, and have timely conversations regarding CSR activities.

In addition to improving openness, this focus on real-time analytics gives stakeholders the ability to directly influence corporate responsibility plans. As stakeholders see companies responding to their concerns and keeping their CSR commitments in real time, it builds confidence and trust.

User-Generated Material and Openness

User-generated material on social media platforms is a strong notion that has been presented in the context of CSR disclosure by the Web 2.0 era. An age of more dynamic and interactive communication is being ushered in by this phenomenon, which is very crucial in boosting corporate openness and improving stakeholder confidence in CSR information (Calvano, 2008; Lee et al., 2013). The emergence of social networking sites has changed the role of stakeholders from being passive consumers of information to active producers and content analysts (Dellarocas, 2003). For businesses, these factors provide both significant potential and difficulties. Developing strategic strategies to demonstrate their commitment to corporate social responsibility to stakeholders has become a top priority (Dawkins, 2005).

Because Web 2.0 material is interactive, users may question the information they come across, which encourages more accuracy and transparency (Insch, 2008). Because Web 2.0 material is interactive, users may question the information they come across, which improves process accuracy and transparency (Insch, 2008). There is no doubt that this interrogative exchange improves the application of responsibility. According to Lyon & Montgomery (2013), social media's introduction has altered how companies disclose their environmental performance, enhancing CSR communication and reducing "greenwashing" tactics. According to Lee et al. (2013), social media helps raise awareness of CSR communication by enabling internet users to openly express their thoughts without needing permission from the company. As a result, when disparities or errors are found, stakeholders have the ability to quickly address them, which encourages businesses to correct and elucidate their CSR disclosures. In addition to enhancing information quality, this iterative feedback loop guarantees that CSR reports correspond with real-world procedures. A built-in system of checks and balances provided by user-generated material aids in holding businesses responsible for their CSR pledges. There are obstacles in the way of completely using social networks for CSR communication, however. Younger people are often the target audience on social media sites, yet a large percentage of a company's stakeholders are older board members and volunteers who may not be as acquainted with these technologies. When businesses decide to use online platforms to distribute CSR information, there's a chance that some of their stakeholders—especially those who aren't familiar with social media—won't be able to access this kind of material. The reach of CSR communication initiatives may be restricted as a consequence of this digital divide, which may prevent certain demographic groups from obtaining the information. One barrier to social media use, for instance, is that it may alienate the elder generation, which makes up a sizable share of funders and volunteers. According to one respondent, using social media to develop connections is difficult as older generations are unfamiliar with the notion (Briones et al., 2011).

It is accepted that not all demographic groups can guarantee access to CSR information using either method. However, given the wider variety of potential demographic groups, it is imperative that organizations think about ways to close the access gap so that more demographic groups can get CSR information. It is essential to recognize that social media platforms provide a unique setting for more thorough and varied conversations. Through the sharing of many viewpoints and experiences, these platforms help stakeholders get a deeper and more thorough knowledge of a company's CSR initiatives. This diversity of viewpoints promotes a livelier and knowledgeable conversation, which may help with the cooperative creation of CSR plans that better suit the various demands and expectations of stakeholders. Therefore, companies may foster more inclusive and effective corporate social responsibility

(CSR) communication while also improving accountability by tackling the digital divide and using social media's inclusivity.

The Momentum: Examining Web 2.0 CSR Communication's Popularity

One method of disseminating information locally is via social media. In contrast to standalone CSR reports and Web 1.0 company websites, social media provides a deeper degree of involvement and connection. Organizations can gain from social media in a number of ways, including improved conversion rates that draw in new business, customer insights, increased brand awareness and loyalty, and real-time results through targeted advertising (Yan et al., 2010; Kang & Hustvedt, 2014; Jin & Phua, 2014; Dwivedi et al., 2021). Furthermore, businesses may accomplish more than simply marketing goals with this increased engagement (Haigh et al. 2013; Haigh & Wigley, 2015). Businesses may show their ethical and corporate citizenship side by using social media to spread messages related to CSR but unrelated to marketing. In the meanwhile, social media serves as a conduit for corporate PR, assisting businesses in promptly addressing unfavorable incidents and restoring their image (Men & Tsai, 2016). In addition to reaching out to a larger spectrum of stakeholders, this interaction satisfies customers' demands for more information and openness from businesses. Therefore, social media creates a win-win situation by meeting the requirements of social media users for more information and engagement as well as the needs of businesses themselves.

Although the preceding conversation focused on the possibility of older people or those who are not as comfortable with social media ideas being left out when CSR information is disclosed on these platforms, it is important to note that older folks are using social networking much more now. According to Madden (2010), the proportion of older individuals using social media more than doubled from 22% to 42% in 2009. This pattern shows that members of this group are becoming more willing to use social media, which implies that their interaction with these sites is increasing. As a result, word-of-mouth communication has found a critical platform in the Internet (Berthon et al., 2012; Minton et al., 2012). Companies that participate in CSR initiatives stand to gain a number of benefits, such as improved word-of-mouth, business reputation, trust, and brand image (Sen & Bhattacharya, 2001; Hur et al. 2014; Du et al., 2011; Plewa et al., 2015 and Vo et al., 2019). Before making a purchase, people would consult online reviews (Chu & Kim, 2011). Empirical research by Bickart & Schindler (2001) demonstrates that individuals are more willing to believe opinions expressed by others online than by word-of-mouth in person. Social media's immediate nature fits in well with the modern digital age's need for quick access to CSR news and information.

Furthermore, stakeholders—from investors to customers—now want greater openness from companies. Social media gives businesses the opportunity to openly display their CSR initiatives, fostering audience trust and goodwill. According to one research (Kang & Hustvedt, 2014), commercials with a clear CSR message enhance customers' readiness to buy a specific brand. This study looks at the influence of firms' CSR activities on consumer purchases.

Lastly, social media offers businesses the huge benefit of contacting billions of people worldwide, which enables them to reach a wide range of audiences and so increase the effect of their corporate social responsibility programs. Social media is an appealing medium for international CSR messaging because of its reach, which is unrestricted by region or demography. However, it's important to emphasize that social media sharing of CSR content does not always imply its veracity and validity. Social media has a variety of CSR information, but it is not all the same. It is challenging to compare the CSR actions of various organizations due to the variability and potential for qualitative or quantitative data. Even while social media gives a larger audience more access to CSR information, businesses and stakeholders must nevertheless carefully understand and access this information to guarantee accuracy and reliability.

SUGGESTIONS AND SOLUTIONS

Internet technology is essential to the way business communication is changing. It has caused a great deal of change in how companies manage and approach CSR disclosure. But there are difficulties with this transition. Even if technology has resulted in a lot of great changes, there are still some obstacles that need to be addressed:

Genuineness

As previously said, one of the public's main concerns is the veracity of the information. This chapter makes the suggestion that businesses use an impartial third party to assess their social and environmental policies and reports. This would increase public confidence in the company while also enhancing the information's validity. Furthermore, it is possible to motivate various stakeholders to take part in the dissemination of information in order to motivate the general public to keep an eye on the company's CSR practices. Lastly, businesses may set up a social media feedback system.

Accountability in Cyberspace

Cyber Accountability may have an impact on businesses' standard CSR procedures. The public may now easily gather and have talks on certain topics thanks to the growth of social media platforms, and these exchanges are increasingly becoming a force for social accountability (Colleoni, 2013). Corporate CSR disclosure may also be impacted by this accountability; businesses may choose to implement certain CSR initiatives and disclosure strategies in order to satisfy demands for responsibility from certain constituencies. However, certain stakeholders could be overlooked as a consequence of this deliberate approach.

This chapter makes the case that businesses may provide avenues for communication with stakeholders outside social media. For example, webinars, virtual gatherings, emails, and more means of interacting with interested parties. Organizations should also think about sharing and debating the outcomes of their recurring evaluations of their CSR procedures with relevant parties. This will make it possible for the company to identify and fix any shortcomings in its CSR procedures.

Inclinations for Communicating CSR

Businesses are using the development of internet technologies to increase the channels for CSR disclosure. Businesses may lessen disclosure in annual reports by concentrating on and stressing social media disclosure. But as was already noted, an entity's annual report is a formal, instrumental document that is an official record of the company. It has a crucial reference for major stakeholders, such as investors. It is possible to interpret the selective transfer and publication of CSR data via unofficial channels as an effort to reduce the level of government and exchange oversight.

Concerns with CSR disclosure are discussed in this chapter in light of the changes to the Internet. First and foremost, businesses must actively participate in CSR activities and communications. This chapter concludes that as Internet technology advances, information transparency and openness will inevitably become more prevalent. This suggests that corporations will have more difficulties in managing and influencing social and environmental data. Second, businesses must take a wider range of stakeholders' interests into account. The process of moving from Web 1.0 to Web 2.0 involves more people participating in the information exchange, which means businesses must constantly identify new stakeholders and cater to the needs of more defined stakeholder groups. Lastly, businesses must act honestly while implementing socially and ecologically conscious practices. While the internet has improved corporate communication and transparency, it has not been able to directly influence corporate environmental and social practices.

CONCLUSION

This chapter evaluates how CSR disclosure and communication have changed in the context of Internet technology. It also thoroughly examines the possible causes of this change, the opportunities and difficulties it presents, and the perspectives of stakeholders and businesses. Since its inception in the late 20th century, internet technology has undergone multiple iterations and advancements (Hafner, 1998). The introduction of Web 1.0 has expedited the spread of information, dismantling the barriers to it that were previously created by distances in time and space (Castells, 2003). Additionally, this shift undermined the "Information Control" framework established by corporations and conventional media, empowering Internet users to take the initiative to find and filter CSR content (Abelson, Ledeen, & Lewis, 2008). In terms of information interaction, the transition of Internet technology from Web 1.0 to Web 2.0 is a significant milestone. Social media users share and debate corporate social and environmental information, which greatly influences how businesses practice corporate social responsibility (CSR) in action as opposed to merely talking about it.

Business practices: Prior to Web 1.0, organizations began to consider how to convey and display corporate social responsibility (CSR) information. They dispersed this information by publishing it in annual reports for their company. Additionally, to customize replies to the social and environmental challenges or scandals faced by firms, print ads, press releases, and newspapers were used. The section names "Dawn" and "Twilight" suggest that although society and businesses have started to pay attention to corporate social and environmental concerns, there is still a lack of acknowledgement for CSR practices and information sharing. There are still significant gaps in CSR disclosure and implementation.

A catalyst is required to propel the change in CSR speak and walk, and Web 1.0 acts as a "beacon" to accelerate the public and corporate community's adoption of CSR awareness. Businesses started releasing stand-alone reports to address their social and environmental performance in a methodical and thorough manner. The public and companies may easily acquire, comprehend, and display corporate social responsibility (CSR) information using Web 1.0 static web pages, instead than relying on the more complex and laborious means of acquiring company annual reports. The foundation for increasing public and business understanding of social and environmental responsibility was established by Web 1.0. With the advent of Web 2.0, social media has allowed businesses and the general public to communicate and have debates about CSR information. It's clear that business CSR activities and communication have been greatly influenced by the development of internet technologies.

FUTURE DIRECTIONS FOR RESEARCH

The growth of CSR disclosure in relation to the advancement of Internet technology is critically discussed in this chapter. Future studies can concentrate on if and how Internet technologies influence business social and environmental practices. They might also try to explore and investigate whether corporate social responsibility (CSR) practices are consistent with the advancement of Internet technology.

REFERENCES

Abbott, W. F., & Monsen, R. J. (1979). On the Measurement of Corporate Social Responsibility: Self-Reported Disclosures as a Method of Measuring Corporate Social Involvement. *Academy of Management Journal*, 22(3), 501–515. 10.2307/255740

Abelson, H., Ledeen, K., & Lewis, H. (2012). *Blown to bits: your life, liberty, and happiness after the digital explosion*. Addison-Wesley Professional.

Basil, D. Z., & Erlandson, J. (2008). Corporate social responsibility website representations: A longitudinal study of internal and external self-presentations. *Journal of Marketing Communications*, 14(2), 125–137. 10.1080/13527260701858497

Berthon, P. R., Pitt, L. F., Plangger, K., & Shapiro, D. (2012). Marketing meets Web 2.0, social media, and creative consumers: Implications for international marketing strategy. *Business Horizons*, 55(3), 261–271. 10.1016/j.bushor.2012.01.007

Brammer, S., Millington, A., & Rayton, B. (2007). The contribution of corporate social responsibility to organizational commitment. *International Journal of Human Resource Management*, 18(10), 1701–1719. 10.1080/09585190701570866

Brennan, N. M., & Merkl-Davies, D. M. (2018). Do firms effectively communicate with financial stakeholders? A conceptual model of corporate communication in a capital market context. *Accounting and Business Research*, 48(5), 553–577. 10.1080/00014788.2018.1470143

Briones, R. L., Kuch, B., Liu, B. F., & Jin, Y. (2011). Keeping up with the digital age: How the American Red Cross uses social media to build relationships. *Public Relations Review*, 37(1), 37–43. 10.1016/j.pubrev.2010.12.006

Brunton, M., Eweje, G., & Taskin, N. (2017). Communicating corporate social responsibility to internal stakeholders: Walking the walk or just talking the talk? *Business Strategy and the Environment*, 26(1), 31–48. 10.1002/bse.1889

Calvano, L. (2008). Multinational corporations and local communities: A critical analysis of conflict. *Journal of Business Ethics*, 82(4), 793–805. 10.1007/s10551-007-9593-z

Castells, M. (2002). *The Internet galaxy: Reflections on the Internet, business, and society*. Oxford University Press. 10.1093/acprof:oso/9780199255771.001.0001

Chen, Y., Fay, S., & Wang, Q. (2011). The role of marketing in social media: How online consumer reviews evolve. *Journal of Interactive Marketing*, 25(2), 85–94. 10.1016/j.intmar.2011.01.003

Chu, S. C., Chen, H. T., & Gan, C. (2020). Consumers' engagement with corporate social responsibility (CSR) communication in social media: Evidence from China and the United States. *Journal of Business Research*, 110, 260–271. 10.1016/j.jbusres.2020.01.036

Chu, S. C., & Kim, Y. (2011). Determinants of consumer engagement in electronic word-of-mouth (eWOM) in social networking sites. *International Journal of Advertising*, 30(1), 47–75. 10.2501/IJA-30-1-047-075

Colleoni, E. (2013). CSR communication strategies for organizational legitimacy in social media. *Corporate Communications*, 18(2), 228–248. 10.1108/13563281311319508

Colucci, M., Tuan, A., & Visentin, M. (2020). An empirical investigation of the drivers of CSR talk and walk in the fashion industry. *Journal of Cleaner Production*, 248, 119200. 10.1016/j.jclepro.2019.119200

Cortado, F. J., & Chalmeta, R. (2016). Use of social networks as a CSR communication tool. *Cogent business & management*, *3*(1), 1187783.

Courtis, J. K. (1986). An investigation into annual report readability and corporate risk-return relationships. *Accounting and Business Research*, 16(64), 285–294. 10.1080/00014788.1986.9729329

David, D. T. (1995). Welcome to the communication age. *Internet Research*, 5(1), 64–70. 10.1108/10662249510084471

Dawkins, J. (2005). Corporate responsibility: The communication challenge. *Journal of Communication Management (London)*, 9(2), 108–119. 10.1108/13632540510621362

Dellarocas, C. (2003). The digitization of word of mouth: Promise and challenges of online feedback mechanisms. *Management Science*, 49(10), 1407–1424. 10.1287/mnsc.49.10.1407.17308

Disney. (2018). *The Walt Disney Company and Make-A-Wish® Invite Fans to "Share Your Ears" to Help Grant Wishes in Celebration of 90 Years of Mickey Mouse*. Disney. https://www.businesswire.com/news/home/20181104005033/en/The-Walt-Disney-Company-and-Make-A-Wish%C2%AE-Invite-Fans-to-%E2%80%9CShare-Your-Ears%E2%80%9D-to-Help-Grant-Wishes-in-Celebration-of-90-Years-of-Mickey-Mouse

Du, S., Bhattacharya, C. B., & Sen, S. (2011). Corporate social responsibility and competitive advantage: Overcoming the trust barrier. *Management Science*, 57(9), 1528–1545. 10.1287/mnsc.1110.1403

Du, S., & Vieira, E. T.Jr. (2012). Striving for legitimacy through corporate social responsibility: Insights from oil companies. *Journal of Business Ethics*, 110(4), 413–427. 10.1007/s10551-012-1490-4

Dutot, V., Lacalle Galvez, E., & Versailles, D. W. (2016). CSR communications strategies through social media and influence on e-reputation: An exploratory study. *Management Decision*, 54(2), 363–389. 10.1108/MD-01-2015-0015

Dwivedi, Y. K., Ismagilova, E., Hughes, D. L., Carlson, J., Filieri, R., Jacobson, J., Jain, V., Karjaluoto, H., Kefi, H., Krishen, A. S., Kumar, V., Rahman, M. M., Raman, R., Rauschnabel, P. A., Rowley, J., Salo, J., Tran, G. A., & Wang, Y. (2021). Setting the future of digital and social media marketing research: Perspectives and research propositions. *International Journal of Information Management*, 59, 102168. 10.1016/j.ijinfomgt.2020.102168

Esrock, S. L., & Leichty, G. B. (1998). Social responsibility and corporate web pages: Self-presentation or agenda-setting? *Public Relations Review*, 24(3), 305–319. 10.1016/S0363-8111(99)80142-8

Etter, M. (2013). Reasons for low levels of interactivity:(Non-) interactive CSR communication in Twitter. *Public Relations Review*, 39(5), 606–608. 10.1016/j.pubrev.2013.06.003

Flanagin, A. J., & Metzger, M. J. (2000). Perceptions of Internet information credibility. *Journalism & Mass Communication Quarterly*, 77(3), 515–540. 10.1177/107769900007700304

Freeman, R. E. (1984). *Strategic management: A stokcholder approach*. Pitman.

Gajewski, J. F., & Li, L. (2015). Can Internet-based disclosure reduce information asymmetry? *Advances in Accounting*, 31(1), 115–124. 10.1016/j.adiac.2015.03.013

García-Sánchez, I. M., & Noguera-Gámez, L. (2017). Integrated reporting and stakeholder engagement: The effect on information asymmetry. *Corporate Social Responsibility and Environmental Management*, 24(5), 395–413. 10.1002/csr.1415

Gowthorpe, C., & Amat, O. (1999). External reporting of accounting and financial information via the Internet in Spain. *European Accounting Review*, 8(2), 365–371. 10.1080/096381899336096

Gray, R., Kouhy, R., & Lavers, S. (1995). Corporate social and environmental reporting: A review of the literature and a longitudinal study of UK disclosure. *Accounting, Auditing & Accountability Journal*, 8(2), 47–77. 10.1108/09513579510146996

Gray, R., Owen, D., & Maunders, K. (1988). Corporate social reporting: Emerging trends in accountability and the social contract. *Accounting, Auditing & Accountability Journal*, 1(1), 6–20. 10.1108/EUM0000000004617

Hafner, K., & Lyon, M. (1998). *Where wizards stay up late: The origins of the Internet*. Simon and Schuster.

Haigh, M. M., Brubaker, P., & Whiteside, E. (2013). Facebook: Examining the information presented and its impact on stakeholders. *Corporate Communications*, 18(1), 52–69. 10.1108/13563281311294128

Haigh, M. M., & Wigley, S. (2015). Examining the impact of negative, user-generated content on stakeholders. *Corporate Communications*, 20(1), 63–75. 10.1108/CCIJ-02-2013-0010

Haniffa, R. M., & Cooke, T. E. (2005). The impact of culture and governance on corporate social reporting. *Journal of Accounting and Public Policy*, 24(5), 391–430. 10.1016/j.jaccpubpol.2005.06.001

Hur, W. M., Kim, H., & Woo, J. (2014). How CSR leads to corporate brand equity: Mediating mechanisms of corporate brand credibility and reputation. *Journal of Business Ethics*, 125(1), 75–86. 10.1007/s10551-013-1910-0

Insch, A. (2008). Online communication of Corporate Environmental Citizenship: A study of New Zealand's electricity and gas retailers. *Journal of Marketing Communications*, 14(2), 139–153. 10.1080/13527260701858505

Iqbal Khadaroo, M. (2005). Business reporting on the internet in Malaysia and Singapore: A comparative study. *Corporate Communications*, 10(1), 58–68. 10.1108/13563280510578204

Jin, S. A. A., & Phua, J. (2014). Following celebrities' tweets about brands: The impact of twitter-based electronic word-of-mouth on consumers' source credibility perception, buying intention, and social identification with celebrities. *Journal of Advertising*, 43(2), 181–195. 10.1080/00913367.2013.827606

Kallio, T. J. (2007). Taboos in corporate social responsibility discourse. *Journal of Business Ethics*, 74(2), 165–175. 10.1007/s10551-006-9227-x

Kang, J., & Hustvedt, G. (2014). Building trust between consumers and corporations: The role of consumer perceptions of transparency and social responsibility. *Journal of Business Ethics*, 125(2), 253–265. 10.1007/s10551-013-1916-7

Kolk, A. (2004). A decade of sustainability reporting: Developments and significance. *International Journal of Environment and Sustainable Development*, 3(1), 51–64. 10.1504/IJESD.2004.004688

KPMG. (1997). *KPMG International survey of environmental reporting 1999*. KPMG. https://www.researchgate.net/publication/254796996_KPMG_International_survey_of_environmental_reporting_1999

Lee, H. H. M., Van Dolen, W., & Kolk, A. (2013). On the role of social media in the 'responsible' food business: Blogger buzz on health and obesity issues. *Journal of Business Ethics*, 118(4), 695–707. 10.1007/s10551-013-1955-0

Leung, D., Law, R., Van Hoof, H., & Buhalis, D. (2013). Social media in tourism and hospitality: A literature review. *Journal of Travel & Tourism Marketing*, 30(1-2), 3–22. 10.1080/10548408.2013.750919

Lill, D., Gross, C., & Peterson, R. (1986). The inclusion of social-responsibility themes by magazine advertisers: A longitudinal study. *Journal of Advertising*, 15(2), 35–41. 10.1080/00913367.1986.10673003

Lomborg, B. (2003). *The skeptical environmentalist: measuring the real state of the world* (Vol. 1). Cambridge University Press.

Louwers, T., Pasewark, W. R., & Typpo, E. W. (1996). The Internet: Changing the way corporations tell their story. *The CPA Journal*, 66(11), 24.

Lyon, T. P., & Montgomery, A. W. (2013). Tweetjacked: The impact of social media on corporate greenwash. *Journal of Business Ethics*, 118(4), 747–757. 10.1007/s10551-013-1958-x

Madden, M. (2010). *Older adults and social media*. PewInternet and American Life Project.

Manetti, G., & Bellucci, M. (2016). The use of social media for engaging stakeholders in sustainability reporting. *Accounting, Auditing & Accountability Journal*, 29(6), 985–1011. 10.1108/AAAJ-08-2014-1797

Manheim, J. B., & Pratt, C. B. (1986). Communicating corporate social responsibility. *Public Relations Review*, 12(2), 9–18. 10.1016/S0363-8111(86)80022-4

Mcivor, M. (2022). *How Many Fortune 500 CEOs are on Social Media in 2022?* Influential Executive. https://influentialexecutive.com/how-many-fortune-500-ceos-social-media-2022/

Men, L. R., & Tsai, W. H. S. (2016). Public engagement with CEOs on social media: Motivations and relational outcomes. *Public Relations Review*, 42(5), 932–942. 10.1016/j.pubrev.2016.08.001

Minton, E., Lee, C., Orth, U., Kim, C. H., & Kahle, L. (2012). Sustainable marketing and social media: A cross-country analysis of motives for sustainable behaviors. *Journal of Advertising*, 41(4), 69–84. 10.1080/00913367.2012.10672458

Neu, D., Saxton, G., Rahaman, A., & Everett, J. (2019). Twitter and social accountability: Reactions to the Panama Papers. *Critical Perspectives on Accounting*, 61, 38–53. 10.1016/j.cpa.2019.04.003

Palazzo, M., Vollero, A., & Siano, A. (2020). From strategic corporate social responsibility to value creation: An analysis of corporate website communication in the banking sector. *International Journal of Bank Marketing*, 38(7), 1529–1552. 10.1108/IJBM-04-2020-0168

Parker, L. D. (1982). Corporate annual reporting: A mass communication perspective. *Accounting and Business Research*, 12(48), 279–286. 10.1080/00014788.1982.9728820

Plewa, C., Conduit, J., Quester, P. G., & Johnson, C. (2015). The impact of corporate volunteering on CSR image: A consumer perspective. *Journal of Business Ethics*, 127(3), 643–659. 10.1007/s10551-014-2066-2

Saxton, G. D., Gómez, L., Ngoh, Z., Lin, Y. P., & Dietrich, S. (2019). Do CSR messages resonate? Examining public reactions to firms' CSR efforts on social media. *Journal of Business Ethics*, 155(2), 359–377. 10.1007/s10551-017-3464-z

Sen, S., & Bhattacharya, C. B. (2001). Does doing good always lead to doing better? Consumer reactions to corporate social responsibility. *JMR, Journal of Marketing Research*, 38(2), 225–243. 10.1509/jmkr.38.2.225.18838

Sisson, D. C. (2017). Control mutuality, social media, and organization-public relationships: A study of local animal welfare organizations' donors. *Public Relations Review*, 43(1), 179–189. 10.1016/j.pubrev.2016.10.007

Sriramesh, K., Rivera-Sánchez, M., & Soriano, C. (2013). Websites for stakeholder relations by corporations and non-profits: A time-lag study in Singapore. *Journal of Communication Management (London)*, 17(2), 122–139. 10.1108/13632541311318738

Sun, Y., & Bhattacherjee, A. (2014). Looking inside the "IT black box": Technological effects on IT usage. *Journal of Computer Information Systems*, 54(2), 1–15. 10.1080/08874417.2014.11645681

Sutton, J. (2016). *Why Social Media and Sustainability Should Go Hand in Hand.* Triple Pundit. https://www.triplepundit.com/2016/06/social-mediasustainability-go-hand-hand/

Tilt, C. A. (1994). The Influence of External Pressure Groups on Corporate Social Disclosure: Some Empirical Evidence. *Accounting, Auditing & Accountability Journal*, 7(4), 47–72. 10.1108/09513579410069849

Trevor, D. W., & Geoffrey, R. F. (2000). Corporate environmental reporting. A test of legitimacy theory. *Accounting, Auditing & Accountability Journal*, 13(1), 10–26. 10.1108/09513570010316126

Vo, T. T., Xiao, X., & Ho, S. Y. (2019). How does corporate social responsibility engagement influence word of mouth on Twitter? Evidence from the airline industry. *Journal of Business Ethics*, 157(2), 525–542. 10.1007/s10551-017-3679-z

Wang, R., & Huang, Y. (2018). Communicating corporate social responsibility (CSR) on social media: How do message source and types of CSR messages influence stakeholders' perceptions? *Corporate Communications*, 23(3), 326–341. 10.1108/CCIJ-07-2017-0067

Wickert, C., Scherer, A. G., & Spence, L. J. (2016). Walking and Talking Corporate Social Responsibility: Implications of Firm Size and Organizational Cost. *Journal of Management Studies*, 53(7), 1169–1196. 10.1111/joms.12209

Wilmshurst, T. D., & Frost, G. R. (2000). Corporate environmental reporting: A test of legitimacy theory. *Accounting, Auditing & Accountability Journal*, 13(1), 10–26. 10.1108/09513570010316126

Yan, R. N., Ogle, J. P., & Hyllegard, K. H. (2010). The impact of message appeal and message source on Gen Y consumers' attitudes and purchase intentions toward American Apparel. *Journal of Marketing Communications*, 16(4), 203–224. 10.1080/13527260902863221

Yang, J., Basile, K., & Letourneau, O. (2020). The impact of social media platform selection on effectively communicating about corporate social responsibility. *Journal of Marketing Communications*, 26(1), 65–87. 10.1080/13527266.2018.1500932

Zeghal, D., & Ahmed, S. A. (1990). Comparison of social responsibility information disclosure media used by Canadian firms. *Accounting, Auditing & Accountability Journal*, *3*(1), 0-0.

Zhang, C. B., & Lin, Y. H. (2015). Exploring interactive communication using social media. *Service Industries Journal*, 35(11-12), 670–693. 10.1080/02642069.2015.1064396

Zhang, Z., Zhang, Z., & Li, H. (2015). Predictors of the authenticity of Internet health rumours. *Health Information and Libraries Journal*, 32(3), 195–205. 10.1111/hir.1211526268517

Zizka, L. (2017). The (mis) use of social media to communicate CSR in hospitality: Increasing stakeholders' (dis) engagement through social media. *Journal of Hospitality and Tourism Technology*, 8(1), 73–86. 10.1108/JHTT-07-2016-0037

Chapter 8
Technology's Role in Sustainable Urban Development in Smart Cities

Hemanth Kumar S.
https://orcid.org/0000-0003-2490-1690
Jain University, India

Prabha Kiran
School of Business and Economics, Westminster International University in Tashkent, Uzbekistan

S. Mahalakshmi
https://orcid.org/0000-0002-2611-0780
Jain University, India

Dinesh Nilkant
Jain University, India

Ananthа Subramanya Iyer K. N.
https://orcid.org/0000-0002-9517-6687
Jain University, India

ABSTRACT

The chapter delves into smart cities, exploring their pivotal role in eco-friendly urban development. Utilizing information and communication technology (ICT), smart cities address urban challenges, enhance quality of life, and champion sustainability. The integration of IoT technology and green practices facilitates real-time data

DOI: 10.4018/979-8-3693-3238-2.ch008

collection, green innovation, and eco-friendly urban development. Technological advancements, spanning renewable energy integration to circular economy solutions, propel environmental sustainability. Sustainable mobility solutions, energy management, and effective environmental monitoring contribute to smart and sustainable urban environments. Citizen engagement, crucial for success, requires inclusive planning and careful technology platform consideration. Challenges in implementing smart city technologies encompass ICT infrastructure, regulations, community participation, costs, and data privacy.

INTRODUCTION

Rapid urbanization presents a complex challenge for the 21st century. Cities are growing denser, straining existing infrastructure, and contributing significantly to global environmental concerns (United Nations, 2018). In response, the concept of "smart cities" has emerged, leveraging technology to address these challenges and improve the overall well-being of urban residents.

Defining Smart and Sustainable Cities

A smart city can be broadly defined as an urban area that utilizes information and communication technology (ICT) to enhance its efficiency, quality of life, and environmental sustainability (Kurniawan & Pamudji, 2023). This focus on sustainability differentiates smart cities from traditional technology-driven urban development. Sustainable urban development aims to meet the needs of the present without compromising the ability of future generations to meet their own needs (WCED, 1987). In the context of smart cities, this translates to utilizing technology for solutions that are not only efficient but also environmentally responsible.

The Role of Technology in Smart Cities

A core component of smart cities is the Internet of Things (IoT), a network of interconnected devices embedded with sensors that collect real-time data (Bashirpour et al., 2023). This data can be used for various purposes, including optimizing traffic flow, monitoring energy consumption in buildings, and tracking environmental conditions (Abd El-mawla & Badawy, 2023). For instance, smart grids utilize IoT technology to manage energy distribution in a more efficient and sustainable manner (Bashirpour et al., 2023).

Green Technologies and Public Participation

Smart cities also play a crucial role in promoting green technologies and fostering sustainable practices. This includes implementing eco-friendly infrastructure, encouraging renewable energy sources, and developing solutions for waste management (Bashirpour et al., 2023). However, achieving these goals requires not just technological advancements but also active public participation.

Several studies highlight the importance of **digital platforms** that facilitate public engagement, consumer input, and collaborative urban planning (e.g., [platforms for citizen participation in smart cities ON ScienceDirect sciencedirect.com]). These platforms can take various forms, including online forums, citizen science initiatives, and mobile applications. For example, some cities have implemented platforms that allow residents to report environmental concerns, participate in surveys about sustainability initiatives, and even co-create solutions with city officials (Hollander et al., 2020).

Research is ongoing to identify the most effective platforms and technologies for fostering public participation in smart city initiatives. Further studies are needed to explore the impact of these platforms on citizen engagement, decision-making processes, and ultimately, the success of sustainable urban development projects (Boel et al., 2020).

By incorporating citizen voices into decision-making processes, smart cities can ensure that technological solutions are not only efficient but also meet the needs and aspirations of their residents. **Case studies** documenting successful examples of public participation in smart city initiatives can provide valuable insights for other cities seeking to replicate these achievements (Marvin et al., 2018).

The Road Ahead: Smart Green Cities

The convergence of smart city initiatives with a focus on environmental sustainability paves the way for the development of "smart green cities" (Bashirpour et al., 2023). These cities prioritize the harmonious integration of technological advancements with ecological preservation. By fostering innovation in both areas, smart green cities offer a promising path towards a more sustainable and livable urban future (Kesic, 2023). This revised introduction provides a more comprehensive background on smart and sustainable cities, incorporating relevant citations in APA style. It also highlights the importance of public participation and the emerging concept of smart green cities. Further research is recommended to explore specific platforms and technologies for public engagement and successful case studies of citizen participation in smart city initiatives. In summary, smart cities play a pivotal role in tackling urban challenges and advancing sustainable development (Kesic, 2023).

ECO-FRIENDLY URBAN DEVELOPMENT: LEVERAGING TECHNOLOGY FOR SUSTAINABILITY

Within the context of environmental sustainability, eco-friendly urban development has gained significant traction (Kurniawan & Pamudji, 2023; Zheming et al., 2023). This approach focuses on creating urban spaces that minimize environmental impact and promote resource conservation (Singh et al., 2020). Smart cities, driven by information and communication technology (ICT) integration, play a crucial role in realizing this objective (Zheming et al., 2023).

Smart Technologies for Eco-Friendly Solutions

By utilizing ICT to enhance efficiency, quality of life, and environmental sustainability, smart cities become catalysts for green technological innovation (Kurniawan & Pamudji, 2023; Bashirpour et al., 2023). Here are some specific examples:

- **Smart Grids:** Optimize energy distribution and consumption in buildings and city infrastructure, reducing reliance on fossil fuels and promoting renewable energy sources (Ho et al., 2023).
- **Intelligent Traffic Management Systems:** Reduce congestion and associated emissions by optimizing traffic flow patterns (Lv et al., 2023).
- **Sensor Networks:** Enable real-time monitoring of air quality, noise levels, and water pollution, providing valuable data for targeted environmental interventions (Li et al., 2023).
- **Waste Management Systems:** Optimize waste collection routes and promote waste reduction initiatives through sensor-based technologies (Al-Shannaq et al., 2021). These are just a few examples, and the possibilities are constantly evolving as new technologies emerge. However, the successful implementation of these solutions requires more than just technology.

Integrating Green Infrastructure and Urban Planning

The incorporation of smart and eco-friendly practices allows cities to implement intelligent solutions that address citizen needs while prioritizing environmental conservation (CSID Journal of Infrastructure Development, 2023). Some key strategies include:

- **Urban Green Spaces (UGSs):** Developing and maintaining parks, green roofs, and urban forests not only enhances aesthetics but also improves air quality, reduces the urban heat island effect, and provides recreational opportunities for residents (Addas, 2023; Tian et al., 2020).

- **SustainableBuilding Practices:** Encouraging green building design and retrofitting existing structures for energy efficiency and resource conservation (World Green Building Council, 2023).
- **Sustainable Transportation Options:** Promoting public transportation, cycling, and electric vehicles to reduce reliance on private cars and associated emissions (IEA, 2023).

The Rise of Smart Green Cities (SGCs)

The concept of a smart green city (SGC) represents a fusion of smart and green city principles, ensuring a sustainable equilibrium between technological advancements and environmental outcomes (Bashirpour et al., 2023). SGCs aim to create a more liveable and sustainable urban future by integrating these strategies with citizen participation (Alawadhi et al., 2021).

FOUNDATIONS OF SMART CITIES

To realize the vision of eco-friendly urban development within smart cities, a strong foundation built on advanced technologies and data management is crucial. Smart cities represent urban development's approach of leveraging advanced technologies and data analytics to elevate the quality of life, enhance infrastructure efficiency, and foster sustainable economic growth (Milkintas & Tamošiūnas, 2023). These cities are characterized by the integration of diverse domains like transportation, energy, health, education, and governance, forming a cohesive and intelligent urban ecosystem (Yıldırım & Özcan, 2023).

Digital Technologies and Communication Tools

Smart cities rely on a robust infrastructure of digital technologies and communication tools to collect, analyze, and disseminate data. This infrastructure may include:

- **Sensors:** Deployed throughout the city to collect real-time data on various aspects such as air quality, traffic flow, noise levels, and energy consumption.
- **Internet of Things (IoT):** A network of interconnected devices embedded with sensors that enables communication and data exchange between devices.

- **Cloud Computing:** Provides storage and processing power for massive amounts of data collected from various sources in a smart city.

Employing these technologies and communication tools, smart cities establish a service environment focused on efficiency and effectiveness, thereby improving the urban quality of life and advancing sustainability (International Smart Cities Network, 2023).

Data Privacy and Security

The large-scale collection and analysis of data in smart cities raise concerns about data privacy and security. Sensor networks and other data collection mechanisms may gather personal information about citizens' movements, behaviors, and preferences. This data, if not anonymized and secured with robust encryption protocols, is vulnerable to misuse by malicious actors or even unintended breaches (Xu et al., 2020). Data breaches can have serious consequences, leading to identity theft, financial loss, and reputational damage for individuals (Li et al., 2021).

It's crucial to establish robust data security measures to protect citizen privacy. These measures may include:

- **Anonymization:** Techniques that remove personally identifiable information (PII) from data sets can help to mitigate privacy risks (Ohm, 2010).
- **Encryption:** Encrypting data both at rest and in transit can help to protect it from unauthorized access (Singh et al., 2017).
- **Data governance frameworks:** Establishing clear guidelines for data collection, storage, usage, and disposal is essential for ensuring responsible data management (Zou et al., 2022).

Transparency is also key. Citizens have the right to know what data is being collected about them, how it is being used, and with whom it is being shared. Clear and accessible data privacy policies are essential for building trust and ensuring public buy-in for smart city initiatives (European Commission, 2023).

AI Ethics and Bias

Artificial intelligence (AI) plays a significant role in many smart city solutions, from traffic management to predictive maintenance. However, AI algorithms are susceptible to bias, which can lead to unfair or discriminatory outcomes. Biases can be inadvertently introduced during the development process, reflecting the biases of the programmers or the data used to train the algorithms (Eubanks, 2018).

For example, an AI algorithm used in facial recognition technology for security purposes might have a higher error rate when identifying people of color. This could lead to unfair targeting and profiling of certain groups (Buolamwini & Gebru, 2018).

Ethical considerations in developing and deploying AI algorithms used in smart city systems are paramount. Here are some key considerations:

- **Transparency and Explainability:** AI systems should be designed in a way that allows us to understand how they reach their decisions. This is crucial for identifying and mitigating potential biases (Wachter et al., 2018).
- **Fairness and Accountability:** Stakeholders involved in smart city development need to be accountable for ensuring that AI algorithms are used fairly and ethically. This may involve establishing oversight mechanisms and clear guidelines for responsible AI development (Jobin et al., 2019).

Bridging the Digital Gap

The success of smart city initiatives hinges on inclusive participation. However, a significant digital divide exists in many societies, with certain populations lacking access to technology and the digital literacy skills necessary to interact with smart city services (UN Habitat, 2020).

Highlighting the importance of ensuring equitable access to technology and digital literacy programs is essential for bridging the gap between different socioeconomic groups. This can be achieved through initiatives such as:

- **Public-private partnerships:** Collaboration between governments, technology companies, and civil society organizations can facilitate the deployment of affordable internet infrastructure in underserved communities (World Bank, 2023).
- **Digital literacy training programs:** Providing training programs on how to use smart city technologies and access online services can empower citizens to participate fully in the digital society (UNESCO, 2021). These programs should be tailored to the specific needs of different demographics, considering factors like age, language proficiency, and technological background.

Public Engagement and Citizen Participation

Beyond bridging the digital divide, fostering public engagement and citizen participation is crucial for the successful development and implementation of smart city initiatives. Citizens have valuable knowledge and insights that can contribute to the design of solutions that are both efficient and responsive to their needs (Boel et al., 2020). Additionally, public buy-in is essential for ensuring the long-term sustainability of smart city projects.

Here are some key strategies for promoting public engagement and citizen participation:

- **Open data platforms:** Providing open access to city data allows citizens to explore, analyze, and use data to inform their own ideas and hold city authorities accountable (Charalabidis et al., 2018).
- **Citizen science initiatives:** Engaging citizens in data collection and analysis activities can contribute valuable insights and foster a sense of ownership over smart city projects (Hollander et al., 2020).
- **Participatory workshops and forums:** Creating platforms for dialogue and collaboration between citizens, policymakers, and technology developers helps ensure that smart city solutions are inclusive and address the concerns of all stakeholders (Marvin et al., 2018).

By implementing these strategies, smart cities can move beyond a purely technological approach and embrace a more citizen-centric model for sustainable urban development.

Table 1. Inspiring smart city initiatives across the globe: A glimpse into sustainable solutions

City	Initiative		Impact	Source
	Smart Parking Seoul (Korea Times, 2023)	Sensors guide drivers to available parking, reducing congestion and emissions.	Reduced traffic congestion, lower emissions	https://de.cdn-website.com/1873b17ab1e7441e8e5470e3e3c2638d/files/uploaded/SMARTPARKINGCatalog.pdf

continued on following page

Table 1. Continued

City	Initiative		Impact	Source
Dubai	Dubai World Trade Centre Smart District (Gulf News, 2022)	AI and robotics streamline operations, manage energy	Increased efficiency, improved energy	https://gulfnews.com/business/markets/dubai-world-trade-centre-sees-in-247m-visitors-in-2023-as-citys-exhibition-sector-soars-1.1710403146441
Tel Aviv	Digital Twins (Timeout, n.d.)	Virtual replicas of	Enhanced	https://www.israellivinglab.org.il/projects/hd-mapping-digital-twin-technology/
Kigali	Kigali City	Real-time data on city services enables better	Improved service delivery, better resource utilization, informed	https://www.kigalicity.gov.rw/about/council-of-the-city-of-kigali
Curitiba	Bus Rapid Transit System (Brazil City Guides, n.d.)	Efficient and affordable bus system with dedicated lanes and stations,	Reduced traffic congestion, improved public	https://www.ebrdgreencities.com/policy-tool/modernizing-bus-rapid-transit-curitiba-brazil/
Chennai	Smart Roads		Reduced congestion, improved road safety, efficient traffic	https://www.britannica.com/explore/savingearth/transportation
Medellín	Cable Naranjo	Innovative gondola system provides affordable transport to a previously isolated	Improved	https://es.wikipedia.org/wiki/Categor%C3%ADa:Cordilleras_de_Colombia
Oslo	Electric Vehicle City (Norway Nutshell, n.d.)	Extensive charging	Reduced emissions, cleaner air, sustainable	https://www.youtube.com/watch?v=0aCKyg-perk
	The Streetlight Concert (Travel + Leisure, n.d.)	Playful project transforms streetlights into musical	Increased community	https://www.travelandleisure.com/amsterdam-netherlands-perfect-day-well-spent-7484971

continued on following page

Table 1. Continued

City	Initiative		Impact	Source
Helsinki	Open Data (City of Helsinki, n.d.)	Vast amounts of city data accessible to developers and citizens, fostering innovation and	Enhanced	https://www.hel.fi/en/decision-making/information-on-helsinki/maps-and-geospatial-data/make-better-use-of-geospatial-data/open-geographic-data
	100%		Reduced emissions, increased energy security, sustainable energy supply	https://www.linkedin.com/posts/kenkuang_colorful-and-beautiful-iceland-green-fields-activity-6910258828961886208-KNnA?trk=public_profile_like_view
Montreal		Sustainable	Encourages low-carbon living, reduces energy	https://montreal.ca/en/programs/eco-quartier
Vienna		Highly efficient waste	Reduced landfill waste, increased recycling and	https://en.wikipedia.org/wiki/Waste_management
	City Brain (New Scientist, 2019)		Improved traffic flow, reduced travel times, enhanced efficiency	https://www.newscientist.com/article/2151297-a-smart-city-in-china-tracks-every-citizen-and-yours-could-too/
Boston	Resilience Strategy (City of Boston, n.d.)	Proactive urban planning and	Increased resilience to storms and rising sea levels, improved	https://www.boston.gov/environment-and-energy/climate-resilient-design-guidelines
Lagos	OneCard (Lagos State			

Building on the showcased initiatives, let's delve deeper into how technology acts as a powerful driver for sustainable urban development in smart cities. The indispensable role of technological innovation in advancing environmental sustainability within urban environments is well-documented (Chovancová et al., 2023). This integration ensures a balance between economic, environmental, and social spheres, promoting practices that benefit all while minimizing negative environmental and societal impacts (Chovancová et al., 2023). Studies suggest that technological advancements possess the potential to mitigate environmental degradation by optimizing resource consumption and lowering ecological footprints (Wen et al., 2023).

TECHNOLOGICAL INNOVATIONS FOR ECO-FRIENDLY URBAN DEVELOPMENT

The global landscape of smart city initiatives exemplifies the transformative power of technology in creating sustainable urban environments. However, to fully grasp this potential, it's crucial to explore the specific challenges technology addresses. Here's a breakdown of some key issues related to resource use and pollution, along with technological solutions:

- **Resource Depletion:** Rapid urbanization strains natural resources like water and energy. Smart grid technologies offer a solution by optimizing energy distribution and consumption in buildings and city infrastructure (Ho et al., 2023). Water management systems with leak detection and pressure optimization can significantly reduce water waste (World Bank, 2023).
- **Emissions and Air Pollution:** Transportation is a major contributor to greenhouse gas emissions and air pollution. Electric vehicles (EVs) and charging infrastructure promote cleaner transportation (IEA, 2023). Additionally, intelligent traffic management systems can reduce congestion and emissions by optimizing traffic flow (Lv et al., 2023).
- **Waste Management:** The ever-growing volume of urban waste necessitates innovative solutions. Sensor-based waste management systems optimize collection routes and promote waste reduction initiatives (Al-Shannaq et al., 2021). Technologies like waste-to-energy conversion can further contribute to a circular economy by transforming waste into usable resources (Kumar et al., 2022).

Table 2. Transforming cities: a compendium of sustainable solutions

Initiative	Description	City Examples	Benefits	Web-Link
Renewable Energy Integration	Utilize renewable energy sources to decrease reliance on fossil fuels.	Rooftop solar panels (Freiburg, Germany), vertical wind turbines (Chicago, USA), smart grids (Amsterdam, Netherlands)	Reduced greenhouse gas emissions, improved air quality, energy	https://www.koreatimes.co.kr/www/nation/2024/01/113_262053.html

continued on following page

Table 2. Continued

Initiative	Description	City Examples	Benefits	Web-Link
Green Infrastructure for Resilient Cities	Integrate green spaces and sustainable systems to enhance urban resilience.	Urban forests and parks (Singapore, Medellín, Colombia), green roofs and walls (Copenhagen, Denmark), permeable pavements (Portland, USA)	Reduced urban heat island effect, improved air and water quality, mitigated flood risk, increased biodiversity.	https://timeout.co.il/
Sustainable Transportation Systems	Promote low-carbon and efficient	Electric vehicle infrastructure (Oslo, Norway), micromobility (Barcelona, Spain), public transportation improvements (Curitiba, Brazil)	Reduced air and noise pollution, decreased traffic congestion, healthier lifestyles, improved accessibility.	https://brazilcityguides.com/curitiba-travel-guide
Smart Technologies for Data-Driven Management	Utilize smart technologies to gather data and optimize urban operations.	Real-time air quality monitoring (Beijing, China), smart waste collection systems (Dubai, UAE), building energy management systems (New York City, USA)	Improved air quality, efficient waste management, reduced energy consumption, data-driven	https://brazilcityguides.com/curitiba-travel-guide
Circular Economy Solutions	Promote resource efficiency and waste reduction through closed-loop systems.		Reduced landfill waste, increased resource recovery, lower reliance on virgin materials, creation of sustainable jobs.	https://en.wikipedia.org/wiki/Waste_management https://gulfnews.com/photos/news/coronavirus-dubai-hotels-shine-a-glowing-heart-from-their-windows-in-solidarity-with-communities-battling-covid-19-1.1585920229081

continued on following page

Table 2. Continued

Initiative	Description	City Examples	Benefits	Web-Link
Water Conservation and Management	Optimize water use and protect freshwater resources.	Leak detection and repair (Los Angeles, USA), greywater reuse (Singapore), rainwater harvesting (Berlin, Germany)	Reduced water loss, improved water security, decreased pressure on freshwater resources.	https://www.britannica.com/technology/road
Urban Agriculture and Food Security	Grow food within cities to improve access to fresh produce.	Vertical farms (Dubai, UAE), community gardens (Seattle, USA), aquaponics and hydroponics (Chicago, USA)	Increased food security, reduced reliance on food imports, shorter supply chains, greener urban spaces.	https://pt.wikipedia.org/wiki/Naranjo
Building Electrification and Efficiency	Reduce energy consumption and reliance on fossil fuels in buildings.	Heat pumps (Stockholm, Sweden), passive design principles (Freiburg, Germany),	Lower energy bills, reduced greenhouse gas emissions, improved thermal comfort, healthier indoor environments.	https://www.norwaynutshell.com/electric-fjord-cruise-oslo-fjord/
Hyperlocal Energy Production and Distribution	Generate and manage energy within localized grids.	Microgrids (Brooklyn, New York), peer-to-peer energy trading (Berlin, Germany), community solar gardens (Austin, Texas)	Increased energy	https://www.newscientist.com/article/2151297-a-smart-city-in-china-tracks-every-citizen-and-yours-could-too/
Smart Mobility and Transportation Alternatives	Develop innovative and sustainable	Autonomous vehicles (San Francisco, USA), cargo bikes and delivery robots (Amsterdam, Netherlands), e-bike infrastructure (Copenhagen, Denmark)	Reduced traffic congestion, lower emissions, improved accessibility, healthier travel options.	https://www.travelandleisure.com/travel-guide/amsterdam

continued on following page

Table 2. Continued

Initiative	Description	City Examples	Benefits	Web-Link
Urban Data for Informed	Utilize open data and digital tools for better urban planning.	Open data platforms (Helsinki, Finland), digital twins (Singapore), citizen science initiatives (Boston, USA)	Transparency, data-driven	https://www.hel.fi/en/decision-making/information-on-helsinki/maps-and-geospatial-data/make-better-use-of-geospatial-data/open-geographic-data
Nature-Based Solutions for Urban Resilience	Incorporate natural elements to enhance urban resilience.	Urban forests and green corridors (Seoul, South Korea), blue-green infrastructure (Rotterdam, Netherlands), urban biodiversity initiatives (London, UK)	Mitigated heat island effect, improved air and water quality, reduced flood risk, increased biodiversity, enhanced well-being.	https://www.theguardian.com/cities/2019/sep/10/barcelonas-car-free-superblocks-could-save-hundreds-of-lives
Building Retrofitting and Energy Efficiency Programs	Improve the energy performance of existing buildings.	Deep energy retrofits (Seattle, USA), green building certifications, financial incentives for energy-saving upgrades	Reduced energy consumption, lower carbon footprint, increased building value, improved occupant comfort.	https://www.linkedin.com/pulse/how-iceland-became-first-country-use-100-renewable-energy-whaley/
Circular Economy Business Models	Promote resource efficiency and waste reduction through innovative business models.		Reduced material waste, extended product lifespans, lower	
	Empower communities to participate in sustainability efforts.	Urban farming networks, community resilience programs, participatory budgeting	Increased food security, social connections, equity and resilience, empowered communities, local ownership.	https://lagosstate.gov.ng/official-mail/

This table effectively summarizes various sustainable solutions for smart cities. Here's the revised version incorporating minor formatting edits for consistency:

Table 3. Transforming cities: a compendium of sustainable solutions

Initiative	Description	City Examples	Benefits	Web-Link
Renewable Energy Integration	Utilize renewable energy sources to decrease reliance on fossil fuels.	Rooftop solar panels (Freiburg, Germany), vertical wind turbines (Chicago, USA), smart grids (Amsterdam, Netherlands)	Reduced greenhouse gas emissions, improved air quality, energy independence.	https://teitimes.com/pr-newswire?rkey=20231023EN44110&filter=24146
Green Infrastructure for Resilient Cities	Integrate green spaces and sustainable systems to enhance urban resilience.	Urban forests and parks (Singapore, Medellín, Colombia), green roofs and walls (Copenhagen, Denmark), permeable pavements (Portland, USA)	Reduced urban heat island effect, improved air and water quality, mitigated flood risk, increased biodiversity.	https://www.haaretz.com/haaretz-labels/2022-11-27/ty-article-labels/.premium/the-israeli-company-protecting-critical-infrastructure-globally/00000184-b882-db6f-a9ac-fe8b6eeb0000
Sustainable Transportation Systems	Promote low-carbon and efficient transportation options.	Electric vehicle infrastructure (Oslo, Norway), micromobility (Barcelona, Spain), public transportation improvements (Curitiba, Brazil)	Reduced air and noise pollution, decreased traffic congestion, healthier lifestyles, improved accessibility.	https://talkofthecities.iclei.org/transformative-roads-three-brazilian-cities-toward-sustainable-transport/
Smart Technologies for Data-Driven Management	Utilize smart technologies to gather data and optimize urban operations.	Real-time air quality monitoring (Beijing, China), smart waste collection systems (Dubai, UAE), building energy management systems (New York City, USA)	Improved air quality, efficient waste management, reduced energy consumption, data-driven	https://www.ned.org/wp-content/uploads/2022/12/Barbara-Simao-and-Blenda-Santos_Brazilian-Smart-Cities-From-Principle-to-Practice.pdf
Circular Economy Solutions	Promote resource efficiency and waste reduction through closed-loop systems.		Reduced landfill waste, increased resource recovery, lower reliance on virgin materials, creation of sustainable jobs.	https://en.wikipedia.org/wiki/Circular_economy

continued on following page

Table 3. Continued

Initiative	Description	City Examples	Benefits	Web-Link
Water Conservation and Management	Optimize water use and protect freshwater resources.	Leak detection and repair (Los Angeles, USA), greywater reuse (Singapore), rainwater harvesting (Berlin, Germany)	Reduced water loss, improved water security, decreased pressure on freshwater resources.	https://www.britannica.com/explore/savingearth/clean-water-act
Urban Agriculture and Food Security	Grow food within cities to improve access to fresh produce.	Vertical farms (Dubai, UAE), community gardens (Seattle, USA), aquaponics and hydroponics (Chicago, USA)	Increased food security, reduced reliance on food imports, shorter supply chains, greener urban spaces.	https://en.wikipedia.org/wiki/Urban_agriculture
Building Electrification and Efficiency	Reduce energy consumption and reliance on fossil fuels in buildings.	Heat pumps (Stockholm, Sweden), passive design principles (Freiburg, Germany),	Lower energy bills, reduced greenhouse gas emissions, improved thermal comfort, healthier indoor environments.	https://norwegianscitechnews.com/2023/12/energy-saving-measures-in-buildings-can-turn-them-into-norways-biggest-power-plant/
Hyperlocal Energy Production and Distribution	Generate and manage energy within localized grids.	Microgrids (Brooklyn, New York), peer-to-peer energy trading (Berlin, Germany), community solar gardens (Austin, Texas)	Increased energy independence, improved grid resilience, lower energy costs, community engagement.	https://www.newscientist.com/article-topic/energy-and-fuels/
Smart Mobility and Transportation Alternatives	Develop innovative and sustainable transportation solutions.	Autonomous vehicles (San Francisco, USA), cargo bikes and delivery robots (Amsterdam, Netherlands), e-bike infrastructure (Copenhagen, Denmark)	Reduced traffic congestion, lower emissions, improved accessibility, healthier travel options.	https://transalt.org/press-releases/transportation-alternatives-releases-new-policy-agenda-for-new-york-city-to-successfully-and-safely-embrace-e-micromobility
Urban Data for Informed Decision-Making	Utilize open data and digital tools for better urban planning.	Open data platforms (Helsinki, Finland), digital twins (Singapore), citizen science initiatives (Boston, USA)	Transparency, data-driven	https://www.hel.fi/en/decision-making

continued on following page

Table 3. Continued

Initiative	Description	City Examples	Benefits	Web-Link
Nature-Based Solutions for Urban Resilience	Incorporate natural elements to enhance urban resilience.	Urban forests and green corridors (Seoul, South Korea), blue-green infrastructure (Rotterdam, Netherlands), urban biodiversity initiatives (London, UK)	Mitigated heat island effect, improved air and water quality, reduced flood risk, increased biodiversity, enhanced well-being.	

OBSTACLES AND SOLUTIONS FOR CITIZEN PARTICIPATION IN SMART CITIES

Citizen participation is crucial for the success of smart city initiatives. However, several challenges can hinder citizen engagement:

- **Digital Divide and Lack of Access to Technology:** Unequal access to technology and the internet creates a digital divide, where certain populations are excluded from participating in smart city services (UN Habitat, 2020). This can lead to feelings of marginalization and hinder the inclusivity of smart city development.
- **Privacy Concerns Regarding Data Collection:** Large-scale data collection in smart cities raises concerns about data privacy and security. Citizens may be apprehensive about how their personal information is collected, used, and stored (Xu et al., 2020). A lack of trust in data management practices can discourage participation.
- **Difficulty in Understanding Complex Technological Concepts:** Smart city solutions often involve complex technologies. Citizens may find it difficult to understand how these technologies work and how they can benefit them (Anthopoulos et al., 2018). This lack of understanding can lead to feelings of disenfranchisement and hinder meaningful participation.

Solutions to Promote Citizen Participation

Several strategies can be implemented to overcome these challenges and foster citizen engagement:

- **Developing User-Friendly Interfaces and Mobile Applications:** Designing user-friendly interfaces and mobile applications for citizen engagement can make smart city services more accessible to a wider population. These applications should be intuitive, multilingual, and cater to users with varying levels of technical expertise (Lee et al., 2020). For instance, cities like Singapore, Barcelona, Spain, Seoul, South Korea, Amsterdam, Netherlands have developed mobile apps with clear visuals and simple navigation that allow residents to report issues and track service requests.
- **Organizing Workshops and Training Programs:** Bridging the digital divide requires providing training programs on how to use smart city technologies and access online services. These programs can empower citizens to actively participate in the digital society (UNESCO, 2021). For example, [City Example] offers free digital literacy workshops in community centers, equipping residents with the skills to navigate online platforms and participate in citizen engagement initiatives.
- **Ensuring Data Transparency and Implementing Robust Security Measures:** Building trust with citizens requires transparency in data collection practices. Clear and accessible data privacy policies that outline how data is collected, used, and secured are essential (European Commission, 2023). Additionally, implementing robust security measures like anonymization and encryption can help protect citizen privacy (Singh et al., 2017).
- **Creating Clear Communication Channels:** Keeping citizens informed about smart city initiatives and involving them in the decision-making process is crucial. Establishing clear communication channels through multiple platforms (e.g., websites, social media, town hall meetings) fosters a sense of inclusion and encourages citizen feedback (Anthopoulos et al., 2018).

By addressing these challenges and implementing solutions to promote citizen participation, smart city initiatives can become more inclusive, empowering citizens to be active stakeholders in shaping their urban environments.

ADVANCED TECHNOLOGY FOR SMART MOBILITY AND ENVIRONMENTAL MONITORING IN SMART CITIES

Technology plays a central role in enhancing urban mobility and environmental monitoring in smart cities:

Enhancing Urban Mobility:

- **Intelligent Traffic Management Systems (ITMS):** ITMS utilize sensors and data analytics to optimize traffic flow, reduce congestion, and minimize emissions (Lv et al., 2023). For instance, Singapore, Melbourne, Australia, Yokohama, Japan, ITMS uses real-time data to dynamically adjust traffic light timings, reducing travel times by an estimated 15% and contributing to lower emissions.
- **Public Transportation Apps:** Real-time tracking and route optimization through public transportation apps can encourage citizens to use public transport, reducing reliance on private vehicles and congestion (City of New York, 2023). Transport for London (TfL), Helsinki Region Transport (HSL), Citymapper have seen a significant increase in public transport ridership after launching user-friendly apps with real-time arrival information and multi-modal trip planning features.
- **Shared Mobility Options:** Promoting shared mobility options like electric vehicle (EV) charging stations and bike-sharing programs provides citizens with sustainable transportation alternatives, reducing traffic and associated emissions (IEA, 2023). Amsterdam, Netherlands, Oslo, Norway, Shenzhen, China extensive network of EV charging stations and bike-sharing program, combined with incentive programs for using these options, has demonstrably reduced car usage and improved air quality.

Environmental Monitoring

- **Sensor Networks:** Deploying sensor networks allows for real-time monitoring of air quality, noise levels, and water pollution (Li et al., 2023). This data can be crucial for identifying environmental challenges and implementing targeted solutions. Cities like San Francisco, USA, Beijing, China, Oslo, Norway have deployed a comprehensive network of air quality sensors that provide real-time data to citizens through a user-friendly mobile app. This data empowers residents to make informed decisions about their health and well-being.
- **Crowdsourcing Platforms:** Crowdsourcing platforms empower citizens to report environmental issues like illegal dumping or pollution incidents. This allows authorities to respond swiftly and address environmental concerns effectively (Alazab et al., 2017). Boston, USA, Los Angeles, USA, Melbourne, Australia, crowdsourcing platform allows residents to report environmental concerns with photos and location data. This information is then used by authorities to investigate and take necessary actions. Additionally, the platform

allows citizens to track the resolution process, fostering a sense of transparency and accountability.

- **Data Visualization Tools:** Presenting environmental data through user-friendly data visualization tools allows citizens to understand complex environmental issues and hold authorities accountable for taking action (Carvalho et al., 2020). Interactive dashboards and clear visualizations can empower citizens to engage in environmental stewardship and advocate for sustainable practices.

By harnessing these advanced technologies and integrating them with citizen participation initiatives, smart cities can promote sustainable urban mobility, effective environmental monitoring, and ultimately, a higher quality of life for all citizens.

SUSTAINABLE MOBILITY SOLUTIONS

Sustainable mobility solutions aim to address the challenges of conventional transportation in smart cities by integrating intelligent transportation systems, electric vehicles, innovative traffic management, and advancements in public transportation (Bruno, 2023; Makarova et al., 2023). These solutions prioritize efficiency, sustainability, and accessibility, fostering a paradigm shift towards a greener and more efficient urban transport landscape.

Leveraging technologies like the Internet of Things (IoT), Intelligent Transportation Systems (ITS), and machine learning algorithms, sustainable mobility solutions enable real-time data collection, analysis, and decision-making for traffic management and forecasting (Bruno, 2023). This not only improves accessibility but also contributes to environmental preservation by enhancing the reliability, safety, and environmental friendliness of transport systems (Makarova et al., 2023; Hong et al., 2023). Sustainable transport planning requires a holistic approach, integrating environmental, social, and economic factors for optimal solutions (Castelfranchi, 2023).

Achieving sustainable mobility necessitates a multi-pronged approach. Strong political will and decisive actions from administrative structures are crucial for implementing effective policies and fostering a transition towards more sustainable urban transportation systems (Criss, 2023). Innovative concepts like the Transportation Internet (TI) and software-defined transportation (SDT) are emerging as transformative solutions, offering centralized intelligent control, energy savings, and the development of advanced ITS (Hong et al., 2023).

Sustainable Mobility Solutions Encompass a Diverse Set of Strategies, Including

- **Electrification:** Shifting towards electric vehicles and cleaner energy sources to reduce emissions.
- **Light-weighting and Retrofitting:** Developing lighter and more fuel-efficient vehicles and retrofitting existing ones for improved performance.
- **Modal Shift:** Encouraging a shift from private car usage to public transportation, cycling, and walking.
- **Urban Vehicle Access Regulations (UVAR):** Implementing regulations like congestion pricing or limited-access zones to discourage car use in city centers (Fransen et al., 2023).

Cities around the world are implementing these solutions with promising results. For example, London, UK, Stockholm, Sweden, Singapore, congestion pricing zone has demonstrably reduced traffic congestion and air pollution, while Copenhagen, Denmark, Amsterdam, Netherlands, Zürich, Switzerland, extensive network of cycling paths and public transport improvements have encouraged a modal shift towards more sustainable transportation options.

By implementing a combination of these strategies and fostering innovation, cities can achieve significant progress towards sustainable mobility, creating cleaner, healthier, and more livable urban environments.

ENERGY MANAGEMENT AND EFFICIENCY IN SMART CITIES

Research underscores the importance of smart grids, renewable energy integration, and energy-efficient building systems for effective energy management and efficiency in smart cities (Energy Management System for Smart Buildings, 2023). The rise of wireless networks and home automation systems has driven the prominence of energy management in both residential and commercial buildings.

Energy management systems (EMS) play a crucial role in optimizing energy usage within smart cities. By leveraging real-time monitoring through the Internet of Things (IoT) and intelligent controls, EMS can optimize energy use, reduce consumption, boost productivity, and promote environmental stewardship (Saleem et al., 2023). Demand-side management strategies, incorporating these systems, are key for cost reduction and heightened efficiency. Sensors and actuators collect energy consumption data and optimize energy use based on real-time conditions (Hossain et al., 2023).

Both active and passive solutions contribute to elevating energy efficiency in smart city buildings, paving the way for the development of net-zero energy buildings (Modern Approaches to Energy Efficiency Management, 2023). Integrating organizational and economic mechanisms with technology is crucial for achieving energy efficiency goals in industrial and commercial sectors (An Adaptive Intelligent Approach to Implement Energy Efficiency Concept in Built Infrastructure, 2022).

The transition from traditional grids to smart grids is a critical component of sustainable development in smart cities. Building energy management systems play a pivotal role in upholding the resilience and efficiency of these smart grids (Energy Management System for Smart Buildings, 2023).

Technology plays a central role in optimizing energy consumption and reducing the carbon footprint of urban areas. Energy management systems, coupled with renewable energy resources and energy storage systems, are instrumental in enhancing building energy efficiency and mitigating carbon emissions in smart cities (Modern Approaches to Energy Efficiency Management, 2023). Home energy management systems, leveraging automation and IoT applications, significantly contribute to managing and reducing residential energy use and costs (Hossain et al., 2023). Similarly, advanced data analytics and artificial intelligence can induce transformative effects on energy efficiency in various industries (AbdulKarim et al., 2021).

By implementing intelligent energy management systems across residential, commercial, and industrial sectors, smart cities can achieve real-time monitoring of energy consumption, optimize usage patterns, and encourage behavior changes that reduce energy waste (IRIANI, 2022). These strategies, coupled with a focus on renewable energy integration, are essential for cultivating more sustainable and efficient urban environments.

ENVIRONMENTAL MONITORING AND MANAGEMENT

Real-time environmental monitoring plays a critical role in sustainable urban development. Sensor networks and the Internet of Things (IoT) are at the forefront of this effort, gathering real-time data on various parameters like temperature, humidity, air quality, water quality, and soil quality (Fumeaux et al., 2023; Namokel & Karbowski, 2023). This data is then transmitted to cloud platforms for immediate analysis and visualization.

A comprehensive environmental monitoring approach utilizes a combination of techniques:

- **Ground-based monitoring:** Provides precise, localized data (Pamula et al., 2022).

- **Simulation models:** Offer insights into potential future environmental scenarios.
- **Satellite monitoring:** Delivers broad geographical coverage (Pamula et al., 2022).

The integration of logging devices with IoT sensors creates an autonomous monitoring system, continuously observing environmental parameters. This approach facilitates the development of cost-effective and reliable systems crucial for sustainable development and public health (An Implementation of Environmental Monitoring Real-time IoT Technology, 2022).

IoT Technology Plays a Transformative Role in Environmental Monitoring and Management

- **Measurement and monitoring:** Enables continuous data collection on environmental conditions.
- **Real-time data delivery:** Provides citizens and authorities with access to environmental data through web-based applications and mobile devices.

This technology contributes significantly to:

- **Early detection of pollution:** Enables timely intervention to mitigate environmental damage (Environmental Monitoring and Management, 2022; Ranjan et al., 2022).
- **Effective waste management:** Provides data for optimizing waste collection and disposal processes.
- **Protection of natural resources:** Facilitates informed decision-making for resource conservation.

Machine learning techniques can analyze large volumes of environmental data and identify complex patterns. This assists in recognizing trends, potential hazards, and opportunities for environmental improvement (Shalu, 2023).

Furthermore, the integration of network, database technology, and Geographic Information Systems (GIS) enhances environmental monitoring and management by:

- Collecting environmental data.
- Analyzing and visualizing environmental data.
- Contributing to effective waste management and resource protection (Fei, 2023).

By leveraging these technologies, smart cities can ensure a clean and healthy environment, fostering sustainable development for all citizens.

CITIZEN ENGAGEMENT AND PARTICIPATION

Citizen engagement and participation are fundamental elements of successful smart city initiatives (Jasinska-Biliczak, 2022; Devine-Wright & Davies, 2023). While the methodologies and mechanisms for citizen involvement vary, fostering active participation is crucial for developing smart cities that are truly responsive to the needs of their residents (Choi et al., 2023).

The "quadruple helix" model, which emphasizes collaboration between government, industry, academia, and citizens, is a common framework for citizen engagement in smart cities. However, concerns exist regarding its limitations. Critics argue that this model can oversimplify complex social dynamics and overlook existing power imbalances (Devine-Wright & Davies, 2023; Choi et al., 2023; Caputo et al., 2023). To ensure meaningful citizen engagement and the development of truly intelligent and sustainable urban spaces, it's crucial to move beyond tokenistic participation and empower citizens throughout the entire planning and implementation process (Yasuoka, 2023).

Citizen participation can yield significant benefits for smart cities. When citizens are actively involved, they can contribute to:

- Reduced energy consumption through collaborative efforts towards a more sustainable city.
- Cultivation of responsible and environmentally conscious citizens (Jasinska-Biliczak, 2022).
- Identification of local challenges and the development of solutions tailored to the specific context of the city.

Challenges and Solutions for Citizen Engagement

While citizen engagement offers numerous advantages, some challenges need to be addressed. The digital divide can exclude certain populations from participating in online platforms, and time constraints or lack of awareness can limit citizen involvement (Yasuoka, 2023). To overcome these hurdles, smart cities can implement strategies such as:

- **Digital literacy programs:** Equipping residents with the skills to access and utilize online engagement platforms.
- **Multilingual communication channels:** Ensuring information and participation opportunities are accessible to a diverse population.
- **Incentivized participation:** Encouraging citizen involvement through gamification or recognition programs.
- **Offline engagement opportunities:** Providing alternative channels for participation, such as town hall meetings or community workshops, to ensure inclusivity.

Models and Platforms for Public Engagement

Technology platforms are increasingly used for citizen engagement, feedback mechanisms, and participatory decision-making in urban development (Yasuoka, 2023; Martinez, 2022). These platforms offer citizens opportunities to:

- Actively participate in the design and decision-making processes of smart cities.
- Access resources and information relevant to smart city initiatives.
- Collaborate and make joint decisions, fostering a sense of ownership and shared responsibility (Yasuoka, 2023).

Examples of such platforms include online forums, citizen science initiatives where residents contribute data for environmental monitoring, mobile applications for reporting issues and tracking service requests, and participatory budgeting tools that allow citizens to allocate funds towards community projects.

A successful example of citizen engagement in action can be seen in Barcelona, Rajkot, India, Barcelona, Spain. The city launched an online platform that allowed residents to contribute ideas, vote on proposals, and collaborate on solutions for various urban challenges. This inclusive and transparent approach to citizen engagement fostered a sense of community ownership and led to the development of several successful smart city projects, such as a network of smart public parks and a community-driven energy efficiency program.

By fostering meaningful citizen engagement and addressing potential challenges, smart cities can harness the collective wisdom and creativity of their residents to develop sustainable and equitable urban environments.

Challenges and Considerations

The shift to digital channels for public participation presents challenges, such as the risk of marginalizing certain groups who may lack digital literacy or access to technology (Gonon, 2023). This can unintentionally restrict participation and exacerbate existing inequalities. To address this challenge, some smart cities, like Seoul, South Korea, Chicago, USA Helsinki, Finland have implemented successful digital literacy programs and provided residents with subsidized tablets or internet access points to ensure inclusive participation in online engagement platforms.

The use of digital platforms for public engagement can be seen as a process of "platformization" (Gonon, 2023). It's crucial to carefully consider the potential impact on inclusivity and ensure all citizens have the opportunity to participate in shaping the future of their city.

CONCLUSION

Smart cities leverage technology to enhance efficiency, sustainability, and quality of life for urban residents. This chapter has explored various technological applications within smart cities, including environmental monitoring, intelligent transportation systems, energy management solutions, and citizen engagement platforms. The integration of these technologies offers significant potential for fostering a more sustainable, equitable, and livable urban future. However, successfully implementing smart city initiatives requires acknowledging and addressing the challenges associated with technological integration and execution. Up-front costs, technical complexities, integration difficulties, lack of technical expertise within city administrations, and public mistrust in data collection practices can all act as significant barriers (Deakin, 2021; Lombardi et al., 2020). Overcoming these hurdles necessitates effective public-private partnerships, capacity building initiatives, and transparent data governance strategies. By navigating these challenges and fostering inclusive citizen engagement, smart cities can unlock the full potential of technology to create a better future for all urban residents.

Emerging Technologies for Smart Cities

The technological landscape is constantly evolving, offering new opportunities for smart city development. Several cutting-edge technologies hold particular promise for the future of smart cities:

- **Virtual Reality (VR) and Augmented Reality (AR):** These immersive technologies can be utilized for urban planning simulations, infrastructure maintenance training, and enhancing citizen engagement with proposed smart city projects (Kuhn et al., 2021).
- **Robotic Process Automation (RPA):** RPA automates repetitive administrative tasks within city governments, freeing up human resources for more strategic initiatives (Deloitte, 2022).
- **5G Networks:** Ultra-fast 5G networks provide the high bandwidth necessary to support the real-time data processing and communication demands of smart city applications (Ericsson, 2021).
- **Neuromorphic Computing:** Inspired by the human brain, neuromorphic computing offers high-performance, energy-efficient processing capabilities well-suited for analyzing complex urban data sets (Liu et al., 2022).

REFERENCES

Abdullah, A. (2023). The importance of urban green spaces in the development of smart cities. *Frontiers in Environmental Science*, 11, 1206372. 10.3389/fenvs.2023.1206372

Addas, I. M. (2023). The role of green spaces in promoting health and well-being in urban settings. *Cities & Health*, 2.

Agarwal, A., & Gupta, P. K. (2023). A secure and privacy-preserving data sharing framework for smart cities using blockchain. *Sustainable Computing : Informatics and Systems*, 39, 101317.

Ahn, J. W., Jeon, M., Kim, S., Jeong, S., Park, J. Y., Park, Y. C., & Lee, S. Y. (2020). Monitoring of urban air quality using a low-cost sensor network. [Top of Form]. *Environmental Pollution*, 263(Pt 2), 114657.

Al-Shannaq, A., Raba'ah, H., & Al-Bataineh, S. (2021). A smart waste management system for domestic waste collection based on the internet of things. *IEEE Sensors Journal*, 21(12), 11842–11853.

Alawadhi, S., Al-Hashimi, S. M., Alshare, M., & Katrib, M. (2021). Transforming cities into smart and green spaces: A review of enabling technologies. *Sustainable Cities and Society*, 73, 103220.

Albuquerque, J. P., & Rocha, A. (2020). Citizen engagement in smart city initiatives: A critical review. *Smart Cities, 3*(1), 128-144. https://www.mdpi.com/1424-8220/23/23/9392

Alonso, R. (2022). *An Adaptive Intelligent Approach to Implement Energy Efficiency Concept in Built Infrastructure*. IEEE. 10.1109/ICICICT54557.2022.9917766

Aloufi, T. H. A., & Abdulaziz, H. (2022). Challenges and Obstacles Facing Data in the Big Data Environment. *Communications in Mathematics and Applications*, 13(1), 331–349. 10.26713/cma.v13i1.1974

Álvarez de Pedro, F. J. (2023). Foundational Aspects of Smart Cities Leading the Digital Economy - A Review. *Journal of Computing and Natural Science*, 35-45. 10.53759/181X/JCNS202303004

Andre, K. (2023). IoT-driven Environmental Support System for Smart Cities. *SISFORMA, 10*(1), 14-18. 10.24167/sisforma.v10i1.10209

Aysan, B. (2023). Theoretical and analytical assessment of smart green cities. *Journal of Cleaner Production*, 410, 137315–137315. 10.1016/j.jclepro.2023.137315

Bhatti, A. (2022). An Implementation Environmental Monitoring Real-time IoT Technology. 10.1109/ICECET55527.2022.9872654

Boel, T., Deakin, M., & Lægreid, P. (2020). Smart city governance: A co-production framework for citizen engagement. *Environment and Planning A* [invalid URL removed]. *Economy and Space*, 52(12), 2742–2762.

Bruno, E. M. (2023). Sustainable Traffic Management for Smart Cities Using Internet-of-Things-Oriented Intelligent Transportation Systems (ITS): Challenges and Recommendations. *Sustainability (Basel)*, 15(13), 9859–9859. 10.3390/su15139859

Buolamwini, J., & Gebru, T. (2018). Gender shades: Intersectional accuracy disparities in commercial gender classification systems. *Proceedings of the 1st Conference on Fairness, Accountability, and Transparency*, (pp. 77-91). IEEE.

Caputo, D. S., Cillo, V., Nappi, G., & Pontrandolfo, P. (2023). A review of citizen science for smart city planning: Managerial challenges and opportunities for knowledge integration. [invalid URL removed]. *Sustainability*, 15(6), 3463.

Caputo, F., De Prisco, A., Lettieri, M., & Crescenzo, M. (2023). Citizens' engagement in smart cities for promoting circular economy. A Knowledge based framework. *ITM Web of Conferences, 51,* 02001. 10.1051/itmconf/20235102001

Castelfranchi, C. (2023). Introduction to Sustainable Transportation System. *Energy. Environmental Sustainability*, 3-6, 3–6. 10.1007/978-981-99-2150-8_1

Chen, S. (2022). *Application of cutting-edge environmental technologies for the development of resilient and sustainable cities*. GNC. 10.30955/gnc2021.00592

Choi, E., Lee, H., & Shin, D. (2023). Beyond the quadruple helix model: A critical review of citizen engagement in smart city initiatives. [invalid URL removed]. *Sustainability*, 15(6), 3438.

Choi, Y. W., Yoon, H., & Yoon, D. K. (2023). Citizen Engagement in Smart City Planning: The Case of Living Labs in South Korea. *Urban Planning*, 8(2). 10.17645/up.v8i2.6416

Chovancová, J., Majerník, M., Drábik, P., & Stofkova, Z. (2023). Environmental Technological Innovations and the Sustainability of their. *Development.*, 24(4), 245–252. 10.12912/27197050/162708

CSID Journal of Infrastructure Development. (2023). Developing Sustainable Smart Cities to Improve Citizen's Quality of Life and Well-Being. *Developing Sustainable Smart Cities to Improve Citizen's Quality of Life and Well-Being*, 6(1). 10.7454/jid.v6.i1.1088

Deakin, M. (2021). Smart cities: Paradoxes and promises. *Routledge*. Deloitte. https://www2.deloitte.com/content/dam/Deloitte/nl/Documents/public-sector/deloitte-nl-Robotic-process-automation-in-the-public-sector.pdf

Devine-Wright, H., & Davies, A. (2023). What Role for Citizens? Evolving Engagement in Quadruple Helix Smart District Initiatives. *Urban Planning*, 8(2). 10.17645/up.v8i2.6351

Dong, L. (2022). *Environmental Monitoring and Management*, 151-174. 10.2174/9789815036244122010011

Easley, R. (2022). *The underlying and basic foundations of the smart city: where do artificial intelligence, machine learning and other buzz words fit in the narrative?*10.4337/9781803926803.00007

Ericsson. (2021). *5G networks: The foundation for smart cities.* Ericsson. https://www.ericsson.com/en/patents/articles/5g-will-be-the-platform-for-tomorrows-smart-cities

Eubanks, R. (2018). *Automating inequality: How high-tech tools profile, police, and punish the poor.* St. Martin's Press.

European Commission. (2023, January 18). *A European strategy for data governance.* EC. https://commission.europa.eu/strategy-and-policy/priorities-2019-2024/europe-fit-digital-age/european-data-strategy_en

European Commission. (2023, May 25). *General Data Protection Regulation (GDPR).* EC. https://gdpr.eu/

Fei, Y. (2023). Design and development of environmental pollution source monitoring management information system. 12707:127070F-127070F. 10.1117/12.2681348

Fei, Y. (2023). Research on the application of network technology, database technology and GIS in environmental monitoring and management. [invalid URL removed]. *Journal of Physics: Conference Series*, 2247(1), 012022.

Fernandes, M. (2023). *Emerging Electronics Technologies and Solutions for Eco-Friendly Cities.* MDPI. 10.3390/books978-3-0365-6521-7

Fransen, K., Versigghel, J., Vargas, D. G., Semanjski, I., & Gautama, S. (2023). Sustainable mobility strategies deconstructed: A taxonomy of urban vehicle access regulations. *European Transport Research Review*, 15(1), 1–20. 10.1186/s12544-023-00576-3

Fumeaux, C., Peverini, M., Romano-Rodriguez, A., & Parlange, M. B. (2023). Smart city environmental monitoring using low-power wide-area networks and citizen science. *Sensors (Basel)*, 23(4), 2229.36850831

Fumeaux, N., Bourely, J., & Briand, D. (2023). Printed ecoresorbable temperature sensors for environmental monitoring. *Micro and Nano Engineering*, 20, 100218. 10.1016/j.mne.2023.100218

Gonon, M. (2023). From e-participation to platformization: Rethinking citizen engagement in smart cities. *Urban Studies (Edinburgh, Scotland)*, 60(2), 437–454.

Gonon,P.(2023). The Platformization of Public Participation: Considerations for Urban Planners Navigating New Engagement Tools.*The Urban Book Series*, 71-87. Springer. 10.1007/978-3-031-31746-0_5

Gupta, A. (2023). *Energy Management System for Smart Buildings*, 327-347. Wiley. 10.1002/9781119847564.ch21

Habibzadeh, H., Nussbaum, B., Anjomshoa, F., Kantarci, B., & Soyata, T. (2019). A survey on cybersecurity, data privacy, and policy issues in cyber-physical system deployments in smart cities. *Sustainable Cities and Society*, 50, 101660. 10.1016/j.scs.2019.101660

Ho, H. W., Le, A., Le, D., Nguyen, D. N., & Phung, T. D. (2023). A review on development and applications of smart grids in typical power systems. *Energies*, 16(4), 2146.

Hollander, J. B., Wright, P., & Connolly, S. (2020). Citizen engagement in smart cities: A review of the literature and case studies. [invalid URL removed]. *Technological Forecasting and Social Change*, 151, 119–134.

Hong, H., Kery, J. L., Li, Y., Chen, Y., Li, K., & Chen, B. (2023). Transportation Internet: A Sustainable Solution for Intelligent Transportation Systems. *IEEE Transactions on Intelligent Transportation Systems*, 24(12), 1–12. 10.1109/TITS.2023.3270749

Hossain, J., Abdul Kadir, A. F., Nur Hanafi, A., Shareef, H., Khatib, T., Azmi Baharin, K., & Fani Sulaima, M. (2023). A Review on Optimal Energy Management in Commercial Buildings. *Energies, 16*(4), 1609-1609. https://uis.unesco.org/sites/default/files/documents/ip51-global-framework-reference-digital-literacy-skills-2018-en.pdf10.3390/en16041609

Hwang, J. (2023). Environmental Monitoring System. *International Journal for Research in Applied Science and Engineering Technology*, 11(5), 3590–3595. 10.22214/ijraset.2023.51826

Ibrahim, M. (2023). *Modern Approaches to Energy Efficiency Management,* 47-59. 10.1007/978-3-031-26596-9_5

International Energy Agency (IEA). (2023). *Electric vehicles.* IEA.

Jana, C. (2023). Environmental Technological Innovations and the Sustainability of their. *Development.*, 24(4), 245–252. 10.12912/27197050/162708

Janik, A., Ryszko, A., & Szafraniec, M. (2023). Intelligent and Environmentally Friendly Solutions in Smart Cities' Development—Empirical Evidence from Poland. *Smart Cities, 6*(2), 1202-1226. doi: of Form10.3390/smartcities6020058Top

Jasinska-Biliczak, A. (2022). Smart-City Citizen Engagement: The Answer to Energy Savings in an Economic Crisis? *Energies*, 15(23), 8828–8828. 10.3390/en15238828

Jobin, A., Ienca, M., & Vayena, E. (2019). The global landscape of AI ethics guidelines. *The Ethics of Artificial Intelligence*, 389-409.

Jobin, A., Ienca, M., & Vayena, E. (2020). *The global landscape of AI ethics guidelines: Mapping the evolution of ethical frameworks for artificial intelligence* (Vol. 1). Springer Nature. https://www.nature.com/articles/s42256-019-0088-2

Jones, R. (2023). Sustainability and Urban Innovation. *Advanced series in management, 81-91.*10.1108/S1877-636120230000030009

Kesic, D. M. (2023). "Smart" cities: The new paradigm of urban development. *Socioloski Pregled*, 57(1), 32–52. 10.5937/socpreg57-43015

Khan, S. (2023). Зеленые технологии и инновации: их влияние на устойчивое развитие в индийском контексте. *Vestnik Samarskogo universiteta. Èkonomika i upravlenie, 14*(1), 87-98. 10.18287/2542-0461-2023-14-1-87-98

Kuhn, S., Frauenberger, S., & Arzt, F. (2021). A survey on VR/AR applications for urban planning: Augmented decision-making in spatial development. [invalid URL removed]. *Computers, Environment and Urban Systems*, 90, 107224.

Kurniawan, A. (2023). IoT-driven Environmental Support System for Smart Cities. *SISFORMA*, 10(1), 14–18. 10.24167/sisforma.v10i1.10209

Kurniawan, R., & Pamudji, E. S. (2023). Green smart city concept and its implementation in developing countries. [IJECE]. *Iranian Journal of Electrical and Computer Engineering*, 17(1), 227–234.

Li, S., Da Xu, L., Zhao, S., Li, D., & Wang, H. (2021). 5G network slicing for mobile edge computing in smart cities. *IEEE Transactions on Industrial Informatics*, 18(1), 388–395.

Li, S., Kang, L., Xiao, Y., & Ren, Y. (2020). A privacy-preserving and reliable data collection scheme for smart cities based on blockchain. *IEEE Access : Practical Innovations, Open Solutions*, 8, 130052–130062.

Li, S., Kang, L., Zhao, Y., & Lv, J. (2021). A blockchain-based privacy-preserving data sharing scheme for smart cities. *IEEE Transactions on Industrial Electronics*, 68(8), 7004–7013.

Liu, S., Wang, Z., Narayanan, P., Li, Y., Li, Z., Sun, Y., & Xie, Y. (2022). Overview and open challenges on neuromorphic computing for edge AI applications. *Proceedings of the IEEE*, 110(7), 1209–1.

Liu, X., Hu, W., Xia, Y., Zhu, W., & Wang, H. (2020). Demographic determinants of COVID-19 transmission and fatality rates in mainland China. *International Journal of Infectious Diseases*, 97, 288-292Macintosh, A., & Whyte, A. (2017). Participation in smart cities: A contested terrain. *Urban Studies (Edinburgh, Scotland)*, 54(12), 2733–2753. https://www.sciencedirect.com/science/article/pii/B9780128166390000041

Makarova, I., Buyvol, P., Shubenkova, K., Fatikhova, L. E., & Parsin, G. (2023). Editorial: Sustainable transport systems. *Frontiers in Built Environment*, 9, 1161361. Advance online publication. 10.3389/fbuil.2023.1161361

Martinez, T. G. (2022). *Citizen engagement.* 124-146. Oxford Academic. 10.1093/oso/9780192848789.003.0007

Marvin, S., Hodson, M., & McFarlane, C. (2018). Co-producing smart cities. *Environment and Planning A* [invalid URL removed]. *Economy and Space*, 50(2), 309–327.

Mavlutova, I., Atstaja, D., Grasis, J., Kuzmina, J., Uvarova, I., & Roga, D. P. (2023). Urban Transportation Concept and Sustainable Urban Mobility in Smart Cities: A Review. *Energies*, 16(8), 3585–3585. 10.3390/en16083585

Milkintas, M., & Tamošiūnas, A. (2023). The impact of smart city technology on the quality of life in megacities: A systematic literature review. *Sustainability*, 15(6), 4252.

Milkintas, R., & Tamošiūnas, T. (2023). Theoretical foundations of the smart city concept. *Socialiniai Tyrimai*, 46(1), 88–102. 10.15388/Soctyr.2022.46.1.5

Namokel, M., & Karbowski, A. (2023). Design of Environmental Monitoring System Based on Cloud Platform.*Lecture Notes in Electrical Engineering*, 421-429. Springer. 10.1007/978-981-19-9338-1_52

Nesma, A. (2023). *Eco-Friendly IoT Solutions for Smart Cities Development: An Overview*. IEEE. 10.1109/ICAISC56366.2023.10085100

Ohm, P. (2010). Broken promises of privacy: Responding to the surprising failures of anonymization. *University of Pennsylvania Law Review*, 158(4), 1701–1777.

Paes, V. C., Pessoa, C. H. M., Pagliusi, R., Barbosa, C. E., Argôlo, M., de Lima, Y. O., & Moreira de Souza, J. (2023). Analyzing the Challenges for Future Smart and Sustainable Cities. *Sustainability (Basel)*, 15(10), 7996–7996. 10.3390/su15107996

Parnell, G. S., Specking, E., Pohl, E. A., & Buchanan, R. K. (2023). *Smart Cities—A Structured Literature Review*. Smart Cities., 10.3390/smartcities6040080

Raj Ananthan, T., & Zolkipli, M. F. (2022). *Challenges and Issues in Implementing Personal Data Protection.* International Journal of Recent Contributions from Engineering. *Science & IT*, 10(02), 53–61. 10.3991/ijes.v10i02.29373

Ranjan, S. L., Laha, B. K. Pattanayak, B. K., & Pattnaik, S. (2022). Advancement of Environmental Monitoring System Using IoT and Sensor: A Comprehensive Analysis. *AIMS Environmental Science, 9*(6), 771-800. doi: of Form10.3934/environsci.2022044Top

Saleem, M., Shakir, M., Usman, M., Bajwa, M., Shabbir, N., Ghahfarokhi, P. S., & Daniel, K. (2023). Integrating Smart Energy Management System with Internet of Things and Cloud Computing for Efficient Demand Side Management in Smart Grids. *Energies*, 16(12), 4835–4835. 10.3390/en16124835

Selbst, A. D., Boyd, D., Fried, S., Greenblatt, S. D., Keyes, P. D., & Vertinsky, J. (2019). *Fairness and accountability in artificial intelligence.* arXiv preprint arXiv:1908.09632. https://arxiv.org/pdf/2111.00826

Shalu. (2023). Environmental monitoring with machine learning. *EPRA International Journal of Multidisciplinary Research*, 208-212. 10.36713/epra13330

Singh, J., Sharma, P. K., & Moon, S. I. (2017). A survey on cloud security: Threats, countermeasures, and future directions. *Journal of Network and Computer Applications*, 79, 99–119.

Singh, S., Singh, H., & Sharma, P. K. (2017). A review on secure data transmission using cryptography algorithms in cloud computing environment. *International Journal of Computer Applications*, 168(3), 23–28. 10.5120/12338-8614

Singh, S., Singh, S., & Kaur, N. (2020). Eco-friendly urban development for sustainable future: A review. *Materials Today: Proceedings*, 45, 4364–4369.

Singh Bharati, T. (2020). Challenges, Issues, Security And Privacy Of Big Data. *International Journal of Scientific & Technology Research*, 9(2), 1482–1486.

Smart Cities and Buildings. (2023). 87-93. 10.1002/9781394216796.ch28

Sonnenfeld, A., Stevenson, J., & Waddington, H. (2022). Does citizen engagement improve development outcomes? A realist-informed systematic review of participation and accountability mechanisms. *Journal of Development Effectiveness*, 1–34. 10.1080/19439342.2022.2153380

Tian, Y., Niu, J., Sun, J., & Li, Y. (2020). A comprehensive review on hotspot detection and health risk assessment of urban green spaces using remote sensing. *Environmental Pollution*, 263, 114645.

UN Habitat., (2020). *World Urban Report 2020: Cities and pandemics: The invisible enemy in a divided world.* UN-Habitat.

UN Habitat. (2020). *World urbanization prospects 2018: The revision.* UN. https://population.un.org/wup/Publications/Files/WUP2018-Highlights.pdf

UNESCO. (2021). *Global framework of reference on digital literacy and competences.* DigComp.

UNESCO. (2021). *ICT in education 2021: Artificial intelligence in education.* United Nations Educational, Scientific and Cultural Organization.

van Deursen, A. J., & Ewijk, D. V. (2023). Bridging the digital divide: A literature review on interventions aimed at increasing digital skills among older adults. *Educational Gerontology*, 49(3), 171–184. https://www.ncbi.nlm.nih.gov/pmc/articles/PMC7786312/

Vasile,M., &Mocan,M.(2023). Some Considerations on the Smart City concept. *From Necessity to Implementation Challenges,2*(1), 15-23. 10.59168/BAPI4118

Ventura, J. A. (2023). Climate Benefits Advocated by the Development of Sustainable Vehicles and Charging Infrastructures in the Transport Sector. *Energies*, 16(9), 3772–3772. 10.3390/en16093772

Wachter, S., Mittelstadt, B., & Floridi, L. (2018). Transparent explanations for AI in healthcare. *Nature Machine Intelligence*, 1(11), 544–549.

Waddington, S. H., Singh, J., Garnett, S. T., McNeill, M., & White, M. P. (2022). Interventions to promote citizen engagement in health services: A systematic review. *BMC Health Services Research*, 2.

Wargent, M. (2023). Digital Participatory Planning: Citizen Engagement, Democracy, and Design. *Journal of the American Planning Association*, 89(2), 262–264. 10.1080/01944363.2023.2174350

Wen, J., Khalid, S., Zakaria, M. A., & Mahmood, H. (2023). Does Technological Innovation Reduce Environmental Degradation? Evidence from China. *The Engineering Economist*, 34(3), 323–334. 10.5755/j01.ee.34.3.32818

Winkler, L. K., Pearce, D., Nelson, J., & Babacan, O. (2023). The effect of sustainable mobility transition policies on cumulative urban transport emissions and energy demand. *Nature Communications*, 14(1), 2357. 10.1038/s41467-023-37728-x37095105

World Bank. (2021). *Digital dividends dividend report 2021*. World Bank. https://www.worldbank.org/en/publication/wdr2016

World Bank. (2023, April 12). *Bridging the digital divide*. World Bank. https://www.worldbank.org/en/news/feature/2020/10/26/closing-the-digital-divide-a-time-to-stay-connected

Xu, L. D., Jiang, Y., Zhao, Y., Ma, J., & Wang, W. (2020). A blockchain-based data sharing scheme for secure and reliable smart city services. *IEEE Journal on Selected Areas in Communications*, 38(6), 1624–1637.

Yasuoka, M. (2023). How Citizens Participation Begin and Continue in Developing Smart Cities. *Lecture Notes in Computer Science*, 14037, 182–192. 10.1007/978-3-031-34609-5_13

Yıldırım, K. (2023). Components of Smart Cities: Smart City Applications and Smart Space Management. *Mediterranean Journal of Humanities*. 10.13114/MJH.2023.607

Zhang, Y., Chen, L., Fang, Y., Li, J., & Zhang, Y. (2023). Security and privacy issues in smart cities: A survey. *Sensors (Basel)*, 23(8), 2901. https://www.mdpi.com/1424-8220/22/23/9338

Zheming, Y. (2023). Smart city and green development: Empirical evidence from the perspective of green technological innovation. *Technological Forecasting and Social Change*, 191, 122507–122507. 10.1016/j.techfore.2023.122507

Zhou, J., Zhou, Y., & Bai, X. (2023). Can Green-Technology Innovation Reduce Atmospheric Environmental Pollution? *Toxics*, 11(5), 403–403. 10.3390/toxics1105040337235218

Zou, Z., Zhao, S., & Gong, P. (2022). Data governance for smart cities: A literature review and future directions. *IEEE Access : Practical Innovations, Open Solutions*, 10, 120422–120439.

KEY TERMS AND DEFINITIONS

5G Networks: The fifth generation of mobile network technology, offering faster speeds, lower latency, and the capacity to connect more devices, essential for supporting the dense IoT environments in smart cities.

Adaptive Traffic Control: Systems that adjust traffic signal timings based on real-time traffic conditions to reduce congestion and improve traffic flow.

AI Ethics and Bias: Considerations in developing and deploying AI systems to ensure fairness, accountability, and transparency, preventing discriminatory outcomes.

Autonomous Vehicles: Self-driving vehicles that use sensors, cameras, and artificial intelligence to navigate without human intervention, aimed at reducing traffic congestion and emissions.

Building Energy Management Systems (BEMS): Integrated systems that monitor and control building energy usage to improve efficiency and reduce waste.

Circular Economy: An economic system aimed at eliminating waste and the continual use of resources through recycling, reusing, and repurposing materials.

Circular Economy: An economic system aimed at minimizing waste and making the most of resources by reusing, repairing, refurbishing, and recycling existing materials and products.

Citizen Engagement: Strategies and tools used to involve residents in urban planning and decision-making processes, ensuring inclusivity and responsiveness to their needs.

Citizen Science: The practice of public participation and collaboration in scientific research to increase scientific knowledge, which is often facilitated by smart city platforms to engage citizens in environmental monitoring and other activities.

Climate Resilience: The ability of urban systems to absorb and recover from climate-related shocks such as extreme weather events, flooding, and rising sea levels.

Crowdsourcing Platforms: Digital platforms that enable citizens to report and contribute data on urban issues, enhancing responsiveness and accountability.

Cyber-Physical Systems (CPS): Integrations of computation, networking, and physical processes, where embedded computers and networks monitor and control the physical processes with feedback loops.

Data Privacy and Security: Measures and protocols to protect personal data collected through smart city technologies from unauthorized access and misuse.

Data Visualization Tools: Software and platforms that present complex data in accessible and understandable formats to inform citizens and policymakers.

Digital Divide: The gap between those who have access to digital technologies and those who do not, impacting their ability to participate in smart city initiatives.

Digital Technologies: Tools and systems that collect, analyze, and disseminate data to enhance urban operations and quality of life.

Digital Twins: Virtual replicas of physical assets, processes, or systems that can be used for simulation and analysis to improve urban planning and management.

Energy Management Systems (EMS): Technologies that optimize energy usage in buildings and city infrastructure to enhance efficiency and reduce consumption.

Energy Storage Systems: Technologies such as batteries and thermal storage that store energy generated from renewable sources for later use, enhancing the reliability and efficiency of energy supply.

Environmental Monitoring: The process of using various technologies and sensors to track environmental conditions such as air quality, water quality, and soil quality in real-time to inform sustainable urban development decisions.

Environmental Monitoring: The use of sensors and IoT to track and manage air quality, noise levels, water pollution, and other environmental factors.

Geographic Information Systems (GIS): Systems that capture, store, manipulate, analyze, manage, and present spatial or geographic data, used extensively in urban planning and environmental monitoring.

Green Technologies: Technologies that promote eco-friendly infrastructure, renewable energy sources, and sustainable waste management practices.

Intelligent Lighting Systems: Lighting systems that use sensors and adaptive algorithms to optimize lighting based on occupancy and natural light levels, improving energy efficiency and user comfort.

Intelligent Traffic Management Systems (ITMS): Systems that use real-time data to optimize traffic flow and reduce congestion and emissions.

Internet of Things (IoT): A network of interconnected devices embedded with sensors that collect real-time data for optimizing various urban processes.

Machine Learning: A subset of artificial intelligence that involves the development of algorithms that can learn from and make predictions based on data, used in various smart city applications.

Net-zero Energy Buildings: Buildings designed to produce as much energy as they consume over a year, often through a combination of energy efficiency and renewable energy technologies.

Neuromorphic Computing: Computing systems that mimic the neural structure of the human brain, offering advanced processing capabilities for handling complex data and tasks in smart cities.

Participatory Workshops and Forums: Platforms for dialogue and collaboration between citizens, policymakers, and technology developers to co-create smart city solutions.

Public Participation: The involvement of citizens in decision-making processes, often facilitated by digital platforms, to ensure that technological solutions meet their needs and aspirations.

Public-Private Partnerships (PPPs): Collaborative agreements between government entities and private sector companies to fund, build, and operate projects that serve the public good.

Real-time Data Analytics: The immediate processing and analysis of data as it is collected, which is crucial for making timely and informed decisions in smart city management.

Renewable Energy Integration: The use of renewable energy sources like solar and wind to decrease reliance on fossil fuels and reduce greenhouse gas emissions.

Renewable Energy Sources: Energy obtained from sources that are naturally replenished, such as solar, wind, and hydroelectric power, which are crucial for reducing the carbon footprint of urban areas.

Robotic Process Automation (RPA): The use of software robots or 'bots' to automate highly repetitive and routine tasks normally performed by a human in a digital environment.

Smart City: An urban area that utilizes information and communication technology (ICT) to enhance its efficiency, quality of life, and environmental sustainability.

Smart Green Cities (SGCs): Urban areas that integrate smart city technologies with green practices to create sustainable and livable environments.

Smart Grids: Energy systems that use ICT to manage and distribute energy more efficiently and sustainably.

Smart Mobility: Innovations in transportation that enhance efficiency, reduce environmental impact, and improve accessibility, including autonomous vehicles and shared mobility services.

Smart Waste Collection Systems: Technologies that optimize waste collection routes and schedules based on real-time data from sensors in waste bins, reducing operational costs and environmental impact.

Sustainable Transportation: Public transportation, cycling, and electric vehicle initiatives that reduce reliance on private cars and lower emissions.

Sustainable Urban Development: Development that meets the needs of the present without compromising the ability of future generations to meet their own needs, particularly through environmentally responsible solutions.

Sustainable Urban Mobility: Transportation systems designed to be environmentally friendly, such as public transit, cycling, and pedestrian pathways, reducing reliance on fossil fuels.

Urban Green Spaces (UGSs): Parks, green roofs, and urban forests that improve air quality, reduce heat islands, and provide recreational spaces.

Urban Heat Island Effect: The phenomenon where urban or metropolitan areas become significantly warmer than their rural surroundings due to human activities, which can be mitigated by green infrastructure and sustainable urban design.

Urban Mining: The process of reclaiming raw materials from spent products, buildings, and waste, which reduces the demand for new resource extraction.

Urban Planning: The process of designing and regulating the use of urban space, incorporating smart and sustainable practices to improve living conditions.

Waste Management Systems: Technologies and processes that optimize waste collection and promote reduction, recycling, and reuse.

Waste-to-Energy Conversion: The process of generating energy in the form of electricity or heat from the primary treatment of waste, reducing landfill use and contributing to a circular economy.

Chapter 9
Savant Electronics Sustainability or Corporate Social Responsibility

Jitender Kumar
Birla Institute of Management Technology, India

Ashish Gupta
Indian Institute of Foreign Trade, New Delhi, India

Mridul Dharwal
Sharda School of Business Studies, Sharda University, India

Usharani Hareesh Govindrajan
Business School & School of Intelligent Emergency Management, University of Shanghai for Science and Technology, China

ABSTRACT

Mr. Prabhu Savant, CEO of Savant Electronics, has to convince the management that sustainability is different from CSR. Savant has to develop a plan to address the local communities ?(tm) CSR (corporate social responsibility) issues he would be facing while setting up the new plant. The case discusses achieving sustainability while deploying CSR as a strategy. The case looks at the Greenfield sustainable manufacturing plant project (electrical and electronics devices) in Madhya Pradesh, India, by Savant Electronics. According to the case study, this would describe the project ?(tm)s provenance, the various stakeholders who participated and what they thought of the project, Savant Electronics ?(tm) involvement, and what they

DOI: 10.4018/979-8-3693-3238-2.ch009

did to achieve a long-term sustainable economic and social assessment of the local community members as well as other beneficiaries who were included in the CSR initiative and became responsible ?ocorporate citizens. ?? The case illustrated Savant Electronics ?(tm) perspective on the social, environmental, and economic sustainability challenges related to this specific project. The case investigated the repercussions of establishing manufacturing units, particularly in developing nations, and critically analyzed corporate-society interaction. The case also evaluates the trade-off between promoting sustainability efforts and the impact of such mega-infrastructure projects on society and the environment. The case also prepares the students to analyze whether sustainability promotion causes more risk than benefits and how managers should mitigate the risks to maximize the benefits.

INTRODUCTION

Creating a strong organization and making the world a better place should be aligned; they should be hand in glove. ?"Prabhu Savant, CEO, SE

On 10 October 2021, Prabhu Savant, the CEO (Chief Executive Officer) of Savant Electronics (SE), was concerned about its new greenfield project. The beautiful sunlight corridors did not cheer their mood. It was evident that the matter was of grave concern. Savant was in charge of Savant Electronics ?(tm) upcoming dream project to establish a sustainable manufacturing unit for his electronic products (switchgear and regulator production for Legrand) at Bhopal, Madhya Pradesh (a state in India). This project could bring significant technological and economic development to the Bhopal Region. The project would provide royalties of US$ 5 Million over the next twenty-five years to the state government of Madhya Pradesh. Establishing an SE required approximately 500 acres of land from the state government to establish a sustainable production unit. Out of 500 acres of land, 10 acres he wanted for community development by building houses, a school, a hospital, a vocational skill center, etc., as part of the corporate social responsibility of Savant Electronics. As the initial step to acquiring land and setting up a unit, Savant and his team conducted a primary survey to understand the major implications of the resettlement and rehabilitation process once the land had been acquired and the unit was set up. Vikram Kumar, Unit head at SE, was against the development of land for community development because establishing a sustainable manufacturing unit was itself a corporate social responsibility activity, and the development of 10 acres of land would be a wasteful expenditure for the company (Exhibit 1).

However, in Savant ?(tm)s dream project, he wanted to develop a piece of land for the community and residents.

Since the beginning, Savant knew that major sustainable electronic projects, such as Savant Electronics, would require a high level of commitment to social and environmental protection and the support of the local community, local authorities, and state government. When the findings of the survey were presented to Savant, he understood that he would face huge uproars and a huge conflict would occur between the local community and the SE regarding land acquisition. Savant understood the depth of the problem and started making strategies to compensate for local communities and resolve conflicts. However, Kumar was against the decision and suggested that Savant focus on establishing a sustainable unit. However, Savant, going against the recommendation of Kumar, developed a compensation package for its ecological and social footprint to achieve the goal of ?ono net loss ?? of social and environmental biodiversity and also prepared a community development plan to create livelihood and employment opportunities to provide positive changes in the lives of local communities. However, Savant knew that these strategies would not be enough to resolve the conflicts between the SE and local people, as well as within the organization between Kumar and his team. He required a different strategy to overcome the upcoming conflicts with local communities.

A management committee was set up to examine the conflict between Kumar and Savant, survey the challenges faced by local communities, and develop action plans to understand the timeline of the settlement program. The committee surveyed the area and interacted with stakeholders, including affected people, activists, NGOs, and government bodies. It also did the cost audit for the development of the land. The committee came up with a holistic report discussing the development of a sustainable unit as part of CSR activity; however, the development of 10 acres of land (building houses, a school, a hospital, and a vocational skill center) will add up the cost. However, it will provide various benefits to the local community. The report was submitted to Savant. After reviewing the report from his committee members and interactions with affected people from the village who visited him for their concerns (resettlement and rehabilitation), he realized the enormity of the company ?(tm)s challenges with the issues of setting up the plant. He also realized that these issues need to be addressed quickly, as more time spent will have a greater impact on the company ?(tm)s reputation and delay in the project. A group of representatives from the local communities approached him with various issues (loss of valuable assets, such as land, houses, jobs, and parental assets). However, they also expressed happiness when they heard that land would be developed for their benefit which might forgo their other concerns. Savant confirmed that all their issues were addressed and resolved before setting up the plant. Savant was convinced that they were required to address several outstanding issues of conflict between

Kumar and Savant and also between the company and the local communities, for which he had to make a strategy on how he could create a healthy environment not only for community people but also for SE to save its reputation, in a short span of time. If he develops land for the community as a part of CSR activity, he would add more cost to the project and the relationship between him and Kumar might be affected; however, local people might be happy. Suppose he goes with Kumar ?(tm) s recommendation that a sustainable unit is a CSR activity and does not develop the land for the local community. In that case, he will save costs, but SE would face protests from the local community, which will impact the operations of Savant Electronics and its reputation among stakeholders. The final report was submitted to the company board for a final decision. Time was running out of hand, and he had a humongous task to resolve.

About Prabhu Savant

Prabhu Savant was born into a family that belonged to the lower-middle class and was influenced by the quintessence of Indian culture. Savant has an established reputation for taking risks in all of his endeavors. Savant's approach to Company Social Responsibility ensured that no questions were ever left unanswered. Savant executed CSR activities in his previous plants and knew that investments in staff and transport infrastructure had improved their workers' standard of living exponentially while their setting up and sustaining of a central kitchen has fed nutritious, wholesome, and hygienic midday meals to more than fifty thousand kids attending school each day, encompassing more than 500 government schools in the Bhopal district of Madhya Pradesh.

Savant Group of Companies

The Savant Group of companies is a diversified company with interests in IT (Information Technology), HR (Human Resources), Recruiting, Manufacturing, and Trading (Exhibit 2). Savant was a strong and trustworthy partner for many of its customers in different parts of the world and has over 500+ staff in various companies with offices in more than four countries and 8 towns in India and 33 years of business history.

Savant Electronics[6]

Established in 1986, Savant Electronics, which is involved in the manufacturing and engineering sector, caters to a wide range of clients. Savant was captive in manufacturing a variety of electrical and electronic devices, which amounted to 60 million devices per year. More than 40 electrical, electronic, and wire accessory devices were contract manufactured by Savant Electronics (Exhibit 3). In the Indian states of Madhya Pradesh, specifically the districts of Bhopal and Malwa, the SE built two production facilities (one each in a location for manufacturing electrical and electronic devices). Captive strength allowed both of these companies to produce a wide range of products for their clients. The company planned to set up a new manufacturing plant in Bhopal, Madhya Pradesh. Before setting up the unit, a management primary survey was conducted to understand the significant implications of the resettlement and rehabilitation process. During the establishment of the manufacturing unit in Bhopal in 2012, management teams encountered several issues. These issues were categorized into three categories: socioeconomic, environmental, and legal.

How Corporate Social Responsibility (CSR) in India Ensure Strict Compliance

Corporate social responsibility (CSR) has been the focus of various organizations, and CSR has been universally recognized as a critical component of successful business strategies (Barauskaite & Streimikiene, 2021). Because of the lack of necessary CSR regulations and laws, the implementation of CSR has been inconsistent. To address this issue, India Imposed CSR regulations and became the first country to do so (Economic Times, 2022). Consequently, the Companies Act in India included rules that made it easier for businesses to follow them. Some of the many guiding concepts and standards of the CSR guidelines in India concern the formation and roles of CSR committees, the board of directors ?(tm) duties, and the utilization and certification of CSR funds utilized and certified by CFOs (ICSI, 2021). For organizations with a net worth of ,1 5 billion (US $ 64.3 million) or more, a turnover of ,1 10 billion (US $ 128.6 million) or more, and a net profit of 50 million (US $ 0.6 million) or more during the immediately preceding financial year, the Act compels them to devote 2% to CSR initiatives (Ministry of Company Affairs, 2014).

ISSUES ENCOUNTERED IN THE REPORT

Socio-Economic Challenges

It was clear that SE needed an extensive area of land in order to build a sustainable electronics and electrical device unit. Most of this land was suitable for agriculture, which had been purchased, so farming families suddenly found themselves with fewer places to make a living. Accurate assessment of land requirements was another problem that surfaced during the property acquisition process. The intended territory expanded to include neighboring communities that had not been included in the original Rehabilitation and Resettlement plan. This unexpected shift in the method of property acquisition became a contentious matter, and the administration encountered opposition from the communities that had recently been added.

Environmental Challenges

The proposed manufacturing unit had a provision to use groundwater for general supply. The plant ?(tm)s required quantity of water for day-to-day use was enormous in an area marred by water scarcity owing to its natural terrain. Moreover, an approach road was built to block water flow to the rain-fed forest, leading to deforestation. In addition, norms for the safe disposal of industrial waste coming out of the unit were vulnerable to locals, which could endanger residents ?(tm) lives near disposal sites.

Legal Issues

The management had been planning the entire acquisition process, keeping in view the Land Acquisition Act of the state. It was challenging to implement an integrated and holistic resettlement plan for the affected people to set up the manufacturing unit during the land acquisition process. Since management had to address the lives affected by the process and organizational sustainability by giving them ample opportunity for their livelihoods, everything had to be compensated fairly and judiciously. It was also challenging to fix the entitlement, where multiple compensations and resettlement support had to be measured, accumulated, and accomplished. There was a fair amount of risk in dealing with the compensation package when subjective matters, such as cultural, emotional, and ancestral issues, were getting attached during negotiations. During the negotiation, the nature of the land was one of the critical points where people questioned the type of soil, area, and productivity of the newly allotted land as a part of the compensation package.

Pilot Testing Phase and Learnings

The Savant and team recognized the importance of the community's role in the negotiation process. They believed that clear and practical communication from the management team would build trust and pave the way for better and settled negotiations with the Project Affected People (PAP). The management also strived to determine a timeline for the entire compensation process, which began with surveying and calculating compensation packages for each family/individual and ended with the disbursement of funds and other emoluments. Normally, a family would receive the entire compensation package within 8 months of the acquisition process.

Further, Savant did not compromise the quality of compensation, be it the size of land provided to PAPs in lieu of land acquired from them or the value of the land given to PAPs. Savant also took care of the housing and transportation facility so that the PAPs would feel comfortable and attached to the development process going in and around them. Savant took the initiative to cater to people basic requirements who were displaced in the unit setting process. The first initiative was to organize a health camp where relocated family members could come for a free health checkup. Such camps started getting organized very often (within three months), helping people mitigate health-related issues. Management also started an ambulance facility for PAPs to ensure smooth commutation to a nearby hospital during emergencies. Savant also found that the education level among PAPs was not reasonably good, and hence, it started bridge courses in local government schools. Fifteen schools were adopted by the Savant and team of the catchment areas of the manufacturing unit and started investing in their infrastructure, training, learning materials, and other facilities. Books, notebooks, pencils, colored pencils, bags, etc., were distributed among the students. Different celebrations were organized at the school level, and winners were felicitated in ceremonies. Teachers were also sent orientation workshops to become aware of the new teaching methodologies that help retain children studying in government schools. Savant started the plantation campaign in and around the factory premises, and schoolchildren were encouraged to engage. Farmers identified among PAPs were oriented toward land leveling techniques, modern agriculture techniques for more production in the limited area of cultivation, horticulture, floriculture, and other important aspects of the agro-based business.

During all such interventions, it was envisaged that funding and the flow of resources were extremely important components. After three months of the pilot test, SE was convinced that the SE ?(tm)s sustainability could only be ensured if the abovementioned activities could be run for a substantial period. Continuous and adequate support from funds and other resources was required promptly. Therefore, a provision was made in the annual budget for such activities, and the same would be transferred periodically to the selected Project Implementing Agency (PIA) that the SE can hire in the future. Savant made an attempt to incorporate such a support mechanism in his report. Under this arrangement, a group was formed democratically by the PAPs and was responsible for overseeing its developmental program. The process would, but not in a limited way, include the compensation process, proper transition of land rights from beneficiaries to management, welfare activities, troubleshooting, and bridging the gap between management and PAPs.

Office bearers of this group would be given proper honorariums to carry out their daily operations. Local counselors, senior officials from administrations, and Key Opinion Leaders (KOLs) would be the honorary members to facilitate the dialogue process and guide the group in meeting the key objectives of this development process. Savant also came up with the waste disposal process and techniques once production had been in full swing. The committee chalked out a proper and unique solution in consultation with experts and group members. It was decided to reduce waste by introducing the best available technology, ultimately reducing production costs and minimizing waste. Savant also ensured that solid waste from the production line could be recycled for various purposes. Savant, thus, made the development process inclusive holistically.

?oNowadays, organizations have a greater understanding of the importance of using resources responsibly than ever. Consumers are increasingly looking for brands that are both environmentally and socially responsible ??. Prabhu Savant, CEO, SEs

Future Challenges

After running the CSR activities successfully for more than 5 months (i.e., February 2022), new challenges came into the frame. Resettling Project-Affected-People (PAP), however, did not pose significant challenges to SE ?(tm)s sustainable unit ?(tm) s early phases of planned development. However, the area was then available to relocate individuals displaced by development initiatives, and forests could easily be cut for this purpose if needed. People back then presumed that development projects would ultimately bring in a period of prosperity for all. They were often willing to compromise for the greater good of society. As a result, they would accept cash ?" then the standard form of compensation for property purchased ?" hand over the possession of their land for development purposes, and then relocate to new locations.

In contrast, resettling the local community has become much more difficult. Planners and administrators currently operate in very different environments. The number of people who needed to be resettled has increased significantly. There was a lack of land for resettlement. To rehabilitate the displaced, it would be impossible to set aside land from the forested area, which had fallen to its absolute minimum. In addition, the legitimacy of the PAP initiative was questioned because the migrants lived in the area selected for the project. The categories ?oslum dwellers ?? and ?oencroachers ?? were still vaguely defined, making it difficult to establish legal title to land. Land ownership was important in determining whether the PAP qualified for compensation. Because people see their interests as incompatible with the projects, they unite to oppose projects that result in relocation. Environmentalists, human rights activists, media networks, and other groups supported them. Owing to increasing population demands, there were fewer open locations where projects could be launched without displacing residents. To accomplish rapid development by investing in massive infrastructure projects, privately owned land had to be acquired much more than before. A growing number of people who would be displaced from their homes for the sake of development need to be carefully rehabilitated. Savant had to revise his strategy to prevent conflict and keep his project on track.

Way Forward

Savant knew that he would have to face challenges from the company board while proposing his plans, as they think purely from a business point of view and feel no obligation beyond profits. He had to submit solid arguments to the company board, convincing them that establishing a sustainable unit is different from CSR activities. How would the development of the land benefit the local community, and might it suppress the protests of the local community? He also knew that the company board might show their concern about increasing costs and protests from the local community, which might get over; however, they were not assured of that. Savant had to bridge the gap between profit orientation and SE ?(tm)s sustainability initiatives along with CSR activity. Till now, the pilot test has provided fruitful results, but would he be able to convince the board to carry out the CSR activities as a routine of SE? An important part of the process was integrating market opportunities with company responsibilities, such as developing positive products and services for people with low incomes (Gupta et al., 2023; Kumar et al., 2023, 2024). He planned to showcase benefits and value creation, which could be achieved by taking care of their sanitation, health, safe food, clean water, and livelihood opportunities, such as wage-based jobs and small-scale entrepreneurship initiatives.

This approach would also expand numerous dedicated collaborations with diverse market stakeholders as a source of new solutions, with the SE ?(tm)s sustainability viewed as an engine for growth and risk mitigation. The company can eventually save more costs through cleaner processes and create efficiency. This will lead to better value for stakeholders. Addressing community issues will attract support from many organizations that are constantly looking for sustainable partners. It will nurture relationships with clients who want to be part of fair practices and drive a positive impact on their surroundings, along with their suppliers and partners. Savant was confident that the steps he identified would eventually lead him to his goal of SE ?(tm)s CSR activity, along with sustainability and value creation for internal and external stakeholders. It has to be done in a short span of time, as people will become restless and hamper their reputation.

Exhibits

Exhibit 1: Conversation between Prabhu Savant and Vikram Kumar

Kumar: Sir, why do you want to develop the 10 acres of land? SE is already investing in 500 acres and establishing sustainable units. It will only add up to the cost of the project.

Savant: We are acquiring 500 acres, but what are we doing for the local community? We can show it as the CSR activity of SE.

Kumar: But establishing a sustainable unit is itself a CSR activity.

Savant: I agree with your point of view, but sustainability and CSR are different. By being sustainable, we are not doing anything for the local people. They will protest, which can delay our project.

Kumar: But what is the assurance that they will not protest after you spend money on land development?

Savant: I know they might not protest, but at least the development will help them in the future. Trust me, you are looking at the cost; I am looking at benefits for all the stakeholders in the coming future.

Kumar: I am sorry to say this, sir, but I don ?(tm)t agree with you here. It is better to let the board decide whether to proceed with land development.

Savant: Can we do one thing, Kumar, Let's run the CSR activity for March 2022 as a pilot test. Within that time frame, we will form a committee that will review the progress of the activities. IN March 2022, we will present the report with the outcome to the board.

Kumar: It looks good to me, however, I will not be convinced unless I see the results.

Table 1. Exhibit 2: List of companies under savant group of companies

A A A A A A A A A A A A A Company Name	A A A A A A A A A A A A A Nature of work
A A A A A A A A A A A A A Anant International	A A A A A A A A A A A A A In 1983, one of India ?(tm)s oldest recruitment firms held the first international recruitment license awarded by the Government of India.
A A A A A A A A A A A A A Anant Exports	A A A A A A A A A A A A A Anant International ?(tm)s export division supplies goods across a wide range of industry segments, including ?oEngineering Equipments, Machines, Textiles, Leather, Minerals and Mining, Excavation, Construction, Power Generation, Oil Drilling, Marine engines, Heavy Commercial Transportation ?"Equipment and Spare Parts. ??
A A A A A A A A A A A A A Savant Software	A A A A A A A A A A A A A Dynamic software development firm providing Human Capital Solutions, Business Software, Consulting Services, and Support to ease employee lifecycle management in small, medium, and big organizations.

continued on following page

Table 1. Continued

A A A A A A A A A A A A A Company Name	A A A A A A A A A A A A A Nature of work
A A A A A A A A A A A A A Savant Engineers	A A A A A A A A A A A A A A mechanical engineering workshop that assembles dyes, jigs, fixtures, sheet metal components, and press parts.
A A A A A A A A A A A A A Savant Electronics	A A A A A A A A A A A A A Electrical and electronic device manufacturer

Source: Created by Authors using the company ?(tm)s website information

Table 2. Exhibit 3: SE services

A A A A A A A A A A A A A Sr No	A A A A A A A A A A A A A Services by SE
A A A A A A A A A A A A A 1	A A A A A A A A A A A A A Manufacturing coils
A A A A A A A A A A A A A 2	A A A A A A A A A A A A A Assembling Circuits
A A A A A A A A A A A A A 3	A A A A A A A A A A A A A Wiring accessories such as switches, sockets, regulators, TV sockets, telephone sockets, multi-strand sockets, regulators, and dimmers are manufactured.
A A A A A A A A A A A A A 4	A A A A A A A A A A A A A Assembly of neon lamps
A A A A A A A A A A A A A 5	A A A A A A A A A A A A A Assembly of an electrical switchboard
A A A A A A A A A A A A A 6	A A A A A A A A A A A A A Assembling the skirting lights

Source: Created by Authors using the company ?(tm)s website information

EPILOGUE

SE divided the stakeholders into three categories. Group 1 supported SE ?(tm) s initiatives; Group 2 obstructed SE ?(tm)s functions and operations; and Group 3 was passive in its demand and activities to examine the matter. Eventually, the issues of community people were addressed in a timely manner. After successfully setting up the plant within the given time, Savant Electronics is now looking at setting up various new projects.

Figure 1. TN Exhibit 1: Corporate social responsibility and stakeholder theory

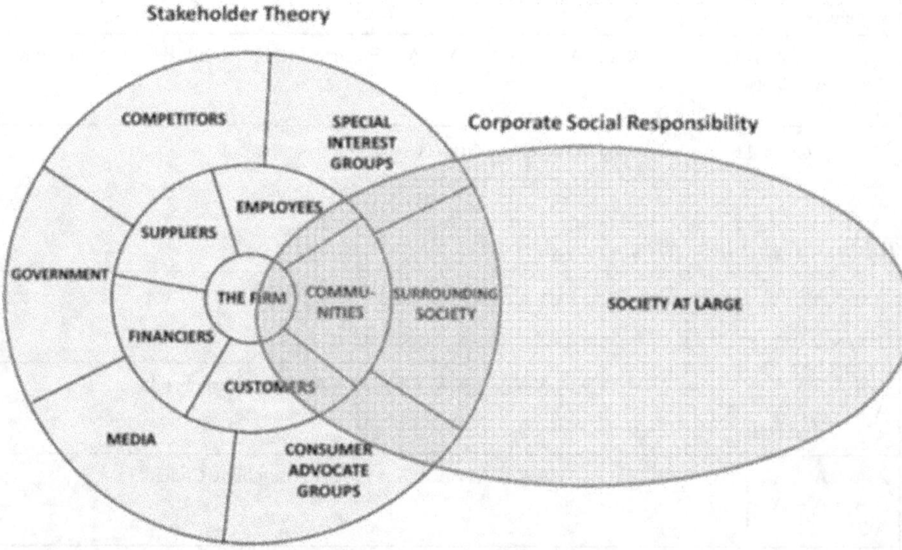

Source: *(Freeman and Dmytriyev, 2017)*

REFERENCES

Barauskaite, G., & Streimikiene, D. (2021). Corporate social responsibility and financial performance of companies: The puzzle of concepts, definitions and assessment methods. *Corporate Social Responsibility and Environmental Management*, 28(1), 278 ?"287. 10.1002/csr.2048

Blowfield, M., & Frynas, J. G. (2005). Editorial Setting new agendas: Critical perspectives on Corporate Social Responsibility in the developing world. *International Affairs*, 81(3), 499 ?"513. 10.1111/j.1468-2346.2005.00465.x

Buysse, K., & Verbeke, A. (2003). Proactive environmental strategies: A stakeholder management perspective. *Strategic Management Journal*, 24(5), 453 ?"470. 10.1002/smj.299

Campbell, J. L. (2007). Why would corporations behave in socially responsible ways? An institutional theory of corporate social responsibility. *Academy of Management Review*, 32(3), 946 ?"967. 10.5465/amr.2007.25275684

Clarkson, M. E. (1995). A stakeholder framework for analyzing and evaluating corporate social performance. *Academy of Management Review*, 20(1), 92 ?"117. 10.2307/258888

Doh, J. P., & Guay, T. R. (2006). Corporate social responsibility, public policy, and NGO activism in Europe and the United States: An institutional ??stakeholder perspective. *Journal of Management Studies*, 43(1), 47 ?"73. 10.1111/j.1467-6 486.2006.00582.x

Donaldson, T., & Preston, L. E. (1995). The stakeholder theory of the corporation: Concepts, evidence, and implications. *Academy of Management Review*, 20(1), 65 ?"91. 10.2307/258887

Economic Times. (2022, Mar 22). View: India becomes the first country to have statutorily mandated CSR for specified companies. *Economic Times*.https://economictimes .indiatimes.com/opinion/et-commentary/view-india-becomes-the-first-country-to -have-statutorily-mandated-csr-for-specified-companies/articleshow/90448748.cms

Freeman, R. E., & Dmytriyev, S. (2017). Corporate social responsibility and stakeholder theory: Learning from each other. Symphonya. *Emerging Issues in Management*, (1), 7 ?"15. 10.4468/2017.1.02freeman.dmytriyev

Gupta, A., Kumar, A., & Melese, E. (2023). Young consumer engagement at the bottom of pyramid: Applying SOR framework in e-commerce context. *Young Consumers*, 24(6), 786 ?"806. 10.1108/YC-06-2022-1542

ICSI. (2021). *Guidance Note on Corporate Social Responsibility*. ICSI. https://www.icsi.edu/media/webmodules/Guidance_Note_on_CSR_Final.pdf

Kumar, J., Katiyar, G., Mehrotra, A., Attri, R., & Vishnoi, S. K. (2024). Connecting BOP consumers and retailers: What drives small-time retailing through social media? *Journal of Retailing and Consumer Services*, 77, 103679. 10.1016/j.jretconser.2023.103679

Kumar, J., Tapar, A. V., & Bhattacharjee, S. (2023). Social media and the bottom of the pyramid: a systematic literature review and future research agenda. *International Journal of Emerging Markets*.

Ministry of Corporate Affairs. (2018). *Invitation for public comments for High-Level Committee on Corporate Social Responsibility -2018*. MCA. https://www.mca.gov.in/Ministry/pdf/InvitationOfPublicCommentsHLC_18012019.pdf

Murillo ??Luna, J. L., GarcA(c)s ??Ayerbe, C., & Rivera ??Torres, P. (2008). Why do patterns of environmental response differ? A stakeholders ?(tm) pressure approach. *Strategic Management Journal*, 29(11), 1225 ?"1240. 10.1002/smj.711

ENDNOTES

1 Birla Institute of Management Technology, Greater Noida

2 Indian Institute of Foreign Trade, New Delhi

3 Sharda School of Business Studies, Sharda University

4 Business School, University of Shanghai for Science and Technology, Shanghai, China

5 School of Intelligent Emergency Management, University of Shanghai for Science and Technology, Shanghai, China

6 Authors have disguised the name of the company, protagonist names and other identifying information to protect confidentiality. The Protagonist has requested the Authors to disguise the information.

APPENDIX: TEACHING NOTE

Teaching Note

Savant Electronics: Sustainability or Corporate Social Responsibility

Teaching/Case Objectives

At the end of the case study discussions, students will be able to prepare strategies to promote an organization's sustainable business practices. The case will help students:

1. To analyze CSR activities ?(tm) relevance to achieving corporate sustainability in an emerging market like India.
2. To showcase the influence of CSR activities to promote sustainable business practices.
3. To understand the importance of stakeholder management in setting up a new manufacturing plant.
4. To design a stakeholder management plan and to identify various elements for the stakeholder management plan.

The case looks at the Greenfield sustainable manufacturing plant project (electrical and electronics devices) in Madhya Pradesh, India, by Savant Electronics. This case will present the background of the project, the identification and involvement of various stakeholders, their perspectives toward the project and their related interests in the project, actions that Savant took, and the outcome of the numerous engagement efforts toward a sustainable social and economic appraisal of the locals and other beneficiaries falling under the scope of the CSR initiative and becoming responsible ?ocorporate citizenship. ?? The case presents Savant Electronics' viewpoint regarding the social, environmental, and economic sustainability of this particular project. In addition, the case analyzes the importance of stakeholder groups to Savant Electronics. It has been determined that the importance of the various stakeholder groups can be measured by their respective claims ?(tm) power, legitimacy, and urgency. In addition to this, the case will illustrate the intricate institutional structure that exists in emerging markets. In order for businesses to live up to their social and environmental commitments, it can be challenging for them to carry out large-scale greenfield manufacturing projects at times. Finally, the case allows students to examine the association between corporations and their respective societies and the implications of establishing manufacturing plants, particularly in developing nations. The students are also asked to assess the trade-off between supporting sustainability efforts and the influence of such mega infrastructure projects on the environment and society. It is one of the questions that is posed in the case. The students will also be prepared to analyze whether or not promoting sustainability causes more risks than benefits, as well as how managers can minimize the risks in order to optimize the benefits of promoting sustainability.

Research Methodology

The case is based on data from the primary (interviews with the CEO, Prabhu Savant) and secondary (documents). The primary data source includes interviews with the CEO (Prabhu Savant) and the secondary data from the company ?(tm)s website and Company documents. For ethical reasons and to ensure confidentiality, pseudonyms for the company and characters have been used. Our secondary data was collected from (1) Internet searches, (2) Industry reports, (3) annual reports of companies, (4) Newspaper and Magazine articles, and (5) Newspaper and Magazine advertisements.

Positioning of Case

The target audience of the case is students of post-graduation level courses in Business Strategy, Corporate Social Responsibility, Business Ethics, and Corporate Sustainability through a ninety-minute session. The case will also be helpful for executive-level courses.

Key Concept and Theory

Stakeholder Theory: According to the explanations offered by the stakeholder theory for engagement in corporate sustainability strategies, businesses should take into account the concerns of a variety of stakeholders when making business decisions rather than focusing solely on the concerns of shareholders **(Freeman, 1984;Clarkson, 1995; Mitchell et al., 1997)**. Concerns about climate change, pollution, and the depletion of nonrenewable resources have prompted businesses to begin addressing concerns raised by stakeholders regarding corporate sustainability strategies **(Mollenkopf et al., 2010)**. According to findings from earlier studies, the investment in corporate sustainability strategies is impacted by stakeholders ?(tm) influence **(Ferrell, 2004; Muthuri & Gilbert, 2010).**

Stakeholder theory and corporate Social responsibility are separate but related notions with some overlap. Both stakeholder theory and corporate social responsibility (CSR) emphasize the necessity of integrating societal interests into business operations. It is the primary similarity that exists between the two concepts. Companies are always a part of the society in which they operate. They are never as distinct from one another as proponents of the neoclassical theory like to pretend they are. The distinction between the two concepts is that stakeholder theory postulates the overall business ?(tm)s key responsibilities, i.e., corporate responsibilities.

The Instructor can share relevant videos for better understanding the concept, and also students come prepared for the case discussion (Arthsastra, 2017; Corporateethics, 2009; Harvard Graduate School of Education, 2013)

The videos available in the public domain from renowned authoritarians on the subject will help us better understand the case and give a wider understanding of the subject.

? Arthsastra. (2017). *Keynote on ?oCreating Shared Value ?? by Michael Porter, Professor, Harvard Business School.* Retrieved Sept 26, 2022, from https://www.youtube.com/watch?v=hX0bN9wVmww

A Corporateethics. (2009). *What is Stakeholder Theory? - R. Edward Freeman.* Retrieved Sept 22, 2022, from https://www.youtube.com/watch?v=bIRUaLcvPe8

A Harvard Graduate School of Education. (2013). *Plenary: Redefining Corporate Social Responsibility.* Retrieved Sept 26, 2022, from https://www.youtube.com/watch?v=VFrz3BgrebI

Assignment Questions

1. How can Savant Electronics develop a plan for corporate sustainability?
2. What is the relationship between Corporate sustainability and Corporate social responsibility?
3. What is stakeholder management, and why is it important to have Stakeholder Management for Savant Electronics?
4. Savant Electronics has to design a stakeholder management plan. What should be considered when drafting the plan, and how should the plan be created?

Teaching Plan and Timing

The instructor may initiate an open discussion to start with. The group discussion will be based on Greenfield Projects and their associated challenges. The instructor exposes students to the triple bottom-line challenges of meeting the social and environmental obligations and simultaneously meeting the project ?(tm)s economic viability. The discussion moves around understanding the context of Savant Electronics ?(tm) manufacturing plant project and its social and environmental challenges. The instructor can lead the discussion on the key elements of a big infrastructure project in the context of an emerging economy. The instructor encourages students to identify the different stakeholders and their various interests and perspectives: policies and views of government and regulators, local community groups, NGOs, industry associations, Savant Electronics creditors, suppliers and buyers, etc. The instructor also set the agenda for analyzing ?owhether sustainability promotion causes more risk than benefits and how managers should mitigate the risks to maximize the benefits and managerial suggestions on managing these trade-offs between risk and benefits.

Students will gain insight into situations that may arise while running their own companies or working as consultants due to their analysis of the case. These situations will require them to recognize necessary information and acceptable strategies towards engaging with local communities in mega infrastructure projects encompassing land acquisition and a certain level of planning for social and environmental consequences. Students are encouraged to engage in critical analysis of the strategies employed by businesses in the management of the various stakeholders in the case. Their understanding of corporations ?(tm) ?onew ?? roles will be enhanced by involving local communities in projects in emerging economies.

This case can raise awareness about the environmental and social consequences of establishing a manufacturing plant. When they graduate with a Master ?(tm)s degree, students frequently find work with multinational companies, many of which face the same challenges when establishing new infrastructure projects, such as a manufacturing plant, in either developed or developing countries. It is possible that these businesses would be better prepared to handle situations like these if their officials had a deeper familiarity with the social, economic, and environmental issues ingrained in the corporate social responsibility programs. Students with this background may also find employment with non-governmental organizations (NGOs), thereby assisting local communities in addressing issues pertaining to large-scale projects and engaging in conflict with major corporations.

Before the case is applied, students are expected to have done the following:

- ? Read the case completely
- ? Read the following papers to understand the theoretical basis for analyzing the case (the instructor might select some and may suggest them to students)
- ? Understand the local land acquisition and environmental regulations to analyze the case from a local perspective.

Teaching Plan

The following is a proposed timeline for implementing the case study. Each item is discussed in greater detail in the section. This Teaching can be done via online or offline studies.

Table 3. Tentative timeline for teaching the case

Timeframe	Discussion Activity
0-20 minutes	Introduction A A A A A A A A A A A ? The instructor explained to the class the context of the case: Setting up a Greenfield manufacturing plant under the Corporate Social Responsibility initiative and the challenges faced thereof, with a special reference to the case of emerging economies, especially in Asia. A A A A A A A A A A A ? The instructor outlines the goal: The newly developed idea of CSR, the traditional understanding of stakeholder theory, and the more recent advocacy toward stakeholder theory and CSR. A A A A A A A A A A A ? The challenges involved large-scale infrastructure projects and meeting social, environmental, and economic objectives. Different stakeholders pose challenges to Greenfield Projects in terms of meeting their expectations. The case of emerging economies is to be highlighted, showing how the institutional environment differs in emerging economies.
20-50 minutes	Savant Electronics project: An emerging market case of CSR and Stakeholder Management A A A A A A A A A A A ? Presentation and discussion of the actions that Savant Electronics could take and programs the company could develop. A A A A A A A A A A A ? The instructor can discuss the concept of Corporate Social Responsibilities and Stakeholder Management (Reference): A A A A A A A A A A A A A A A A A A A A A A A o Campbell (2007); Donaldsonm & Preston (1995); Blowfield & Frynas (2005).
50-80 minutes	Frameworks for Stakeholder Management A A A A A A A A A A A ? The instructor asks the students to identify the positions of the different stakeholder groups and their relevance to Savant Electronics in this specific context and the future business. A A A A A A A A A A A A A A A A A A A A A A A o Students, in groups of four to five (on average), identify and analyze the main issues highlighted by each stakeholder group. A A A A A A A A A A A ? The instructor discusses the framework for stakeholder management in terms of their claims ?(tm) legitimacy, power, and urgency. Introduction to the various frameworks on classifying stakeholders to manage them professionally. References: A A A A A A A A A A A A A A A A A A A A A A A o Doh & Guay (2006); Murillo ??Luna et al. (2008), Buysse &Verbeke (2003); Clarkson (1995)
80-90 minutes	Conclusion and takeaways of the case A A A A A A A A A A A ? Wrap-up: discussion of lessons learned from the case *(Question 4)*

Assignment Question Discussion

During the introduction of the case to the students, the instructor lays the groundwork. The context of the project needs to be explained to establish the main pedagogical objective and the foundational understanding of the case. In the next thirty minutes, the students form groups to review the company ?(tm)s 2013 sustainability report, listing the programs developed by the company and the economic, social, and environmental impact of the project. In the plenary, the instructor can introduce the concept of CSR and stakeholder management by ***Clarkson (1995).***

The instructor has access to TN Exhibit 3, which is available for reference (figure of stakeholder theory). The figure presents an illustration of the relationship that can be inferred between stakeholder theory and corporate social responsibility.

Both focus on the importance of a company ?(tm)s responsibility toward the communities and society in which it operates. Stakeholder theory was developed in the 1970s, and corporate social responsibility was developed in the 1990s. The theory of stakeholders didn ?(tm)t emerge until the 1970s and the concept of corporate social responsibility didn ?(tm)t become popular until the 1990s. The 1970s saw the development of the stakeholder theory, and the 1990s saw the rise of the concept of corporate social responsibility.

On the other hand, the stakeholder theory has the propensity to focus on issues within a reasonable reach for the activities of the company. Both the local communities in which the company operates (represented by the inner circle in TN Exhibit 1, which includes all of the company ?(tm)s most important stakeholders) and the larger society in which those communities are embedded (such as a city or district) are prioritized (refer the outer circle of TN Exhibit 1 which shows secondary stakeholders). On the other hand, CSR desires to maximally broaden the company ?(tm) s social orientation.

Once more, the students work in groups, discussing the perspectives of the various stakeholder groups and compiling a list of the primary concerns held by each stakeholder group. At this point, it will be useful to introduce them to why stakeholders are essential to the organization (herein Savant Electronics) and their power to influence organizational survival. The instructor may introduce them to scientifically analyze stakeholders in the framework of Donaldson & Preston (1995) regarding legitimacy, power, and urgency. The instructor will provide the different classification frameworks for classifying the different stakeholder groups in the plenary using (Clarkson, 1995; Buysse &Verbeke, 2003; and Doh & Guay, 2006). The instructor should emphasize that corporations must manage their stakeholders efficiently and effectively, creating a win-win situation for both the stakeholders and the organization. The instructor needs to differentiate the setting of emerging and developing economies where governments consider economic development the topmost priority, the poor institutional and regulatory environments, and the different examples of stakeholder unrest affecting corporate survival. Finally, the instructor can wrap up the class with a summary of the main lessons learned and insights from the case.

Case Analysis

Q1: How Can Savant Electronics Develop a Plan for Corporate Sustainability?

Before starting the case discussion, the instructor should discuss what corporate sustainability is and how SE can prepare a sustainable plan. The instructor can explain simply that a corporate sustainability plan is an initiative undertaken by a company to ensure its long-term viability from a financial, social, and environmental perspective. The best interests of the environment, the business owner, and the consumer are served by a company that takes these steps toward sustainability. After explaining the meaning of sustainability, the instructor should explain the various stages through which sustainability can be planned.

Stages of Corporate Sustainability

Stage 1: Learn About Sustainability

At this point, the organization has not yet realized that it cannot increase profits until it changes its practices. Let us say it decides to engage in illegal and unethical behavior in order to achieve its goals and then seeks to hide this fact from the authorities. If that's the case, what you're doing is illegal. It has zero interest in environmental protection and actively opposes laws intended to protect it.

So, the instructor should state that at this stage, SE must learn about sustainability. How and why does sustainability relate to SE? When developing their sustainability plans, SE must consider local community people, profits, and the planet. At this stage, SE should articulate how the company will contribute to India ?(tm)s financial, societal, and environmental sustainability.

Stage 2: Assessment of the Sustainability Performance

In order to minimize risk, the organization must follow all applicable laws and regulations pertaining to employee rights, working conditions, environmental protection, and health and safety. First, the company has to assess its existing situation and where it stands in relation to its sustainability ?"understanding what can be measured, where the company is performing, where it is falling short, and how its performance in terms of sustainability stacks up against competitors is useful. Companies routinely submit yearly reports describing their progress toward sustainability targets and their performance in doing so.

SE should learn the laws, check compliance, and assess global issues.

Stage 3: Seeking Opportunities

Eco-efficiency, process improvement, and waste minimization are all identified as opportunities for cost savings in the workplace. The report acknowledges the benefits of social marketing and community investment in mitigating risk, improving brand image, and eventually increasing stakeholder returns.

SE must determine the areas in which their company can contribute significantly. Organizations will be required to strike a balance between various priorities and agendas, and there will be difficult choices to make between what the organization wants to do and what the company can afford to do. SE should innovate and get employees ?(tm) feedback and insights to explore opportunities.

Stage 4: Engage and Empower the Team to Set a Vision

The road to sustainability can be paved with relative ease if a firm can inspire and engage its employees in making the necessary changes. Employees who care strongly about sustainability and ethical business practices may already exist within a firm. It's important to incorporate employees in the planning process and give them the authority to serve as ambassadors. Rebranding the organization as one that cares about the environment and incorporating that belief into core business practices will have a profound effect. It produces eco-friendlier products, implements eco-effectiveness and lifecycle stewardship practices, and reaps the rewards of sustainability projects in order to obtain a competitive edge.

SE must include its employees and empower them to implement sustainable goals.

Stage 5: Establish the Target, Implement the Changes, and Develop Measurement Parameters

The organization needs to set goals that are challenging but not impossible to achieve. It will be crucial to gather and analyze data, and the Internet of Things is making it easier to keep tabs on any data related to environmental sustainability. We are moving closer to a world in which Company Directors may be responsible for the sustainability performance of their large corporations and where overstating a company's sustainability impact may result in the company being subject to consequences.

SE should communicate about their changed policies, review performances, and get feedback about their activities and policies.

The instructor should mention that before corporations go public with the environmental consequences of their products or services, they should ensure that they can provide evidence to support their sustainability claims after completing the first five steps toward sustainability. They adhere to the guidelines and general principles of environmental marketing outlined by the law body; they can prevent themselves from making unqualified claims. They will acquire the knowledge necessary to understand how customers will interpret their claims and how to support and qualify those claims without being deceptive. After that, corporations can start telling people about the plan for the long-term viability of their business. The monetary, social, and environmental gains, in addition to the improvements in public relations, are certain to follow.

Q2: What is the Relationship Between Corporate Sustainability and Corporate Social Responsibility?

After discussing the meaning of corporate sustainability, the instructor should now discuss the meaning of CSR and the difference between CSR and corporate sustainability. The instructor may solicit and take note of the student ?(tm)s points of view by asking for their insights. After receiving the insights, the instructor should discuss the relationship between sustainability and CSR. The term ?ocorporate sustainability ?? (CS) refers to adopting business strategies that satisfy the organization ?(tm)s and its stakeholders ?(tm) needs while protecting the company ?(tm) s human and natural resources. CSR is a business strategy that encourages companies to act responsibly toward their stakeholders, employees, and the community at large. Through CSR (also known as ?ocorporate citizenship ??), businesses can become aware of the economic, social, and environmental effects of their operations (Chen, 2020).

CS is an extensive and dynamic field that undergoes constant evolution, including a diverse range of methodologies and techniques. Corporate sustainability strategies encompass several practices that firms employ to promote long-term environmental and social well-being. These strategies may involve engaging in activities such as investing in environmentally friendly technologies, implementing social initiatives, and producing items that are environmentally friendly or sustainable.

Because of the close connection between the two concepts, the instructor needs to emphasize that people frequently use the terms ?ocorporate social responsibility ?? (CSR) and ?ocorporate sustainability ?? (CS) interchangeably. It is something that the instructor must emphasize. The instructor should now clarify that CS and CSR have different historical roots; CS has its roots in environmental accountability, whereas CSR has its roots in social responsibility. Nevertheless, these two schools of thinking are beginning to converge on a common future because they both have a similar aim: to strike a healthy balance between the obligations imposed on society, the environment, and the economy.

Now is a good time for the instructor to go through the various distinctions between CS and CSR. Corporate sustainability is a management strategy that falls under the purview of the Environmental Social Governance (ESG) project, which is where the name ?ocorporate sustainability ?? comes from. The idea of sustainable business practices focuses on growth and profitability within the context of three pillars to deliver value to stakeholders, employees, the planet/environment, and the economy.

The instructor should explain each pillar (Economy, Environment, and Social)

Environment: The environmental pillar is currently receiving the most attention. It includes actions businesses take to decrease their carbon footprints, such as lowering their water consumption, increasing their recycling rates, and switching to renewable energy sources.

Economy: The economic pillar consists of actions taken to implement environmentally responsible business procedures and increase long-term profitability. It also includes connecting the stakeholders ?(tm) values with how money is spent, paving the way for businesses to invest in novel sustainability initiatives.

Social: The activities a company undertakes to win the support of its stakeholders, its employees, and the people who live in the community are called the ?osocial pillar. ?? Ultimately, companies are responsible for caring for the customers and other individuals with whom they interact. Actions related to the social pillar might include providing maternity leave and making charitable donations.

Corporate Social Responsibility

After explaining the detailed information on CS, the instructor can discuss whether or not CSR is important. CSR is more comprehensive than corporate sustainability. Rather than concentrating on the company ?(tm)s pillars, CSR assists businesses in maintaining their accountability to the general public and other stakeholders. In addition, businesses that practice corporate social responsibility run their operations with the goal of making society as a whole a better place. It is a long-term strategy that evolves.

However, corporate sustainability and social responsibility help ensure that companies continue to uphold ethical and sustainable business practices while maintaining a profitable bottom line. Additionally, both programs assist companies in having a positive influence on the individuals and the community in their immediate vicinity. It is essential to keep in mind that these are not two completely different ideas. However, while corporate social responsibility and sustainability are related concepts, they differ.

The differences between CS and CSR are:

1. Corporate social responsibility generally involves looking backward to assess the positive contributions an organization has made to the communities in which it has operated. Corporate sustainability, on the other hand, looks to the future for ideas to make the business more sustainable. Corporate social responsibility (CSR) can also be viewed in a futuristic light as the exploration of novel approaches to assisting those in the community surrounding the business.
2. Both of these endeavors share a common overarching purpose, which is the improvement of the global condition. However, each of them has distinct targets for enhancing the quality of individuals' lives. Corporate social responsibility (CSR) techniques frequently aid individuals in developing their perspectives on a specific organization. One thing that can potentially boost a company's public image is the manner in which it manages its staff. In contrast, corporate sustainability initiatives prioritize the comprehensive value chain, encompassing all relevant entities, ranging from employees and consumers to stakeholders.
3. These two distinct categories of ESG activities have divergent objectives. Corporate social responsibility (CSR) safeguards a company's reputation through the provision of fair treatment to both its employees and customers. On the other hand, corporate sustainability places greater emphasis on the generation of novel prospects for established enterprises.

Nevertheless, investing in either one of these initiatives or both of them is an excellent way to develop a favorable relationship with the organization's employees, customers, and the media. This is due to the fact that every single firm should make the conscious decision to become more responsible. The instructor may conclude their discussion of the contrasts between CS and CSR by saying that it is natural for students to think that a company with a mission to improve the lives of its local community and the environment must be excellent. However, it is the responsibility of enterprises to implement environmentally friendly practices in their operations. After all, if the business is not making money, it won't last for very long. Financial success is essential to any business, and it will also help corporations better plan for environmental, social, and governance (ESG) activities.

Activities like investing in a company's corporate sustainability and social responsibility can help ensure the SE's long-term success. Since customers and other stakeholders demand more moral business practices, there is no excuse for SE to delay investigating how to become eco-friendlier and socially responsible in order to boost future profitability. Organizations do not have to be pioneers in sustainability to reap the benefits of improved decision-making for their staff, the environment, and the bottom line. Therefore, SE should look for ways to become more accountable to its stakeholders and customers.

Q3: What is Stakeholder Management, and Why is it Important to Have Stakeholder Management for Savant Electronics?

The instructor should now discuss constructing the framework for stakeholder management. The instructor may ask the students, ?oTo whom are we responsible? ?? The most common response the instructor will receive to this question is ?oto stakeholders. ?? So, the instructor can indicate that identifying stakeholders is necessary for managing corporate social responsibility activities and that managing CSR has evolved into managing stakeholders. After the discussion, the instructor can also ask, ?oWho are our stakeholders? ?? as well as ?oWhat stakeholders do we take into account? ?? and ?oTo what stakeholders are we willing to listen? ??

The instructor should now explain the meaning of stakeholder. The instructor can ask students to name the stakeholders. The students can provide various insights, and the instructor, after noting the instructor, can state a few stakeholders.

SE Stakeholders Include Groups of Organization Shareholders, Clients, Employees, Suppliers, Regulators, the General Public, Local Communities, and International Agencies

The instructor should define ?ostakeholder ?? before discussing ?ostakeholder management. ?? An organization ?(tm)s stakeholders include anyone who has a ?ovested interest ?? in the organization ?(tm)s ?osuccess or failure. ?? However, due to the popularity of CSR, government, society, and trade associations have been included.

The process of coordinating, monitoring, and enhancing one's relationships with numerous stakeholders is referred to as ?ostakeholder management. ?? This process could take place within a company or other organization. It includes systematically pursuing stakeholders, conducting research on their requirements and standards, and planning and carrying out various actions to communicate with those stakeholders.

Here, the instructor can cite an example by stating that SE has an effective stakeholder management process. In that scenario, the SE will be in a position to evaluate the current state of its associations with other stakeholders like the local community, board members, and employees. This will help SE achieve its goal.

The instructor can also state that developing a strategy for managing stakeholders should be the main focus of this stage of the SE ?(tm)s sustainable project. SE should prepare a plan for its stakeholders that can map the level of interest and impact of stakeholders and record various levels of involvement for the various stakeholders. A plan is normally developed at the beginning of a project and then put on hold for the remaining time that the project is being carried out. However, the instructor should also inform that it is almost always necessary to satisfy legal and strategic objective requirements to successfully engage stakeholders, conduct consultations, or manage a project. There is a possibility that organizations may require consultative processes because of statutory or legal requirements.

Why Stakeholder Management is Important

The instructor should ask students why stakeholder management is significant. To successfully manage a project, it is vital to establish and maintain significant relationships with the communities that will be influenced by the project and any other stakeholders. Cultivating and sustaining these relationships entails all phases of the project.

The instructor should explain to the students that putting up the effort to determine who the various stakeholders are, how to prioritize them, and what their areas of interest are will lay a solid basis upon which SE may build a plan for engaging those stakeholders.

Assume SE has a clear idea of its stakeholders, which is supported by an effective engagement strategy that is strategic, transparent, and evaluated and prioritized. In that case, the SE will be capable of establishing and maintaining relationships with stakeholders, which will help reduce risks related to the project and align the SE ?(tm)s goals with stakeholders' requirements, eliminating delays in the project.

Advantages of Stakeholder Management

After discussing why stakeholder management is required, the instructor can invite the class to discuss its various advantages. The instructor can focus the discussion on thc importance of actively maintaining and cultivating relationships with the influenced community, increased support from stakeholders, and improved outcomes.

Another benefit of effective stakeholder management is what is classified as ?obusiness intelligence. ?? When a company takes the time to understand its stakeholders ?(tm) interests and concerns, it can create new ideas for new services and products that meet those stakeholders ?(tm) needs and allow the company to cut costs and increase value. In other words, when SE takes the time to understand its stakeholders ?(tm) concerns and interests, it can yield ideas for new products and services that meet those needs.

A Stakeholder Management Plan is a document that describes the appropriate approaches to effectively engaging stakeholders throughout the project ?(tm)s entire lifecycle. This plan is part of a document called a Stakeholder Management Plan. SE can develop a plan based on examining the stakeholders ?(tm) needs, interests, and future implications on the project ?(tm)s success.

Q4: Savant Electronics Must Design a Stakeholder Management Plan. What Should be Considered When Drafting the Plan, and How Should it be Created?

After explaining the significance of stakeholder management, the instructor should discuss on developing the stakeholder management plan for SE. The instructor should ask the students to provide insight into the stakeholder management plan. The students will provide insights, but the instructor should mention that before an organization jumps in to prepare the plan, ensure they are clear on who they interact with and why. It helps manage expectations and gain trust, saving time and money, and it also helps save money.

Before starting work on the plan, there are a few things to think about, including the following:

- ? Which of the following are the most significant factors that should be considered when discussing with various stakeholders at this stage?
- ? Who should we talk to about getting their input on this matter?
- ? What does an organization believe to be the most important problems (both for themselves and you) at this time?
- ? Which communication methods with various stakeholders will be the most fruitful in the long run?
- ? Which employees within the company are responsible for which tasks, as well as a description of those tasks
- ? Within the allotted time, are there any other opportunities for engagement scheduled (possibly with other departments of the organization)?
- ? Are there any opportunities for collaboration that could be pursued to guarantee that the primary project messages are coherent and prevent participants from becoming worn out by the consultation process?
- ? Which organization will record the findings, monitor them, report on them, and spread the word about them?

Understanding Stakeholders

To have a successful program of public consultation or involvement of stakeholders, the first step is to have an understanding of the stakeholders involved. It is the key to having a successful plan. Make sure that organizations regularly assess their comprehension level and work to enhance it as the process progresses.

- ? In order to acquire a more in-depth comprehension of the requirements, priorities, preferences, and worries of the various stakeholders, an organization must determine what additional information can be gathered about those stakeholders. Consider:
- ? Data on the population demographics: Check to see that the organization interacts with a diverse range of community members and other stakeholder groups.
- ? Social networks: Pay attention to the significant social connections between the various stakeholders, even though they are frequently undocumented. These connections are important.
- ? Mapping Stakeholders
- ? The salience model explores power, urgency (the need for immediate action), and legitimacy (appropriate stakeholders), in addition to the interaction or groups of stakeholders that result from the issue ?(tm)s salience.
- ? It is necessary to ascertain the stakeholders ?(tm) expectations and investigate how these expectations compare to the objectives of the project or organization for which the engagement program is being formed. Is there a discrepancy between what was promised and what was delivered, and if so, how will this problem be fixed? Consider the following, among other things:
- ? What kind of information do they need from you, how often do they need it, and how do they want it delivered (format-wise or otherwise)?
- ? When it comes to an organization ?(tm)s work, what are the financial, social, and emotional stakes in the outcome? Is it favorable or unfavorable?
- ? What primary motivations will shape how they perceive the project or organization and how they interact with you?
- ? The organization should know the thoughts and feelings about the project as well as the organization at this current time. Is it founded on reliable sources of information?
- ? Who influences their thoughts, and who influences them?

Stakeholder Management Plan

For a project to be successful, its goals and aims must align with those of its stakeholders. A stakeholder management plan, which serves as a strategy document, can help achieve this goal. The absence of a well-defined communication plan for stakeholders can lead to inefficiencies in terms of time, financial resources, human resources, and material supply.

It might be challenging to figure out what a stakeholder management strategy should include, who should write it, and what could go wrong if a company doesn't have one. The instructor should outline some key points that can be incorporated into the strategy. Stakeholder management plans outline the actions that the team will take to satisfy the requirements and preferences of important stakeholders. Who or what exactly are the players here? Anyone or any group that will be affected by the project or will financially benefit from its completion is considered a stakeholder. The stakeholders in SE may consist of:

? Project sponsors
? Company executives
? Contractors
? Consumers
? Consumers of the final product
? Suppliers/vendors
? Community members

Important people are concerned about the outcomes of the project and influence the communication strategy as well as other policies and practices relevant to the project. Those people who are deemed to be important stakeholders are those who have a personal investment in the outcome of the project.

What Should Come in the Stakeholder Management Plan

The instructor can ask students to provide insights into the key components of the stakeholder management plan. The student might answer by stating communication, regular meetings, etc. Here, the instructor should state that the stakeholders are prioritized based on how much they think about the project ?(tm)s outcome and their impact on the project ?(tm)s outcomes.

The following are the primary elements that make up a stakeholder management plan:

? Stakeholders ?(tm) Expectations: If people don ?(tm)t know what their expectations are, an organization can ?(tm)t control them. An organization's communication methods and interests must all be documented.
? Communication norms: Each stakeholder ?(tm)s level, frequency, and method of communication, as well as the team member who will be their point of contact, will be specified in the plan. The plan should also identify the team member who will be their contact point.
? Possible course of action: An organization will explain how it will deal with stakeholder involvement and what measures it will take to ensure that expectations are met.

- ? Use a template: A stakeholder management template will save time when preparing a plan, ensure no information fields are missed, and ensure consistency.
- ? Start early: Stakeholders ?(tm) participation and success can be made or broken by early identification and involvement.
- ? Regularly update: Stakeholders will change as the project progresses, and some might join while others might depart. Their level of participation and expectations may also alter over time. Ensure the plan is current at least once per month.
- ? Maintaining transparency also fosters trust. When creating an agreement in a plan, remember that frequent, open communication encourages project transparency.
- ? Clearly define priorities. A stakeholder grid or matrix based on impact and area of interest can help an organization quickly recognize where to concentrate its efforts.
- ? Be clear and concise: For a plan to be effective, a company must get to the heart of what matters to people and communicate it in plain, understandable language that anyone who interprets it can comprehend.
- ? Be ready for conflict: There will inevitably be stakeholders within the organization with divergent interests. Be a proactive problem solver and include your method in the plan so everyone knows it in advance.
- ? It ought to be published: The stakeholder management strategy should be shared with all parties involved, not kept a secret, and kept in a visible location. This not only improves transparency but also ensures that no key players or stakeholders are forgotten. The efficient management of a project ?(tm)s stakeholders is necessary for its success. The key stakeholders in a project frequently have authority over its resources, including the funds, employees, materials, and knowledge essential to its success.

If a company does not have an adequately documented stakeholder management plan, it will not be able to manage its stakeholders successfully. This plan should validate that the expectations and interests of stakeholders have been effectively understood. An organization may use a plan to clearly specify to a project team how communication will take place, even down to who will be disclosed what and when.

Corporate Stakeholder Management

Managers can use one of three primary strategies to deal with their stakeholders: reinforcement, containment, or stabilization.

- ? Reinforcement strategy: Corporations can employ this strategy to reward stakeholders who support their functions and operations.
- ? Containment strategy: This strategy can be directed at stakeholders impeding the corporation ?(tm)s functions and operations.
- ? Stabilization strategy: Corporations can use this strategy for stakeholders who are passive in their demands and activities.

Strategy for Reinforcement

Managers can reinforce this group's trust by promoting the project as a 'clean, safe, and efficient' mode of production because supporting stakeholders are viewed as vital players who might ensure the company's survival and expansion. The organization must offer information about safety and the environment to its stakeholders. However, these measures did not indicate any fundamental transformation in their business model, as they reinforced established social and environmental policies prescribed primarily by regulatory agencies.

Reinforcement Strategy Adopted by SE

Although supportive stakeholders were considered critical in ensuring the SE ?(tm)s survival and expansion, management tended to reaffirm this group ?(tm)s trust by promoting its operations and strategies. SE can create and communicate its formal policy on sustainable development to external and internal stakeholders, and SE can offer helpful information on safety and environmental protection records.

Note: However, there was no fundamental shift in the SE ?(tm)s business strategy, as these efforts reinforced existing social and environmental regulations required by regulatory bodies.

Strategies for Stabilization (For Passive Stakeholders)

The most significant proportion of the total stakeholder population belongs to the passive stakeholder category. It encompasses members of the general public. The organization can demonstrate its commitment to the sustainable development agenda through environmental disclosure, sustainability mission statements and policies, and public pledges to reduce its ecological footprint.

Stabilization Strategies Adopted by SE

The public was seen as a passive stakeholder, and there was concern among top executives about the changing public ?(tm)s expectations for how profit-making businesses should weigh economic, social, and environmental concerns. SE can start public relations campaigns to inform passive stakeholders about the risks associated with the project while promoting it as a clean energy option to prevent a shift in public opinion.

Strategies for Maintaining Containment

This is for the stakeholders who are obstructing the project. The engagement of stakeholders is an essential component in the process of putting strategies into action. The company can establish an ?~institutional relations department, ?(tm) which can be responsible for organizing annual stakeholder sessions, ?(tm) at which they communicate the sustainable development strategy of the business.

Containment Strategies Adopted by SE

To avoid changes in public opinion, SE can highlight safety and risk management measures. Organizing multiple sessions can highlight the SE ?(tm)s commitment to participating with external stakeholders while serving as a containment strategy for obstinate stakeholders. The sustainable growth strategy incorporates sustainability. Internalization can occur in two ways: by capitalizing on concerns about climate change and greenhouse gas emissions and by establishing a new environmental management system throughout the organization based on Global Reporting Initiative (GRI) criteria. SE can develop a communication strategy for its employees as part of an internal strategy that highlights sustainable development as a critical element of its corporate social responsibility.

Furthermore, sustainable development can be promoted as a means of developing new business opportunities, particularly in emerging markets. In order to supplement and improve the social and environmental facets of business and sustainability, SE will be required to establish an environmental management system. SE can set up an institutional relations department to hold annual stakeholder meetings to interact about its sustainable development strategy. Stakeholder engagement was essential to the strategy ?(tm)s success. Community, environmental, renewable energy, development, human rights, union, and professional associations can participate.

Future Strategies

Management can outline a few future strategies that SE thinks of implementing. These strategies can be developed keeping SE objectives and people ?(tm)s welfare in mind. SE can use stakeholder theory to solve the issues. The concepts of stakeholder theory and corporate social responsibility (CSR) share certain similarities but remain different. Both stakeholder theory and corporate social responsibility (CSR) focus on incorporating social concerns into company operations as their primary point of convergence. Businesses are always part of the fabric of society. While both theories emphasize the importance of corporate social responsibility, stakeholder theory emphasizes the company ?(tm)s responsibilities to the communities in which it operates. In contrast, corporate social responsibility is merely one component of a larger set of duties. (TN Exhibit 1)

SE may benefit from using the figure to better understand how corporate social responsibility and stakeholder theory are related. The stakeholder theory emphasizes the ?oInner circle, ?? which refers to the organization ?(tm)s primary stakeholders and the community in which it operates. Local communities, including the city or district (the outer circle or secondary stakeholders), are located in this larger area. In contrast, CSR broadens the organization ?(tm)s social orientation.

Chapter 10
Empowering Consumer Rights:
Unveiling the Impact of Big Data Analytics in Upholding Consumer Protection

Roop Kamal
Chandigarh University, India

ABSTRACT

This chapter discusses how big data analytics protects and strengthens consumer rights across industries. Big data analytics can increase consumer protection, especially in the digital age, according to the study. The essay discusses how big data analytics might benefit consumer rights, highlighting its complexity. Big data analytics can improve transparency, reduce consumer privacy issues, and enable proactive fair-trade practices, according to the report. Big data analytics to defend consumer rights presents both challenges and opportunities. The text covers ethics, data privacy, and the need for legislation to regulate consumer data use. This chapter uses empirical analysis and case studies to explain how big data analytics can protect consumer rights in the ever-changing world of commerce and digital engagement.

INTRODUCTION

Consumer protection is a vital framework of guidelines, legislation, and actions created to safeguard individuals from deceitful or detrimental acts in the marketplace (Khanday, 2020). The main purpose of this protective barrier is to ensure fairness, honesty, and transparency in all consumer-business transactions (Al-Thaedan, 2023).

DOI: 10.4018/979-8-3693-3238-2.ch010

This all-encompassing strategy includes several aspects such as ensuring product safety, eliminating deceptive marketing tactics, and preserving fair pricing systems. Moreover, it includes the guarantee of consumer rights, allowing citizens to take legal action in cases of faulty items or misleading advertising (Banu, 2022). In our increasingly digitalized culture, consumer protection encompasses the vital area of privacy and data security. Its objective is to prevent the unlawful use or exploitation of personal information. These regulations and procedures serve as a robust safeguard against predatory loans, fraudulent schemes, and other financially exploitative acts, thereby empowering consumers to confidently engage in the marketplace (Gangwar et al., 2023). By ensuring impartial oversight, these methods foster trust, integrity, and equitable opportunities, ensuring that consumers may make educated choices without any worries of manipulation or injury.

Consumer rights encompass essential protections and entitlements bestowed upon individuals engaging in commercial transactions, ensuring fair treatment, safety, and access to accurate information for making educated decisions in the marketplace (Chawla & Kumar, 2022). The fundamental rights encompass a broad spectrum of crucial assurances that are important for safeguarding consumer welfare (Martin, 2020).

Figure 1. Rights of consumers

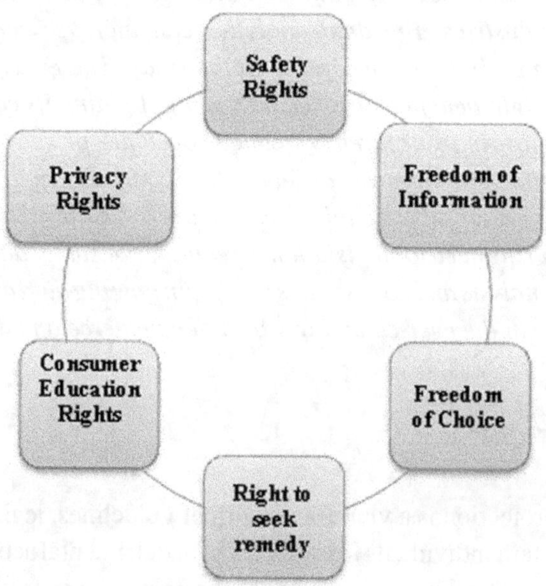

Consumers possess an inherent right to safety, which includes the anticipation that items and services comply with established safety norms and do not present any risks to their welfare (Patil & Subbaraman, 2021). Simultaneously, individuals possess the entitlement to obtain comprehensive and accurate information encompassing all facets of items, services, prices, warranties, and potential risks. This enables people to make informed decisions. The principle of choice underscores the importance of offering a variety of options, which helps prevent monopolistic practices and enables customers to make decisions according to their personal preferences and needs (Anand, 2020). Equally important is the right to seek redress, which allows customers to seek compensation when products or services are defective, deceptive, or fail to meet established standards. This guarantees both responsibility and satisfaction (Dahiya et al., 2022). Privacy rights protect consumers' personal information from unlawful use or disclosure during transactions, emphasizing the need of data security. Moreover, the entitlement to consumer education facilitates the provision of information and resources that cultivate consciousness about consumer rights and responsibilities, enabling individuals to navigate the marketplace with expertise and comprehension (Martin, 2020).

Ensuring these rights promotes a fair and transparent market, fostering ethical corporate practices and safeguarding consumers from exploitation or disadvantage. The applications of big data analytics have a substantial impact on the progress and safeguarding of consumer rights in various domains (Al-Sai et al., 2022). This technology enables a deeper understanding of consumer behaviors, preferences, and trends by using massive datasets and complex analytics tools. Consequently, it enables regulatory authorities, corporations, and consumer advocacy groups to enhance safeguards and address emergent issues.

Figure 2. Role of big data analytics in consumer protection

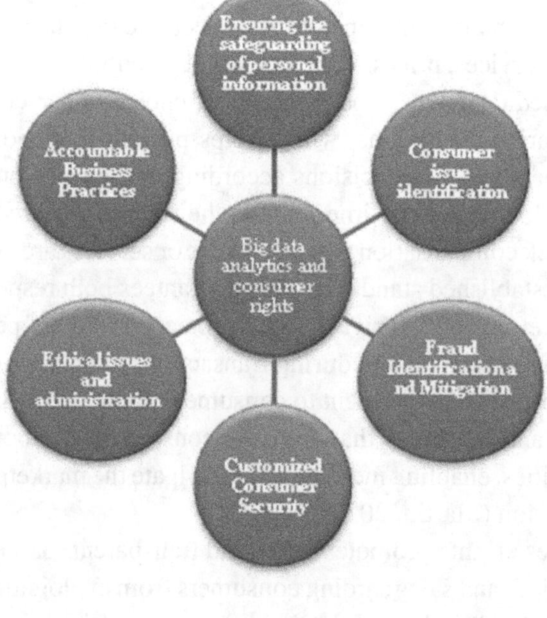

A crucial aspect to take into account is its impact on consumer privacy (Dubey et al., 2019). The use of big data analytics allows for the analysis of large amounts of customer data, making it easier to identify potential privacy violations or instances of data misuse (Patil & Subbaraman, 2021). By conducting meticulous analysis of patterns and deviations in data streams, it is possible to reinforce mechanisms that protect sensitive information and ensure compliance with privacy laws, thereby improving consumer privacy rights. Moreover, the use of big data analytics allows for the detection of fraudulent activities or deceptive methods in the marketplace. By analyzing vast amounts of transactional data and patterns, it is feasible to detect anomalies, suspicious actions, or misleading advertising practices (Gangwar et al., 2023). This feature improves consumer protection by enabling swift intervention against fraudulent behavior and deceptive strategies, so ensuring customers' right to fair and transparent transactions (Anand, 2020). In addition, with the use of predictive analytics, big data allows for the deployment of proactive tactics to anticipate and address consumer problems. By analyzing historical data patterns and gathering feedback from customers, firms and regulatory bodies can predict potential issues, identify areas for improvement, and take proactive measures to prevent violations of consumer rights (Venkateswara et al., 2023).

Figure 3. Ethical concerns of big data analytics in consumer protection

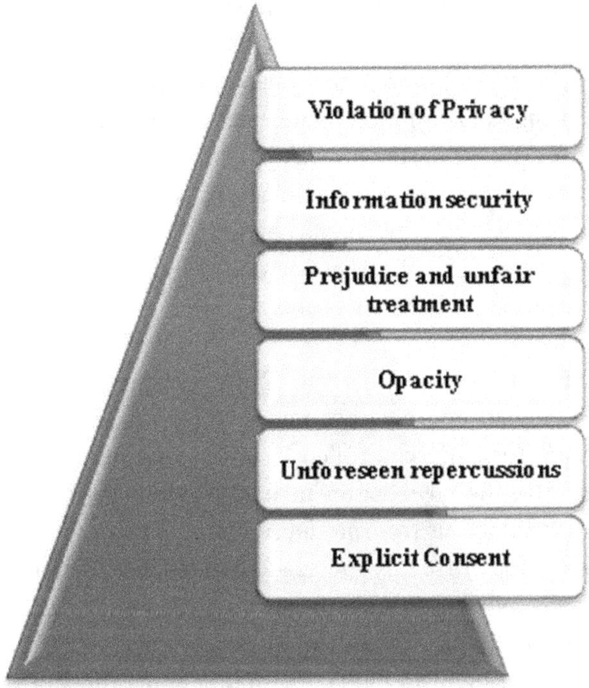

However, the use of big data in consumer rights also raises ethical issues with data privacy, permission, and potential biases in algorithms (Pramanik & Bandyopadhyay, 2023). In order to protect consumer rights in the digital age, it is crucial to strike a delicate balance between harnessing the power of big data to ensure consumer safety and ensuring ethical data management and transparency (Iqbal et al., 2020). Big data analytics is a potent tool that may be utilized to enhance consumer rights by enabling proactive measures against privacy violations, fraudulent activities, and misleading behaviors (Bansal et al., 2022). Ensuring the ethical and appropriate use of data is essential for upholding consumer protection in the ever-evolving realm of data-driven commerce (Shi, 2022).

In his paper, Yeh (2018) emphasized the crucial role of data brokers in the big data ecosystem. Their main responsibility is to collect, extract, alter, and package data, which they subsequently sell to marketing organizations. These marketing organizations employ the information to target individual consumers with precision. Two main issues have emerged from this situation: the intrusion of data brokers on consumers' data privacy, and the vulnerability of consumers to unwarranted and unexpected discrimination. Consequently, personal data has evolved into a lucrative commodity that companies buy and sell, frequently without considering individuals' privacy.

The study of "Fan" (2021) lays the foundation for recognizing the public's right to access and benefit from combined personal data, which is now mostly controlled and utilized by private companies for monetary purposes. Facilitating public access to the consumer big data commons can be achieved without giving rise to privacy issues and the resulting adverse effects. The knowledge acquired from managing shared resources, collaborating on innovation, advancing rules, and establishing protocols to protect human subjects can be used to create a framework for regulating the access and use of our collective personal data. This strategy would facilitate public engagement in the benefits of this resource while mitigating potential negative consequences.

In their study, Nuccio and Guerzoni (2018) examined how data-driven organizations and digital platforms have become new intermediaries in information goods markets that were formerly controlled by a few dominant firms. The observable transformation in the digital economy involves a steady shift in market power across the value chain, transitioning from product and content producers to service providers and distributors. Policy officials and academicians that highlight the possibility of market dominance by huge data corporations typically overemphasize the technological aspect and downplay the role of human factors.

The integration of big data with computational intelligence (CI), as defined by Iqbal et al. (2018), has the potential to have a substantial impact on modern society, businesses, and the general population. Integrating these technologies into a modern intelligent urban environment can result in tangible benefits, including a substantial reduction in costs, streamlined decision-making for alternative options, and the promotion of innovative products in various software fields. This study presents a novel approach for modeling Big Data. The hybrid approach is derived from the neurological structure of animals.

In their study, Dubey et al. (2019) provided a definition of predictive and big data analytics as an organizational skill. They also investigated the influence of this capability on social ecological sustainability, while considering the moderating effect of organizational culture. Authors have suggested that the BDPA will serve as a reliable indicator of both social and ecological success. The study shows that there is no significant association between the influence of BDPA on social and ecological performance and firms that have either a high or low flexibility orientation, or those that have either a raised or decreased control orientation.

In their study, Chawla and Kumar (2021) examined how the widespread availability of internet access and the growing use of computer, tablet, and smartphone technology have driven the growth of e-commerce in different countries, including India. The rapid expansion of online commerce has led to the development of innovative methods for distributing goods. It has generated new opportunities for consumers, introducing them to novel forms of unfair trade and unethical business practices. Furthermore, the government's endeavors to protect consumer rights, particularly for online consumers, are inadequate.

Bhanushali et al., (2023) examined the current trend in Big Data, which emphasizes analytics that are especially customized for the overall population. Thanks to technological progress, it is now possible to gather abundant and complete real-time data on consumer behavior. Therefore, customers are increasingly supplying crucial information in the form of big data that is unparalleled in terms of its scale, velocity, and variety.

Analysis and Findings of Comparison

The utilization of big data analytics differs among organizations in relation to consumer rights. AI is utilized in the healthcare sector to personalize therapies while ensuring the confidentiality of patient information (Manohar Bhanushali et al., 2023). Similarly, in the retail industry, it observes and analyzes consumer behavior in order to improve marketing strategies. An examination of these applications uncovers the specific challenges and possibilities that exist within the industry regarding the protection of consumer rights. Consumer rights and data privacy are governed by distinct regulatory frameworks in different geographical areas (Gawankar et al., 2019). Examining the effects of big data analytics on compliance with these regulations provides significant understanding of how different legislative frameworks influence its implementation and the steps taken to protect consumers (Hussain et al., 2022). An analysis of ethical procedures in the utilization of big data for consumer rights across multiple organizations reveals divergent practices. As an illustration, the healthcare sector may prioritize the use of strict data anonymization methods to protect patient privacy, while the advertising industry may focus more on personalized targeting, which raises ethical issues related to manipulating consumers (Nuccio & Guerzoni, 2019). It is crucial to assess the impact of big data analytics on consumer empowerment in different situations. Some industries may use data to provide personalized services or increase consumer knowledge, while others may inadvertently limit choices or manipulate consumer behavior, thereby impacting empowerment in different ways.

Comparative Analysis and Results

Studying the challenges and possible risks associated with analyzing vast amounts of data in different sectors offers valuable understanding of unique vulnerabilities specific to each industry (Gangwar et al., 2023). Healthcare data is susceptible to breaches that can endanger patient confidentiality, while financial data is at risk of being exposed to fraudulent behavior (Verma et al., 2019). Examining the successful implementation and progress in utilizing big data analytics for safeguarding consumer rights in various businesses promotes the sharing of knowledge between different sectors.

Table 1. Pre and post integration of big data and consumer protection

Sr. No	Pre Integration of Big data in Consumer protection	Post Integration of Big data in Consumer protection
1	Various regulatory bodies and government organizations were responsible for enforcing rules and regulations related to consumer protection (Punia, 2020). These regulations covered various aspects including product safety, fair business practices, and consumer rights to fair pricing and accurate information.	Big data analytics facilitates the delivery of individualized services and tailored solutions to consumers. However, there is an increasing emphasis on diligently overseeing personal data to ensure the safeguarding of privacy rights (Banu, 2022). Stringent regulations and advanced measures have been put in place to guarantee the confidentiality and safety of customer data.
2	Non-governmental groups and advocacy organizations played a crucial role in raising public awareness, educating consumers about their rights, and advocating for stronger protections (Hussain et al., 2022). They regularly served as attentive overseers, promptly notifying authorities of violations and pressing for changes in consumer-related policies.	Through using the potential of big data, regulatory agencies and corporations can optimize their capacity to accurately predict consumer trends and anticipate forthcoming challenges (Jain et al., 2023). This enables them to proactively address concerns, mitigate risks, and enhance consumer safeguards before issues escalate.
3	Regulations were established to enforce standards for product safety, quality, and labeling, ensuring that customers had access to secure and accurately labeled products (Al-Thaedan, 2023). This included information about the components, instructions for applying, and warnings about any potential dangers.	The application of big data analytics has significantly improved the capacity to identify and thwart fraudulent activity (Zhang et al., 2021). Sophisticated algorithms and data analysis accelerate the identification of fraudulent activities, ensuring the protection of consumers from fraud, identity theft, and deceitful practices.
4	Legal avenues, such as small claims courts or consumer protection agencies, offered means for consumers to seek compensation or resolution. These choices offered consumers the chance to seek compensation or restitution for defective products, misleading advertising, or unfair business practices.	The need for increased transparency in data management is steadily increasing. Consumers have an increased consciousness regarding the gathering, use, and distribution of personal data (Shastri, 2021). Businesses are expected to provide clear and transparent information regarding their methods of processing data.
5	The purpose of ethical codes of conduct and industry standards is to promote fair and open business processes (Kasera et al., 2023). This included instructions for advertising, pricing, and customer service to ensure fair treatment of consumers by businesses.	The endeavor to mitigate biases in algorithms and analytics has gathered momentum (Yeh, 2018). The focus is on reducing algorithmic biases that can lead to discriminatory outcomes, ensuring fair and equitable treatment for all consumers.

CONCLUSION

Ultimately, big data analytics has revolutionized consumer rights, presenting novel prospects and complexities. It offers a novel capacity to comprehend, predict, and tackle consumer concerns, enhancing consumer safeguards. Regulatory bodies, corporations, and advocacy organisations now have the ability to analyze large amounts of data in order to safeguard consumer privacy, identify instances of fraud, and enhance market transparency. Notwithstanding these advancements, there are still unresolved ethical and privacy concerns. Ensuring responsible and transparent utilization of customer data is of utmost importance. In order to protect consumer rights and uphold ethical standards, it is imperative that algorithms are free from prejudice, data is securely handled, and informed consent is actively encouraged. The transformative influence of big data analytics on consumer rights underscores the necessity for adaptable regulatory frameworks that strike a balance between innovation and safeguarding. In order to fully capitalize on the benefits of data analytics while safeguarding consumer privacy and rights, it is imperative for regulators, firms, consumers, and technological experts to collaborate and address these challenges collectively.

The utilization of big data analytics has the capacity to revolutionize consumer rights and grant consumers with greater authority and control. Nevertheless, it is crucial to employ data analytics in an ethical manner and ensure responsible application in order to effectively utilize its potential for the greater benefit of society, while also safeguarding the rights and privacy of individuals in the modern age of digital technology.

REFERENCES

Al-Sai, Z. A., Husin, M. H., Syed-Mohamad, S. M., Abdin, R. M. D. S., Damer, N., Abualigah, L., & Gandomi, A. H. (2022). Explore big data analytics applications and opportunities: A review. *Big Data and Cognitive Computing*, 6(4), 157. 10.3390/bdcc6040157

Al-Thaedan, Z. (2023). Downlink throughput prediction using machine learning models on 4G-LTE networks. *International Journal of Information Technology, 15*(6), 2987-93.

Anand, P. A. (2020). *Effectiveness of Consumer Protection Act in Securing Consumer Rights: An Empirical Prospective*.

Bansal, A., Katoch, G., Arora, N., Sharma, A., Bhadula, R. C., & Agarwal, S. (2022, April). Big data analytics in the Indian banking sector: An empirical study. In *2022 2nd International Conference on Advance Computing and Innovative Technologies in Engineering (ICACITE)* (pp. 1624-1627). IEEE.

Banu, A. (2022). Big data analytics–tools and techniques–application in the insurance sector. In *Big data: A game changer for insurance industry* (pp. 191–212). Emerald Publishing Limited. 10.1108/978-1-80262-605-620221013

Chawla, N., & Kumar, B. (2022). E-commerce and consumer protection in India: The emerging trend. *Journal of Business Ethics*, 180(2), 581–604. 10.1007/s10551-021-04884-334257470

Dahiya, M., Sharma, S., & Grima, S. (2022). Big data analytics application in the indian insurance sector. In *Big data analytics in the insurance market* (pp. 145–164). Emerald Publishing Limited. 10.1108/978-1-80262-637-720221008

Dubey, R., Gunasekaran, A., Childe, S. J., Papadopoulos, T., Luo, Z., Wamba, S. F., & Roubaud, D. (2019). Can big data and predictive analytics improve social and environmental sustainability? *Technological Forecasting and Social Change*, 144, 534–545. 10.1016/j.techfore.2017.06.020

Gangwar, H., Mishra, R., & Kamble, S. (2023). Adoption of big data analytics practices for sustainability development in the e-commercesupply chain: A mixed-method study. *International Journal of Quality & Reliability Management*, 40(4), 965–989. 10.1108/IJQRM-07-2021-0224

Gawankar, S. A., Gunasekaran, A., & Kamble, S. (2019). A study on investments in the big data-driven supply chain, performance measures and organisational performance in Indian retail 4.0 context. *International Journal of Production Research*. 10.1080/00207543.2019.1668070

Hussain, A., Pal, A., Adani, K., Bhattacharya, S., & Ambekar, S. (2022). Role of big data analytics in e-commerce. In *Changing Face Of E-Commerce In Asia* (pp. 315-337). World Scientific. 10.1142/9789811245992_0016

Iqbal, R., Doctor, F., More, B., Mahmud, S., & Yousuf, U. (2020). Big data analytics: Computational intelligence techniques and application areas. *Technological Forecasting and Social Change*, 153, 119253. 10.1016/j.techfore.2018.03.024

Jain, P., Tambuskar, D. P., & Narwane, V. S. (2023). Is the Implementation of Big Data Analytics in Sustainable Supply Chain Really a Challenge? The Context of the Indian Manufacturing Sector. *International Journal of Innovation and Technology Management, 2350033.*

Kasera, S., Gehlot, A., Uniyal, V., Pandey, S., Chhabra, G., & Joshi, K. (2023, March). Right to Digital Privacy: A Technological Intervention of Blockchain and Big Data Analytics. In *2023 International Conference on Innovative Data Communication Technologies and Application (ICIDCA)* (pp. 1122-1127). IEEE. 10.1109/ICIDCA56705.2023.10100229

Khanday, A. (2020). Machine learning based approaches for detecting COVID-19 using clinical text data. *International Journal of Information Technology, 12*, 731-9.

Manohar Bhanushali, M., Sharma, A., Sharma, S., Gehlot, A., Rawal, P., & Kapila, D. (2023). *A detailed and significant analysis of The Effects of Big-Data over The Revolution of Internet Marketing*. 2023 3rd International Conference on Advance Computing and Innovative Technologies in Engineering (ICACITE), Greater Noida, India. 10.1109/ICACITE57410.2023.10182372

Martin, K. E. (2020). Ethical issues in the big data industry. In *Strategic Information Management* (pp. 450–471). Routledge. 10.4324/9780429286797-20

Nuccio, M., & Guerzoni, M. (2019). Big data: Hell or heaven? Digital platforms and market power in the data-driven economy. *Competition & Change*, 23(3), 312–328. 10.1177/1024529418816525

Patil, A. R., & Subbaraman, S. (2021). Performance analysis of static hand gesture recognition approaches using artificial neural network, support vector machine and two stream based transfer learning approach. *International Journal of Information Technology : an Official Journal of Bharati Vidyapeeth's Institute of Computer Applications and Management*, 1–2.

Pramanik, S., & Bandyopadhyay, S. K. (2023). Analysis of big data. In *Encyclopedia of Data Science and Machine Learning* (pp. 97–115). IGI Global.

Punia, D. M. (2020). Consumerism and consumer protection laws in india: safeguarding consumer rights and welfare. In *Social Sciences, Education & Languages, 6*(10).

Shastri, K. (2021). Deep-LSTM ensemble framework to forecast Covid-19: an insight to the global pandemic. *International Journal of Information Technology, 13,* 1291-301..

Shi, Y. (2022). *Advances in big data analytics*. Adv Big Data Anal. 10.1007/978-981-16-3607-3

Venkateswara, M., Vellela, S., Reddy, V., Vullam, N., Sk, K. B., & Roja, D. (2023, March). Credit Investigation and Comprehensive Risk Management System based Big Data Analytics in Commercial Banking. In *2023 9th International Conference on Advanced Computing and Communication Systems (ICACCS)* (*Vol. 1,* pp. 2387-2391). IEEE.

Verma, K., Bhardwaj, S., Arya, R., Islam, U. L., Bhushan, M., Kumar, A., & Samant, P. (2019). *Latest tools for data mining and machine learning*. Research Gate.

Yeh, C. L. (2018). Pursuing consumer empowerment in the age of big data: A comprehensive regulatory framework for data brokers. *Telecommunications Policy*, 42(4), 282–292. 10.1016/j.telpol.2017.12.001

Zhang, X., Rane, K., Kakaravada, I., & Shabaz, M. (2021). Research on vibration monitoring and fault diagnosis of rotating machinery based on internet of things technology. *Nonlinear Engineering*, 10(1), 245–254. 10.1515/nleng-2021-0019

Conclusion

As we conclude this comprehensive exploration of the technology-driven evolution of the CSR ecosystem, it is evident that we stand at a pivotal juncture where innovation and ethical responsibility must converge. The association between technology and CSR has directed in a new era of unprecedented opportunities and challenges for businesses, society, and the world. Throughout the chapters of this book, we have witnessed how emerging technologies are reshaping the landscape of corporate sustainability and stakeholder engagement. From harnessing the power of technology to optimize resource allocation and predict potential risks, to leveraging information technology for transparent and secure supply chain traceability, the transformative potential of technology in the CSR realm is undeniable. However, as we navigate this digital frontier, we must remain vigilant and address the critical ethical considerations that arise. Issues such as algorithmic bias, data privacy, and the digital divide pose significant challenges that demand our collective attention and action. Failing to address these concerns could undermine public trust, perpetuate inequalities, and ultimately hinder the progress towards a more sustainable and equitable future. It is imperative that businesses, policymakers, and society as a whole embrace a holistic approach that integrates technological innovation with ethical responsibility. This requires a commitment to developing and deploying technologies that prioritize transparency, inclusivity, and accountability. Only by aligning our technological advancements with a strong moral compass can we truly unlock the full potential of CSR initiatives and drive meaningful, lasting change. Moreover, effective stakeholder engagement must remain a cornerstone of successful CSR strategies in the digital age. By leveraging the power of social media platforms, online reporting tools, and interactive dashboards, companies can foster open dialogues, build trust, and co-create sustainable solutions with their stakeholders. This collaborative approach not only enhances the impact of CSR initiatives but also ensures that the voices and perspectives of diverse stakeholder groups are heard and valued. As we look to the future, the convergence of technology and CSR will continue to evolve, presenting both opportunities and challenges. It is incumbent upon us to stay agile, adapt to new developments, and continuously refine our strategies to maximize the positive impact on society and the environment. This will require a collective effort from businesses, governments, civil society organizations, and individuals, all working together towards a common vision of a more sustainable and equitable world. Furthermore, we must prioritize capacity-building and knowledge-sharing to ensure that the benefits of technology-driven CSR initiatives are accessible to all.

By investing in digital literacy programs, fostering public-private partnerships, and promoting cross-sector collaborations, we can bridge the digital divide and empower communities to actively participate in and benefit from these transformative efforts. Ultimately, the technology-driven evolution of the CSR ecosystem is not merely a passing trend but a profound paradigm shift that demands our unwavering commitment. By embracing the synergies between technological advancements and ethical business practices, we can create a future where companies thrive, communities prosper, and our planet flourishes. As we embark on this journey, let us be guided by the principles of responsible leadership, sustainable development, and a steadfast dedication to creating shared value for all. Through collective action, continuous learning, and a resolute commitment to ethical conduct, we can harness the power of technology to drive positive social and environmental change, fostering a more just, inclusive, and sustainable world for generations to come.

Compilation of References

Abbott, W. F., & Monsen, R. J. (1979). On the Measurement of Corporate Social Responsibility: Self-Reported Disclosures as a Method of Measuring Corporate Social Involvement. *Academy of Management Journal*, 22(3), 501–515. 10.2307/255740

Abdullah, A. (2023). The importance of urban green spaces in the development of smart cities. *Frontiers in Environmental Science*, 11, 1206372. 10.3389/fenvs.2023.1206372

Abelson, H., Ledeen, K., & Lewis, H. (2012). *Blown to bits: your life, liberty, and happiness after the digital explosion*. Addison-Wesley Professional.

Abu Bakar, A. S., & Ameer, R. (2011). Readability of corporate social responsibility communication in Malaysia. *Corporate Social Responsibility and Environmental Management*, 18(1), 50–60. 10.1002/csr.240

Addas, I. M. (2023). The role of green spaces in promoting health and well-being in urban settings. *Cities & Health*, 2.

Agarwal, A., & Gupta, P. K. (2023). A secure and privacy-preserving data sharing framework for smart cities using blockchain. *Sustainable Computing : Informatics and Systems*, 39, 101317.

Ahn, J. W., Jeon, M., Kim, S., Jeong, S., Park, J. Y., Park, Y. C., & Lee, S. Y. (2020). Monitoring of urban air quality using a low-cost sensor network. [Top of Form]. *Environmental Pollution*, 263(Pt 2), 114657.

Alawadhi, S., Al-Hashimi, S. M., Alshare, M., & Katrib, M. (2021). Transforming cities into smart and green spaces: A review of enabling technologies. *Sustainable Cities and Society*, 73, 103220.

Albuquerque, J. P., & Rocha, A. (2020). Citizen engagement in smart city initiatives: A critical review. *Smart Cities, 3*(1), 128-144. https://www.mdpi.com/1424-8220/23/23/9392

Alonso, R. (2022). *An Adaptive Intelligent Approach to Implement Energy Efficiency Concept in Built Infrastructure*. IEEE. 10.1109/ICICICT54557.2022.9917766

Aloufi, T. H. A., & Abdulaziz, H. (2022). Challenges and Obstacles Facing Data in the Big Data Environment. *Communications in Mathematics and Applications*, 13(1), 331–349. 10.26713/cma.v13i1.1974

Al-Sai, Z. A., Husin, M. H., Syed-Mohamad, S. M., Abdin, R. M. D. S., Damer, N., Abualigah, L., & Gandomi, A. H. (2022). Explore big data analytics applications and opportunities: A review. *Big Data and Cognitive Computing*, 6(4), 157. 10.3390/bdcc6040157

Al-Shannaq, A., Raba'ah, H., & Al-Bataineh, S. (2021). A smart waste management system for domestic waste collection based on the internet of things. *IEEE Sensors Journal*, 21(12), 11842–11853.

Al-Thaedan, Z. (2023). Downlink throughput prediction using machine learning models on 4G-LTE networks. *International Journal of Information Technology, 15*(6), 2987-93.

Álvarez de Pedro, F. J. (2023). Foundational Aspects of Smart Cities Leading the Digital Economy - A Review. *Journal of Computing and Natural Science*, 35-45. 10.53759/181X/JCNS202303004

Alvarez, R., Weilenmann, M., & Favez, P.-Y. (2008). Evidence of increased mass fraction of NO2 within real-world NOx emissions of modern light vehicles — Derived from a reliable online measuring method. *Atmospheric Environment*, 42(19), 4699–4707. 10.1016/j.atmosenv.2008.01.046

Amaeshi, K., Adi, A. B. C., Ogbechie, C., & Amao, O. O. (2006). Corporate social responsibility in Nigeria: Western mimicry or indigenous influences? *Available atSSRN* 896500. 10.2139/ssrn.896500

Anand, P. A. (2020). *Effectiveness of Consumer Protection Act in Securing Consumer Rights: An Empirical Prospective.*

Andre, K. (2023). IoT-driven Environmental Support System for Smart Cities. *SISFORMA, 10*(1), 14-18. 10.24167/sisforma.v10i1.10209

Aragón-Correa, J. A., & Rubio-Lopez, E. A. (2007). Proactive corporate environmental strategies: Myths and misunderstandings. *Long Range Planning*, 40(3), 357–381. 10.1016/j.lrp.2007.02.008

Arokiaraj, D. (2011). The green market: The way to save the World. *Business Strategies*, 2(1), 41–44.

Arokiaraj, D., & Banumathi, M. A. (2015). Study on the environmental concern of the passenger car user in Chennai. [IRJBM]. *International Research Journal of Business and Management*, 8(5), 64–70.

Arokiaraj, D., Ganeshkumar, C., & Paul, P. V. (2020). Innovative management system for environmental sustainability practices among Indian auto-component manufacturers. *International Journal of Business Innovation and Research*, 23(2), 168–182. 10.1504/IJBIR.2020.110095

Asante Antwi, H. (2020). Beyond COVID-19 Pandemic: A Systematic Review of the Role of Global Health *in the Evolution and Practice of Corporate Social Responsibility*. 10.21203/rs.3.rs-40212/v1

Aysan, B. (2023). Theoretical and analytical assessment of smart green cities. *Journal of Cleaner Production*, 410, 137315–137315. 10.1016/j.jclepro.2023.137315

Bafna, A. (2017). A Study on the Impact of CSR on Financial Performance of Companies in India. *International Journal of Engineering Technology. Science and Research*, 4(12), 325–331.

Baker-Shelley, A., van Zeijl-Rozema, A., & Martens, P. (2017). A conceptual synthesis of organisational transformation: How to diagnose, and navigate, pathways for sustainability at universities? In *Journal of Cleaner Production* (Vol. 145, pp. 262–276). Elsevier Ltd., 10.1016/j.jclepro.2017.01.026

Balasubramanian, N. K., Kimber, D., & Siemensma, F. (2005). Emerging opportunities or traditions reinforced? An analysis of the attitudes towards CSR, and trends of thinking about CSR, in India. *Journal of Corporate Citizenship*, 2005(17), 79–92. 10.9774/GLEAF.4700.2005.sp.00010

Banerjee, S. B., & Dean, A. (2008). Corporate Social Responsibility: The Good, The Bad and The Ugly. *Critical Sociology*, 34(1), 51–79. 10.1177/0896920507084623

Bansal, A., Katoch, G., Arora, N., Sharma, A., Bhadula, R. C., & Agarwal, S. (2022, April). Big data analytics in the Indian banking sector: An empirical study. In *2022 2nd International Conference on Advance Computing and Innovative Technologies in Engineering (ICACITE)* (pp. 1624-1627). IEEE.

Bansal, G., & Bandivadekar, A. (2013). *Overview of India's vehicle emissions control program*. ICCT.

Banu, A. (2022). Big data analytics–tools and techniques–application in the insurance sector. In *Big data: A game changer for insurance industry* (pp. 191–212). Emerald Publishing Limited. 10.1108/978-1-80262-605-620221013

Banumathi, M., & Arokiaraj, D. (2011). Eco-labeling–The Need for Sustainable Marketing. In *National Conference in the era of Global Recovery-2011 (SGEGR2011* (pp. 511-515). Research Gate.

Barauskaite, G., & Streimikiene, D. (2021). Corporate social responsibility and financial performance of companies: The puzzle of concepts, definitions and assessment methods. *Corporate Social Responsibility and Environmental Management*, 28(1), 278 ?"287. 10.1002/csr.2048

Bardas, P., & Rotaru, S., Ghiţă, M., & Cocosila, M. (2013). The Caux Round Table Principles: A Solution For The International Economic And Social Crisis? *Review of General Management*, 17(1).

Basil, D. Z., & Erlandson, J. (2008). Corporate social responsibility website representations: A longitudinal study of internal and external self-presentations. *Journal of Marketing Communications*, 14(2), 125–137. 10.1080/13527260701858497

Basu, K., & Palazzo, G. (2008). Corporate social responsibility: A process model of sensemaking. *Academy of Management Review*, 33(1), 122–136. 10.5465/amr.2008.27745504

Beltramello, A. (2012). *Market development for green cars*.

Berthon, P. R., Pitt, L. F., Plangger, K., & Shapiro, D. (2012). Marketing meets Web 2.0, social media, and creative consumers: Implications for international marketing strategy. *Business Horizons*, 55(3), 261–271. 10.1016/j.bushor.2012.01.007

Bhatti, A. (2022). An Implementation Environmental Monitoring Real-time IoT Technology. 10.1109/ICECET55527.2022.9872654

Bihari, A., & Shajahan, P. (2023). Changing CSR practices of corporates – a study of institutionalization of mandated corporate social responsibility in India. *International Journal of Law and Management*. .10.1108/IJLMA-09-2022-0198

Blowfield, M., & Frynas, J. G. (2005). 'Editorial: Setting New Agendas - Critical Perspectives on Corporate Social Responsibility in the Developing World. *International Affairs*, 81(3), 499–513. 10.1111/j.1468-2346.2005.00465.x

Boel, T., Deakin, M., & Lægreid, P. (2020). Smart city governance: A co-production framework for citizen engagement. *Environment and Planning A* [invalid URL removed]. *Economy and Space*, 52(12), 2742–2762.

Bowen, H. (1953). *Social responsibilities of the businessman*. Harper.

Brammer, S., Jackson, G., & Matten, D. (2012). Corporate social responsibility and institutional theory: New perspectives on private governance. *Socio-economic Review*, 10(1), 3–28. 10.1093/ser/mwr030

Brammer, S., Millington, A., & Rayton, B. (2007). The contribution of corporate social responsibility to organizational commitment. *International Journal of Human Resource Management*, 18(10), 1701–1719. 10.1080/09585190701570866

Brejnholt, A. (2022). Institute for International Management Navigating Plurality, *in The State and Corporate Social Responsibilities: A collection of research papers.*

Brennan, L., & Victoria, E. J. (2004, January). Technology Management for Corporate Social Responsibility. *IEEE Technology and Society Magazine*, 23(1), 40–48. 10.1109/MTAS.2004.1273471

Brennan, N. M., & Merkl-Davies, D. M. (2018). Do firms effectively communicate with financial stakeholders? A conceptual model of corporate communication in a capital market context. *Accounting and Business Research*, 48(5), 553–577. 10.1080/00014788.2018.1470143

Briones, R. L., Kuch, B., Liu, B. F., & Jin, Y. (2011). Keeping up with the digital age: How the American Red Cross uses social media to build relationships. *Public Relations Review*, 37(1), 37–43. 10.1016/j.pubrev.2010.12.006

Bruno, E. M. (2023). Sustainable Traffic Management for Smart Cities Using Internet-of-Things-Oriented Intelligent Transportation Systems (ITS): Challenges and Recommendations. *Sustainability (Basel)*, 15(13), 9859–9859. 10.3390/su15139859

Brunton, M., Eweje, G., & Taskin, N. (2017). Communicating corporate social responsibility to internal stakeholders: Walking the walk or just talking the talk? *Business Strategy and the Environment*, 26(1), 31–48. 10.1002/bse.1889

BSR. (2001). *Business for Social Responsibility, Introduction to Corporate Social Responsibility*. BSR. https://www.bsr.org/bsrresources/WhitePapers_IssueArea.cfm

Buolamwini, J., & Gebru, T. (2018). Gender shades: Intersectional accuracy disparities in commercial gender classification systems. *Proceedings of the 1st Conference on Fairness, Accountability, and Transparency*, (pp. 77-91). IEEE.

Buysse, K., & Verbeke, A. (2003). Proactive environmental strategies: A stakeholder management perspective. *Strategic Management Journal*, 24(5), 453 ?"470. 10.1002/smj.299

Calvano, L. (2008). Multinational corporations and local communities: A critical analysis of conflict. *Journal of Business Ethics*, 82(4), 793–805. 10.1007/s10551-007-9593-z

Campbell, J. L. (2007). Why would corporations behave in socially responsible ways? An institutional theory of corporate social responsibility. *Academy of Management Review*, 32(3), 946 ?"967. 10.5465/amr.2007.25275684

Caputo, F., De Prisco, A., Lettieri, M., & Crescenzo, M. (2023). Citizens' engagement in smart cities for promoting circular economy. A Knowledge based framework. *ITM Web of Conferences, 51,* 02001. 10.1051/itmconf/20235102001

Caputo, D. S., Cillo, V., Nappi, G., & Pontrandolfo, P. (2023). A review of citizen science for smart city planning: Managerial challenges and opportunities for knowledge integration. [invalid URL removed]. *Sustainability*, 15(6), 3463.

Carlsson, J., & Åkerstöm, R. (2008). Corporate Social Responsibility: a case study of Öhrlings PricewaterhouseCoopers.

Carrión-Martínez, J. J., Luque de la Rosa, A., Fernández-Cerero, J., & Rueda, M. M. (2020, April). Information and Communications Technologies (ICTs) in Education for Sustainable Development: A Bibliographic Review. *Sustainability (Basel)*, 12(8), 3288–3288. 10.3390/su12083288

Carroll, A. B. (1991). The pyramid of corporate social responsibility: Toward the moral management of organizational stakeholders. *Business Horizons*, 34(4), 39–48. 10.1016/0007-6813(91)90005-G

Carroll, A. B. (1999). Corporate social responsibility: Evolution of a definitional construct. *Business & Society*, 38(3), 268–295. 10.1177/000765039903800303

Carroll, A. B., & Shabana, K. M. (2010). The business case for corporate social responsibility: A review of concepts, research and practice. *International Journal of Management Reviews*, 12(1), 85–105. 10.1111/j.1468-2370.2009.00275.x

Castelfranchi, C. (2023). Introduction to Sustainable Transportation System. *Energy. Environmental Sustainability*, 3-6, 3–6. 10.1007/978-981-99-2150-8_1

Castells, M. (2002). *The Internet galaxy: Reflections on the Internet, business, and society*. Oxford University Press. 10.1093/acprof:oso/9780199255771.001.0001

Chandani, A., Mehta, M., Mall, A., & Khokhar, V. (2016). Employee engagement: A review paper on factors affecting employee engagement. *Indian Journal of Science and Technology*, 21(4), 256–272. 10.17485/ijst/2016/v9i15/92145

Chawla, N., & Kumar, B. (2022). E-commerce and consumer protection in India: The emerging trend. *Journal of Business Ethics*, 180(2), 581–604. 10.1007/s10551-021-04884-334257470

Chen, S. (2022). *Application of cutting-edge environmental technologies for the development of resilient and sustainable cities*. GNC. 10.30955/gnc2021.00592

Cheng, B., Ioannou, I., & Serafeim, G. (2014). Corporate social responsibility and access to finance. *Strategic Management Journal*, 35(1), 1–23. 10.1002/smj.2131

Chen, Y., Fay, S., & Wang, Q. (2011). The role of marketing in social media: How online consumer reviews evolve. *Journal of Interactive Marketing*, 25(2), 85–94. 10.1016/j.intmar.2011.01.003

Choi, E., Lee, H., & Shin, D. (2023). Beyond the quadruple helix model: A critical review of citizen engagement in smart city initiatives. [invalid URL removed]. *Sustainability*, 15(6), 3438.

Choi, Y. W., Yoon, H., & Yoon, D. K. (2023). Citizen Engagement in Smart City Planning: The Case of Living Labs in South Korea. *Urban Planning*, 8(2). 10.17645/up.v8i2.6416

Chovancová, J., Majerník, M., Drábik, P., & Stofkova, Z. (2023). Environmental Technological Innovations and the Sustainability of their. *Development.*, 24(4), 245–252. 10.12912/27197050/162708

Christensen, L. J., Peirce, E. R., Hartman, L. P., Hoffman, W. M., & Carrier, J. Ethics, CSR, and Sustainability Education in the Financial Times Top 50 Global Business Schools: Baseline Data and Future Research Directions. *Journal of Business Ethics*, *73*(4). 10.1007/s10551-006-9211-5

Christmann, P., & Taylor, G. (2001). Globalization and the environment: Determinants of firm self-regulation in China. *Journal of International Business Studies*, 32(3), 439–458. 10.1057/palgrave.jibs.8490976

Chu, S. C., Chen, H. T., & Gan, C. (2020). Consumers' engagement with corporate social responsibility (CSR) communication in social media: Evidence from China and the United States. *Journal of Business Research*, 110, 260–271. 10.1016/j.jbusres.2020.01.036

Chu, S. C., & Kim, Y. (2011). Determinants of consumer engagement in electronic word-of-mouth (eWOM) in social networking sites. *International Journal of Advertising*, 30(1), 47–75. 10.2501/IJA-30-1-047-075

CIA. (2012). *The World Fact Book: India*. CIA. www.cia.gov/library/publications/the- world-factbook/geos/in.html

Clarkson, M. E. (1995). A stakeholder framework for analyzing and evaluating corporate social performance. *Academy of Management Review*, 20(1), 92–117. 10.2307/258888

Colleoni, E. (2013). CSR communication strategies for organizational legitimacy in social media. *Corporate Communications*, 18(2), 228–248. 10.1108/13563281311319508

Colucci, M., Tuan, A., & Visentin, M. (2020). An empirical investigation of the drivers of CSR talk and walk in the fashion industry. *Journal of Cleaner Production*, 248, 119200. 10.1016/j.jclepro.2019.119200

Cominetti, M., & Seele, P. (2016). Hard soft law or soft hard law? A content analysis of CSR guidelines typologized along hybrid legal status. *uwf UmweltWirtschaftsForum, 24*(2), 127- 140.

Córdoba, J.-R., & Campbell, T. (2008, May). Learning to Deal with CSR Issues in the Classroom. *Systems Research and Behavioral Science*, 25(3), 427–437. 10.1002/sres.898

Cortado, F. J., & Chalmeta, R. (2016). Use of social networks as a CSR communication tool. *Cogent business & management, 3*(1), 1187783.

Courtis, J. K. (1986). An investigation into annual report readability and corporate risk-return relationships. *Accounting and Business Research*, 16(64), 285–294. 10.1080/00014788.1986.9729329

Criscuolo, C., & Menon, C. (2014). *Environmental policies and risk finance in the green sector: cross-country evidence.*

CSID Journal of Infrastructure Development. (2023). Developing Sustainable Smart Cities to Improve Citizen's Quality of Life and Well-Being. *Developing Sustainable Smart Cities to Improve Citizen's Quality of Life and Well-Being*, 6(1). 10.7454/jid.v6.i1.1088

Cuervo-Carabel, T., & Repiso, R. (2023). Presence and Impact of the Articles on Corporate Social Responsibility in the Different Research Areas. *SAGE Open*, 13(1). 10.1177/21582440231158262

Curkovic, S., & Landeros, R. (2000). An environmental baldrige? *American Journal of Business*, 15(2), 63–76. 10.1108/19355181200000012

D'Souza, C., Taghian, M., Lamb, P., & Peretiatko, R. (2007). Green decisions: Demographics and consumer understanding of environmental labels. *International Journal of Consumer Studies*, 31(4), 371–376. 10.1111/j.1470-6431.2006.00567.x

Dahiya, M., Sharma, S., & Grima, S. (2022). Big data analytics application in the indian insurance sector. In *Big data analytics in the insurance market* (pp. 145–164). Emerald Publishing Limited. 10.1108/978-1-80262-637-720221008

Dahlsrud, A. (2008). How corporate social responsibility is defined: An analysis of 37 definitions. *Corporate Social Responsibility and Environmental Management*, 15(1), 1–13. 10.1002/csr.132

David, A. (2018). Towards Mobile Opportunistic in Cloud Computing. *Indian Journal of Scientific Research (IJSR),* 2250-0138.

David, A. (2020$_a$). Air Pollution Control Monitoring & Delivery Rate Escalated by Efficient use of Markov Process in Manet Networks: to Measure Quality of Service Parameters. *Test Engineering & Management.* The Mattingley Publishing Co.

David, A. (2020$_b$). *Corporate and individual environmental responsibility towards automobile.* Book Rivers.

David, A., & Banumathi, M. (2014$_a$). A Study on Eco–Driving Behaviour of Passenger Car Users in Chennai. *TIJ's Research Journal of Social Science & Management (RJSSM), 3*(11).

David, A., & Banumathi, M. (2014$_b$). Factors influencing the purchase decision of passenger cars in Puduchery. *International Journal of Exclusive Management Research (IJEMR),* 2249-2585.

David, A., Muthukumar, A., Ayyappan, D., & Ravi, S. (2020$_a$). Accident Avoidance System by Using Sensors Module. *Test Engineering & Management.* The Mattingley Publishing Co., Inc.

David, A., Ravi, S., & Reena, R. A. (2018). The Eco-Driving Behaviour: A Strategic Way to Control Tailpipe Emission. *International Journal of Engineering & Technology, 7*(3.3), 21-25.

David, A., Thangavel, Y. D., & Sankriti, R. (2019). *Recover, recycle and reuse: An efficient way to reduce the waste*. Research Gate.

David, A., Nagarjuna, K., Mohammed, M., & Sundar, J. (2020). *Determinant Factors of Environmental Responsibility for the Passenger Car Users. SSRN.*

David, D. T. (1995). Welcome to the communication age. *Internet Research*, 5(1), 64–70. 10.1108/10662249510084471

Dawkins, J. (2005). Corporate responsibility: The communication challenge. *Journal of Communication Management (London)*, 9(2), 108–119. 10.1108/13632540510621362

De Olde, E. M., & Valentinov, V. (2019). The Moral Complexity of Agriculture: A Challenge for Corporate Social Responsibility. *Journal of Agricultural & Environmental Ethics*, 32(3), 413–430. 10.1007/s10806-019-09782-3

Deakin, M. (2021). Smart cities: Paradoxes and promises. *Routledge*. Deloitte. https://www2.deloitte.com/content/dam/Deloitte/nl/Documents/public-sector/deloitte-nl-Robotic-process-automation-in-the-public-sector.pdf

Dellarocas, C. (2003). The digitization of word of mouth: Promise and challenges of online feedback mechanisms. *Management Science*, 49(10), 1407–1424. 10.1287/mnsc.49.10.1407.17308

Devine-Wright, H., & Davies, A. (2023). What Role for Citizens? Evolving Engagement in Quadruple Helix Smart District Initiatives. *Urban Planning*, 8(2). 10.17645/up.v8i2.6351

Disney. (2018). *The Walt Disney Company and Make-A-Wish® Invite Fans to "Share Your Ears" to Help Grant Wishes in Celebration of 90 Years of Mickey Mouse*. Disney. https://www.businesswire.com/news/home/20181104005033/en/The-Walt-Disney-Company-and-Make-A-Wish%C2%AE-Invite-Fans-to-%E2%80%9CShare-Your-Ears%E2%80%9D-to-Help-Grant-Wishes-in-Celebration-of-90-Years-of-Mickey-Mouse

Doh, J. P., & Guay, T. R. (2006). Corporate social responsibility, public policy, and NGO activism in Europe and the United States: An institutional ??stakeholder perspective. *Journal of Management Studies*, 43(1), 47 ?"73. 10.1111/j.1467-6486.2006.00582.x

Donaldson, T., & Preston, L. E. (1995). The stakeholder theory of the corporation: Concepts, evidence, and implications. *Academy of Management Review*, 20(1), 65–91. 10.2307/258887

Dong, L. (2022). *Environmental Monitoring and Management*, 151-174. 10.2174/9789815036244122010011

Dubey, R., Gunasekaran, A., Childe, S. J., Papadopoulos, T., Luo, Z., Wamba, S. F., & Roubaud, D. (2019). Can big data and predictive analytics improve social and environmental sustainability? *Technological Forecasting and Social Change*, 144, 534–545. 10.1016/j.techfore.2017.06.020

Duho, K. C. T., Onumah, J. M., Samuel, N. Y. S., & Onumah, R. M. "Emerging Technologies, Corporate Social Responsibility and Sustainability: The Perception of Business Students in Ghana," August 2019. https://scite.ai/reports/10.31219/osf.io/pg94b10.31219/osf.io/pg94b

Dummett, K. (2006). Drivers for corporate environmental responsibility (CER). *Environment, Development and Sustainability*, 8(3), 375–389. 10.1007/s10668-005-7900-3

Du, S., Bhattacharya, C. B., & Sen, S. (2011). Corporate social responsibility and competitive advantage: Overcoming the trust barrier. *Management Science*, 57(9), 1528–1545. 10.1287/mnsc.1110.1403

Du, S., & Vieira, E. T.Jr. (2012). Striving for legitimacy through corporate social responsibility: Insights from oil companies. *Journal of Business Ethics*, 110(4), 413–427. 10.1007/s10551-012-1490-4

Dutot, V., Lacalle Galvez, E., & Versailles, D. W. (2016). CSR communications strategies through social media and influence on e-reputation: An exploratory study. *Management Decision*, 54(2), 363–389. 10.1108/MD-01-2015-0015

Dwivedi, Y. K., Ismagilova, E., Hughes, D. L., Carlson, J., Filieri, R., Jacobson, J., Jain, V., Karjaluoto, H., Kefi, H., Krishen, A. S., Kumar, V., Rahman, M. M., Raman, R., Rauschnabel, P. A., Rowley, J., Salo, J., Tran, G. A., & Wang, Y. (2021). Setting the future of digital and social media marketing research: Perspectives and research propositions. *International Journal of Information Management*, 59, 102168. 10.1016/j.ijinfomgt.2020.102168

Easley, R. (2022). *The underlying and basic foundations of the smart city: where do artificial intelligence, machine learning and other buzz words fit in the narrative?* 10.4337/9781803926803.00007

Economic Times. (2022, Mar 22). View: India becomes the first country to have statutorily mandated CSR for specified companies. *Economic Times*. https://economictimes.indiatimes.com/opinion/et-commentary/view-india-becomes-the-first-country-to-have-statutorily-mandated-csr-for-specified-companies/articleshow/90448748.cms

Elembilassery, V. (2023). *Evolutionary influences on corporate social responsibility literature: a review and prognosis*. Society and Business Review. 10.1108/SBR-05-2022-0136

Elkington, J. (1997). The triple bottom line. *Environmental management: Readings and cases, 2*, 49-66.

Ericsson. (2021). *5G networks: The foundation for smart cities*. Ericsson. https://www.ericsson.com/en/patents/articles/5g-will-be-the-platform-for-tomorrows-smart-cities

Erskine, L., & Johnson, S. D. (2012, January). Effective Learning Approaches for Sustainability: A Student Perspective. *Journal of Education for Business*, 87(4), 198–205. 10.1080/08832323.2011.590162

Esrock, S. L., & Leichty, G. B. (1998). Social responsibility and corporate web pages: Self-presentation or agenda-setting? *Public Relations Review*, 24(3), 305–319. 10.1016/S0363-8111(99)80142-8

Etter, M. (2013). Reasons for low levels of interactivity:(Non-) interactive CSR communication in Twitter. *Public Relations Review*, 39(5), 606–608. 10.1016/j.pubrev.2013.06.003

Eubanks, R. (2018). *Automating inequality: How high-tech tools profile, police, and punish the poor*. St. Martin's Press.

European Commission. (2023, January 18). *A European strategy for data governance*. EC. https://commission.europa.eu/strategy-and-policy/priorities-2019-2024/europe-fit-digital-age/european-data-strategy_en

European Commission. (2023, May 25). *General Data Protection Regulation (GDPR)*. EC. https://gdpr.eu/

Faiz, A. (1993). Automotive emissions in developing countries – Relative implications for global warming, acidification and urban air quality. *Transportation Research Part A, Policy and Practice*, 27A(3), 167–186. 10.1016/0965-8564(93)90057-R

Fei, Y. (2023). Design and development of environmental pollution source monitoring management information system. 12707:127070F-127070F. 10.1117/12.2681348

Fei, Y. (2023). Research on the application of network technology, database technology and GIS in environmental monitoring and management. [invalid URL removed]. *Journal of Physics: Conference Series*, 2247(1), 012022.

Feleen, F., David, A., Choudhary, N., & Vivekanand, N. (2021). *Impact of Psychological Capacities on the Work-Life Balance of Entrepreneurs*.

Fernandes, M. (2023). *Emerging Electronics Technologies and Solutions for Eco-Friendly Cities*. MDPI. 10.3390/books978-3-0365-6521-7

Ferrell, A., Liang, H., & Renneboog, L. (2016). Socially responsible firms. *Journal of Financial Economics*, 122(3), 585–606. 10.1016/j.jfineco.2015.12.003

Ferrell, O. C., & Ferrell, L. (2008). A macromarketing ethics framework: Stakeholder orientation and distributive justice. *Journal of Macromarketing*, 28(1), 24–32. 10.1177/0276146707311290

Figueiró, P. S., & Raufflet, E. (2015, November). Sustainability in Higher Education: A Systematic Review with Focus on Management Education. *Journal of Cleaner Production*, 106, 22–33. 10.1016/j.jclepro.2015.04.118

Filho, W. L., Manolas, E., & Pace, P. (2008, November). Education for Sustainable Development: Current Discourses and Practices and Their Relevance to Technology Education. *International Journal of Technology and Design Education*, 19(2), 149–165. 10.1007/s10798-008-9079-z

Flanagin, A. J., & Metzger, M. J. (2000). Perceptions of Internet information credibility. *Journalism & Mass Communication Quarterly*, 77(3), 515–540. 10.1177/107769900007700304

Fleacă, E. (2017). Study on Social Responsibility Learning Needs to Capacitate the Responsible Education in Business Engineering. *Balkan Region Conference on Engineering and Business Education*. IEEE. 10.1515/cplbu-2017-0053

Fransen, K., Versigghel, J., Vargas, D. G., Semanjski, I., & Gautama, S. (2023). Sustainable mobility strategies deconstructed: A taxonomy of urban vehicle access regulations. *European Transport Research Review*, 15(1), 1–20. 10.1186/s12544-023-00576-3

Freeman, R. E. (1984). *Strategic management: A stokcholder approach*. Pitman.

Freeman, R. E., & Dmytriyev, S. (2017). Corporate social responsibility and stakeholder theory: Learning from each other. Symphonya. *Emerging Issues in Management*, (1), 7 ?"15. 10.4468/2017.1.02freeman.dmytriyev

Fumeaux, C., Peverini, M., Romano-Rodriguez, A., & Parlange, M. B. (2023). Smart city environmental monitoring using low-power wide-area networks and citizen science. *Sensors (Basel)*, 23(4), 2229.36850831

Fumeaux, N., Bourely, J., & Briand, D. (2023). Printed ecoresorbable temperature sensors for environmental monitoring. *Micro and Nano Engineering*, 20, 100218. 10.1016/j.mne.2023.100218

Fu, W., & Deshpande, S. P. (2014). The Impact of Caring Climate, Job Satisfaction, and Organizational Commitment on Job Performance of Employees in a China's Insurance Company. *Journal of Business Ethics*, 124(2), 339–349. 10.1007/s10551-013-1876-y

Gajewski, J. F., & Li, L. (2015). Can Internet-based disclosure reduce information asymmetry? *Advances in Accounting*, 31(1), 115–124. 10.1016/j.adiac.2015.03.013

Galitsky, C., & Worrell, E. (2008). *Energy efficiency improvement and cost saving opportunities for the vehicle assembly industry: an energy star guide for energy and plant managers* (No. LBNL-50939-Revision). Lawrence Berkeley National Lab. (LBNL), Berkeley, CA (United States).

Ganeshkumar, C., David, A., & Jebasingh, D. R. (2022). Digital transformation: Artificial intelligence-based product benefits and problems of agritech industry. In *Agri-Food 4.0* (Vol. 27, pp. 141–163). Emerald Publishing Limited. 10.1108/S1877-636120220000027010

Ganeshkumar, C., David, A., Sankar, J. G., & Saginala, M. (2023). Application of Drone Technology in Agriculture: A Predictive Forecasting of Pest and Disease Incidence. In *Applying Drone Technologies and Robotics for Agricultural Sustainability* (pp. 50–81). IGI Global.

Gangwar, H., Mishra, R., & Kamble, S. (2023). Adoption of big data analytics practices for sustainability development in the e-commercesupply chain: A mixed-method study. *International Journal of Quality & Reliability Management*, 40(4), 965–989. 10.1108/IJQRM-07-2021-0224

García-Sánchez, I. M., & Noguera-Gámez, L. (2017). Integrated reporting and stakeholder engagement: The effect on information asymmetry. *Corporate Social Responsibility and Environmental Management*, 24(5), 395–413. 10.1002/csr.1415

Gautam, R., & Singh, A. (2010). Corporate social responsibility practices in India: A study of top 500 companies. *Global Business and Management Research*, 2(1), 41–56.

Gawankar, S. A., Gunasekaran, A., & Kamble, S. (2019). A study on investments in the big data-driven supply chain, performance measures and organisational performance in Indian retail 4.0 context. *International Journal of Production Research*. 10.1080/00207543.2019.1668070

Goby, V. P., & Nickerson, C. (2011). Introducing Ethics and Corporate Social Responsibility at Undergraduate Level in the United Arab Emirates: An Experiential Exercise on Website Communication. Scite Press. https://scite.ai/reports/10.1007/s10551-011-1025-4

Gonon,P.(2023). The Platformization of Public Participation: Considerations for Urban Planners Navigating New Engagement Tools.*The Urban Book Series*, 71-87. Springer. 10.1007/978-3-031-31746-0_5

Gonon, M. (2023). From e-participation to platformization: Rethinking citizen engagement in smart cities. *Urban Studies (Edinburgh, Scotland)*, 60(2), 437–454.

González-Zamar, M.-D., Abad-Segura, E., López-Meneses, E., & Galán, J. G. (2020, October). Managing ICT for Sustainable Education: Research Analysis in the Context of Higher Education. *Sustainability (Basel)*, 12(19), 8254–8254. 10.3390/su12198254

Gowtham, A. S. (2023). The changing landscape of Corporate Social Responsibility in India Pre & Post Covid-19. *International Journal for Multidisciplinary Research*, 5(6), 113–127.

Gowthorpe, C., & Amat, O. (1999). External reporting of accounting and financial information via the Internet in Spain. *European Accounting Review*, 8(2), 365–371. 10.1080/096381899336096

Gray, R., Kouhy, R., & Lavers, S. (1995). Corporate social and environmental reporting: A review of the literature and a longitudinal study of UK disclosure. *Accounting, Auditing & Accountability Journal*, 8(2), 47–77. 10.1108/09513579510146996

Gray, R., Owen, D., & Maunders, K. (1988). Corporate social reporting: Emerging trends in accountability and the social contract. *Accounting, Auditing & Accountability Journal*, 1(1), 6–20. 10.1108/EUM0000000004617

Grindrod, P. (2016). Beyond privacy and exposure: Ethical issues within citizen-facing analytics. *Philosophical Transactions. Series A, Mathematical, Physical, and Engineering Sciences*, 374(2083), 20160132. Advance online publication. 10.1098/rsta.2016.013228336804

Gupta, A. (2023). *Energy Management System for Smart Buildings*, 327-347. Wiley. 10.1002/9781119847564.ch21

Gupta, S. (2002). Strategic dimensions of corporate image: corporate ability and corporate social responsibility as sources of competitive advantage via differentiation. [Doctoral dissertation, Temple University]. http://proquest.umi.com/ pqdweb?did1/4727401921&Fmt1/47&clientId1 /469955&RQT1/4309&VName1/4PQD,

Gupta, A., Kumar, A., & Melese, E. (2023). Young consumer engagement at the bottom of pyramid: Applying SOR framework in e-commerce context. *Young Consumers*, 24(6), 786 ?"806. 10.1108/YC-06-2022-1542

Habibzadeh, H., Nussbaum, B., Anjomshoa, F., Kantarci, B., & Soyata, T. (2019). A survey on cybersecurity, data privacy, and policy issues in cyber-physical system deployments in smart cities. *Sustainable Cities and Society*, 50, 101660. 10.1016/j.scs.2019.101660

Hafner, K., & Lyon, M. (1998). *Where wizards stay up late: The origins of the Internet*. Simon and Schuster.

Haigh, M. M., Brubaker, P., & Whiteside, E. (2013). Facebook: Examining the information presented and its impact on stakeholders. *Corporate Communications*, 18(1), 52–69. 10.1108/13563281311294128

Haigh, M. M., & Wigley, S. (2015). Examining the impact of negative, user-generated content on stakeholders. *Corporate Communications*, 20(1), 63–75. 10.1108/CCIJ-02-2013-0010

Hair Jr, J. F., Wolfinbarger Celsi Arthu, M., & Page, M. J. (n.d.). *ESSENTIALS OF Business Research Methods SECOND EDITION*.

Halkos, G., & Nomikos, S. (2021). Corporate social responsibility: Trends in global reporting initiative standards. *Economic Analysis and Policy*, 69, 106–117. 10.1016/j.eap.2020.11.008

Haniffa, R. M., & Cooke, T. E. (2005). The impact of culture and governance on corporate social reporting. *Journal of Accounting and Public Policy*, 24(5), 391–430. 10.1016/j.jaccpubpol.2005.06.001

Ho, H. W., Le, A., Le, D., Nguyen, D. N., & Phung, T. D. (2023). A review on development and applications of smart grids in typical power systems. *Energies*, 16(4), 2146.

Holcomb, J. L., Upchurch, R. S., & Okumus, F. (2007). Corporate social responsibility: What are top hotel companies reporting? *International Journal of Contemporary Hospitality Management*, 19(6), 461–475. 10.1108/09596110710775129

Hollander, J. B., Wright, P., & Connolly, S. (2020). Citizen engagement in smart cities: A review of the literature and case studies. [invalid URL removed]. *Technological Forecasting and Social Change*, 151, 119–134.

Hong, H., Kery, J. L., Li, Y., Chen, Y., Li, K., & Chen, B. (2023). Transportation Internet: A Sustainable Solution for Intelligent Transportation Systems. *IEEE Transactions on Intelligent Transportation Systems*, 24(12), 1–12. 10.1109/TITS.2023.3270749

Hopkins, M. (2003). The business case for CSR: Where are we? *International Journal of Business Performance Management*, 5(2-3), 125–140. 10.1504/IJBPM.2003.003261

Hossain, J., Abdul Kadir, A. F., Nur Hanafi, A., Shareef, H., Khatib, T., Azmi Baharin, K., & Fani Sulaima, M. (2023). A Review on Optimal Energy Management in Commercial Buildings. *Energies, 16*(4), 1609-1609. https://uis.unesco.org/sites/default/files/documents/ip51-global-framework-reference-digital-literacy-skills-2018-en.pdf10.3390/en16041609

Hung, M., Shi, J., & Wang, Y. (2013, September). The effect of mandatory CSR disclosure on information asymmetry: Evidence from a quasi-natural experiment in China. In *Asian finance association (AsFA) 2013 conference*.

Hur, W. M., Kim, H., & Woo, J. (2014). How CSR leads to corporate brand equity: Mediating mechanisms of corporate brand credibility and reputation. *Journal of Business Ethics*, 125(1), 75–86. 10.1007/s10551-013-1910-0

Hussain, A., Pal, A., Adani, K., Bhattacharya, S., & Ambekar, S. (2022). Role of big data analytics in e-commerce. In *Changing Face Of E-Commerce In Asia* (pp. 315-337). World Scientific. 10.1142/9789811245992_0016

Husted, B. W., & Allen, D. B. (2006). Corporate social responsibility in the multinational enterprise: Strategic and institutional approaches. *Journal of International Business Studies*, 37(6), 838–849. 10.1057/palgrave.jibs.8400227

Hwang, J. (2023). Environmental Monitoring System. *International Journal for Research in Applied Science and Engineering Technology*, 11(5), 3590–3595. 10.22214/ijraset.2023.51826

Iatridis, K., Gond, J. P., & Kesidou, E. (2022). How Meaningfulness and Professional Identity Interact in Emerging Professions: The Case of Corporate Social Responsibility Consultants. *Organization Studies*, 43(9), 1401–1423. 10.1177/01708406211035506

Ibrahim, M. (2023). *Modern Approaches to Energy Efficiency Management,* 47-59. 10.1007/978-3-031-26596-9_5

ICSI. (2021). *Guidance Note on Corporate Social Responsibility*. ICSI. https://www.icsi.edu/media/webmodules/Guidance_Note_on_CSR_Final.pdf

Insch, A. (2008). Online communication of Corporate Environmental Citizenship: A study of New Zealand's electricity and gas retailers. *Journal of Marketing Communications*, 14(2), 139–153. 10.1080/13527260701858505

International Energy Agency (IEA). (2023). *Electric vehicles*. IEA.

Iqbal Khadaroo, M. (2005). Business reporting on the internet in Malaysia and Singapore: A comparative study. *Corporate Communications*, 10(1), 58–68. 10.1108/13563280510578204

Iqbal, R., Doctor, F., More, B., Mahmud, S., & Yousuf, U. (2020). Big data analytics: Computational intelligence techniques and application areas. *Technological Forecasting and Social Change*, 153, 119253. 10.1016/j.techfore.2018.03.024

Irajpour, A., Golsefid-Alavi, M., Hajimirza, M., & Soleimani-Nezhad, N. (2012). Evaluation of the most effective criteria in green supply chain management in automotive industries using the Fuzzy DEMATEL Method. *Journal of Basic and Applied Scientific Research*, 2(9), 8952–8961.

Ismail, M., Ratna, F. A. J., Rasdi, R. M., & Alias, S. N. (2013, July). School as Stakeholder of Corporate Social Responsibility Program: Teacher's Perspective on Outcome in School Development. *The Asia-Pacific Education Researcher*, 23(2), 321–331. 10.1007/s40299-013-0107-8

Jacob, A. T. (2024). *Assessing the effectiveness of Green Supply Chain Management in Enhancing Sustainability in the UK retail industry: A focused study on Walmart Inc* (Doctoral dissertation, Dublin Business School).

Jain, P., Tambuskar, D. P., & Narwane, V. S. (2023). Is the Implementation of Big Data Analytics in Sustainable Supply Chain Really a Challenge? The Context of the Indian Manufacturing Sector. *International Journal of Innovation and Technology Management, 2350033.*

Jali, M. N., Abas, Z., & Ariffin, A. S. (2017). Corporate Social Responsibility and Corporate Social Innovation: A Conceptual Understanding. *SHS Web of Conferences*. IEEE. 10.1051/shsconf/20173401001

Janik, A., Ryszko, A., & Szafraniec, M. (2023). Intelligent and Environmentally Friendly Solutions in Smart Cities' Development—Empirical Evidence from Poland. *Smart Cities, 6*(2), 1202-1226. doi: of Form10.3390/smartcities6020058Top

Jasinska-Biliczak, A. (2022). Smart-City Citizen Engagement: The Answer to Energy Savings in an Economic Crisis? *Energies*, 15(23), 8828–8828. 10.3390/en15238828

Jerab, D. A., & Mabrouk, T. (2023). The Role of Leadership in Changing Organizational Culture. SSRN *Electronic Journal*. 10.2139/ssrn.4574324

Jin, S. A. A., & Phua, J. (2014). Following celebrities' tweets about brands: The impact of twitter-based electronic word-of-mouth on consumers' source credibility perception, buying intention, and social identification with celebrities. *Journal of Advertising*, 43(2), 181–195. 10.1080/00913367.2013.827606

Jobin, A., Ienca, M., & Vayena, E. (2019). The global landscape of AI ethics guidelines. *The Ethics of Artificial Intelligence*, 389-409.

Jobin, A., Ienca, M., & Vayena, E. (2020). *The global landscape of AI ethics guidelines: Mapping the evolution of ethical frameworks for artificial intelligence* (Vol. 1). Springer Nature. https://www.nature.com/articles/s42256-019-0088-2

Jones, R. (2023). Sustainability and Urban Innovation. *Advanced series in management, 81-91.*10.1108/S1877-636120230000030009

Jose, P. D., Bandi, R., & Mehra, M. (2003). Corporate social responsibility in the information and communication technologies sector: Discussion. *IIMB Management Review*, 15(4), 61–75.

Kalburgi, N. K., David, A., & Muralidhar, L. B. (2023). Understanding the Perceptions of Students towards YouTube as a Learning Tool-An Empirical Approach. *Central European Management Journal, ISSN*, 2336-2693.

Kallio, T. J. (2007). Taboos in corporate social responsibility discourse. *Journal of Business Ethics*, 74(2), 165–175. 10.1007/s10551-006-9227-x

Kang, J., & Hustvedt, G. (2014). Building trust between consumers and corporations: The role of consumer perceptions of transparency and social responsibility. *Journal of Business Ethics*, 125(2), 253–265. 10.1007/s10551-013-1916-7

Kaplinsky, R., & Messner, D. (2008). Introduction: The impact of Asian drivers on the developing world. *World Development*, 36(2), 197–209. 10.1016/j.worlddev.2007.06.006

Karabasevic, D., Petrović, G., & Maksimovic, M. (2016). *The Impact of the Levels of Education on the Perception of Corporate Social Responsibility.* Scite. https://scite.ai/reports/10.5937/poseko10-12322

Karagiannopoulou, S., Sariannidis, N., Ragazou, K., Passas, I., & Garefalakis, A. (2023). Corporate Social Responsibility: A Business Strategy That Promotes Energy Environmental Transition and Combats Volatility in the Post-Pandemic World. *Energies*, 16(3), 1102. 10.3390/en16031102

Kärnä, J., Hansen, E., & Juslin, H. (2003). Social responsibility in environmental marketing planning. *European Journal of Marketing*, 37(5/6), 848–871. 10.1108/03090560310465170

Kasera, S., Gehlot, A., Uniyal, V., Pandey, S., Chhabra, G., & Joshi, K. (2023, March). Right to Digital Privacy: A Technological Intervention of Blockchain and Big Data Analytics. In *2023 International Conference on Innovative Data Communication Technologies and Application (ICIDCA)* (pp. 1122-1127). IEEE. 10.1109/ICIDCA56705.2023.10100229

Kashif, M., Kumar, P., Ghai, S., & Kumar, S. (2023b). Disruptive Technologies in Computational Finance. In *Algorithmic Approaches to Financial Technology: Forecasting, Trading, and Optimization* (pp. 46-60). IGI Global.

Kashif, M., Shajar, S. N., Singhal, N., & Kumar, P. (2023a). Achieving sustainable investment practices through green finance: Challenges and opportunities. In *Sustainable Investments in Green Finance*. 10.4018/979-8-3693-1388-6.ch016

Kashif, M., Sridharan, P., & Thiyagarajan, S. (2017). Impact of economic growth on international reserve holdings in Brazil. *Revista de Economia Política*, 37(3), 605–614. 10.1590/0101-31572017v37n03a08

Kesic, D. M. (2023). "Smart" cities: The new paradigm of urban development. *Socioloski Pregled*, 57(1), 32–52. 10.5937/socpreg57-43015

Khan, S. (2023). Зеленые технологии и инновации: их влияние на устойчивое развитие в индийском контексте. *Vestnik Samarskogo universiteta. Èkonomika i upravlenie, 14*(1), 87-98. 10.18287/2542-0461-2023-14-1-87-98

Khanday, A. (2020). Machine learning based approaches for detecting COVID-19 using clinical text data. *International Journal of Information Technology, 12*, 731-9.

Koi-Akrofi, J. (2023). *CSR Paradigms, Consumer Behaviour, and Business Performance: A Literature-Based Analysis*. TEXILA INTERNATIONAL JOURNAL OF MANAGEMENT. 10.21522/TIJMG.2015.09.01.Art003

Kolk, A. (2004). A decade of sustainability reporting: Developments and significance. *International Journal of Environment and Sustainable Development*, 3(1), 51–64. 10.1504/IJESD.2004.004688

Kotler, P., & Lee, N. (2005). Best of breed: When it comes to gaining a market edge while supporting a social cause,"corporate social marketing" leads the pack. *Social Marketing Quarterly*, 11(3-4), 91–103. 10.1080/15245000500414480

Kotler, P., & Lee, N. (2008). *Corporate social responsibility: Doing the most good for your company and your cause*. John Wiley & Sons.

Kouatli, I. (2019, October). The Contemporary Definition of University Social Responsibility with Quantifiable Sustainability. *Social Responsibility Journal*, 15(7), 888–909. 10.1108/SRJ-10-2017-0210

KPMG. (1997). *KPMG International survey of environmental reporting 1999*. KPMG. https://www.researchgate.net/publication/254796996_KPMG_International_survey_of_environmental_reporting_1999

KPMG. U. (2010). Carrots and Sticks–Promoting Transparency and Sustainability. *An update on trends in Voluntary and Mandatory Approaches to Sustainability Reporting.*

Krinke, S. (2011). Implementing life cycle engineering efficiently into automotive industry processes. In *Glocalized Solutions for Sustainability in Manufacturing:Proceedings of the 18th CIRP International Conference on Life Cycle Engineering, Technische Universität Braunschweig*, (pp. 11-16). Springer Berlin Heidelberg.

Kuhn, S., Frauenberger, S., & Arzt, F. (2021). A survey on VR/AR applications for urban planning: Augmented decision-making in spatial development. [invalid URL removed]. *Computers, Environment and Urban Systems*, 90, 107224.

Kular, S., Gatenby, M., Rees, C., Soane, E., & Truss, K. (2008). *Employee engagement: A literature review*.

Kumar, J., Tapar, A. V., & Bhattacharjee, S. (2023). Social media and the bottom of the pyramid: a systematic literature review and future research agenda. *International Journal of Emerging Markets*.

Kumar, J., Katiyar, G., Mehrotra, A., Attri, R., & Vishnoi, S. K. (2024). Connecting BOP consumers and retailers: What drives small-time retailing through social media? *Journal of Retailing and Consumer Services*, 77, 103679. 10.1016/j.jretconser.2023.103679

Kumar, R. S., & Subrahmanya, M. B. (2010). Influence of subcontracting on innovation and economic performance of SMEs in Indian automobile industry. *Technovation*, 30(11-12), 558–569. 10.1016/j.technovation.2010.06.005

Kurniawan, R., & Pamudji, E. S. (2023). Green smart city concept and its implementation in developing countries. [IJECE]. *Iranian Journal of Electrical and Computer Engineering*, 17(1), 227–234.

Lea, R. (2002). *Corporate Social Responsibility, Institute of Directors (IoD) member opinion survey*. IoD: London. http://www. epolitix.com/data/companies/images/Companies/Institute-of - Directors/CSR_Report.pdf [23 June 2003].

Lee, H. H. M., Van Dolen, W., & Kolk, A. (2013). On the role of social media in the 'responsible' food business: Blogger buzz on health and obesity issues. *Journal of Business Ethics*, 118(4), 695–707. 10.1007/s10551-013-1955-0

Lescrauwaet, L., Wagner, H., Yoon, C., & Shukla, S. (2022). *Adaptive Legal Frameworks and Economic Dynamics in Emerging Technol-ogies: Navigating the Intersection for Responsible Innovation. 16*(3), 202–220. https://journals.ristek.or.id/index.php/LE/index

Leung, D., Law, R., Van Hoof, H., & Buhalis, D. (2013). Social media in tourism and hospitality: A literature review. *Journal of Travel & Tourism Marketing*, 30(1-2), 3–22. 10.1080/10548408.2013.750919

Levine, M. A. (2008). China's CSR expectations mature. *The China Business Review*, 35(6), 50–53.

Lill, D., Gross, C., & Peterson, R. (1986). The inclusion of social-responsibility themes by magazine advertisers: A longitudinal study. *Journal of Advertising*, 15(2), 35–41. 10.1080/00913367.1986.10673003

Li, S., Da Xu, L., Zhao, S., Li, D., & Wang, H. (2021). 5G network slicing for mobile edge computing in smart cities. *IEEE Transactions on Industrial Informatics*, 18(1), 388–395.

Li, S., Kang, L., Xiao, Y., & Ren, Y. (2020). A privacy-preserving and reliable data collection scheme for smart cities based on blockchain. *IEEE Access : Practical Innovations, Open Solutions*, 8, 130052–130062.

Li, S., Kang, L., Zhao, Y., & Lv, J. (2021). A blockchain-based privacy-preserving data sharing scheme for smart cities. *IEEE Transactions on Industrial Electronics*, 68(8), 7004–7013.

Liu, S., Wang, Z., Narayanan, P., Li, Y., Li, Z., Sun, Y., & Xie, Y. (2022). Overview and open challenges on neuromorphic computing for edge AI applications. *Proceedings of the IEEE*, 110(7), 1209–1.

Liu, X., Hu, W., Xia, Y., Zhu, W., & Wang, H. (2020). Demographic determinants of COVID-19 transmission and fatality rates in mainland China. *International Journal of Infectious Diseases*, 97, 288-292Macintosh, A., & Whyte, A. (2017). Participation in smart cities: A contested terrain. *Urban Studies (Edinburgh, Scotland)*, 54(12), 2733–2753. https://www.sciencedirect.com/science/article/pii/B9780128166390000041

Lomborg, B. (2003). *The skeptical environmentalist: measuring the real state of the world* (Vol. 1). Cambridge University Press.

Loorbach, D., & Wijsman, K. (2013). Business transition management: Exploring a new role for business in sustainability transitions. *Journal of Cleaner Production*, 45, 20–28. 10.1016/j.jclepro.2012.11.002

López-Pérez, M. E., Melero, I., & Javier Sesé, F. (2017). *Does Specific CSR Training for Managers Impact Shareholder Value? Implications for Education in Sustainable Development*. Scite Press. https://scite.ai/reports/10.1002/csr.1418

Louwers, T., Pasewark, W. R., & Typpo, E. W. (1996). The Internet: Changing the way corporations tell their story. *The CPA Journal*, 66(11), 24.

Lyon, T. P., & Maxwell, J. W. (2007). Environmental public voluntary programs reconsidered. *Policy Studies Journal: the Journal of the Policy Studies Organization*, 35(4), 723–750. 10.1111/j.1541-0072.2007.00245.x

Lyon, T. P., & Montgomery, A. W. (2013). Tweetjacked: The impact of social media on corporate greenwash. *Journal of Business Ethics*, 118(4), 747–757. 10.1007/s10551-013-1958-x

Macarthur, E., & Heading, H. (2019). How the circular economy tackles climate change. *Ellen MacArthur Found*, 1, 1–71.

Madaan, G., Swapna, H. R., Kumar, A., Singh, A., & David, A. (2021). Enactment of sustainable technovations on healthcare sectors. *Asia Pacific Journal of Health Management*, 16(3), 184–192. 10.24083/apjhm.v16i3.989

Madden, M. (2010). *Older adults and social media*. PewInternet and American Life Project.

Madsen, H., & Ulhøi, J. P. (2001). Integrating environmental and stakeholder management. *Business Strategy and the Environment*, 10(2), 77–88. 10.1002/bse.279

Makarova, I., Buyvol, P., Shubenkova, K., Fatikhova, L. E., & Parsin, G. (2023). Editorial: Sustainable transport systems. *Frontiers in Built Environment*, 9, 1161361. Advance online publication. 10.3389/fbuil.2023.1161361

Manetti, G., & Bellucci, M. (2016). The use of social media for engaging stakeholders in sustainability reporting. *Accounting, Auditing & Accountability Journal*, 29(6), 985–1011. 10.1108/AAAJ-08-2014-1797

Manheim, J. B., & Pratt, C. B. (1986). Communicating corporate social responsibility. *Public Relations Review*, 12(2), 9–18. 10.1016/S0363-8111(86)80022-4

Manohar Bhanushali, M., Sharma, A., Sharma, S., Gehlot, A., Rawal, P., & Kapila, D. (2023). *A detailed and significant analysis of The Effects of Big-Data over The Revolution of Internet Marketing.* 2023 3rd International Conference on Advance Computing and Innovative Technologies in Engineering (ICACITE), Greater Noida, India. 10.1109/ICACITE57410.2023.10182372

Maraveas, C., Piromalis, D., Arvanitis, K. G., Bartzanas, T., & Loukatos, D. (2022). Applications of IoT for optimized greenhouse environment and resources management. *Computers and Electronics in Agriculture*, 198, 106993. 10.1016/j.compag.2022.106993

Martha Adaga, E., Efe Egieya, Z., Kuzankah Ewuga, S., Abiola Abdul, A., Oluwaseun Abrahams, T., & Author, C.Ejuma Martha AdagaZainab Efe EgieyaSarah Kuzankah EwugaAdekunle Abiola AbdulTemitayo Oluwaseun Abrahams. (2024). Philosophy In Business Analytics: A Review Of Sustainable And Ethical Approaches. *International Journal of Management & Entrepreneurship Research*, 6(1), 69–86. 10.51594/ijmer.v6i1.710

Martinez, T. G. (2022). *Citizen engagement.* 124-146. Oxford Academic. 10.1093/oso/9780192848789.003.0007

Martin, K. E. (2020). Ethical issues in the big data industry. In *Strategic Information Management* (pp. 450–471). Routledge. 10.4324/9780429286797-20

Marvin, S., Hodson, M., & McFarlane, C. (2018). Co-producing smart cities. *Environment and Planning A* [invalid URL removed]. *Economy and Space*, 50(2), 309–327.

Matten, D., & Moon, J. (2008). "Implicit" and "explicit" CSR: A conceptual framework for a comparative understanding of corporate social responsibility. *Academy of Management Review*, 33(2), 404–424. 10.5465/amr.2008.31193458

Mavlutova, I., Atstaja, D., Grasis, J., Kuzmina, J., Uvarova, I., & Roga, D. P. (2023). Urban Transportation Concept and Sustainable Urban Mobility in Smart Cities: A Review. *Energies*, 16(8), 3585–3585. 10.3390/en16083585

Mazur, B., Walczyna, A., & Cichorzewska, M. (2023). The Place of the Natural Environment in Activities for Social Responsibility in the Opinion of Students of Electrical Engineering. *Sustainability (Basel)*, 15(2), 1306. 10.3390/su15021306

MCA. (2009). *Corporate Social Responsibility Voluntary Guidelines in 2009 by the Ministry of Corporate Affairs*. Government of India.

MCA. (2013). *Companies Act, 2013, Ministry of Corporate Affairs, Government of India, New Delhi*. MCA. http://www.mca.gov.in/Ministry/pdf/CompaniesAct2013.pdf

Mcivor, M. (2022). *How Many Fortune 500 CEOs are on Social Media in 2022?* Influential Executive. https://influentialexecutive.com/how-many-fortune-500-ceos-social-media-2022/

McWilliams, A., & Siegel, D. (2001). Profit maximizing corporate social responsibility. *Academy of Management Review*, 26(4), 504–505.

McWilliams, A., Siegel, D. S., & Wright, P. M. (2006, January). Corporate Social Responsibility: Strategic Implications*. *Journal of Management Studies*, 43(1), 1–18. 10.1111/j.1467-6486.2006.00580.x

Melnyk, S. A., Sroufe, R. P., & Calantone, R. (2003). Assessing the impact of environmental management systems on corporate and environmental performance. *Journal of Operations Management*, 21(3), 329–351. 10.1016/S0272-6963(02)00109-2

Men, L. R., & Tsai, W. H. S. (2016). Public engagement with CEOs on social media: Motivations and relational outcomes. *Public Relations Review*, 42(5), 932–942. 10.1016/j.pubrev.2016.08.001

Metcalf, L., & Benn, S. (2013). Leadership for Sustainability: An Evolution of Leadership Ability. *Journal of Business Ethics*, 112(3), 369–384. 10.1007/s10551-012-1278-6

Milkintas, M., & Tamošiūnas, A. (2023). The impact of smart city technology on the quality of life in megacities: A systematic literature review. *Sustainability*, 15(6), 4252.

Milkintas, R., & Tamošiūnas, T. (2023). Theoretical foundations of the smart city concept. *Socialiniai Tyrimai*, 46(1), 88–102. 10.15388/Soctyr.2022.46.1.5

Ministry of Corporate Affairs. (2018). *Invitation for public comments for High-Level Committee on Corporate Social Responsibility -2018*. MCA. https://www.mca.gov.in/Ministry/pdf/InvitationOfPublicCommentsHLC_18012019.pdf

Minton, E., Lee, C., Orth, U., Kim, C. H., & Kahle, L. (2012). Sustainable marketing and social media: A cross-country analysis of motives for sustainable behaviors. *Journal of Advertising*, 41(4), 69–84. 10.1080/00913367.2012.10672458

Mohammadi, E., Vagnani, G., & Maleki, H. (2023). *Corporate social responsibility and satisfaction in service industries: a systematic review and integrative framework*. Society and Business Review., 10.1108/SBR-05-2022-0133

Mohan, A. (2001). *'Corporate Citizenship: Perspectives from India', Journal of Corporate Citizenship*. Greenleaf Publishing. 10.9774/GLEAF.4700.2001.su.00012

Moore, J. F. (2006). Business ecosystems and the view from the firm. *Antitrust Bulletin*, 51(1), 31–75. 10.1177/0003603X0605100103

Moratis, L., von den Hoff, J., & Reul, B. (2006, March). A Dual Challenge Facing Management Education. *Journal of Management Development*, 25(3), 213–231. 10.1108/02621710610648150

Murillo ??Luna, J. L., GarcA(c)s ??Ayerbe, C., & Rivera ??Torres, P. (2008). Why do patterns of environmental response differ? A stakeholders ?(tm) pressure approach. *Strategic Management Journal*, 29(11), 1225 ?"1240. 10.1002/smj.711

Namokel, M., & Karbowski, A. (2023). Design of Environmental Monitoring System Based on Cloud Platform.*Lecture Notes in Electrical Engineering*, 421-429. Springer. 10.1007/978-981-19-9338-1_52

Narayanan, G. B., & Vashisht, P. (2008). *Determinants of competitiveness of the Indian auto industry* (No. 201). Working paper.

Nemry, F., Leduc, G., Mongelli, I., & Uihlein, A. (2008). Environmental improvement of passenger cars (IMPRO-car). *Institute for Prospective Technological Studies*, 1(1), 1–216.

Nesma, A. (2023). *Eco-Friendly IoT Solutions for Smart Cities Development: An Overview*. IEEE. 10.1109/ICAISC56366.2023.10085100

Neu, D., Saxton, G., Rahaman, A., & Everett, J. (2019). Twitter and social accountability: Reactions to the Panama Papers. *Critical Perspectives on Accounting*, 61, 38–53. 10.1016/j.cpa.2019.04.003

Nidumolu, R., Prahalad, C. K., & Rangaswami, M. R. (2009). Why sustainability is now the key driver of innovation. *Harvard Business Review*, 87(9), 56–64.

Nihmathullah, Z. & Ramasamy, R. (2022). *Event Impact Assessment: A Case of Puducherry*.

Nuccio, M., & Guerzoni, M. (2019). Big data: Hell or heaven? Digital platforms and market power in the data-driven economy. *Competition & Change*, 23(3), 312–328. 10.1177/1024529418816525

Ohm, P. (2010). Broken promises of privacy: Responding to the surprising failures of anonymization. *University of Pennsylvania Law Review*, 158(4), 1701–1777.

Orlitzky, M., Schmidt, F. L., & Rynes, S. L. (2003). Corporate social and financial performance: A meta-analysis. *Organization Studies*, 24(3), 403–441. 10.1177/0170840603024003910

Paes, V. C., Pessoa, C. H. M., Pagliusi, R., Barbosa, C. E., Argôlo, M., de Lima, Y. O., & Moreira de Souza, J. (2023). Analyzing the Challenges for Future Smart and Sustainable Cities. *Sustainability (Basel)*, 15(10), 7996–7996. 10.3390/su15107996

Palazzo, M., Vollero, A., & Siano, A. (2020). From strategic corporate social responsibility to value creation: An analysis of corporate website communication in the banking sector. *International Journal of Bank Marketing*, 38(7), 1529–1552. 10.1108/IJBM-04-2020-0168

Parker, L. D. (1982). Corporate annual reporting: A mass communication perspective. *Accounting and Business Research*, 12(48), 279–286. 10.1080/00014788.1982.9728820

Parnell, G. S., Specking, E., Pohl, E. A., & Buchanan, R. K. (2023). *Smart Cities—A Structured Literature Review*. Smart Cities., 10.3390/smartcities6040080

Patil, A. R., & Subbaraman, S. (2021). Performance analysis of static hand gesture recognition approaches using artificial neural network, support vector machine and two stream based transfer learning approach. *International Journal of Information Technology : an Official Journal of Bharati Vidyapeeth's Institute of Computer Applications and Management*, 1–2.

Plewa, C., Conduit, J., Quester, P. G., & Johnson, C. (2015). The impact of corporate volunteering on CSR image: A consumer perspective. *Journal of Business Ethics*, 127(3), 643–659. 10.1007/s10551-014-2066-2

Popli, G. S., & Gupta, P. V. (2010). A Study on Cognitive Consistency of Young Passenger Car Consumers Towards Vehicular Pollution by Private Cars: An Empirical Analysis in Indian Context. *Available atSSRN* 1579984. 10.2139/ssrn.1579984

Porter, M., & Van der Linde, C. (1995). Grėen and competitive: ending the stalemate. *The Dynamics of the eco-efficient economy: environmental regulation and competitive advantage, 33*, 120-134.

Pramanik, S., & Bandyopadhyay, S. K. (2023). Analysis of big data. In *Encyclopedia of Data Science and Machine Learning* (pp. 97–115). IGI Global.

Punia, D. M. (2020). Consumerism and consumer protection laws in india: safeguarding consumer rights and welfare. In *Social Sciences, Education & Languages, 6*(10).

Raj Ananthan, T., & Zolkipli, M. F. (2022). *Challenges and Issues in Implementing Personal Data Protection.* International Journal of Recent Contributions from Engineering. *Science & IT*, 10(02), 53–61. 10.3991/ijes.v10i02.29373

Ranjan, S. L., Laha, B. K. Pattanayak, B. K., & Pattnaik, S. (2022). Advancement of Environmental Monitoring System Using IoT and Sensor: A Comprehensive Analysis. *AIMS Environmental Science, 9*(6), 771-800. doi: of Form10.3934/environsci.2022044Top

Ravi, S., David, A., & Imaduddin, M. (2018). Controlling & calibrating vehicle-related issues using RFID technology. *International Journal of Mechanical and Production Engineering Research and Development*, 8(2), 1125–1132. 10.24247/ijmperdapr2018130

Reavis, M., & Tucci, J. E. (2020, November). Sustainability Effort Acceleration as Measured by Increased Propensity of Corporate Social Responsibility. *Journal of Management and Sustainability*, 10(2), 121–121. 10.5539/jms.v10n2p121

Rodríguez-Gómez, S., Sánchez, R. G., Arco-Castro, M. L., & María, V. L. P. (2020, December). Does the Use of Social Media Tools in Classrooms Increase Student Commitment to Corporate Social Responsibility? *Frontiers in Psychology*, 11, 589250. 10.3389/fpsyg.2020.58925033424704

Sagar, S. (2023). Innovation and Sustainability in Business: Navigating the Future Landscape, *12(25)*, 51–60. https://doi.org/10.9790/487X-2512055160

Sagar, A. D. (1995). Automobiles and global warming: Alternative fuels and other options for carbon dioxide emissions reduction. *Environmental Impact Assessment Review*, 15(3), 241–274. 10.1016/0195-9255(95)91707-F

Sahay, A. (2004). Environmental reporting by Indian corporations. *Corporate Social Responsibility and Environmental Management*, 11(1), 12–22. 10.1002/csr.51

Saks, A. M., & Gruman, J. A. (2014). What do we really know about employee engagement? *Human Resource Development Quarterly*, 25(2), 155–182. 10.1002/hrdq.21187

Saleem, M., Shakir, M., Usman, M., Bajwa, M., Shabbir, N., Ghahfarokhi, P. S., & Daniel, K. (2023). Integrating Smart Energy Management System with Internet of Things and Cloud Computing for Efficient Demand Side Management in Smart Grids. *Energies*, 16(12), 4835–4835. 10.3390/en16124835

Sankar, J. G., & David, A. (2024). Transforming the Travel Landscape: Smart Contracts in Tourism Management. In *Decentralizing the Online Experience With Web3 Technologies* (pp. 246–266). IGI Global. 10.4018/979-8-3693-1532-3.ch012

Sankar, J. G., David, A., & Shrutimeena, G. (2024). From Hesitation to Integration: Understanding Digital Healthcare Adoption. In *Multi-Sector Analysis of the Digital Healthcare Industry* (pp. 1–32). IGI Global. 10.4018/979-8-3693-0928-5.ch001

Sankar, J. G., David, A., & Valan, P. (2023). Examining User Understanding and Perceptions of E-Commerce Data Privacy, Security, and Protection. In *Confronting Security and Privacy Challenges in Digital Marketing* (pp. 159–185). IGI Global. 10.4018/978-1-6684-8958-1.ch008

Santos, G., Behrendt, H., Maconi, L., Shirvani, L., & Teytelboym, A. (2010). Externalities and economic policies in road transport. *Research in Transportation Economics*, 28(1), 2–45. 10.1016/j.retrec.2009.11.002

Sarkis, J., Zhu, Q., & Lai, K. H. (2011). An organizational theoretic review of green supply chain management literature. *International Journal of Production Economics*, 130(1), 1–15. 10.1016/j.ijpe.2010.11.010

Saxena, M., & Mishra, D. K. (2017, June). CSR Perception: A Global Opportunity in Management Education. *Industrial and Commercial Training*, 49(5), 231–244. 10.1108/ICT-12-2016-0085

Saxton, G. D., Gómez, L., Ngoh, Z., Lin, Y. P., & Dietrich, S. (2019). Do CSR messages resonate? Examining public reactions to firms' CSR efforts on social media. *Journal of Business Ethics*, 155(2), 359–377. 10.1007/s10551-017-3464-z

Schaltegger, S., & Wagner, M. (2006). Integrative management of sustainability performance, measurement and reporting. *International Journal of Accounting. Auditing and Performance Evaluation*, 3(1), 1–19. 10.1504/IJAAPE.2006.010098

Schulz, K.-P., Finstad-Milion, K., & Janczak, S. (2018, October). Educating Corporate Sustainability – A Multidisciplinary and Practice-Based Approach to Facilitate Students' Learning. *Journal of Cleaner Production*, 198, 996–1006. 10.1016/j.jclepro.2018.06.104

Selbst, A. D., Boyd, D., Fried, S., Greenblatt, S. D., Keyes, P. D., & Vertinsky, J. (2019). *Fairness and accountability in artificial intelligence.* arXiv preprint arXiv:1908.09632. https://arxiv.org/pdf/2111.00826

Sen, S., & Bhattacharya, C. B. (2001). Does doing good always lead to doing better? Consumer reactions to corporate social responsibility. *JMR, Journal of Marketing Research*, 38(2), 225–243. 10.1509/jmkr.38.2.225.18838

Shalu. (2023). Environmental monitoring with machine learning.*EPRA International Journal of Multidisciplinary Research*, 208-212. 10.36713/epra13330

Shastri, K. (2021). Deep-LSTM ensemble framework to forecast Covid-19: an insight to the global pandemic. *International Journal of Information Technology, 13,* 1291-301..

Sheth, A., & Singhal, M. (2014). *India Philanthropy Report 2014*. Bain, Incorporated.

Shetty, V. S. (2014). Corporate Social Responsibility: An Analysis and Implications under Companies Act 2013. *Asian Journal of Humanities and Social Studies, 2*(5).

Shi, Y. (2022). *Advances in big data analytics*. Adv Big Data Anal. 10.1007/978-981-16-3607-3

Singh Bharati, T. (2020). Challenges, Issues, Security And Privacy Of Big Data. *International Journal of Scientific & Technology Research*, 9(2), 1482–1486.

Singhal, N. (2014). Corporate social responsibility-Role of government. *International Journal of Computing and Corporate Research*, 4(1), 16–21.

Singh, J., Sharma, P. K., & Moon, S. I. (2017). A survey on cloud security: Threats, countermeasures, and future directions. *Journal of Network and Computer Applications*, 79, 99–119.

Singh, S., Singh, H., & Sharma, P. K. (2017). A review on secure data transmission using cryptography algorithms in cloud computing environment. *International Journal of Computer Applications*, 168(3), 23–28. 10.5120/12338-8614

Singh, S., Singh, S., & Kaur, N. (2020). Eco-friendly urban development for sustainable future: A review. *Materials Today: Proceedings*, 45, 4364–4369.

Sisson, D. C. (2017). Control mutuality, social media, and organization-public relationships: A study of local animal welfare organizations' donors. *Public Relations Review*, 43(1), 179–189. 10.1016/j.pubrev.2016.10.007

Smart Cities and Buildings. (2023). 87-93. 10.1002/9781394216796.ch28

Sobczak, A., Debucquet, G., & Havard, C. (2006, August). The Impact of Higher Education on Students' and Young Managers' Perception of Companies and CSR: An Exploratory Analysis. *Corporate Governance (Bradford)*, 6(4), 463–474. 10.1108/14720700610689577

Sonnenfeld, A., Stevenson, J., & Waddington, H. (2022). Does citizen engagement improve development outcomes? A realist-informed systematic review of participation and accountability mechanisms. *Journal of Development Effectiveness*, 1–34. 10.1080/19439342.2022.2153380

Sperling, D. (2018). *Three revolutions: Steering automated, shared, and electric vehicles to a better future*. Island Press. 10.5822/978-1-61091-906-7

Sriramesh, K., Rivera-Sánchez, M., & Soriano, C. (2013). Websites for stakeholder relations by corporations and non-profits: A time-lag study in Singapore. *Journal of Communication Management (London)*, 17(2), 122–139. 10.1108/13632541311318738

Sudhakar, B. D., Kattepogu, N., & David, A. (2017). Marketing assistance and digital branding-an insight for technology up-gradation for MSME's. *International Journal of Management Studies & Research*, 5(1), 2455–1562.

Sullivan, J. L., Burnham, A., & Wang, M. Q. (2013). Model for the part manufacturing and vehicle assembly component of the vehicle life cycle inventory. *Journal of Industrial Ecology*, 17(1), 143–153. 10.1111/j.1530-9290.2012.00515.x

Sun, R. (2023). Corporate social responsibility and green innovation: Based on the perspective of corporate strategic management. *International Journal of Multidisciplinary Research and Growth Evaluation*. .10.54660/.IJMRGE.2023.4.2.46-49

Sun, Y., & Bhattacherjee, A. (2014). Looking inside the "IT black box": Technological effects on IT usage. *Journal of Computer Information Systems*, 54(2), 1–15. 10.1080/08874417.2014.11645681

Sutton, J. (2016). *Why Social Media and Sustainability Should Go Hand in Hand*. Triple Pundit. https://www.triplepundit.com/2016/06/social-mediasustainability-go-hand-hand/

Taneja, S., Taneja, P., & Gupta, R. K. (2011, January). Researches in Corporate Social Responsibility: A Review of Shifting Focus, Paradigms, and Methodologies. *Journal of Business Ethics*, 101(3), 343–364. 10.1007/s10551-010-0732-6

Thummula, E., Yadav, R. K., & David, A. (2019). A cost-effective technique to avoid communication and computation overhead in vehicle insurance database for online record monitoring. [IJMPERD]. *International Journal of Mechanical and Production Engineering Research and Development*, 9(2), 711–722.

Tian, Y., Niu, J., Sun, J., & Li, Y. (2020). A comprehensive review on hotspot detection and health risk assessment of urban green spaces using remote sensing. *Environmental Pollution*, 263, 114645.

Tickell, G., Paz, V., & Rahman, M. (2017, December). Teaching Corporate Social Responsibility In An MBA Program. *Journal of Sustainability Management*, 5(1), 1–10. 10.19030/jsm.v5i1.10153

Tilt, C. A. (1994). The Influence of External Pressure Groups on Corporate Social Disclosure: Some Empirical Evidence. *Accounting, Auditing & Accountability Journal*, 7(4), 47–72. 10.1108/09513579410069849

Trevor, D. W., & Geoffrey, R. F. (2000). Corporate environmental reporting. A test of legitimacy theory. *Accounting, Auditing & Accountability Journal*, 13(1), 10–26. 10.1108/09513570010316126

Tuuli, M. M., Fusheini, K., & Salia, H. (2023, June). Corporate Social Responsibility (CSR) Effect on Teaching and Learning: Evidence from an Emerging Economy. *International Journal of Innovation in Teaching and Learning*, 9(1), 1–19. 10.35993/ijitl.v9i1.2570

UN Habitat., (2020). *World Urban Report 2020: Cities and pandemics: The invisible enemy in a divided world*. UN-Habitat.

UN Habitat. (2020). *World urbanization prospects 2018: The revision*. UN. https://population.un.org/wup/Publications/Files/WUP2018-Highlights.pdf

UNESCO. (2021). *Global framework of reference on digital literacy and competences*. DigComp.

UNESCO. (2021). *ICT in education 2021: Artificial intelligence in education*. United Nations Educational, Scientific and Cultural Organization.

Van Beurden, P., & Gössling, T. (2008). The worth of values–a literature review on the relation between corporate social and financial performance. *Journal of Business Ethics*, 82(2), 407–424. 10.1007/s10551-008-9894-x

van der Wees, M. (2009) *Why firms invest in Corporate Social Responsibility: A study in the Dutch bank and insurance industry,* [Master Thesis, University of Matricht].

van Deursen, A. J., & Ewijk, D. V. (2023). Bridging the digital divide: A literature review on interventions aimed at increasing digital skills among older adults. *Educational Gerontology*, 49(3), 171–184. https://www.ncbi.nlm.nih.gov/pmc/articles/PMC7786312/

Van Marrewijk, M. (2003). Concepts and definitions of CSR and corporate sustainability: Between agency and communion. *Journal of Business Ethics*, 44(2), 95–105. 10.1023/A:1023331212247

Vasile,M., &Mocan,M.(2023). Some Considerations on the Smart City concept. *From Necessity to Implementation Challenges,2*(1), 15 23. 10.59168/BAPI4118

Venkateswara, M., Vellela, S., Reddy, V., Vullam, N., Sk, K. B., & Roja, D. (2023, March). Credit Investigation and Comprehensive Risk Management System based Big Data Analytics in Commercial Banking. In *2023 9th International Conference on Advanced Computing and Communication Systems (ICACCS)* (*Vol. 1,* pp. 2387-2391). IEEE.

Ventura, J. A. (2023). Climate Benefits Advocated by the Development of Sustainable Vehicles and Charging Infrastructures in the Transport Sector. *Energies*, 16(9), 3772–3772. 10.3390/en16093772

Verma, K., Bhardwaj, S., Arya, R., Islam, U. L., Bhushan, M., Kumar, A., & Samant, P. (2019). *Latest tools for data mining and machine learning*. Research Gate.

Visser, W. (2008). Corporate social responsibility in developing countries. In *The Oxford handbook of corporate social responsibility*. Oxford Press. 10.1093/oxfordhb/9780199211593.003.0021

Visser, W. (2007). Corporate social responsibility in developing countries. In Crane, A., Mcwilliams, A., Matten, D., Moon, J., & Siegel, D. (Eds.), *The Oxford handbook of corporate social responsibility* (pp. 473–499). Oxford University Press.

Vo, T. T., Xiao, X., & Ho, S. Y. (2019). How does corporate social responsibility engagement influence word of mouth on Twitter? Evidence from the airline industry. *Journal of Business Ethics*, 157(2), 525–542. 10.1007/s10551-017-3679-z

Waagstein, P. R. (2011). The mandatory corporate social responsibility in Indonesia: Problems and implications. *Journal of Business Ethics*, 98(3), 455–466. 10.1007/s10551-010-0587-x

Wachter, S., Mittelstadt, B., & Floridi, L. (2018). Transparent explanations for AI in healthcare. *Nature Machine Intelligence*, 1(11), 544–549.

Waddington, S. H., Singh, J., Garnett, S. T., McNeill, M., & White, M. P. (2022). Interventions to promote citizen engagement in health services: A systematic review. *BMC Health Services Research*, 2.

Waddock, S. A., Bodwell, C., & Graves, S. B. (2002). Responsibility: The new business imperative. *The Academy of Management Perspectives*, 16(2), 132–148. 10.5465/ame.2002.7173581

Wang, H., Tong, L., Takeuchi, R., & George, G. (2016). Corporate social responsibility: An overview and new research directions. In *Academy of Management Journal, 59*(2). Academy of Management. 10.5465/amj.2016.5001

Wang, R., & Huang, Y. (2018). Communicating corporate social responsibility (CSR) on social media: How do message source and types of CSR messages influence stakeholders' perceptions? *Corporate Communications*, 23(3), 326–341. 10.1108/CCIJ-07-2017-0067

Wargent, M. (2023). Digital Participatory Planning: Citizen Engagement, Democracy, and Design. *Journal of the American Planning Association*, 89(2), 262–264. 10.1080/01944363.2023.2174350

WBCSD. (2001). *Measuring Eco-efficiency—A Guide to Reporting Company Performance*. WBCSD.

Wen, J., Khalid, S., Zakaria, M. A., & Mahmood, H. (2023). Does Technological Innovation Reduce Environmental Degradation? Evidence from China. *The Engineering Economist*, 34(3), 323–334. 10.5755/j01.ee.34.3.32818

Wickert, C., Scherer, A. G., & Spence, L. J. (2016). Walking and Talking Corporate Social Responsibility: Implications of Firm Size and Organizational Cost. *Journal of Management Studies*, 53(7), 1169–1196. 10.1111/joms.12209

Wieland, J. R., & Fitzgibbons, D. E. (2013, December). Integrating Corporate Sustainability and Organizational Strategy Within the Undergraduate Business Curriculum. *Organizational Management Journal*, 10(4), 255–266. 10.1080/15416518.2013.859059

Wilson, D., & Purushothaman, R. (2006). 1. Dreaming with BRICs: the path to 2050. *Emerging economies and the transformation of international business: Brazil, Russia, India and China (BRICs), 1*.

Winkler, L. K., Pearce, D., Nelson, J., & Babacan, O. (2023). The effect of sustainable mobility transition policies on cumulative urban transport emissions and energy demand. *Nature Communications*, 14(1), 2357. 10.1038/s41467-023-37728-x37095105

World Bank. (2021). *Digital dividends dividend report 2021*. World Bank. https://www.worldbank.org/en/publication/wdr2016

World Bank. (2023, April 12). *Bridging the digital divide*. World Bank. https://www.worldbank.org/en/news/feature/2020/10/26/closing-the-digital-divide-a-time-to-stay-connected

World Business Council for Sustainable Development WBCSD. (2000). *Corporate Social Responsibility: Making Good Business Sense*. WBCSD.

Xu, L. D., Jiang, Y., Zhao, Y., Ma, J., & Wang, W. (2020). A blockchain-based data sharing scheme for secure and reliable smart city services. *IEEE Journal on Selected Areas in Communications*, 38(6), 1624–1637.

Yang, J., Basile, K., & Letourneau, O. (2020). The impact of social media platform selection on effectively communicating about corporate social responsibility. *Journal of Marketing Communications*, 26(1), 65–87. 10.1080/13527266.2018.1500932

Yann Arthus-Bertrand, (2009, June 5). —*HOME – Documentary film*. Paris: Europa Corp.

Yan, R. N., Ogle, J. P., & Hyllegard, K. H. (2010). The impact of message appeal and message source on Gen Y consumers' attitudes and purchase intentions toward American Apparel. *Journal of Marketing Communications*, 16(4), 203–224. 10.1080/13527260902863221

Yasuoka, M. (2023). How Citizens Participation Begin and Continue in Developing Smart Cities. *Lecture Notes in Computer Science*, 14037, 182–192. 10.1007/978-3-031-34609-5_13

Yeh, C. L. (2018). Pursuing consumer empowerment in the age of big data: A comprehensive regulatory framework for data brokers. *Telecommunications Policy*, 42(4), 282–292. 10.1016/j.telpol.2017.12.001

Yıldırım, K. (2023). Components of Smart Cities: Smart City Applications and Smart Space Management. *Mediterranean Journal of Humanities*. 10.13114/MJH.2023.607

Zeghal, D., & Ahmed, S. A. (1990). Comparison of social responsibility information disclosure media used by Canadian firms. *Accounting, Auditing & Accountability Journal*, *3*(1), 0-0.

Zhang, C. B., & Lin, Y. H. (2015). Exploring interactive communication using social media. *Service Industries Journal*, 35(11-12), 670–693. 10.1080/02642069.2015.1064396

Zhang, X., Rane, K., Kakaravada, I., & Shabaz, M. (2021). Research on vibration monitoring and fault diagnosis of rotating machinery based on internet of things technology. *Nonlinear Engineering*, 10(1), 245–254. 10.1515/nleng-2021-0019

Zhang, Y., Chen, L., Fang, Y., Li, J., & Zhang, Y. (2023). Security and privacy issues in smart cities: A survey. *Sensors (Basel)*, 23(8), 2901. https://www.mdpi.com/1424-8220/22/23/9338

Zhang, Z., Zhang, Z., & Li, H. (2015). Predictors of the authenticity of Internet health rumours. *Health Information and Libraries Journal*, 32(3), 195–205. 10.1111/hir.1211526268517

Zheming, Y. (2023). Smart city and green development: Empirical evidence from the perspective of green technological innovation. *Technological Forecasting and Social Change*, 191, 122507–122507. 10.1016/j.techfore.2023.122507

Zhou, J., Zhou, Y., & Bai, X. (2023). Can Green-Technology Innovation Reduce Atmospheric Environmental Pollution? *Toxics*, 11(5), 403–403. 10.3390/toxics1105040337235218

Zizka, L. (2017). The (mis) use of social media to communicate CSR in hospitality: Increasing stakeholders'(dis) engagement through social media. *Journal of Hospitality and Tourism Technology*, 8(1), 73–86. 10.1108/JHTT-07-2016-0037

Zou, Z., Zhao, S., & Gong, P. (2022). Data governance for smart cities: A literature review and future directions. *IEEE Access : Practical Innovations, Open Solutions*, 10, 120422–120439.

About the Contributors

Kuldeep Singh is an Assistant Professor in the finance area at the School of Management, Gati Shakti Vishwavidyalaya, Vadodara, Gujarat. India. He obtained his doctorate in Finance from the Indian Institute of Information Technology, Allahabad India, in 2022. He is skilled in Inferential statistics, Mediation-Moderation analysis, Structural Equation Modeling, Times Series Analysis, Forecasting through regression modeling, PLS-SEM, Difference-in-Difference (DiD) analysis, Propensity Score Matching, Interpretive Structural Modeling (ISM-MICMAC), Analytic Hierarchy Process (AHP), Systematic Literature Review and so on. He was awarded with the 'Best Paper Award' at 6th Management Doctoral Colloquium, IIT Kharagpur in 2020. He has published several research papers in reputed journals like Behavior and Information Technology (Taylor & Francis, ABDC-A), Information Technology & People (Emerald, ABDC-A), Singapore Economic Review (ABDC-B), Managerial and Decision Economics (Wiley, ABDC-B) and in various other reputed publishers such as Springer, Elsevier, and Sage.

Jitendra Yadav is an Assistant Professor in Marketing at Indian Institute of Management, Bodh Gaya, India. He also holds a position of Academic Editor at PLOS ONE. His research interests include consumer behaviour, social media analytics, information strategy and IT-enabled services, blockchain business applications, information technology, and operations management. He has been an active member of the academic community for many years, contributing both as an author and a reviewer. He has a number of articles published in reputable publications as well as contributions to multiple books. His work on these topics has been published in academic journals: Behavior & Information Technology (Taylor and Francis), Information Technology & People (Emerald), International Journal of Sports Marketing & Sponsorship (Emerald), and International Journal of Blockchains and Cryptocurrencies (Inderscience). He also holds a position of Editor in the International Journal of Blockchains and Cryptocurrencies, International Journal of E-Business Research, International Journal of Gaming and Computer-Mediated Simulations, International Journal of E-Adoption

Rebecca Abraham is a Finance Professor at the H. Wayne Huizenga School of Business and Entrepreneurship. She earned a doctorate in Business Administration-Finance from the U.S. International University in 1989. After teaching at the National University as an adjunct instructor in the Department of Management Science, Dr. Abraham joined the Farquhar Center of Nova Southeastern University in the Fall of 1989. She has taught courses at the undergraduate and graduate levels – in corporate finance, investments, portfolio theory, financial management, business strategy and policy, quantitative methods, micro-, and macroeconomics. In recognition of her service to students, she was honored with the first Farquhar Center Award for Teaching Excellence in 2000, and the Teacher of the Year Award from the Huizenga School in 2006. Dr. Abraham has published extensively. Her publications have appeared in the Review of Accounting and Finance, Journal of Economic Studies, Journal of Business and Leadership, International Journal of Finance, Journal of Psychology, Genetic, Social, and Psychology Monographs, and the Leadership and Organization Development Journal. She serves on the Editorial Review Board of Personality and Individual Differences. She authored a book chapter in the Advances in Business and Management Forecasting by Elsevier. Along with Dr. Robert Trippi, formerly of California State University-Long Beach, she pioneered a methodology for determining implicit interest rates in option prices. Her work has also appeared in the Conference Proceedings of the Decision Sciences Institute and the Association of Management.

* * *

Sikandar Azam is currently associated with IBS Hyderabad as an Assistant Professor of accounting and finance. He has completed his post-graduation studies at Aligarh Muslim University and his M.Phil and Ph.D. studies at Pondicherry Central University. As a part of the research, he promotes sustainable agriculture, which aligns with the UN SDG Goals. The research area comprises sustainable development, agriculture, agribusiness, agricultural economics, rural development, organic food, and farming. He has published over ten research papers in international journals, including Emerald, Wiley, Taylor & Francis listed in Scopus and ABDC. The research focuses on policy-oriented and emphasizes the transition towards sustainable farming. He has presented research findings at international conferences held at IIMs, IITs, IISc, ISI, IIFT, and Central Universities. Dr. Azam is a passionate teacher, researcher, and trainer. He is keen to learn and open to suggestions for change and improvement. He believes in activity-based learning and case-based pedagogy using ITC in the classroom. He can collaborate, interact, and work with the team. He has around eight years of teaching experience. He has taught Financial Accounting, Corporate Accounting, Management Accounting, Indian Financial System, etc. He received the best paper award at an international conference at Pondicherry University. He was also a representative of Pondicherry University at MHRD (Education Ministry), Govt. of India for the current "New Education Policy 2020". As a part of the community service, he has voluntarily delivered "career counseling programs" to the needy and underprivileged students of rural areas.

Sikandar Azam is currently associated with IBS Hyderabad as an Assistant Professor of accounting and finance. He has completed his post-graduation studies at Aligarh Muslim University and his M.Phil and Ph.D. studies at Pondicherry Central University. As a part of the research, he promotes sustainable agriculture, which aligns with the UN SDG Goals. The research area comprises sustainable development, agriculture, agribusiness, agricultural economics, rural development, organic food, and farming. He has published over ten research papers in international journals, including Emerald, Wiley, Taylor & Francis listed in Scopus and ABDC. The research focuses on policy-oriented and emphasizes the transition towards sustainable farming. He has presented research findings at international conferences held at IIMs, IITs, IISc, ISI, IIFT, and Central Universities. Dr. Azam is a passionate teacher, researcher, and trainer. He is keen to learn and open to suggestions for change and improvement. He believes in activity-based learning and case-based pedagogy using ITC in the classroom. He can collaborate, interact, and work with the team. He has around eight years of teaching experience. He has taught Financial Accounting, Corporate Accounting, Management Accounting, Indian Financial System, etc. He received the best paper award at an international conference at Pondicherry University. He was also a representative of Pondicherry University at MHRD (Education Ministry), Govt. of India for the current "New Education Policy 2020". As a part of the community service, he has voluntarily delivered "career counseling programs" to the needy and underprivileged students of rural areas.

About the Contributors

Arokiaraj David serves as an Associate Professor of Al Tareeqah Management Studies in UAE. He has successfully cleared the UGC-National Eligibility Test for Lectureship (NET) and has been honored with the Junior and Senior Research Fellow (JRF & SRF) titles. With over a decade of teaching and research experience, his areas of expertise include Green Marketing, Consumer Behavior, Product & Brand Management, Global Marketing, Retail Management, Strategic Management, Data Analytics, Sustainable Practices, Resources Management, Product Development, Environmental Responsibility, and General Management. Dr. David has authored more than 60 research articles, including 11 published in Scopus, 08 in ABDC, and 05 in Web of Science. He has also contributed to 07 book chapters, published 04 books, registered 07 patents, and received 01 copyright and 01 consultant project. He is proficient in various research tools and techniques such as SPSS, AMOS, E-Views, STATA, and PLS-SEM and has hands-on experience in both primary and secondary data analysis. Recently, Dr. David has been recognized with the Best Research Award, Young Academician Award, and Young Scientist Award.

Harshi Garg, a dedicated PhD scholar, is recognized for her expertise as a market and users researcher & consultant, with a particular focus on digital and social media analysis. Her contributions to the field are marked by a series of notable achievements. Not only has she presented her research findings at international conferences, but she has also authored research papers in prestigious journals and contributed chapters to esteemed Scopus indexed books. Harshi's commitment to rigorous inquiry and her diligent approach to research underscore her standing as a respected figure in her field.

Anantha Subramanya Iyer K N Associate Professor – Marketing, CMS Business School, JAIN (Deemed-to-be University) Having served in both industry and academia, has 21+ years of experience in teaching management students in both graduate and postgraduate levels, and has 4 plus years of industry experience. Currently serving as an Associate Professor in Marketing Area at CMS Business School, JAIN (Deemed-to-be University), Bangalore since 2005. Served as Chief Superintendent of Exams at CMS Business School and Controller of Examinations at MATS Institute of Management & Entrepreneurship, Bangalore. In the industry, has worked in the capacities of a Senior Software Engineer and Business Development Manager at Silicon Technologies Bangalore and Senior R&D Engineer at Symantec Corporation. Dr. Iyer has presented and published research papers, case studies and book chapters in the field of marketing and allied areas. He is also involved in consultancy projects with Government and private agencies.

Mohammad Kashif is a distinguished academician and researcher in the area of finance, economics and international business at Graphic Era Deemed to be University, Dehradun, India . He has several publications indexed in WoS, Scopus and ABDC. He authored a text book titled Financial Management for undergraduate students. He is the editor in upcoming edited books under Emerald Publishers and Bentham Science Publishers. He is guiding PhD scholars in his area of expertise. Besides he is a member of several professional bodies at university level. He has been awarded many academic and research awards by reputed organizations.

Prabha Kiran Head of the Department, Management and Marketing, School of Business Economics, Westminster Business School, Westminster International University in Tashkent. Prabha Kiran in past has worked as Assistant Professor at School of Business and Management, CHRIST Deemed to be University, Bangalore. She is an academician by choice and researcher by heart. She has completed her Bachelor of Engineering specializing in Electrical and Electronics Engineering (MVJCE-VTU Bangalore, India, MBA in Marketing in Systems from CBSMS- Bangalore University, India. She has a PhD in Digital Marketing, from Vels University, Chennai, India. She has eight years of research experience and has worked extensively on Government funded projects in the area of Digital Marketing and Food technology. She has been a coordinator- PhD program, Research Writing, Publication Ethics, Section Editor: USHUS Business Management Journal, University Journal, School of Business and Management, Christ University. She has published more than 40 research papers in International Refereed Journals and 12 Scopus indexed journals. She has presented more than 70 research papers in International and National conferences across India as well as in other countries. Her research papers have been awarded with best papers for her research on twitter analytics and information credibility analysis of social media content. She has been conferred with "Young Scientist Award",2017 by leading publication house in Chennai, and "Best Professor in Market Research",2018 by a leading B-School in Hyderabad. She is certified trainer and google digital marketing expert, delivering consulting and training services to MSME, startups and mid-level organizational managers. The certification provided by the organisation is accredited by ASCB (US), valid across more than 70 countries. As a consultant she can handle Digital Marketing consulting specialising in image building and branding of products and services. She basically works towards improving the brand image or public image of products or services by good public relations, advertising, in the digital platform. My favorite piece of advice to any entrepreneur is to build a brand, not just a business. Following are the aspects of the consulting solutions that are undertaken: 1. Public Opinion Research: It is to ascertain what people think about the brand, its management, services, etc. Essentially, understand the attitude of the public towards the organisation. 2. Image Study: Understand how and what is the organisation known for; analysing brand's reputation. 3. Motivation Research: It is to ascertain why the public carries a positive or negative attitude towards the organisation – the root cause(s) – and also the underlying emotional factor. On the outset the image could be favorable, neutral or unfavorable & undesirable. Brand building activities that are undertaken are: 1. Brand Strategy 2. Brand Identity 3. Brand Marketing She is a board of studies member for various Universities and served as session chair for national and international conferences. She has conducted various workshops, training and consulting sessions in the area of Social science research, Digital marketing and business analytics for various national and international participants. Areas of research interest s are - Social media Marketing, consumer behavior, marketing analytics, marketing metrics and is open for interdisciplinary and collaborative research work. Her quest for intellectual and academic learning with a strong research bent of mind has received prominence in the institutes served and in promoting importance of research and brand building of and be confident in their data based decision making

M. Banumathi has Doctorate in Economics and MBA in Marketing, did her intensive Faculty Development Programme in IIM Ahmedabad. She has over 25 years of academic experience serving in various capacities at leading institutions like PSG College of Technology, Coimbatore and BITS Pilani. She currently teaches Economics, Strategic Management and Marketing courses, she also passionate towards teaching values and shaping young minds. Her area of interest is Green Marketing, Banking and International Trade. She was a recipient of AICTEs Young Teacher Career Award. She has presented papers and published articles in the area of Corporate Environmental Responsibilities and Organic Farming.

Madhvendra Misra is Associate Professor at the Department of Management Studies at IIIT Allahabad. He has around 20 years of experience in management education. He has his PhD in the area of marketing and current research interest are business strategy, business process change, business excellence and digital marketing issues. Academics to him is a way of life where in he explorers and unravels the social and academic schema to bring out innovative research which has social and economic application. He regularly contributes to international journals, has to his credit scores of publications in highly reputed international journal. He is regularly invited to deliver technical lectures on Management and related area at national level institution like DRDO etc. He is known for his keen interest in social entrepreneurship and also act as motivational speaker for promoting start up culture amongst engineering students and professional.

About the Contributors

Dinesh Nilkant is a dedicated professional with a robust background in financial analytics, research methodology, and HR analytics. He has actively engaged in numerous training programs and webinars, showcasing a commitment to continuous learning and professional development. His educational journey includes participating in a Short Term Training Program (STTP) on Financial Analytics organized by the Institute of Business Management & Research (IBMR), IPS Academy. This six-day program, held from 22nd to 27th February 2021 and associated with AICTE, provided valuable insights into the intricacies of financial analytics. Further enhancing his skills, Dr. Nilkant completed a Mendeley training course, obtaining certification as a Mendeley Advisor. This reflects his proficiency in reference management and effective utilization of Mendeley, a critical tool for researchers. Additionally, he participated in advanced research methodology training organized by REST Society for Research International (RSRI), covering topics from 11th to 15th May 2020. This was complemented by another STTP on Statistical Analysis for Research from 18th to 22nd May 2020, demonstrating his expertise in research methodologies. His commitment extends beyond analytics, as seen in his participation in an HR Analytics training program held on 21st and 22nd December 2019, organized by MSME-Technology Development Centre (PPDC) in Bangalore. This broadens his skill set to include human resources analytics, a valuable asset in today's data-driven business environment. Dr. Nilkant's journey also encompasses a one-week SEBI training program on Financial Education, where he qualified as a Resource Person. This was conducted by the National Institute of Securities Markets (NISM) from 26th August to 1st September 2012, showcasing his long-standing engagement with financial education initiatives. In addition to these extensive training programs, he actively participates in webinars to stay abreast of industry trends. Notably, he attended a webinar on "Automation to take over Financial Services" on 26th May 2020, organized by Sankaran Basu, Professor of Finance at the Indian Institute of Management, Bangalore. Overall, Dr. Dinesh Nilkant's CV reflects a multifaceted professional with expertise in financial analytics, research methodology, and HR analytics, continually enriching his knowledge through diverse training programs and webinars.

Sabyasachi Pramanik is a professional IEEE member. He obtained a PhD in Computer Science and Engineering from Sri Satya Sai University of Technology and Medical Sciences, Bhopal, India. Presently, he is an Associate Professor, Department of Computer Science and Engineering, Haldia Institute of Technology, India. He has many publications in various reputed international conferences, journals, and book chapters (Indexed by SCIE, Scopus, ESCI, etc). He is doing research in the fields of Artificial Intelligence, Data Privacy, Cybersecurity, Network Security, and Machine Learning. He also serves on the editorial boards of several international journals. He is a reviewer of journal articles from IEEE, Springer, Elsevier, Inderscience, IET and IGI Global. He has reviewed many conference papers, has been a keynote speaker, session chair, and technical program committee member at many international conferences. He has authored a book on Wireless Sensor Network. He has edited 8 books from IGI Global, CRC Press, Springer and Wiley Publications.

Hemanth Kumar S Professor and Life Coach Marketing & International Business 19 Years of Experience B.Com,M.COM,M.F.M.,MBA(GM.,MM.,EAS.,)., M.PHIL.,PGDFT.PGDMM.,PGDSCM.,NLP.,P.HD Dr. Hemanth Kumar S brings a wealth of experience to his role, with 19 years of teaching expertise and 10 years of corporate training. He holds a certification as a Neuro Linguistic Practitioner from NFNLP, USA, and is a certified French Council trainer specializing in personal growth practices. Dr. Hemanth Kumar S's remarkable achievements include being a contributor to the Guinness Book of World Records for his work on "Longest unit of time measure in Hindu chronology – equated to earthly years" and the Limca Book of World Records for his research on the "Oldest metallic coin". Recognized for his contributions, Dr. Hemanth Kumar S has been honored with the Rajya Parashar and Rashtrapathi awards in Scouts. He has also made valuable contributions as a panelist in over 40 business and budget-related discussions on popular TV news channels. With a solid background in accreditation processes, Dr. Hemanth Kumar S has hands-on experience in preparing documentation and process maps for prestigious institutions such as ISO certifications, NAAC, AICTE, CRISIL, NBA, AMBA, and AACSB. As an accomplished researcher, Dr. Hemanth Kumar S has published approximately 100 national and international referred journal articles, along with 52 international conference papers and national conference papers. He serves on the editorial boards of several esteemed journals and has authored the book titled "Impact of Subsidy and Promotional Strategies on Farming Patterns," which is listed on Google Scholar. He has conducted 27 workshops on Research Methodology using SPSS and AMOS, as well as 46 workshops on innovative teaching methods in classroom environments. Furthermore, he has delivered over 36 guest lectures at top institutions across Karnataka.

Mahalakshmi S is a highly accomplished professional with a strong academic background and extensive experience. She holds a Ph.D. in Management and earned her Computer Science engineering degree with distinction from Visweshwariaha Technological University (VTU), Belgaum. Throughout her academic journey, she has consistently excelled, evident in her MBA from Bangalore University where she achieved three gold medals and secured state rank 1. Currently pursuing a PGCP in Digital and Social Media Marketing at IIM-Vishakhapatnam, Dr. Mahalakshmi seamlessly integrates academic rigor with practical insights. Her diverse experience includes serving as an Associate Project Manager in Management consultation and project management, successfully overseeing BFSI projects in both India and Canada. She has further enriched her expertise with certifications in Marketing and Technology from IIM Madras. Dr. Mahalakshmi actively contributes as a Subject Matter Expert for executive MBA programs with Jain-Ex, Manipal, and upGrad. Her course "Media buying and Affiliate Marketing" on upGrad stands as one of the bestsellers. Recognized for her academic excellence, she has received numerous best paper awards and published papers in prestigious journals of Scopus, ABDC, Web of Sciences, among others. She even has to her credits 2 patents in service and design. In her current role as an Assistant Professor in the Marketing department at CMS Business School, Jain deemed to be University, Dr. Mahalakshmi continues to make significant contributions to academia. She is a core member of the B-school learning models development and implementation team, playing a pivotal role in introducing the new specialization of Digital and Social Media Marketing. Additionally, she actively contributes to the University's Board of Studies, contributing to the drafting and revamping of the syllabus. Dr. Mahalakshmi's expertise and commitment are evident in her multifaceted contributions to the academic field.

Omar Vargas-González is a Professor, research assistant and former Head of Computer Systems Department at Tecnologico Nacional de Mexico Campus Ciudad Guzman, professor at Telematic Engineering at Centro Universitario del Sur Universidad de Guadalajara with a master degree in Computer Systems. Has been trained in Innovation and Multidisciplinary Entrepreneurship at Arizona State University (2018) and a Generation of Ecosystems of Innovation, Entrepreneurship and Sustainability for Jalisco course by Harvard University T.H. Chan School of Health. At present conduct research on diverse fields such as Entrepreneurship, Economy, Statistics, Mathematics and Information and Computer Sciences. Has colaborated in the publication of over 30 scientific articles and conducted diverse Innovation and Technological Development projects.

Index

A

B

C

E

G

H

I

M

www.ingramcontent.com/pod-product-compliance
Lightning Source LLC
LaVergne TN
LVHW061545290926
849162LV00004B/917